Transfiguring Luther

Transfiguring Luther

The Planetary Promise of Luther's Theology

Vítor Westhelle

Foreword by
David Tracy

CASCADE Books • Eugene, Oregon

TRANSFIGURING LUTHER
The Planetary Promise of Luther's Theology

Copyright © 2016 Vítor Westhelle. All rights reserved. Except for brief quotations in critical publications or reviews, no part of this book may be reproduced in any manner without prior written permission from the publisher. Write: Permissions, Wipf and Stock Publishers, 199 W. 8th Ave., Suite 3, Eugene, OR 97401.

Cascade Books
An Imprint of Wipf and Stock Publishers
199 W. 8th Ave., Suite 3
Eugene, OR 97401

www.wipfandstock.com

PAPERBACK ISBN: 978-1-62564-216-5
HARDCOVER ISBN: 978-1-4982-8881-1
EBOOK ISBN: 978-1-5326-0044-9

Cataloguing-in-Publication data:

Names: Westhelle, Vítor. | Tracy, David, foreword.

Title: Transfiguring Luther : The Planetary Promise of Luther's Theology / Vítor Westhelle ; foreword by David Tracy.

Description: Eugene, OR : Cascade Books, 2016 | Includes bibliographical references and indexes.

Identifiers: ISBN 978-1-62564-216-5 (paperback) | ISBN 978-1-4982-8881-1 (hardcover) | ISBN 978-1-5326-0044-9 (ebook)

Subjects: LCSH: Luther, Martin, 1483–1546. | Lutheran Church—Doctrines. | Economics—Religious aspects—Lutheran Church.

Classification: LCC BR332.5 .W48 2016 (print) | LCC BR332.5 (ebook)

Manufactured in the U.S.A.   05/20/16

For Regina, Wilson, and Mariane:
Remembering Henrique, Waldemar, & Veny,
& those who risk because they trust
& love because they know.

Contents

Foreword by David Tracy | ix
Preface and Acknowledgments | xi
Abbreviations | xv

Introduction | 1

Part One—The Genius of Language: Grammar and Rhetoric

1. The Quest for Language: Engaging the Head and the Heart | 17
2. More than Enough: Letter as Solace | 40
3. Stories That Shape the Story | 58
4. Faith and Love, the Space In-Between: On the Beatitudes | 68

Part Two—Theology Matters

5. On the Playground of God: Justification as Event and Representation | 83
6. Beholding the Core: Reading Chalcedon | 95
7. Enduring the Scandal: *theologia crucis* | 111
8. Cross and Creation | 124
9. The Groaning Mask: Ecojustice and the Human Place in Nature | 133
10. The Church in Eden: On the Priesthood of the Faithful | 145
11. Apocalypse: Yet-Time and Not-Yet | 155

Part Three—The Planet Luther: Transfigurations

12 Globalization and Fragmentation: Lutheran World Federation | 167
13 Transfiguring Lutheranism: Displacing Tradition | 181
14 Lutheranism and Culture in the Americas: A Comparative Study | 195
15 Contextual Hermeneutics | 207
16 A Communion of Teaching and Learning | 219
17 Luther Yet Incomplete: A Global Inquiry | 226
18 Planet Luther: Challenges and Promises | 241

Part Four—Economy and Politics: The Paradigms

19 "The Third Bank of the River": The Challenge of Modernity | 255
20 Two Kingdoms Doctrine: When the Rubber Hits the Road | 262
21 Works, Law, and Faith: Régimes and Event in Luther | 276
22 Power and Politics | 292
23 Lutheran Social Ethics: A Sketch | 304

Conclusion: Inconclusive Final Notes | 317

Bibliography | 321
Author Index | 333
Subject Index | 335

Foreword

MARTIN LUTHER WAS ONE of those rare historical phenomena: a singular individuality in a particular place and time who, in and through his very particularity, became a figure of universal power and significance. Martin Luther was a classic, not a period piece. He is an ever-renewed present not a spent instant. He is not a mere fragment of our common history but a frag-event whose power still fragments and shatters all reified institutions, all "isms." Martin Luther reveals the reality of the justifying, gracious God as the cross of Jesus Christ releases a liberating power in historical situation after situation in ever different cultures. As this brilliant book makes clear, Martin Luther, so grounded in historical fact, is thereby not a symbol but a *figura* which constantly transfigures itself in place after place, culture after culture.

Luther's doctrine of justification remains as emancipatory as when he first rediscovered it in Galatians and Romans of St. Paul. In the Global South, where so many Christians now live (including approximately 40 percent of Lutherans), Luther's emancipatory doctrine of justification has often been united to the strong liberation theologies of justice to provide yet another transfiguration of Luther's figural power beyond earlier European and North American settings.

In this book, Professor Vítor Westhelle significantly adds to his former work focused on Luther's foundational theology of the cross as well as his important work on the import of postcolonial theory for all theology. In this work, Professor Westhelle unites these two studies to show how Luther is now a *figura* in the Global South which can unite theological justification with social-ethical theological justice.

Professor Westhelle, by means of his fine development of the traditional literary category of the *figura* (in Erich Auerbach and others), shows how Martin Luther lives not merely as a symbol in allegory but as a *figura* in a way well beyond earlier North Atlantic, often politically conservative notions of Luther's two kingdoms—Martin Luther as an irreplaceable, very particular historical *figura* whose figure continues its liberating power over and over again in ever new ways. Professor Westhelle does not pretend that Luther was without faults. He faces straightforwardly Luther's disgraceful attitudes toward the Jews as well as his troubling reactions to the peasants in revolt against oppression, and Luther's more than occasional out-of-control polemical rhetoric of excess. This study is not hagiographical.

In sum, like us all only more so given his religious and theological intensity of genius, Martin Luther was both plural (as a *figura* who keeps transforming—there are many Luthers, as this book shows) and ambiguous—that is, disclosing the true and the false, the good and the bad, the holy and the unholy. However, Martin Luther's central theological truth (the doctrine of justification through grace in faith; the theology of the cross not the theology of glory; the *solus Christus* yielding *sola gratia*, *sola fides*, *sola scriptura*) overwhelms his limits and faults. At the same time, Martin Luther demonstrated an integrity in his life, an honesty about himself and us all: ultimately we are all beggars before a gracious God. Professor Westhelle, with his great advantage of living on the border between North and South, in this book shows the richness of plural forms of Lutheranism: many different Lutheranisms of Europe and North America allied to the sometimes explosive new Lutheran theologies of liberation, justification, and justice of the Global South.

Professor Westhelle's own journey—deeply embedded in the theology of the cross and dedicated to the struggle for justice—shows us in this singular book many of the transfigurations in our day attending that irreplaceable *figura* of our common history, Martin Luther. Readers will feel privileged, as I do, to join Vítor Westhelle in his journey with Martin Luther.

David Tracy
The University of Chicago, September 2015

Preface and Acknowledgments

A LUTHER SCHOLAR I claim not to be, but Martin Luther, the man and his theology, has been an integral part of my vocational career, a risk of my choosing. From the first published academic article under my name, four decades ago, to my present recurring involvement with research, teaching, programs, and boards associated with Lutheran theology, the sixteenth-century Reformer intermittently revisits my daily work as a theologian with inter- and transdisciplinary proclivities. Luther's texts, each distinct, with its own hue and shape, are all in movement not synchronically but each at its own pace toward what for Luther was the core—the knowledge of Christ or justice of Christ. To this end I have nudged some of Luther's texts in their movement, taking care not to change their hue or shape but translating them for our times, all the while acknowledging that I might have been a traitor in the process, which I cannot but be.

I will continue to be a chronicler and a translator of Luther, not to iconize him or to replant the sixteenth-century Luther in the twenty-first century but to see him come alive in our contexts. Thus, this book does not enclose Luther between its covers; rather, it presents an interim report on a project that I, along with a score of colleagues laboring in these labyrinthine ambits, received incomplete, and as such will leave it still unfinished for others to put on the mantle when our term is up and the labor done. Nevertheless, the need to publish this intermezzo is of importance even as my research on Luther persists, revealing ever new glimpses into the theology of this enigmatic and yet serendipitous and insightful thinker. These pages are thus both a revisitation of the past and an invitation to a new orientation. It is a revisitation since a glimpse into the past at this juncture is opportune for Lutheran theology and its heritage, where remembrance is done not just for the sake of recollection but to enable a radical encounter with the past so as to take a stance in current history. This intermezzo is thus also an invitation to direct the gaze to a beam of light projected onto trails untrodden and paths often deviating from the highway Lutheranism and Lutheran theology have historically journeyed.

My hope is that the present text will lead to fresh research into new directions; yet this novelty does not necessarily surpass what has been brought to light in other circumstances and for other occasions. To indicate their resilience is the task of chroniclers who raise signals, positioning themselves neither as curators of a monumental memory nor as champions carrying forward the torch of the historical march of a weighty tradition. Chroniclers tell stories as if the chambermaids of those history acclaims as heroes. Their gaze is of a third, neither that of detached "objectivity," of "what really happened," nor that of the cheerleaders of celebrities. They register and store occasions in which transfigurations occurred; historically inscribed circumstances etch their imprint in other settings, coming there to life. Chroniclers acknowledge and commit these transfiguring events to memory.

For disdainful detractors, discontent with Lutheranism and its theology, this text may be awkwardly confessional; yet it is an announcement of the advent of an unsuspected companion for the journey, or rather the detection of its presence. As for the Luther aficionados, these chapters will be seen as affected by improper methodological flâneur, or even heterodoxy, yet they announce that it is time for taking on other templates, as the old are passing away.

Many of the arguments in the text found their way to select publics in previous installments and, importantly, were written for those contexts. Reformulating the essays and lacing them together into a new and cogent whole that is different than the sum of its parts has been rewarding. A good number of these texts have resulted from my engagement with the Lutheran World Federation, especially with the Department of Theology and Public Witness (formerly the Department of Theology and Studies), and I sincerely thank the communion for the privilege to be part of its work in drafting the contours of a living Lutheran theology in the planetary communion. I am also deeply indebted to the following publications/institutions for granting permission to collect the ideas here, presented in a new light:

> Cambridge Scholar's Publishing: "Luther and the Apocalyptic," in *On the Apocalyptic and Human Agency: Conversations with Augustine of Hippo and Martin Luther* (2015);
>
> Pickwick Publications: "Planet Luther: Challenges and Promises for a Lutheran Global Identity," in *Lutheran Identity and Political Theology* (2014);

Lutheran Quarterly: "Communication and the Transgression of Language in Martin Luther" (2003); "Luther on the Authority of Scriptures" (2005); "Justification as Death and Gift" (2010);

Fortress Press: "Power and Politics: Incursions into Luther's Theology," in *The Global Luther: A Theologian for Modern Times* (2009); "The Word and the Mask: Revisiting the Two-Kingdoms Doctrine," in *The Gift of Grace: The Future of Lutheran Theology* (2005);

Word and World: "The Weeping Mask: Ecological Crisis and the View of Nature" (1991).

Mentors and guides, friends and partners in conversation who helped bring my thoughts to fruition are, needless to say, too numerous to mention, and not a few even elude consciousness. Naming always runs the risk of oversight, unintended though it might be. However, past and present companions I bring along—some I have named in the text and footnotes; others have left their imprints anonymously but are nonetheless present. From the named and unnamed I seek leniency if my use of their guidance led me to places they had not intended.

Professor David Tracy honored me with a foreword to this book—to him the thanks of an admirer.

This work would not have found its way to the public were it not for the work of Professor Mary Philip, who is *de facto* editor of this volume and whose dedication to bring it to completion will remain not properly accredited.

I also acknowledge the three institutions where I held concurrent appointments from 2011 to 2015: The Lutheran School of Theology at Chicago; Faculdades EST, in Brazil; and Århus University, in Denmark. To these institutions, their faculty, staff, and administration, my sincere thanks for their invaluable support and friendship.

To Cascade Books, particularly the competent editorial work and support of Charlie Collier and Jacob Martin, my heartfelt gratitude.

As I continue my journey I leave these scripts as signs by the side of the path I am trodding; they are not tombstones, for these signposts point to the horizon ahead.

Abbreviations

ABU	Associação Bíblica Universtitária
CEBI	Centro Ecumênico de Estudos Bíblicos
COMIN	Conselho Indigenista Missionário
CPT	Comissão Pastoral da Terra
DTS	Department of Theology and Studies (of LWF)
JDDJ	Joint Declaration on the Doctrine of Justification
LW	Luther's Works
LWF	Lutheran World Federation
MTS	Movimento do Trabalhadores Rurais Sem Terra
RGG^3	Die Religion in Geschichte und Gegenwart, 3rd ed.
RGG^4	Die Religion in Geschichte und Gegenwart, 4th ed.
RPP	Religion Past and Present
WA	Weimar Ausgabe (Luthers Werke, kritische Gesamtausgabe)
WA Br	Weimar Ausgabe Briefe
WA TR	Weimar Ausgabe Tischenrede

Introduction

Praeterit enim figura huius mundi.
(For the figure of this world passes.)

AD CORINTHIOS I, 7:31

THE POINTED ARCH, THE ribbed vault and the flying buttress, characteristic of Gothic architecture was not any different on that day to the passersby of All Saints Church, known as the Castle Church. The church had become a hub of activity ever since it was commissioned as the chapel of the University of Wittenberg. Students scuttled like squirrels either on the way to classes or for worship. The sound of the pipe organ did not seem to alarm the occasional golden eagle that swooped down to take a swipe at the little birds that fluttered by the doors of the church. Life in and around Wittenberg was mundane.

On that day, October 31, 1517, so goes the legend, a young Augustinian friar, Martin Luther, walked up to the door of the Castle Church in Wittenberg and nailed a set of theses titled "Disputation on the Power and Efficacy of Indulgences," which later became the manifesto of the Reformation. If the legend has historical grounds, the young monk would not have done anything extraordinary, for it was the customary way of precipitating an academic debate with social repercussions in those days. However, what ensued was indeed extraordinary and needless to say not so customary. The preceptorial morphed into a revolution! Known as the Ninety-Five Theses, this document and events that followed boosted and buttressed the inception of the Reformation movement. Some three centuries later appeal to the meaning of that event was evoked, but little related to church or theology: "Just as it was once the monk, so is it now the philosopher in whose brain the revolution begins."¹ Such is one of the receptions of this Augustinian brother's nailing of the Ninety-Five Theses. For Marx the figure of the Reformer passed on to Hegel.

The nailing incident, in itself not especially unusual, achieved its marked significance only retrospectively, since it was followed by a controversial and prolific career of its main actor. Incendiary pamphlets, provocative sermons, Bible translations, catechisms, treatises, and commentaries, all produced in the juncture of politico-ecclesiastical trials, offered a magnifying glass through which that 31st of October became the emblematic turning point for many dimensions of social existence. Chiefly remembered, however, is the schism it produced in Christianity, the most significant since the split of Eastern and Western Christianity in 1054, and arguably the most noteworthy in the whole of the occidental Christian church. The revolution thus metamorphosed into a religious reformation! But its impact, also in political and economic life, was and continued to be notable. The Reformer's name is frequently evoked as a cipher to name revolutionary moments beyond ecclesiastical and theological bounds. The relationship of God's grace to everyday life in many of its dimensions quivered. Solid institutions smelted. Here the term "revolution," when used in the Copernican sense, applies in describing the dislodging of the gravitational center from institutional sacredness to the presence of that which is unique, alone, sole (*solus*). The *solus Christus*—reappearing in *sola gratia, sola fide, sola scriptura*—was the sun (*sol*) that regimented the orbits of the theological, ecclesial, and political "planets." As Copernicus placed the sun at the center of our gravitational system, so did the Reformer with the *solae* for systems of theology and ecclesial autarchies.

The political meaning of the word "revolution," inherited from astronomy as an analogue, emerged only later and was used in association with the modern idea of freedom. Ernst Bloch in 1921 used the term to describe the erstwhile Luther follower and then his opponent, Thomas Müntzer, as theologian of revolution.² However, it has been used as it should be, in my opinion, to frame the figure of the author of *On the Freedom of a Christian*, the third of the major reforming treatises of 1520. To this day ideas of freedom, of protest, dissent, and tenacity are conjured when the name Luther is invoked. The name elicits also images that associate him with socio-political conservativism, theological intransigence, moral prevarications, and ecclesial laxity. Even for contradictory reasons and ambivalent assessment of its accomplishments, the Reformation of the sixteenth century marks a

---

1. Marx, "Critique of Hegel's Philosophy of Right," 3:182.
2. Bloch, *Thomas Müntzer als Theologe der Revolution* (1921).

moment that has been capable of migrating to other times and places. It is invoked in circumstances and contexts that share little with the sixteenth-century Reformation in Saxony, which nonetheless find a point of contact and kindredness. The Reformation reappears in events that appeal to it as warrant or inspiration. In the appeals made to the event a metabolism takes place. There is a yoking of disparate occurrences when the Reformation becomes an insignia for conveying promises associated to it, ideas for which it stood. In return it receives a content that not only enriches but displaces its original context when it emerges in new ones.

Events such as the Reformation, and particularly some gestures of its best known protagonist, Martin Luther, inscribe themselves into the inventory of images, projecting figures and sketching profiles that become catalysts for momentous occasions and characters in other times and other places. History offers an array of such reincarnations that regardless of depth and nuances are evoked to shroud with its figures other events. The depth associated with the occasion evoked lends to the new circumstances thickness and endurance; yet the evocation rests in an Archimedean point powerful enough to be the axis around which the event revolves, but sufficiently spongy to absorb variegated contents. Such is the fate of the historical figure of Luther and the Reformation.

To examine this process of reconfiguration of the Reformation in different contexts is not an easy task when we consider it as a disruptive event; and the Reformation was and should be considered a disruptive event! However, grafted in the subconscious of societies affected by it erstwhile, the Reformation hardened into the institutional patterns of European culture and politics. How does an institutionalized reality become an event again? Or to put it bluntly, can and should "orthodoxy" find its "heretical roots" again? And if it were to, how? The tendency to accommodate difference under the guise of inclusivism, dialogue, and ecumenism can indeed become a blinder to deeper rooted fragmentations resilient to assimilation. How to awaken the "heretic" spirit of the Reformation, and indeed of Luther, even when wicked specters will also come along and bring Luther the anti-Semitic and the reactionary repressor of peasants? And, furthermore, how appropriate is the appeal to the Reformation to frame events far removed from its own time and place?

Luther was by and large a parochial character. He had a very limited sense of the wider world at his time. Aware he was that the inhabited world consisted of Europe, Asia, and Africa, the continents that have a shore to the Mediterranean.[3] But that was about it. Of America, whose European

---

3. WA 31/II, 95, 36: *Sunt 3 mundi parti habitabiles, Asia, Aphrica, Europa.*

extraordinary landfall was no secret all over Europe, there are some vague references to "islands just found."[4] But these few oblique remarks were only done to address the problem regarding the fulfillment of the great commission to the apostles to go to the whole world. Yet those who were conquering the world the Reformer hardly acknowledged were not so oblivious about Luther. In the second quarter of the sixteenth century, during the time of the Inquisition in the New World, public condemnation and execution of heretics included the reading of the *autos-da-fé* which said, "They left this kingdom to become Lutherans." While this was meant to define the heretics, little did they know about Luther's theology. Luther had indeed become a cipher for freedom and rebellion, a cipher for another "kingdom." But those were the times in which the Reformation territories in Europe served as the measuring stick to define heresy, rebellion, freedom, and nonconformity to the hegemonic Holy Roman Empire.

The Reformer's theology for the last five centuries has been almost exclusively researched and interpreted by German, Scandinavian, and US theologians, while the significance of Luther's theology for the global South is rising in the very proportion to which Lutheranism is migrating *en masse* to the south of the planet.

Lutherans are belated in following other large world Christian communions, as Roman Catholics, Anglicans, Presbyterians, and Methodists, to find its majority in the south of the planet. In demographics, the other ecumenical communions have already been severely depleted in regions of the world where they constituted themselves originally, mostly the North Atlantic axis, and their presence outside of this axis well surpasses the 50 percent mark. But Lutherans are following suit. Currently about 45 percent of Lutherans are now outside of what the LWF defined, half a century ago, as the three main blocks: Central Europe, Scandinavia, and the United States. One hundred years ago the Lutheran presence outside of the axis was negligible. The statistics are changing so fast as to presume that very soon the majority of Lutherans will be in nontraditional Lutheran territories. How theology will follow this trend and define Lutheranism not only by the letter of the Weimar edition of Luther's works or the Book of Concord, but by the *viva vox* of an *ecclesia semper reformanda*, is a challenge and an opportunity. These Lutheran people in new contexts that the old barely knows have become the "new heretics." There is no *auto-da-fé* being read now, but a condescending attitude that dismisses the theological competence of these new "heretics" prevails among custodians of the heritage. The time is ripe to acknowledge that translating Luther to new contexts involves a process

---

4. WA 10/III, 139, 20f. See also WA 10/I/i, 20, 16; 53, 169.

of transfiguration by which the old, relevant as it is in its reappearance, also passes away.

These Lutherans in new contexts are becoming the majority of the Lutherans worldwide. However, unlike the ones of the traditional geographical settings of Lutheranism, this upcoming *majority* find themselves in contexts in which they are a *minority* surrounded by other faiths and confessions. And this posits challenges for theology at least as significant as the geographical dislocation alone. The contours of the Reformation now are to be defined over against this new background in which powers and principalities exert control now as they did when the Reformation erupted as a cry for freedom and a call for the gospel. The Reformation defined them then; it is left for us to name them today, yet the spirit is the same.

If the institutional profile of Lutheran identity is one of the significant changes taking place, there is another characteristic that is more salient, and goes beyond identity politics. One thing is to consider Lutheranism in the institutional formation of an identity, but another and entirely different thing is to appeal to the event. Appealing to Lutheranism's emblematic character or characters not for an identity but as occasions that evoke ideas, visions, and inspiration is radically significant. The Reformation and the figure of Luther name events and project characters whose use-value is not subjected to the exchange-value acquired in the controlled economy of the ecclesial and academic market of identity formation. This subversive character to what regulates it and issues the currency for its equivalence is crucial.

When the use-value escapes the control of market-regulated exchange-value the "commodity" is available unleashed, notwithstanding the constant effort to tame it back to a predictable and controllable exchange process regulated either by the academia or the church. With its use-value set free from the market, it is adopted and employed, without having to pay tribute to the curators of the name and the image. The free-floating image henceforth appears in contexts that are not proper to it. In the new contexts these images function without anchorage in conventional academic or ecclesial foundations. These are indeed superficial uses of the image. What matters is precisely the surface in which they appear. Their validity is determined by the use for which they function as apparitions. Such apparitions are banners raised in the name of some ideas, causes, principles, and dispositions the image is endowed with by association. When an image, by virtue of ideals for which it stands, is transferred across borders from remote places and times without customs levies, it is called *figura*. This procedure has been referred to as "figural interpretation" which accounts for the invocation of

Luther or several Reformation motifs without the slightest intent to engage in identity politics or to build strategic allegiances.

Erich Auerbach[5] studied the use of *figura* as a literary trope in Western literature, particularly its use in the Judeo-Christian scriptures. He offers a suggestive option for framing Reformation studies, and particularly Martin Luther. *Figurae* function as ciphers, which the Arabic root designates as the symbol for zero—0. Ciphers by themselves have no value. Yet when compounded with any value it changes its worth exponentially. From there the word *cipher* assumes the connotation of a key or a code. This key or code allows a given reading of characters, events, and circumstances, casting a new light onto them, setting them into a given perspective, bringing to attention facets and edges otherwise passed unnoticed, in a word, deciphering them. *Figura* functions as a cipher, but adds to it rootedness in an original context situated concretely in space and time. But from its original placing it detaches itself to find a new dwelling in remote characters and events.

Figurae, as a trope, share with analogues elements of resemblance. In both there is a connection between two occasions, and they both lift up similarities in their difference. However, while analogues establish a relationship between two circumstances by comparing the parallelism of a series of elements that unfold a similar pattern in a causal chain, a *figura* is evoked to lift up a punctual feature not dependant on the causal nexus of events in its original historical setting.

Two other tropes bear likeness to the *figura*: the symbol and the allegory. In the case of the symbol, in the classical definition of Goethe, "An appearance is transposed into an idea, the idea into an image, and in such a way that the idea remains always infinitely active and unapproachable in the image."[6] The *figura*, while sharing with the symbol the appearance-idea-image process, parts company with it in keeping the idea attached to the image. While making the image mobile, the *figura* binds the idea to its concrete singularity. If, for instance, freedom is the idea and Luther the image functioning as *figura*, the idea remains connected to particular features associated to the image. A symbol would be represented by the image of, say, an eagle in which the idea of freedom is not rooted in the concrete singularity of the bird depicted in the image.

This "attachment to the image's particularity"[7] brings it close to the allegory; between *figura* and allegory "the boundary is fluid."[8] In distinction

---

5. Auerbach, "Figura," in *Scenes from the Drama*, 11–76. See also his classic study of Western literature, *Mimesis*.

6. Goethe, *Maximen und Reflexionen*, 192, my translation.

7. Ibid.

8. Auerbach, "Figura," 47.

to it, however, *figura* does not allow for the idea to be held in the image alone; its content is bipolar with an oscillating reference to both the original event and its present instantiation. Its resurgence endows it with a content that is infused by its appearance in new contexts, enriching the idea with dimensions that saturate the image. In the *figura* the image is overdetermined by content not adduced entirely in the original. The signifier receives an excess of meaning in the signified. "Figural interpretation establishes a connection between two events or persons, the first of which signifies not only itself but also the second, while the second encompasses or fulfills the first."[9] The major distinction from the allegory, with which it shares many characteristics, is that, unlike the allegory, in the *figura* both the signifier and the signified are historically anchored. "The two poles of the figure are separate in time, but both, being real events or figures, are within time, within the stream of history."[10]

Luther as *figura*, as a figure, is something to be understood apart from, or before other specialized doctrinal aspects may be scrutinized and discerned. At least it needs to be acknowledged as a dimension of Luther research that in-depth textual and historic-critical analysis often overlooks or simply ignores, leaving unexplained its enduring significance and recurring effects. The *figurae* have *Wirkungsgeschichte*; they work. The more immersed Luther studies become in the profundity of the thought of the Reformer, the more obscure and neglected becomes his figural significance. The call for a closer reading of the text may arrest the inquiring gaze into historical and philological frames of a picture whose "aura"—to use Walter Benjamin's helpful notion—has long taken flight.

This book is about Luther's theology and practice that has inspired so many across confessional and even religious lines worldwide, or else excite those for whom he displays pathetic (and at times pathological) features of a dubious character, displaying even cases of bigotry untamed. Be it as it may, Luther's theology, his understanding of creation and incarnation, the cross, his affirmation of freedom from ecclesial, economic, and political encroachments, and his distinction between the political reality and the economy, or even his atrocious invectives against Jews and Turks (Muslims) are seen in a new light in societies in which modernization does not mean necessarily secularization, and the intellect (*logos*) is not set in dual opposition to things material. The now century-old European dispute about whether Luther is a late medieval theologian or a beacon of modernity is rendered largely superfluous when the Reformer is read and interpreted in contexts (including

9. Ibid., 53.
10. Ibid., 53f.

to a good extent North America!) that do not share the peculiar cultural and political history of Europe, its orthodoxies, its pietisms, its enlightenments, and its secularisms, which have formed the matrix of so much dispute over Luther's legacy.

The following pages intend to lift up the significance of the Reformer's reception that has not been filtered by the remarkably erudite tradition of Luther research for almost half of a millennium. Certainly the authoritative contributions made by Europe and also North America cannot be bypassed or seen as not deserving utmost deference. However, here is offered a reading of Luther and his legacy that goes beyond, and often sails over, the traditional geopolitics of Luther research, and goes into realities where the Reformer's reception and the latent promise of his theology receive an unsuspected appraisal and a transfigural presence.

The argument that follows is woven, to use a simile, with warps and woofs to produce the fabric, the *texture*, of the contentions. The two strings keep on traversing each other in perpendicular directions finding no resolution, but a text(ure) whose meaning only rests in an irresolute eschatological horizon. The reader is invited to see the meaning in the offing.

These traversing strings of thought, these warps and woofs, can be described as a combination of distinct dimensions of the God-world relation, on the one hand, and by a theologically informed perspectival gaze into human affairs, on the other hand.

The first line, the "warps," in keeping the simile, carries the signature notion of the Reformation. It entails all that pertains to the *coram deo* relationship, constituting all that relates to the spiritual regime. The thoughts on justification, the *solae* (*sola gratia, sola fide, sola scriptura, solus Christus*), and the evangelical criterion of what conveys Christ (*was Christum treibet*) belong to it. These entail ultimate concerns. Transversal "woofs" constitute all theological thoughts that are aided by reason and entail questions concerning the *coram mundo* relation; here matters of justice and the proper use of reason for achieving equitable ends prevail. The latter encompass penultimate concerns that relate to the earthly regime. Between the two there is no causal relationship (notwithstanding the occasional use of the fruit–tree metaphor). They are discernable as distinct strands whose importance is not the yarn by itself but the fabric it constitutes.

During the turbulent years of the beginning of the sixteenth century, before the Reformation movement reached its climax, the quest of the young Augustinian friar, Martin Luther, for a merciful God and even the marvelous answer found was still no more than a bundle of yarn. Its paramount significance was not the discovery of its existence as a thread in and of itself. Its momentous magnitude that lent the Reformation its insignia would only manifest itself in being woven through the "woofs" of challenges in ordinary earthly existence. There it finds its unique and irreducible dimension; by itself it just spins a yarn. Spinning a yarn instead of weaving a fabric has often been the fate of discourses about justification when done in abstract—fine the string, but missing the texture.

The text that follows is about the fabric, the texture that makes Luther a *figura* that has the quality of being transfigured. The question of justification, this article by which all that merits existence stands or falls, will reveal its color and receive its strength precisely in the fabric into which it is intertwined. So it is of import to say in advance, as clearly as possible, that the teachings on justification belong to the nature of the "warps." However, these started to delineate themselves only in the interlacing of the quest of justification with spheres of earthly existence that provided the occasion for the message of God's sole grace to shine through.

The celebrated nailing of the Ninety-Five Theses not only gave the Reformation momentous significance but it was also portentous. In the texture of its fabric a theological principle was making public inroads.

The theological principle manifested itself in a struggle that was fought mostly in three fronts that exposed the three publics Luther had in mind as constitutive of the worldly order of things, the church institutional, the household/economy, and the politico-civil affairs (*ecclesia, oeconomia, politia*). With different theological emphases, each one of these publics displayed fundamental anthropological and sociological dimensions of human earthly existence over against which the message of justification shone. Each one revealed a facet of the scope of oppression of human existence in the world. To the extent that each remains as such into our days, transfiguration shows its effectiveness.

In one way or another, these three publics entered the programmatic agenda of the Reformation opening the fronts by which the Reformation movement defined its most basic social and anthropological agenda. Each one had a significant impact in the theology of the Reformation and its ecclesial and socio-political significance. They represented, in the unfolding of the Reformation, Luther's practical concern with the three basic publics or "orders" of creation for the institutional organization of earthly existence, which roughly correspond to the three basic anthropological faculties since Aristotle—*praxis, poēsis* or productive labor, and *theōria* or intelligible comprehension. However, in the practical articulation of the challenges that they represented, Luther's adoption of the medieval conception of the three orders, or publics (*Dreiständelehre*), showed their interconnectedness and dynamic overlapping features. Each one was a discrete public, and the sphere each public encompasses is unique as to the challenge they represent and the procedures with which each operates; these will be defined by the respective anthropological faculty. Each one, therefore, provides an entrance to the others and, even if distinct, cannot be discretely isolated from each other.

The engagement in the political front can be represented by the fierce debate and tragic outcome of the Peasant Revolt and its subsequent suppression. The struggle led by enthusiast leaders had several aspects. An important one, the dispute over hermeneutics, has been discussed at length in Protestant research focusing mainly on the theology of Thomas Müntzer and Karlstadt. But from the peasants' standpoint, if we take it from the "Twelve Articles" of the peasants, what is by far more decisive is the access to land for hunting, fishing, collecting wood, the demands for fair taxes and rents, and for the abolition of the "death clause" (by which a widow would lose her husband's right to the land upon his death). It was a cry for a vital space in a late feudal society. Luther, who was first called upon by the peasants themselves as a witness to their plea, later supported the repression launched against them. And the reason, in the Reformer's view, is that competencies were being violated. The Word of God was recruited to legislate over "matters for the lawyers to discuss."[11] Implicitly recognizing the justice of the peasants' claims, Luther even counseled them to suffer martyrdom. The miner's son would not recognize in the peasants' protest the struggle to preserve and conquer the basic means of life and work. It was a protest against the world and its injustices for the right of labor and the vital space that ensured it. The peasants' demands were not a "class struggle"; their revolt was against the world as it stood.[12] Luther's insistence on keeping competencies apart has led both to some of the sharpest criticisms he has ever received, as well as praise for an austere modern realism that could have prevented even greater bloodshed.

A second front of the Reformation movement was connected with the emergence of financial capitalism and the practice of usury. Here the Reformation took some ambiguous positions in relation to the official stance of the late medieval Roman Catholic Church. If Calvin condoned usury within certain interest restrictions, the Roman theologians had a legalistic interpretation of Aristotle's notion of the sterility of money, but creatively reinterpreted it to justify interest on the basis of the risk to the lender, and for the maintenance of banking institutions. But Luther, even if not thoroughly

---

11. LW 46:39; WA 18, 337, 13f.

12. Commenting on the characteristics of peasants' revolts as a protest, not against a class, but against the whole "world," Ianni (*Dialética e Capitalismo*, 110) says, "The struggle for land is always also a struggle for the preservation, the conquest . . . of a mode of living and working." See also for the same argument Paz, *Posdata*, 87–92.

consistent, would argue theologically against the exploitation of the poor that usury caused. Accused of revealing only a profound frustration[13] or producing "occasional explosions of a capricious volcano,"[14] the Reformer has indeed revealed a theological concern and rage against the oppression caused by usurers. Usurers are robbers of the means for the sustenance of life, demonic explorers of labor and family. Here Luther's voice in defense of the created goodness of this order is emphatically affirmed.

These two fronts are complemented by a third one, in which the Reformation was most successful and in which Luther had a particular important role to play. He was, first and foremost, the reformer of the church in its earthly (!) task of being an instrument of the Word of God in both its vocal (*viva vox*) and visible (sacraments) form. If the first front represented a cry for a vital space and the second for just social and economic relations for the sustenance of life and biological reproduction, the third opened space in the search for a viable realm of communication between the Word of God and the language(s) of the people to whom, in whom, and through whom the Word communes.

These three fronts that displayed the public engagement of the Reformer, as reflected thorough his life and writings, are one aspect of Luther's theology that refer to and constitute the earthly régime. This régime is juxtaposed by what is called the spiritual régime. But the two are not symmetrical. They entailed discontinuities. The earthly régime involves realities that are posited, institutional apparatuses that imply some permanence. In it reason operates and ethical responsibilities are called for to provide stability. The spiritual régime, however, has an eventual character. While the spiritual dimension refers to presence, the earthly implies *re*-presentation. One encompasses all that pertains to justification; the other is about justice and fairness (equity). While one refers to an event that is ultimately apophatic, the other describes an embodied reality that needs to be cared for and reasoned about even as they pass away.

Luther's thoughts about the two régimes (normally referred to as the two kingdoms doctrine) is what makes his theology at once fascinating, but also disconcerting for some paroxysms it incurs. They are not complementary realities, but they overlap each other without one displacing the other. The relation is somehow analogous to the light that allows us to see colors and discern objects, yet the light as such is not "seen." The genius of the Reformer was to sustain, through and through, a communication between

---

13. Nelson, *Idea of Usury*, 46.

14. The expression is R. H. Tawney's, cited in Preston, *Religion and the Ambiguities*, 141.

presence and representation, between event and institution, between heaven and earth, between passivity and activity, justification and justice. But the trick lies in the irreducible mystery of the communication between the two. Phrasing it by one of Luther's favorite metaphors, there is an organic connection between the right and the left hand of the one God, but without a causal relation between them, so as if the left hand knows not what the right is doing.

This communication between these different qualities is predicated on a reading of the Councils of Constantinople (381) and Chalcedon (451) and the formulation of the doctrine regarding the *communicatio idiomatum*, or the communication of properties or qualities. The concept of the incarnation and its implication lie at the core of Luther's theology. Subsequent Lutheranism organized the Reformer's rendition of the *communicatio* more systematically saying that it included the transmission of divine and infinite qualities to the carnal and finite (*genus majestaticum*), which implies as well the reverse transference of the finite to the infinite (*genus tapeinoticum*). This has been correctly pointed out to be the axial point of Luther's theology, its motor.[15]

However, if this is the point, it beams beyond itself into a horizon that the early sixteenth-century Reformer could hardly envision. If the limit of one's language is the limit of one's world (Wittgenstein), Luther, in the cage of medieval ecclesiastical Latin, had few options to venture beyond into new vistas. Yet, he dared breaking with the conventional use of academic Latin, making incursions into the vernacular, to the point of being acclaimed as the father of modern German language. However, many of his texts blend Latin and German, often inserting also Hebrew and Greek expressions, creating thus a truly hybrid text of a unique character. All this was done as an attempt to get beyond the boundaries of his own language, his own world whose limits he could only scratch the surface, but in so doing he acknowledged the limit as a threshold and not an impervious capsule. Justification is the name he gave to this threshold that is crossed from outside as a light illuminating the earthly régime with its legal institutions, rationalities, and all that results from laborious production that throws their shadows. The light as such cannot be seen, but it can be inferred by the shadows it casts. In this respect traces of Augustine's suggested "ontological argument" for God's existence (and further elaborated by medieval Franciscans) are lurking in the work of Luther. It is through the shadows cast that the light can be discerned, that the infinite reveals its presence in the mere finite. And only

---

15. See Steiger, "The *communicatio idiomatum* as the Axle and Motor of Luther's Theology," 125-58.

there is it given for our inquiry; only in representation is presence given for human scrutiny *a posteriori*.

This book is divided into four parts. In each the weaving is taken up from different perspectives. There is an order in their progression, yet each part offers a different angle from which Luther's *figura* may be observed. It is as if the four parts form quadrants of the same circumference, bidding different watching stations. Most certainly other positions could be taken but these are the ones that in the author's judgment offer decidedly pertinent perspectives and distinctly privileged standpoints. These parts are not lined up like beads on a string but arrayed like a constellation that can simultaneously be observed from different vantage points. From each perspective new light is projected onto the whole, which inevitably will result in overlaps and repetitions. But as to them remains valid the old lesson: *repetitio mater studiorum est*.

Part One deals with Luther's use of language and how he dealt with the letter of the Scriptures. The spirit gives itself as letter; the living voice, *viva vox*, casting its shadow in the written text (*scriptura*). If Part One dwells in the frozen crust of the surface of the "depth of riches" (Rom 11:33), Part Two delves into some of the "riches" even as inscrutable as they remain. The doctrine of justification is examined as the description of an event which can only be addressed in the mirror of its representations. At the core of it lies the examination of the person of Christ as it fully manifests itself in the cross that inculcates itself into the profundity of this natural world revealing its entrails as the "apocalypse of Jesus Christ" (Rev 1:1). Part Three offers an overview of the challenges and the actuality of Luther's transfiguration as it makes its appearance and offers its promises for the planetary challenges of the day. The final part deals specifically with the contributions a Lutheran informed theology makes in framing the contemporary challenges faced by the economic order, or the management of the *oikos*, on the one hand, and the trials of the city, or the ruling of the *polis*, on the other. Luther's incisive distinction of these two dimensions (to which the church comes as the third) is one of the most relevant, if not unique, insights the Reformer offers to a theologically responsible and relevant social ethics for today.

Luther is believed to have said, "One Book is enough, but a thousand books are not too many!" Well, many a book it might take to decipher Luther's theology, but suffice it is to say that the time has come to follow his figure as it is passed on, transfigured. To that end I offer the pages that follow.

Part One

The Genius of Language: Grammar and Rhetoric

1

The Quest for Language

Engaging the Head and the Heart

The time of silencing is over, the time to speak has come.

MARTIN LUTHER

The Word in Words

WHEN THE MIND IS at sea a new word provides a raft, wrote Goethe three hundred years after Martin Luther's time. However, these words could not have been truer for Luther, for the limits of language set the limits of his world. Language constituted the very communicability and linguistic being of human beings.

Martin Luther is celebrated as a virtuoso in the art of translation as well as the architect of the modern German language. This is accepted without significant controversy across the theological and ideological spectrum. While his linguistic adeptness went uncontested, his theological stances, to the contrary, present a different picture. His theology is both championed by followers as well as decried by foes. Such discrepancy in the reception of the Reformer suggests an interesting query. Is the *form* of Luther's thought, as rendered in his use of language, independent from the *content* of his theological contentions? The initial argument here sustains that this is not the case. The form implies the content and vice versa. The creative use of language for the sake of communicating the gospel is tied to Luther's understanding of the communication of the *logos* with the flesh. This is best illustrated with an examination of the language Luther employed.

The Reformation movement and particularly Luther were concerned with the recreation of a language capable of giving voice to the voiceless, of turning unarticulated utterances into meaning, of constituting knowledge for empowerment, because the Word communicates in the medium of language(s), idioms. Between the divine utterance of the addressed Word of God and the language of the people we find the cultural equivalent of the distinctively Lutheran rendition of the Council of Chalcedon's (451 CE) doctrine of *communicatio idiomatum*, the "communication of attributes or properties," in all its three classical Lutheran genres in which it expresses itself (*idiomaticum, apotelesmaticum,* and *majestaticum*).[1] What the *communicatio idiomatum* means for Christology parallels the relationship between the Word and language: the semantics of the Word are meaningful in the vernacular (*genus idiomaticum*); the effective deeds of the Word are performed in language (*genus apotelesmaticum*), and the defiled character of human languages and communication is capable of the sublime Word (*genus majestaticum*). It did not end there. The reverse, complementary process also was true: The broken and diffident quotidian vernacular finds itself totally present in the majestic Word of God rendering it humble and meek (*genus tapeinoticum*).

Luther's understanding of language puts into practice his doctrine of the person of Christ, including the disputes over the Lord's Supper. This is the practice of the *ecclesia*, this earthly order of creation that is the space for a "marvelous exchange" to take place. This celebrated christological axiom[2] finds its linguistic equivalent in his argumentation during an academic disputation in 1537: "All words are made new when they are transferred from their own to another [semantic] context."[3] The new language (*nova lingua*) is the result of this transference. It is not an epiphany, an unambiguous manifestation of the divine. Strictly speaking, there is no epiphany in Luther's theology; the divine manifests itself in debased conditions. And where this communication happens, there is the church. Luther's understanding of the church as the creature of the Word (*ubi verbum, ibi ecclesia*) is grounded on this assumption.[4] For him, the Word cannot exist without the people of

---

1. On the *communicatio idiomatum* in general, see Kolb and Wengert, *Book of Concord*, 622 n. 268. The analogous relationship between Luther's Christology and his understanding of language has been well presented by Steiger, "The *communicatio idiomatum* as the Axle and Motor of Luther's Theology." A similar argument in connection with the sacramental dispute with Zwingli is presented by Thomas Wabel, *Sprache als Grenze*, 257–73

2. *Mirabilem mutacionem.* WA 39/1, 435, 11.

3. *Omnia vocabula fiunt nova, quando e suo foro in alienum transferuntur.* WA 39/1, 231, 1f.

4. The expression Luther used was this: *Ecclesia enim creatura est Evangelii.* WA 2,

God, and neither can the people of God exist without the Word of God.[5] To give it a sharp focus: the question of language in Luther is ultimately about the communication of the Word, and therefore also with the body of the communicative language hosting it. Therefore, to separate the Word of God from the vernacular, or to have a theology of the Word apart from human communication with all the botches of the vernacular is a form of linguistic Nestorianism. This would sustain that the Word attaches itself to human words without becoming the very words spoken in the quotidian argot.

The vernacular with all its limitations, ambiguities, and imprecisions is the host of the Word as Mary carries God in her womb. And the Word is present in the broken vernacular not in spite, but because of its defective character. This defective character in communication theory is dubbed as "noise," which impairs communication. Gregory Nazianzen's maxim that "what is not assumed is not redeemed," finds its linguistic equivalent here. If the Word is not in the "noise," communication can never take place; Babel would prevail.

The limits of one's language are not an impediment to the revelation of the Word just as the corruption of the flesh does not prevent it from receiving the infinite. On the contrary, the whole meaning of the Word becoming flesh lies in the very corruption of the flesh. That Christ has been made sin (2 Cor 5:21) is how Paul phrased it, and one finds in Luther the scandalous definition of Christ as *maximus peccator*. The attempt to make the flesh worthy before it can host the divine is comparable to the cleansing of language from its vernacular "transgressions" in order to make it worthy of the Word. It is no wonder that Luther would find in the contempt shown toward the base vernacular (including his own!) the same attitude he found in his own monastic experience of trying to become worthy of divine righteousness. It is therefore in language and its limits that we will find also Luther's appreciation of glory dwelling in the frailty of the flesh. Any such an attempt to find a prelapsarian language that is scientifically unequivocal (*wissenschaftlich*) and semantically univocal (logical positivism) borders on a form of Gnosticism.

It is in the inability to use one's language or the active suppression of the vernacular's validity as a vehicle of the Word that Luther would find a correlation to clericalism's purported ontological difference between those specially called (*vocati*) and the laity. The result is Luther's "engaged

---

430, 6f. In reference to the church as a continuing creation of the Word, see WA 3, 533, 1; 6, 130, 26; 30/II, 681, 34–38.

5. WA 50, 657–61.The absence of the Word describes the condition of hell: "Also muss yhe widderumb die helle seyn, da Gottis wort nicht ist." WA 10/III, 192, 20f.

literature,"⁶ which is in itself a practice of fighting for language in the very midst of itself. As Luther wrote in a letter to Spalatin early in 1519 ". . . (so it follows) in the midst of common language we have been battling."⁷ And the effects of this struggle reverberate in Luther's own text producing rippling effects of which he is quite aware. In comparing his own language to Melanchthon's, he praises the latter's style, logic, and clarity, which he felt exceeded his own. But then he concludes, "I have been born to take up an open fight with the mob and devils, therefore my books are much more tempestuous and belligerent [than Melanchthon's]."⁸ It is in the midst of the freedom of language that Luther fights against the oppression of language, against its subjection, against the language of oppression.

It is in the axis between language and oppression that some of the most significant contributions of Luther for the Reformation movement can be located. And this finally encompasses all of his theology. In what follows I will suggest that for Luther language is the medium between the constitution of the self (*coram meipso*) and the relation to the Other both individually and collectively (*coram Deo* and *coram hominibus*). Language is what allows one to be placed outside of oneself (*extra se*), to use the image of Luther's eccentric anthropology.⁹ For Luther, the "genius of languages" (*die Art der Sprachen*)¹⁰ is authenticated in its very use by the "common person."¹¹

The focus of Luther's theology was the ordinary folk, their use of language, especially, in how they expressed their relationship to God, to everyday lives and to themselves. The translation of the Bible into the vernacular, the tract literature, etc., an example of this commitment and a pointer to the Reformer's own anticlericalism, and is not to be seen as an idiosyncratic peculiarity. This linguistic gesture brought about the liberation from institutional mediations that controlled the access to the sacred, to life, and to the people. In Luther's case, such liberation happened through the relativizing of institutional orders encoded in linguistic systems and their régimes of truth controlled by the academia and its philosophy, the courtroom and its jurisprudence, politics and its legislations, the market and its economy, and by the church and its "spirituality."

---

6. Stolt, *Studien zu Luthers Freiheitstraktat*, 139.

7. ". . . *mixtim (utfit) vernacula lingua digladiabamur*." WA Br 1, 301, 16f.

8. WA 30/2, 68f.

9. Using Luther's terms, the other two foci of the Reformation movement could be subsumed accordingly under his understanding of the relations *coram mundo* and *coram hominibus*. See Ebeling, *Luther*, 198–200.

10. WA 18, 155, 4f.; LW 40:165.

11. WA 18, 154, 20f.; LW 40:164.

On Language and Oppression

In Luther's linguistic move we find a compelling illustration of the liberating aspects of the way the Reformation situated one's relationship to the world and to God, as well as its impact in distinct semantic realms entailing different rules. Such insight allowed Luther to recognize that for the Word to be heard anew the Word needed to move not only vertically on the relation between God and the world, but also horizontally through different semantic fields of everyday life, from philosophy to the market, from the pulpit to politics, from the kitchen to the court, from the carnival to the children's playground.[12] To transgress these linguistic realms and the limits of their distinct uniqueness and relative legitimacy—to themselves as well as to the Word—destabilized the grip of power held by the régimes of truth of the day and the disciplinary confines into which each of them was secluded.

Anders Nygren has argued that to understand the uniqueness of Luther one needs to recognize "different motif contexts" that operate in his discourse, which changes the meaning when a word moves from one context to another.[13] This "semantic shift"[14] is now well recognized when it pertains to the relationship between theology and philosophy. My argument here is that such semantic displacements do not pertain only to the relation between the spiritual and the earthly régimes, but apply as well to "lateral" semantic moves in which words from diverse everyday-life realms break in and create unexpected meaning. Such lateral semantic transfers free a given context of meaning to entertain newness. And in this liberation offered by the unexpected meaning that breaks in Luther also saw the space for the incursion of the Word of God. It is in the disruption caused by these semantic displacements, in the disquieting "noise" in the midst of communication, that space is opened for the formation of what Luther called a "new language" (*nova lingua*) shaped by the grammar of the Spirit.

The surprise of another word, different than those legislated by the dominant régimes of truth that norm the church, the State, the economy, and the household, breaking into these domains, is for Luther an eschatological event. By the limits, at the *eschata*, of one's régime there is the promise of novelty. Thus in the text of "A Mighty Fortress Is Our God," the so-called

---

12. The prefiguring of Wittgenstein's theory of language-games is well explored in Wabel, *Sprache als Grenze*.

13. Nygren, *Meaning and Method*, 368. Nygren built his case on Wittgenstein's "language games" metaphor, which he renders as "context for meaning." Ibid., 243–64. A pertinent analysis of the construction of meaning within a semantic domain is offered by Bielfeldt, "Luther on Language."

14. The expression is found in Bielfeldt, "Luther, Metaphor, and Theological Language," 123.

Marseillaise of the Reformation, we find these words: "Let this world's tyrant rage; In battle we'll engage! His might is doomed to fail; God's judgment must prevail! One little word subdues him."[15] For Luther this battle with the world is also the strife of words (*pugna verborum*) for the sake of communication, for the sake of allowing the Word to be uttered. Where this does not happen, there "this world's tyrant rage" reigns. The tyrant who imposes a normative language sets the limits to the world, framing it and keeping the Word at bay in well-regulated and disciplined domains. How does this happen? The following digression with the help of some illustrations will etch the contours of the interface between language and oppression.

Dissimulation and Heteroglossy

In a study of popular culture in Brazil, José de Souza Martins pointed to a regular phenomenon that affects subaltern groups in society alienating them from official language. "Metaphor, occultation, dissimulation, silence, remain as the language that documents the persistence of the same violence that caused its origin . . . in the language of the oppressor."[16]

The encoded or canonical official language of hegemonic institutions is not only an instrument for the communication of power, but it is itself the exercise of power that works by depriving other voices of legitimacy. That is the end of communication, the end of conversation, and the transformation of language into a tool of power and control. The end of a conversation always implies the silencing of the other voice. Domination and oppression are, therefore, always constituted in and by the language of the one who dominates. In this sense the imposition of a linguistic system indicates the very demise of the actuality of language, the suppression of vernacular, the language of a group, the silencing and dissembling of the knowledge of the other. This is why under the dominance of a régime of truth that cannot be contested resistance is manifested in the reverse side of language, in occultation, in jest, in silence, in curse, in whispering, or in cries. These are the limiting fields in which language is at the same time suppressed but in its non-actuality, in silence and dissimulation, the emergent other voice, heteroglossy, is documented first by the very fact of its absence. But it is an exclamatory silence, an eloquent reticence!

In Shakespeare's dialogue between Prospero, the conqueror, and Caliban, the native, in *The Tempest*, a late text of 1616, he has Caliban say,

> You taught me language; and my profit on't

---

15. *Lutheran Book of Worship*, Hymn 269, trans. Catherine Winkworth.
16. Martins, *Caminhada no chão da noite*, 116–17.

Is I know how to curse; the red plague rid you,
For learning me your language![17]

The observation is pertinent. Between official languages—the language that imposes power and defines knowledge—and the dissimulated languages of those who survive and resist in dissemblance and silence, there is a cleft that the institutions ignore, suppress, or hide. Mary Douglas' often-quoted remark that "every society is fragile in its margin" is right on target in showing that the margin is not the fragile side of a society, but is where the fragility of any society manifests itself. This is why any instituted society needs to hide its margin to prevent it from becoming visible. And it becomes visible by establishing its own word, by naming its world. The other voice has to be suppressed because it implies the emergence of a new world.

In the prologue to the *Gramática de la lengua castellana*, written by the Spaniard Antonio de Nebrija—published in 1492 (the year of the Spanish conquest of the New World, when the boy Martin Luther was attending school in Mansfeld) and dedicated to the Spanish queen, Isabella—we read the following:

> Language has always accompanied domination . . . and since Your Majesty has imposed your yoke to a number of barbarian peoples and nations of different languages, in consequence of their defeat, they would be obliged to receive the laws that the winner imposes to the defeated, and then, the latter could gain the knowledge of them [the laws] through my grammar.[18]

This *Gramática*, considered the first grammar book in the modern sense of the term, was not by coincidence written on the occasion of the European confrontation with the newly discovered languages of the natives in the New World, languages never encountered before. Language, in its formal sense, has not always accompanied domination, but when it did—and in this Nebrija is right on target—the consequence of domination was the destruction of the very soul of a people, of the possibility of naming their world.

Throughout history the demand for a language has been intrinsically linked to the human search for self-determination and open communication. The silencing of language is a demonic phenomenon.[19] It deprives the subject from emerging and leaves her or him under the control of alien

---

17. Shakespeare, *The Tempest*, I, ii.
18. Quoted in Romano, *Os mecanismos da conquista colonial*, 79. Nebrija's *Gramática* is regarded as the first modern grammar produced in the Western world.
19. See my article "Idols and Demons: On Discerning the Spirits."

forces. António Vieira, Jesuit missionary in Brazil and one of the most acclaimed preachers of the seventeenth century, gave us a poignant description of the relationship between language and oppression.

> The incapability of expressing itself was the situation of Brazil and the main cause of its ills. This is the reason why nothing was more difficult for Christ than to heal a possessed mute. The worst crisis faced by Brazil during its illness was the silencing of its speech.[20]

Even when not mentioning the exegetical grounds for his remark (probably Mark 9:17–29), Vieira was right on the meaning of Jesus' exorcisms. In almost all cases, demonic possession in the New Testament is associated with the incapability of a person to utter an authentic word; either the demon speaks through the person, or the person stutters, or the possessed person is dumb. As much as language provides the limits of one's world (Wittgenstein)[21] or, conversely, provides a home for being (Heidegger),[22] its silencing, or suppression, is a cipher that allows for the possibility of recognizing the limits of one's world. The silencing of a speech documents and reveals (indeed, *sub contraria specie*) the powers of domination. But it is at this very limit that the experience of heteroglossy, by the insurrection of another language, the language of the other, that newness announces itself and attests that another world is indeed possible.

The Insurrection of the Vernacular

There is no great historical event that is not associated with a linguistic phenomenon. The Reformation movement owes its historical impact to the way in which it was able to incorporate the language of the people into its political, religious, and cultural program, expanding it, giving it a dynamic formation and a public character.

It has frequently been stressed that the Reformation's effectiveness cannot be dissociated from the Renaissance's renewal of the classic humanist values. Marked by a return to the classical values of the Western world, the Renaissance represented an elitist move toward the rebirth of classicism within a medieval and feudal world entangled by institutional constraints administered by the church and the empire, and by the emergent powerful financial institutions. There is hardly anything popular about all this. But

---

20. Quoted in Westhelle, "Apresentação," 119–20.

21. Wittgenstein, *Tractatus Logico-Philosophicus*, 148.

22. Heidegger, *Existence and Being*, 276: "It is only language that affords the very possibility of standing in the openness of the existent. Only where there is language, is there world."

in an ironic way the Renaissance also contributed to the insurgence of the "common folk"[23] onto the stage. This coming onto the stage was hastened by the Reformation movement that also helped to shape this movement of common folk providing for a yet richer and more variegated choreography.

As Mikhail Bakhtin demonstrated well in his study of Rabelais,[24] the Middle Ages at the dawn of the Renaissance was divided by the split between popular national languages and medieval Latin—in his terms, between "popular" and "official" language. Medieval Latin attempted to adjust as much as it could to the regional linguistic variations, resulting in a feeble cosmetic attempt at "official contextualization" (certainly a contradiction in terms). The Renaissance's renewal brought back a classic, Ciceronian Latin that had the merit of exposing the syncretistic efforts of corrupt Medieval Latin by manifesting its very limits and its deformed face; it had failed to give voice to the people, to allow for heteroglossy, for different voices to enter the conversation. In the words of Bakhtin, "the very desire that the Renaissance had of re-establishing Latin in its antique and classic purity turned it into a dead language." At the same time, it also unmasked the ideological trick of Latin alchemists eager to transform it into a workable, everyday language. Bakhtin continues, "The Latin of Cicero illuminated the true character of medieval Latin, its true face, that people saw practically for the first time: until then they had their language (Medieval Latin), without perceiving its deformed and limited face."[25]

The Renaissance opened and revealed the cleft between two cultures, the popular and the official, a cleft somehow disguised by Latin as *lingua franca*. The end of the fifteenth century and the beginning of the sixteenth were marked by this twofold phenomenon: the emergence of classic humanism alongside the dissemination of popular vernacular literature and folk legends. Renaissance humanism, observed Franz Lau, "was the discoverer not only of the antique languages, but also of the language of the people."[26] If the first was an appeal to the past and the recovery of classic human values for the construction of the present, the second was an invocation of the present and the affirmation of nationhood for the reconstruction of the past. In this way, as A. G. Dickens pointed out, they both acted as "midwifes of the Lutheran Reformation."[27]

---

23. For the role of popular imagery in the theology of the Reformation, see Scribner, *For the Sake of Simple Folk*.

24. Bakhtin, *A cultura popular na Idade Média e no Renascimento*.

25. Ibid., 411.

26. Lau, *Luther*, 90.

27. Dickens, *German Nation and Martin Luther*, 21–22.

The twofold process is never as simultaneous and interconnected as in the humanist emphasis on the biblical languages together with the re-emergence of popular myths and folk-legends. The recovery of particular myths to sustain the national identity was even read into the biblical text, as with the story of Tuisco ("*Teutsch*"), a legendary postdiluvian offspring of Noah, conceived to be the founding hero of Germany.[28] In another myth that linked the popular with the biblical past we have the story that before "tongues became diversified at the tower of Babel, the human race had spoken German."[29]

If every nation, as Octavio Paz often remarked, is based upon a myth, it was the reconstruction of the German mythology that gave voice and identity to the people by providing them with a language. "Through the myths," observes Paz, "each man and woman of the group felt part of the totality of a natural and supernatural time, for all the dead were also members of the tribe."[30]

Opposing Germany to France (where people and culture would presumably have an original identity) Nietzsche regarded the Reformation as the moment in which a primordial power inhabiting an abyss beneath cultural life came forth and surfaced. Identity became for a moment visible. Luther embodied this affirmation and was its emblematic figure. He was for Nietzsche the one "to whom we shall be indebted for the rebirth of the German myth."[31] And this was for Nietzsche the myth of the people and not of the empire.

In this context, the Reformation movement began to build its own program. Far from being unified, it was nonetheless able to give expression (even if for a short period before it became itself institutionalized) to the imagination of a people, long suppressed by the very limits imposed by the prevailing institutions that through language established the limits of the world (among these institutions the church). Concealed in an array of dialects, the dissimulated languages have their power and knowledge submersed in the strict limits of contexts of meaning closed to otherness.

A Kind of Little Discourse

The most revealing face of the emergence of the vernacular, along with myths and folk-legends that it brought to light, was the remarkable development of

---

28. Ibid., 23–24.
29. Ibid., 16.
30. Paz, *La otra voz*, 72.
31. Nietzsche, *Birth of Tragedy*, 136–37.

the publication of leaflets and pamphlets (*Flugschriften*). The publication of leaflets and pamphlets was known before the Reformation. It was the literature of the masses, breaking with the pattern of aristocratic book production, and was greatly facilitated by the printing press.[32] Yet the early years of the Reformation in particular were marked by an astonishing increase in the production of pamphlets indicating that a new birth was in labor and coming into life. Between 1518 and 1525 the number of pamphlets published in Germany increased six-fold.[33] Latin continued to be used as a language also for the larger public, but the radically new phenomenon that catapulted the literary production was the massive output of German texts.[34] These were the years of pamphleteering. However this new literature was not only *aimed* at the larger public; it facilitated the emergence of a new class of authors. Martin Arnold in a fascinating study has pointed to this new phenomenon, not to be found in the years before 1523: people belonging to the working class, including women, could be counted as authors in a business previously dominated mostly by the clergy.[35]

In this context Luther made a major contribution, being quite conscious of his own intentions even when his pamphleteering practice led him to be discredited and held with suspicion and contempt, as we can read in the opening paragraphs of the *Treatise on Good Works*:

> And although I know full well and hear every day that many people think little of me and say that I only write little pamphlets and sermons in German for the uneducated laity, I do not let that stop me. I believe that if I were of a mind to write big books of their kind, I could perhaps, with God's help, do it more readily than they could write my kind of little discourse.[36]

But for Luther pamphleteering does not mean simply the selection of the public to whom the text is addressed at the exclusion of others. Against Karlstadt he argued that knowledge should not be limited to the confinement of a dissimulated language of a group unable to articulate itself efficaciously against the hegemonic powers.[37] In his "Introduction" to the *German Mass* he laments what has happened to the Bohemian Waldensians who ended up "hiding their faith in their own language to such a degree

---

32. Dickens, *German Nation and Martin Luther*, 105 See also Arnold, *Handwerker als theologische Schriftsteller*, 43.

33. Arnold, *Handwerker*, 38–41; Dickens, *German Nation and Martin Luther*, 106.

34. Dickens, *German Nation and Martin Luther*, 46.

35. Arnold, *Handwerker*, 43–44, 327.

36. WA 6, 203, 5–14; LW 44:22.

37. Dickens, *German Nation and Martin Luther*, 33.

of not being able any longer to speak to anyone in a clear way."[38] Certainly the mechanism of dissimulation was operative among the Waldensians after centuries of atrocious persecution. Luther might have missed that, but he certainly believed that with the Reformation the time to speak out publicly had arrived, and the time to dissimulate turned into an opportune moment and a venue for people to speak their word. In his defense of public education, the emphasis on the instruction of biblical languages was not intended as moving away from Latin (which he did regard a great poetic language), but as an enhancement of knowledge for the benefit of the youth among whom he (following in this Erasmus) included women, who were traditionally marginalized from formal education (with the exception of those who through religious orders could pursue intellectual endeavors).[39]

Language as Communication

The importance of Luther for the normative nature of the German language is widely recognized and celebrated. However, even for those who assess Luther's view of language as an external expression of an existential language-event (as in Gerhard Ebeling) or for those who follow a cultural-linguistic interpretation (as in George Lindbeck), little attention has been given to the importance of language as the articulation of popular aspirations and desires in the semantically dynamic historical context of late-medieval Europe. These two assessments of Luther's use of language, exemplified by Ebeling and Lindbeck, have a history in linguistic theory that reaches back a few centuries but finds its origin in the late-medieval opposition between realism and nominalism. While medieval realism regarded language as the formal principle that constituted reality as such, nominalism approached it as a functional expression of the world in socio-cultural established conventions. In classic modern linguistic theory, we find it for example in the distinction that Wilhelm von Humboldt suggested between seeing language as either *ergon* (a work) or as *energeia* (an activity). Humboldt favored a view that language is "the continual intellectual effort to make the articulated sound capable of expressing thought."[40] Thus, for him, *energeia* (and not *ergon*) was the true expression of the nature and craft of language. Language

---

38. WA 19, 74, 13–16; LW 53:63.

39. Wiberg Pedersen, "Can God Speak the Vernacular?," notes the remarkable use of the vernacular as a theological language in the writing of religious women three centuries before the Reformation, suggesting it as a gesture that prefigures the Reformation itself.

40. Quoted in Morse, *New World Soundings*, 12.

in this case is the outer hardened crust of an inner vitality. The locus of truth that ought to be sought is the inner experience out of which the external expression ensues.

This existentialist and expressivist interpretation of language is a position that in the contemporary research on theological language has been associated with the name of Gerhard Ebeling and has had a significant impact on all those who followed his lead in Luther research. For Ebeling, "the authority to use the language of faith is a matter of experience. Language arises only from experience."[41] Conversely what can be regarded as meaningful at the semantic level must be traced back and reconstituted as a subjective experience. Experience is what alone authenticates language.

The opposite view was inspired in modern times by the structural approach to language as presented in Ferdinand Saussure's distinction between *langue* and *parole*, analogous to Humboldt's *ergon* and *energeia*. For Saussure *langue* represented a structurally stable and formative set of rules that was rather the cause and not the effect of experience, while *parole* was regarded as particular, even idiosyncratic, deviations from the norm. Here the external has priority over the internal. George Lindbeck, working with the distinction between a linguistic-cultural model (language as *ergon*) and an experiential-expressive model (language as *energeia*) says "that the former reverses the relation of the inner and the outer. Instead of deriving external features of religious language from inner experience, it is inner experiences which are viewed as derivative."[42] Grammar conditions and controls semantics; meaning presupposes assent to abiding rules.[43]

Are we bound to these two options for our reading of Luther's own view of language? *Tertium non datur* in this binary alternatives? In relation to the contextual situation of Luther's time and the problems issuing from the confrontation between official languages and their régimes of truth, on the one hand, and the popular insurgence of heteroglossic "transgression," on the other, either of the options fails to help. The experiential approach is

---

41. Ebeling, *Introduction to a Theological Theory*, 206. See also his distinction between "pontentiality" and "act": "even the most perfect distillation of a language into vocabulary and grammar must ultimately concede victory . . . to the living and concrete use of language" (ibid., 90).

42. Lindbeck, *Nature of Doctrine*, 34.

43. Ibid., 17–18. This dual option certainly has a significant genealogy of analogical binaries in Christian theology, which can be traced back to Paul's distinction between "letter" and "spirit," the medieval opposition between "love" (as *exemplum*) and "work" (as *sacramentum*), the Protestant debate between the orthodox defense of the *fides quae* and the Pietist case for the *fides qua*, and other distinctions more vaguely related. What characterizes the present debate is that it is applied to religious language and doctrine as such.

incapable of accounting for the power-relation in the confrontation among languages, especially between popular and official usages. It will have to regard some of the boorish expressions in Luther's parlance as idiosyncratic oddities. The cultural structural approach, in its turn, detects well the process of restoration of doctrine as a foundational grammar buried in cultural misrepresentations, official or popular, but is unable to recognize the dynamic nature of language, and the displacements of meaning it produces by moving through different semantic fields.

I would like to suggest an alternative approach, following an insight of Mikhail Bakhtin in his reactions against both the subjectivist experiential position that views language as the objective expression of a subjective drive or experience (*energeia*), and the cultural-linguistic analysis that focuses on the codified norms of linguistic systems (*ergon*). Criticizing the opposition between spontaneous versus formal language that is presupposed in both schools respectively, Bakhtin suggested that what is at stake is communication, not language as such. And in communication one needs to focus on the emergence of utterances under the contextual conditions within which they appear. An utterance "will have a meaning different than it would have under any other conditions; all utterances are heteroglot, in that they are functions of a matrix of forces practically impossible to recoup, and therefore impossible to resolve."[44]

What Bakhtin is looking for in language is neither its systemic, grammatical character nor the experiential well out of which it springs, but precisely the emergence of voices that are other than the system (yet they do appear at the surface of language). These voices, these appearances, disturb and institute meaning *in loco*. However, this meaning is created because of the shock issuing from the clash among different semantic fields and not as a new spontaneous creation. This is what his understanding of heteroglossy amounts to: "Heteroglossia is as close a conceptualization as is possible of that locus where centripetal and centrifugal forces collide; as such it is that which a systematic linguistics must always suppress."[45] Bakhtin's concern is with the insurrection of language. Language is not the formal principle of reality or an outer manifestation of inner experience, it neither structures reality nor is it a husk of its inner being. Language is always a function of communication, it is the attempt to keep in tension the relation between the heteronomy of linguistic rules and norms that want to institute reality (Bakhtin's "centripetal forces"), and the autonomous drive toward "reinventing" it (Bakhtin's "centrifugal forces"). Communication emerges neither

---

44. Bakhtin, *Dialogic Imagination*, 428.
45. Ibid.

when the linguistic forms break down nor when we just pour our hearts out. If language is about communication, then language fulfills its purpose when there is a transgression of a restricted semantic domain, a "collision of senses."[46] In the words of Bakhtin,

> Thus at any given moment of its historical existence, language is heteroglot from top to bottom: it represents the co-existence of socio-ideological contradictions between the present and the past, between differing epochs of the past, between different socio-ideological groups in the present, between tendencies, schools, circles and so forth . . .[47]

In other words, communication happens in and through language not because people are united under an Esperanto, or share the same experiences; it happens unexpectedly at the moment when one listens to another's language and wonders, "How is it that we understand it?" (Acts 2:7-8). Communication is always a linguistic surprise precisely because it happens in the midst of "noise." What makes sense is first something unheard-of; it sensitizes.

As an event of communication,

> language . . . lies on the borderline between oneself and the other. The word in language is half between oneself and the other. The word in language is half someone else's . . . It exists in other people's mouths, in other people's contexts, serving other people's intentions: it is from there that one must take the word and make it one's own.[48]

Apart from the reference to the people's mouth, which is also Luther's metaphor for language, it is important to realize that communication implies a transgression of confined semantic domains, a moving of utterances from one realm to another. This lies at the very core of Luther's above-mentioned comment: "All words are made new when they are transferred from their own to another [semantic] context."[49] Different from "poetry," from the creation of language (which is still pre-communicative[50]), linguistic

---

46. Bielfeldt, "Luther, Metaphor, and Theological Language," 127.

47. Bakhtin, *Dialogic Imagination*, 291.

48. Ibid., 293-94.

49. *Omnia vocabula fiunt nova, quando e suo foro in alienum transferuntur.* WA 39/I, 231, 1-3, A I]. The context of the discussion is the meaning of "works" when used *coram deo* or *coram mundo*.

50. This is why poetry, strictly speaking, cannot be translated. It is pre-commumcative but not anti-communicative. It is to communication what bricks are to a building. See Bakhtin, *Dialogical Imagination*, 296-98.

communication happens not in creation of language but in this transgressive movement across semantic domains.[51]

Luther Laughing at the Devil

Nietzsche defined the Reformation movement as the stupendous moment of the stirring of primordial powers underneath a cultural shell.[52] Although this was not the work of Luther alone, he became its emblematic figure. This emblematic character of Luther—who, however, claimed he did not want to be a master[53]—has all to do with this mixture of humanist sophistication, erudition and piety blended together with grotesque profanity in style. In a certain way, he represented and unified the very contradictions of the cultural context of the time. And with this he was able to bridge the cleft that separated the heart of the people from the sterile official culture, creating what Bakhtin called the locus of collision. In the words of Agnes Heller:

> Luther essentially differed from all previous renewers of religion, not because he was oriented toward the world (many others had been as well), but because the notion of election had no part in his ideology and practice . . . He was a man un-shamed of his particularity, unlike St Augustine; on the contrary, he accepted it.[54]

Luther could be content in calling the German people fools or himself a barbarian or a sack of worms or a prideful idiot, and so forth. Some of these

---

51. The difficulty of maintaining the dialectical relationship and a steady focus on the locus of collision (Bakhtin) between linguistic system and language-event will reveal also the somewhat conservative trends in Luther's understanding of institutions. While the Reformer recognized the relative character of institutions, he was not yet able to regard them as transient. This ambiguity in relation to institutions is the same that will show itself in the doctrine of the inspiration of the Scriptures, where the oscillation between inerrancy and hermeneutics remains unresolved. See Ruokanen, *Doctrina divinitus inspirata*. For an appraisal of Luther's disregard for institutions, see Wolin, *Politics and Vision*, 162–64. But the ambiguity of Luther's early "modern" attitude yet still caught in a medieval world is classically presented by Troeltsch, *Protestantism and Progress*. See also chapter 19 below.

52. Nietzsche, *Birth of Tragedy*, 136.

53. WA 8, 685, 14; LW 45:71.

54. Heller, *Renaissance Man*, 203. Heller's comments about election and vocation not playing a role in Luther seem to be off the mark, considering the role that both had in Luther's theology. What I read Heller saying is that by leveling all callings and no longer accepting a special vocation that separated clergy from laity he was in fact including himself among those who did not have any calling that essentially distinguished him from anyone else.

expressions could be taken as typical of medieval penitential utterances and practices if it were not for the obvious ironic sense embedded in them. The point is not so much humility (false or not) as it is a carnival-like attitude toward everything.[55] He showed the fearlessness of a fool, but in everyday life and not in the midst of a feast when jest and satire were tolerated and even expected. With his language, Luther brought the carnival to academia, to the pulpit, to the square, breaking down the disciplined frontiers in which these utterances were allowed. He could as much laugh at Melanchthon's dedication to astrology (still a respected discipline, not clearly distinguished from astronomy), saying that he would profit more sitting by a keg of beer,[56] as he could show his rage against his enemies calling them apostles of the devil or simple asses. In fact he regarded himself to be even more foolish in believing he could teach them anything. Such remarks can be multiplied.[57]

The point, however, is not to show idiosyncrasies in Luther's personality, but to indicate that his burlesque attitude is to be taken as a central characteristic of his own theological practice and not occasional odd deviations. A world divided between the official pomp of the instituted language of the church and the grotesque humor of the lower strata of society that provided the motifs for the carnivals was combined by Luther's jests and theological subtleties. Boorish and burlesque motifs invaded the controlled realm of theological discourse. If we take even the most serious and somber of Luther's texts (mostly those in Latin) although the form does not reveal his attitudes of mockery and jest, the motifs do. The classical remarks in Luther's theology of creation about the mask or wrapping (*larva* or *involucrum*) of God[58] represent theologically a rupture with the representational attitude that prevailed in theology. The metaphor of the mask is not simply a new way of speaking about God. It broke with the medieval realism going simultaneously beyond the parsimonious and skeptical stance of the nominalists. It touched the people's imagery in which the mask had a very concrete and popular significance, and it was not the *prosopon* of the Greek theater. To elucidate the images evoked by the mask trope in a context not distant from Luther's own, Bakhtin offers the following commentary:

> The motif of the mask . . . is full of meaning within popular culture. Masks translate the gayness of alteration and reincarnation, the happy relativity, the happy negation of identity and

---

55. On Luther's scatological language, see Oberman, *Luther*, 106-10.

56. WA TR I, 7, 9f. (nr. 17).

57. Plenty of such illustrations are provided by Oberman, *Luther: Man between God and the Devil*.

58. See WA 40/I, 173-74; LW 26:95-96.

singleness of meaning, the negation of the stupid coincidence with oneself; the mask is the expression of transference, of the metamorphoses, of the violation of the natural frontiers . . . the mask incarnated the principle of the life-game; it is based on a peculiar interrelation of reality and image, characteristic of the most ancient rites and performances. The complex symbolism of the mask is copious.[59]

"In every line that Luther wrote," commented Karl Holl, "it is apparent what unusual compulsion toward imagery possessed him."[60] And certainly here the verb "possess" has an allusive meaning.

Luther's possession by imagery had the very character of possession, of being occupied by the imagery of popular culture, to the point of breaking linguistically with the dichotomous views of society, between the official and the popular. The burlesque in Luther's theology is what allowed the people's imagery to break into and out of the official language of ecclesial and political institutions.

There is a technique of reversals applied ingeniously by Luther that links him to the popular burlesque of the carnivals, not however in the feast of fools, where it would be routine, but rather in the interdicted space of the pulpit, of academia, and of publications. Expressions like "God cannot be God without being first the devil," present a reversal that corresponds to this other reversal: "the devil will not be the devil before being God."[61] Such reversals are typical of the transvaluation of popular culture in the realm of the festivals, in breaking with established dominant conceptions: the fool is king, the king is fool.[62] The enraged monk said to have thrown a pot of ink at the devil would later in a libel against the Duke of Braunschweig say that he is "laughing at the devils."[63]

The burlesque character of Luther's language has amused a number of commentators, and he is here and there quoted on behalf of courageous defiance. But would this not be a way of shifting the focus away from the deeper core of his burlesque, turning it into a mere idiosyncratic jest? Or else, is Luther not all too frequently submitted to a Romantic transformation of the burlesque into satire, with its negative and lugubrious humor

---

59. Bakhtin, *Cultura Popular*, 35. On the motif of the mask, see chapter 8 below.
60. Holl, *Cultural Significance of the Reformation*, 147.
61. WA 31/I, 250, 24–25; LW 14:32.
62. For examples of these reversals in popular culture, see Scribner, *For the Sake of Simple Folk*, 59–94
63. WA 51, 469, 23; LW 41:185.

surrendering the open laughter of the text?⁶⁴ In Luther, the ambivalence of the polarities in his humorous reversals is not a reified antithesis. This brings him rather close to the grotesque with its regenerating comic attitude toward the subject matter. Bakhtin defines the grotesque as "the style in which the corporeal and material principle is perceived as universal and popular, opposed to all separation of the corporeal and material roots of the world from . . . all that has an ideal and abstract character, from all that has pretension of meaning detached and independent from earth and the body."⁶⁵

And such is the character of Luther's remarks when he talks about (scholastic) reason, calling it a harlot, or when he says that the church is the great whore (*magna peccatrix*). To take the latter as an analytic remark on the nature of the church, as it is often done with the former on the matter of reason, makes it evident how the point is missed completely.

In the same spirit he ridicules those who separate heaven and earth as distinct sites.⁶⁶ The burlesque and even the grotesque in Luther brings forth his sensitivity toward the mentality of the people that can, in life and language, live with the *complexio oppositorum*. This acceptance of paradoxes can turn the noble into the most scorned and make of manure a pleasant sight. In the following quotation from the attack on the Duke Henry of Braunschweig/Wolfenbüttel, entitled "Against Hanswurst," Luther uses a German carnival figure (*Hanswurst*) who in the festivals carries a long leather-made sausage around his neck, wearing a colorful clown-like costume in typical farcical vulgar burlesque. And there he writes: "You should not write a book before you have heard an old sow fart; and you should then open your jaws with awe saying, 'Thank you, lovely nightingale, that is just the text for me!'"⁶⁷

This is what I mean by the popular grotesque in Luther's language and style. While much has been said about the importance of Luther for the German language, his theological burlesque has been regarded more as an attitude of jest or contempt than as a carnival-like subversion of institutionalized values, in order to open space for the dissimulated language of the people to emerge and even to authorize it. And this coheres with his theological program. The quote from Klopstock is frequently cited: "No one who knows what a language is can come face to face with Luther without venerating him."⁶⁸ But particularly the Romantic appraisal of Luther's lan-

64. On the distinction between the burlesque character of the medieval popular language and its satirical reappropriation in modern Romanticism, see Bakhtin, *Cultura Popular*, 35.

65. Ibid., 17.

66. LW 37:280-81; cf. WA 49, 224, 30f.: *Quando dico Celum celi domini, non intelligo celum situ et loco distincto terra, sed ich meine das regiment mit.*

67. WA 51, 561, 25-28; LW 41:250.

68. Ebeling, *Introduction to a Theological Theory*, 28. For the classical Romantic

guage has been notorious in failing to recognize his appeal to the popular grotesque as constitutive not only of style and form but of the very theological practice he was engaged in.

When Luther argued that "Christian theology does not start at the top, in the highest altitudes, . . . but there at the bottom, in the deepest profundity,"[69] he refers to the very core of the language he uses, to the utterly vulgar and pamphleteering character of his writings. In a style marked by the popular boor, Luther intentionally wanted his pamphlets to provide for a transgressive language through which the people could articulate their feelings and longings. It can only be understood in this locus of collision (Bakhtin) in which communication takes place.

Yet in all of this he was not only a practitioner of communication breaking through semantic domains to elicit new meanings. He was also a poet engaged in unearthing what Bakhtin called pre-communicative utterances to which his hymns attest. Poetry, said Heidegger, is what "first makes language possible."[70] And this concern comes explicitly to the fore when Luther laments not having read more poetry: "How I regret now that I did not read more poets and historians, and that no one taught me them! Instead, I was obliged to read at great cost, toil, and detriment to myself, that devil's dung, the philosophers and the sophists, from which I have all to purge myself."[71]

Looking People in the Mouth

The importance of Luther's linguistic subversion is correctly associated with his translation of the Bible. Luther was not the first to translate the Bible into German, but he was certainly the first one to make vernacular German into the normative principle for the whole translation of the Scriptures. "I don't know of any other ground," he said in reference to the validity of norms for uttering theological statements, "than the one offered by the genius of languages as God has created them."[72]

---

appraisals of Luther in the literature, see Bornkamm, *Luther im Spiegel der deutschen Geistesgeschichte.*

69. WA 40/I, 79, 25–26; LW 26:30.

70. Heidegger, *Existence and Being*, 283.

71. WA 15, 46, 18–21; LW 45:370. Luther's poetics is a theme of itself that cannot be dealt with here. It suffices to mention that poetry is to communication what metaphors are to language insofar as it discloses new semantic associations. See Brecht, *Luther als Schriftsteller.*

72. WA 18, 155, 4–5; LW 40:165.

What is important in the translation of the Bible was not the effort of making the message of the Scriptures understandable, but rather of articulating the people's imagery in biblical language. This is exemplarily expressed then in his essay "On Translation."[73] There he reacts against the attack he received for his German rendering of Romans 3:28 with the expression "only by faith." In the original Greek, the adverb "only" is not present. In beautiful examples drawn from vernacular expressions he justifies his introduction of the adverb as necessary for the translation to be in good German for people to grasp the intended meaning. Accusing the Papists of knowing German less than an ass, he summons all who want to judge his Bible translation to learn the language people speak and how they speak in everyday life:

> We must not, like these asses, ask the Latin letters how we are to speak German; but we must ask the mother in the home, the children in the street, the common man in the market place about this, and look them in the mouth to see how to speak, and afterwards do our translation.[74]

Hegel recognized the magnitude of this effort well when he said: "for the Christians in Germany to have the book of their faith translated into their mother tongue is the greatest revolution that could happen. Only when uttered in the mother tongue is something my property."[75] Even if Luther did not know the Italian play of words—*traduttore/tradittore*—that makes a translator a traitor, he certainly knew the Greek verb *paradidōmi* which can mean both handing over in an act of treason or passing on the tradition (cf. Mark 14:10 and 1 Corinthians 11:23 where the same verb is used for Judas' treason and Paul's conveyance of the words that Jesus spoke at the last supper). And it goes unavoidably in both ways: the translator

---

73. WA 30/II, 632-646; LW 35:181-202.

74. WA 30/II, 638; LW 35:190. In defense of the use of the neutral in referring to the bread as the body of Christ, Luther was not concerned to show the literal accuracy of the neutral Greek but pointed to the fact that this was the way a German would speak: "Nu wyr wollen ursach sagen, Warumb Christus 'Tuto' odder 'Das' und nicht 'Der' vom brot saget. Ynn Deutscher zungen gibts die art der sprache, das, wenn wyr auff eyn ding deutten, das fur uns ist, so nennen und deutten wyrs eyn Das, es sey sonst an yhm selbst eyn Der odder Die, alls wenn ich spreche: Das ist der man, davon ich rede, Das ist die Jungfraw, die ich meyne.... Hier beruffe ich mich auff alle Deutschen, ob ich auch deutsch rede. Es ist ye die rechte mutter spräche, und so redet der gemeyne man ynn Deutschen landen." WA 18, 154, 12-21; LW 40:164.

75. Hegel, *Werke*, 20:16-17; "Erst in der Muttersprache ausgesprochen is etwas mein Eigentum."

becomes a traitor and the traitor becomes a translator. Luther claimed the latter in his defense of translating Romans 3:28.

Language is the "mirror of the heart," said Luther quoting a popular expression.[76] But it is more and less than that. It is more because it opens a possibility for an encounter with otherness in the transference of semantic realms, as we have seen. However, it is also less, because it is also the heart's prison, the limit of one's world. There is no justification through language alone. Language only spans the space that the heart inhabits and in which it gains a profile and a mask that joyfully reveals and answers its secrets and longings and simultaneously conceals and hides mystery. Language is the earthly stuff with which the ecclesial régime conveys and conceals the presence of the Word in a similar way as equity (*Billigkeit*) does for the economy, and reason does for the political régime. These three—reason in *politia*, equity in *oeconomia*, and language in *ecclesia*—are the vortexes in and through which God's justification can be both revealed and hidden in the midst of the stations of life we journey through. As such they form the matrix in which Christ's *parousia*, the eschatological moment, announces itself.

Luther's criticism of medieval realism—language as the formal principle of reality—brought him closer to nominalism—language as the arbitrary signifying accident of reality itself. However, he would not stay attached to nominalism either. He went beyond, envisioning language and particularly the vernacular as the score for the inscription of the melody of the Spirit. Luther said it well: "The Holy Spirit has its own grammar; people who grammatically speak falsely, may, regarding the sense of it, speak the truth."[77] That means: new meanings and realities are not only given shape, but also brought about through language in its heteroglot dynamic movement.

Such a stance in Luther's theology has been called a mixture of philosophical nominalism and theological realism.[78] Through it, Luther contributed to the liberation of the desires and aspirations of the people hidden by the instituted linguistic régimes and kept away from the public sphere. By looking people in the mouth, Luther brought the vernacular, the language of the people, out of the confinement of privacy into the public and allowed its grotesque character to invade the official realm. The carnival was brought to the pulpit and to academia. All of this was entirely consistent with his theological program of letting God be God. Although Luther's search for language is inextricably linked to his theology, his main accomplishment was to free language from the confines of its disciplined domains. And in

---

76. WA 11, 408–416; LW 29:305–14.
77. WA 39/II, 104.
78. Työrinoja, "Nova vocabula et nova lingua."

this lateral move of displacing words among and across its semantic (and heteroglot) domains, new meanings were produced. What was kept silent and hidden could then find an utterance; words conveyed the Word, communication was won in and through the "noise."

In its indebtedness to the nominalist's supra-structural view of language, the existential-expressivist school of contemporary Luther-reading misses the point in its attempt to trace the Reformation's insight to some grounding experience; it misses that which cannot be reduced to inner experience, but arrives coming from other semantic domains as an advent. Much of the Reformers' insights came not from subjective experiences surfacing at the level of language, but from transgressing semantic fields and bringing words along. This linguistic displacement evinces unexpected new meanings (as the example of the mask illustrates). And, in their indebtedness to medieval realism's formation of reality out of the rules and grammar of language, the cultural linguists' reading of Luther miss the fact that language and communication are heteroglot through and through, as Bakhtin insisted. For Luther, the grammar of faith is always a transgression of its own domains. Whatever is secured in language, as in the writing of a book, is simultaneously also concealed by it: "That one must write books is already a great transgression and an infirmity of the spirit."[79]

The consequence of these remarks for the study of Luther seems to be self-evident. The point is not primarily to know how the dogmatic content of Luther's theology can restore a doctrinal nucleus or to find in it a new expression of faith experience. It is how the principle by which Luther articulated his theological thought offered space for the people to articulate the language concerning their relationship to themselves, to the world, and to God, beyond the confines of the régimes that controlled and regulated the proper use of language, creatively transgressing and crossing them.

While many regret the fact that Luther's theology was not more systematic, I am suggesting that the "unsystematic" nature of his writings cannot be dissociated from his theological program of "looking people in the mouth" and giving back to them, like one who lifts a mirror, authentic words, stories that raise them out of silence and dissimulation, constantly transgressing disciplinary domains. In the Reformer there is "systematic" indisposition against systems. That is what prompted him to speak. As Luther said in the presentation of his treatise *To the Christian Nobility*, "the time of silencing is over, the time to speak has come."[80]

---

79. WA 10/I, 627, 1f.
80. WA 6, 404, 11–12; LW 44:123.

2

More than Enough

Letter as Solace

> So I opened my mouth, and he gave me the scroll to eat.
> He said to me, Mortal, eat this scroll that I give you and
> fill your stomach with it. Then I ate it; and in my mouth
> it was as sweet as honey.
>
> —Ezekiel 3:2–3

LUTHER'S CREATIVE ENDEAVOR IN exploring language to its limits and innovating it is driven by his pneumatological motivation for creating new possibilities for evangelical rhetoric. Nevertheless, the spirit is evanescent without the letter. This is a lesson that was engraved in the Wittenberg theologians since the tragic events culminating in the 1525 peasant revolt backed by a theology that did not consider the distinction (though in simultaneity) of régimes by which the work of the spirit did not cancel or supersede accomplishments in the secular sphere where the letter of the law, guided by reason, was to reign to bring about equity (*Billigkeit*). While the revolt raged havoc in the name of the spirit's freedom, by a stroke of irony Luther was at the Wartburg tied up with the translation of the Bible. He was absorbed by the letter! For Müntzer, the prominent leader of the disastrous revolt of 1525, the work of Luther in translating the Bible to the language of the people was commendable, but ultimately superfluous since the spirit could speak directly to the believer. As we have seen, Luther would agree to the extent that the appeal to the letter is an "infirmity of the spirit." Yet without the letter the spirit is empty air; it would be analogous to breath in order to speak, but without physical vocal cords.

The letter of the Scriptures offers the compass for the spirit's roving. This is what is entailed in the exemplary irony of Luther's seclusion in the Wartburg while, in the name of the spirit, anarchy reigned outside. This was one of the functions that led to the principle of the *sola scriptura*. But the second one, and of decisive importance, is that the scriptural principle was a declaration of liberation from the institutional ties that controlled biblical interpretation and its dissemination. By this principle there is no instituted office authorized to mediate the relationship between the Word and the enfleshment in the vernacular.[1]

Fundamentalism and Foundationalism: The Enlightenment

Between the Reformation's understanding of *sola scriptura* and the understanding of this Reformation mantra in the present day stand the traumatic events unleashed by the European Enlightenment of the eighteenth century, events that changed our views of science, of politics, and of religion. As far as Protestant theology is concerned, *sola scriptura* (or the scriptural principle, as it is known) seems to have been the first casualty. When Luther and the *Confessions* describe the Scriptures as entailing law and promises, the Scriptures present it through prophets and apostles. Prophecy is what points to the gospel, the fulfillment of which is testified by the apostles as witnesses of the life, deeds, death, and resurrection of Jesus Christ, as attested in the Scriptures. This understanding was grounded in two fundamental assumptions that have remained unchallenged throughout Christendom until the time of the Enlightenment. The first was that Jesus Christ is the fulfillment of the Old Testament prophecies. The second was that the miracle accounts, particularly the resurrection of Jesus, were factual events and should be regarded as such today. The Enlightenment brought about the erosion of these two fundamental assumptions.

The philological work of Hermann Samuel Reimarus (1694–1768) is responsible for launching the criticism of taking for granted that the New Testament is the fulfillment of the Old.[2] Gotthold Ephraim Lessing (1729–81) furthered and radicalized his predecessor's work rendering the truth claim of the miracle stories and the resurrection as undemonstrable

---

1. However, see Saler, *Between Magisterium and Marketplace*, for a highly informative study of how liberation from the magisterium exposes theological authorship to the whims of the market.

2. Reimarus, *Fragments*, particularly the chapter "On Miracles and Prophecies," 69–83.

by reason. This left two options for those who felt the impact and wanted to remain faithful to the Christian message. One was to surrender reason, a *sacrificium intellectus*, and cling to the literal sense of the Scriptures, no matter what reason might argue or whatever critical history might be able to corroborate. This gave birth to what is known as *fundamentalism*. The other was to ground Christian faith on some foundation other than the Scriptures, such as a moral postulate, a feeling of absolute dependence, a ground of being, authentic existence, on universal history as revelation, and so forth, of which the Scriptures would be a dated and circumstantial expression. This has been called *foundationalism*. Both fundamentalism and foundationalism are products of the Enlightenment. One kept the *sola scriptura* but subjected it to an anachronistic misreading; the other simply evaded it. Much of the current debate over the authority of the Scriptures is a debate over these two options, with the participants not realizing that the responses offered still leave the basic question unchallenged. Both foundationalism *and* fundamentalism are, in fact, celebrations of the Enlightenment's biblical criticism. Both are a concession to Lessing's celebrated thesis that "accidental truths of history can never become the proof of necessary truths of reason."[3] Fundamentalism opted for the truths of history without the aid of reason, whereas foundationalism sought the truths of reason without the historical claims of the Bible. Both were an affirmation of Lessing's thesis, though they were validated through the different truths Lessing proposed—truths of history and truths of reason—as exclusive and exclusionary options. However both remained separated by Lessing's "ugly broad ditch" (*ein garstiger, breiter Graben*).

The problem that plagues both answers, prompting the modern alternative of either having reason (along with will and feelings) alone as arbiter, or requiring blind assent to the letter, lies in Lessing's thesis itself, insofar as it is assumed that it addresses the *sola scriptura* principle. But, in fact, to superimpose the Enlightenment's agenda on the scriptural principle turns out to be a blatant anachronism.

The scriptural principle for the Reformers addressed an entirely different problem from the one that prompted Lessing's quest for truth against or apart from biblical-historical claims. The Reformers' question was not one that concerned primarily reason, logic or even historicity. It was a question of *power*, namely: Who controls evangelical rhetoric, the art of proclaiming the gospel in its universality, its catholicity? Once this is understood, the answers that foundationalism and fundamentalism gave to the Enlightenment become the fallacies of a misplaced question. The irony in all of

3. Lessing, *Lessing's Theological Writings*, 53.

this controversy is that the *sola scriptura* principle as it was used by the Reformers was an attempt to prevent precisely the fallacy produced by both fundamentalism and foundationalism, that is, to ground the teachings and practice of Christianity anywhere else but in grace, in faith, in Christ as attested by the apostolic witness and registered in the Scriptures. *Sola scriptura* is "alone" only insofar as alone is faith, alone is grace, alone is Christ, *sola fide, sola gratia, solus Christus*. This is the reason why, since August Twesten (1789–1876) in the early nineteenth century coined the expressions,[4] we speak of *sola scriptura* as the "formal principle" of evangelical Protestantism, while justification, signified by the expressions *sola fide, sola gratia*, and *solus Christus*, is called the material principle. In other words, the scriptural principle is the apostolic principle, that is, what was attested by the apostles as inculcating Christ and him crucified and resurrected. For the Reformers the "successors" of the apostles are all those or anyone who brings the prophetic and apostolic witness to be heard and read by their contemporaries. Bringing the Scriptures as the yardstick for the teaching of faith entails primarily two functions; one carries on the work on negation, the second implies a positive procedure.

Sola Scriptura: The Negative Function

The *sola scriptura* principle is not an invention of the Reformation. It had a pre-history in medieval theology, preaching, and philosophy, as did many other *theologoumena* normally associated with the Reformation.[5] Such was the case with the *sola sciptura*. It was used with different emphases and nuances by Roger Bacon, John Wyclif, John Hus, Marsilius of Padua, William Occam, Jean Gerson, Wessel Gansfort, and others. All of them, like Luther, used it primarily as a negative principle to oppose the claims of a special and independent authority as argued by the Roman Curia.[6]

The first time this argument was explicitly stated was when Basil of Caesarea in his treatise *On the Spirit* (374) explained the institution

---

4. Twesten, *Vorlesungen über die Dogmatik*, 280–82, where he distinguishes an "objective material principle" (*objective materiale Princip*) as the doctrine of justification and a "formal principle" (*formale Princip*) as the Scriptures. He then (284) identifies a third "subjective or generative principle" (*subjective or erzeugende Princip*), which he describes as the "alertness of conscience" (*Regsamkeit des Gewissens*). See the informative essay by Heen, "The Distinction 'Material/Formal Principles' and Its Use in American Lutheran Theology," 329–54.

5. See Oberman, *Forerunners of the Reformation*.

6. See Westhelle, *Church Event*, 47–58.

of practices like crossing oneself or turning to the east in prayer that he regarded as normative and divinely ordained. Here Basil is relying on a fundamental distinction between *dogma* and *kerugma*, where the former is a silent reverential observance and the latter a proclamation to the entire world.[7] The reason for the distinction is to permit dogma to interpret *and supplement* Scripture. This distinction has been preserved in most of Orthodox and Roman Catholic theology. Modern Protestant theology has also invoked it, as in the nineteenth-century proposal by Karl Friedrich Kahnis to introduce an "ecclesial principle" alongside the formal and material principles distinction proposed by Twesten.[8] Carl Braaten has since suggested an insertion to augment the Reformation's clear and exclusive distinction between *ius divinum* and *ius humanum*: the introduction of a third concept of law, which he called *ius ecclesiasticum*.[9]

Luther objected forcefully to this argument for a "silent" or "secret" (Basil's words) tradition entailing the assumption of divinely sanctioned rites. And he made his objection very clear in his writings in the *Bondage of the Will*. Luther, as it is well known, was arguing with Erasmus who was unable to join the Reformation cause, though being initially sympathetic toward it, precisely because he could not abandon Basil's argument for a secret knowledge kept in the episcopal office of which the Scriptures are silent. Thus Luther writes, "I have attacked the pope, in whose kingdom nothing is more commonly stated or more generally accepted than the idea that the scriptures are obscure and ambiguous, so that the spirit to interpret them must be sought from the Apostolic See of Rome."[10] And he concludes the argument: "The Scriptures are perfectly clear."[11] This does not mean that the Scriptures are self-evident. Laborious dedication, study are necessary: "It is true that for many people much remains abstruse; but this is not due to the obscurity of Scripture, but to the blindness and indolence of those who will not take the trouble to look at the very clearest truth."[12]

The clarity and sufficiency of the Scriptures is an old theme in Christian theology, and it first emerged in the struggle against Gnosticism. And much before Luther, in the late second century, Irenaeus had already refuted these secretive private assumptions and asserted that there was nothing obscure in the Scriptures, and that it was understandable by all though not

---

7. Basil, *On the Spirit*, 41–42.
8. See Cloege, "Schriftprinzip," in RGG[3].
9. Braaten, *Mother Church*, 97.
10. LW 33:90.
11. LW 33:99.
12. LW 33:27.

believed by all. For Irenaeus the apostolic witness left in print, the Scriptures, was more than enough to anchor the faith of the church: "... the entire Scriptures, the prophets, and the Gospels can be clearly, unambiguously, and harmoniously understood by all, although all do not believe them."[13] This is the tradition in which Luther stands.

Scripture as Interpreter Itself: The Positive Function

Luther's often quoted thesis that "Scripture interprets itself" (*scriptura sui ipsius interpres*) is well known.[14] Gerhard Forde,[15] Oswald Bayer,[16] and Steven Paulson[17] have independently phrased this notion well when they say that we do not interpret Scripture, but Scripture interprets us. But how is this brought about? The common English translation (that the Scriptures interpret themselves) is not precise and suggests that one should be using the Scriptures against the Scriptures in order to find the correct meaning. This is in fact a post-Enlightenment translation, which, although not completely wrong, misses the sharpness of the literal translation. It should literally be translated as "Scripture is in itself the interpreter." The word *interpres* in Latin is a noun, designating that which stands between two values or "prices" (*inter-pres*). The etymology of the word points to the exchange of merchandise in markets of antiquity. It was often the case that because of differences in the languages or dialects spoken by the merchants bargaining for the value of their goods an interpreter was needed to convey the value or the price asked by a merchant of another in the process of negotiating an exchange. Analogously, the thesis that Scripture interprets itself has the precise meaning that it is not interpreted but is the interpreter itself. Scripture stands between two "values" and allows for the exchange to happen.

What are those values? Luther's concise definition of what theology is about says it all: *homo peccator et Deus salvator*, or simply: Jesus Christ and us. Scripture interprets this exchange, Christ in our stead and we in the stead of Christ. That is why Luther could call it a happy or marvelous exchange.[18] As our interpreter, Scripture makes intelligible to us a language that for us is foolishness (*moria*, 1 Cor 1:18). We come to the "market" with

13. *Against Heresies* 2.27.2 (*ANF* 1:398).
14. WA 7, 97, 20–22 is the locus classicus for the expression.
15. Forde, *More Radical Gospel*, 71.
16. Bayer, *Gott als Autor*, 298.
17. Paulson, "Lutheran Assertions Regarding Scripture," 381.
18. *Mirabilis mutatio.* WA 31/II, 435, 11; LW 17:225.

the notion that we can barter with the valuables we think we have and the interpreter tells us that they are worth nothing. Yet the other party is giving even herself to us. What is this if not a foolish and scandalous exchange? Nothing for all, all for nothing! If we try to do something, even that little we suppose we retain (*facere quod in se*) in this exchange, we destroy the gift, and the happy exchange turns into a miserable deal. A gift can only be given if it is free and without any reciprocity; otherwise it is no longer a gift. Its sheer reception is called faith. Hence the *sola scriptura* stands between two other *solae*, *solus Christus* and *sola fide*, the gift and the reception conveyed by grace alone, *sola gratia*.

The problem with foundationalism in all its liberal colors is that it took Scripture to be negotiated by the theologian or philosopher, who stands between Scripture and its reader and gives the hermeneutic key to knowing its worth, that is, the worth of Scripture, not the worth of Christ. The fundamentalist with all shades of biblical legalism does the same thing as the negotiator, asserting its immense purchase value, but in the exchange loses Christ. Between the two, foundationalism and fundamentalism, it is only the price tag that each puts on Scripture that is different, but it still is merchandise in the market of ideas and morals. For each, Scripture is a value in and of itself and no longer the interpreter. In contrast, to say that Scripture is itself the interpreter does not put a price tag on Scripture. Therefore Scripture, like the interpreter in the marketplace, does not have a value in itself. Its importance is to make possible the exchange, a very foolish yet happy exchange at that. Hence it is not valueless, but value free. Such is Luther's conception of the economy of salvation.[19]

More than Enough: Rhetoric and Dialectics

So, is *sola scriptura* sufficient? Is only enough? Simply put, no! It is not enough because it is more than enough! If I were to just say that it is not

19. Worth noticing is that this process in which the means of exchange become the end of a bargain is a modern phenomenon typical to capitalist economies. And it is not surprising that this problem of the Scriptures turning into a commodity is a phenomenon that coincides with the triumph of capitalism. In precapitalist economies the "interpreter," i.e., money, is a means and not an end in itself; it exists only to make possible the exchange of goods. In capitalism a reversal occurs. As Marx put it in his classical description of this transition to capitalism, we move from the formula C-M-C' (commodity-money-commodity) to M-C-M', by which money is transformed into capital. Accumulation thus becomes an end in itself. Fundamentalism and foundationalism are approaches to Scripture ruled by a similar capitalist ethos. While the reformers conceived of the reader under the law facing Scripture to be the reader under the gospel (R-S-R'), foundationalism and fundamentalism see Scripture under examination by the reader to be transformed into Scripture interpreted (S-R-S').

enough, lurking behind that statement would be the suspicion that we need a further knowledge to complement what is lacking or not clearly exposed in it. This would be equivalent to Gnosticism, a position that Irenaeus and a number of theologians leading to the Reformers so often criticized and that foundationalists are reintroducing. But if I were to say that it is simply enough, lying in wait would be the suspicion that Scripture is no longer the interpreter but a value, or the value in itself, as fundamentalist merchants of Scripture advertise. Luther prevented both options by suggesting that Scripture is in fact more than enough.

Grammatically speaking, the expression "more than enough," can have, however, two meanings. In a *rhetorical* sense, we can use the expression to denote something that exceeds expectations. A gift that comes with no strings attached; and only in this way is it a gift. So, let us suppose a gift that enriches our lives beyond what we had envisioned, a gift that is in excess to what we deem necessary and sufficient. Such a gift can be described as "more than enough" in this rhetorical sense; it is something that comes by sheer grace. But "more than enough" can also be interpreted in a *logical* sense as that which exceeds a condition set or a requirement made, and the excess is superfluous or overcharged.

What would be the right choice between these two senses of "more than enough"? Can both be true? In fact, Scripture is more than enough, as it is the interpreter that presents the story of a gift that is self-surpassing, which we call gospel, and all that points to it and inculcates Christ (*was Christum treibet*). It is the story of God who becomes flesh and dies the death of a sinner, of the greatest sinner (*maximus peccator*), so as to meet us on our terms, we who have nothing to bargain, we who stand condemned by the law, we to whom all is given, even God's own self. This is the rhetorical sense of "more than enough."

But the logical sense to "more than enough" is also true. There is plenty in the Scriptures that exceeds what for us is necessary and sufficient, even as it is salutary for times and places in which it was promulgated and will serve us as examples if correctly understood, that is, according to its "grammatical, historical meaning," as Luther insists.[20] This is what Luther says clearly in "How Christians Should Regard Moses" (1525):

> One must deal cleanly with the Scriptures. From the very beginning the word has come to us in various ways. It is not enough simply to look and see whether this is God's word, whether God has spoken it; rather we must look and see to whom it has been spoken, whether it fits us. That makes all the difference between

---

20. LW 39:181.

night and day. . . . The word in Scripture is of two kinds: the first does not pertain or apply to me, the other kind does. . . . The false prophets pitch in and say, "Dear people, this is the word of God." This is true; we cannot deny it. But we are not the people.[21]

The Universal Word Speaks Dialect

The question is to whom are the words addressed? If the words are spoken to the one who is totally sinner (*totus peccator*) and entails the promise of Christ that makes us wholly righteous (*totus iustus*), this is the word for all of us that Scripture interprets. Now, if the word addresses a particular individual or group of people, and is bound to that particular situation and context, it is a different and distinct kind of word; it is equally the word of God, but we might not be the people to whom it is addressed. If it is not the universal word that brings us to Christ in the midst of our *totus peccator* condition, if it is a particular word that addresses a political, economic, social, familial, gender, race, or sexual situation, then this word needs translation (*trans-latio*, bringing over from a given context to another context), because the universal Word for us speaks dialect.[22] This is the distinction between what is apostolic and what is not, even if spoken by an apostle. In one of his many criticisms of the book of James, Luther said,

> And this is the true test by which to judge all books, when we see whether or not they inculcate Christ. For all the scriptures show us Christ, Romans 3 [21]; and St. Paul will know nothing but Christ, I Corinthians 2 [2]. Whatever does not teach Christ is not [yet] apostolic, even though St. Peter or St. Paul does the teaching. Again, whatever preaches Christ would be apostolic, even if Judas, Annas, Pilate or Herod were doing it.[23]

Even Christ's own command when he bids the ten healed lepers "go to the priest and make sacrifice does not pertain to me," does not pertain to us. And Luther adds: "The example of their faith, however, does pertain to me; I should believe Christ, as did they."[24]

---

21. LW 35:170.

22. The expression is from Casaldáliga, *Creio na justiça e na esperança*, 211.

23. LW 35:396. This is also the reason that Luther in criticizing the spiritual (allegorical, tropological, and anagogical meaning) exegesis argues that "literal meaning" (which is the fourth meaning) is "not a good term" and prefers "grammatical, historical meaning." LW 39:181.

24. LW 35:174.

Is Luther contradicting himself in saying that the Scriptures stand alone and are clear for those who dedicates themselves to their study, on one hand, but then adding an external criterion to determine what pertains to us, on the other? Had he not made the case that the Scriptures are themselves the interpreter, as argued above? And does he now also claim that they need to be translated, brought over to see if they meet our condition? Legalists and liberals alike would charge Luther with trying to have it both ways. And so he does, because, for him, interpretation is not translation. And it is important to stress the meaning of each.

The Scriptures are both the interpreter and also that which needs translation, depending on the use implied. The Scriptures are our immediate interpreter insofar as their words are for us, both as the universal word that condemns us and leads us to the promise, and as the civic mandate that pertains to worldly affairs. And these two coincide when we are brought by them to Christ.

However, the Scriptures need to be translated whenever the dialect employed does not speak to us. This distinction between the theological and the political discourse remains through the *eschaton*: *Duplex est forum, theologicum et politicum.*[25] There are two distinct semantic spheres, one theological and the other political. In a given dialect of today we would say that theology and ideology are different orders of discourse. One pertains to the ultimate, the other to penultimate realities. One is the Word that alone speaks, promises, and delivers; the other is a dialect that the Word speaks for circumstances demarcated by time and space. One does what it says, which would be the Reformer's meaning of *sacramentum*, the gift of presence; the other exemplifies what the doing implies for a given context, which is called *exemplum*.[26]

Yes, the Word speaks dialect, a specific mode of carrying a conversation confined to a given context and addressing particular issues that pertain to and are demarcated by that context. From the same root *dialect* we have the word dialectics which, before Hegel gave it an ontological meaning, was one of the ancient basic human arts in what was called the *trivium*, in which it was complemented by grammar and rhetoric. Dialectics was the art of mastering the logic or rationality of a given dialect, a conversation within a given context. For example, varied are the dialects of the court room, a market place, a street gang gathering, church liturgies, a session of parliament, or an academic convention, and so forth. Each entails its own rules and logic, which are bound to the very context of the dialect employed.

---

25. WA 39/I, 320, 2–3.
26. For a typical description of the distinction, see WA 5, 639, 13–16.

Luther used the distinction between the Word, as law and gospel that pertains to all, and other narratives that address only some, and under given and different circumstances. Thus he describes them as two different linguistic arts: rhetoric and dialectics. Dialectics for Luther was what we would call the logic of an argument, by which a postulate, proposition, or mandate is put forward, sets and begs its counterpart, and demands a fitting response. In a commandment a proposition is made and a response is expected. It presupposes an exchange, an interaction that might not be a happy one. Dialectics was regarded as the art of reasoning within the rules of conversation in the context of a given "dialect." It is the craft Luther employed in the many disputations he was part of. A disputation implies an understanding and discernment of the rules and the context in which a debate takes place. The context in which it happens must be specified by reading it grammatically and historically.[27] Luther's criticism of the spiritual meaning in biblical exegesis as a tool of interpretation was precise and incisive because "spiritual" exegesis (entailing allegorical, tropological, or anagogical meaning) sought a universal meaning in a particular dialect and did not "deal cleanly with Scripture." Rhetoric, on the other hand, is just telling the story, proclaiming the promise. Such is the gospel, which Luther again and again defined simply as a discourse or story about Christ that grasps us as the overwhelming gift of God. It does not make a proposition to be argued, neither is it about a conversation among different parties. It is pure deliverance in both senses of the term: it dispenses and releases in the same act.

The Rule of Grammar

How do we discern these two genres? It is vital to know if the text is "for me." But could one not be in denial? For Luther this discernment is made possible by the primary liberal art and the most important of the *trivium* (grammar, rhetoric, and dialectic) for theology as theology (but not for proclamation!): grammar. "Among the human sciences devised, the most useful for the theological propagation is grammar."[28] Why grammar? Because it is grammar that reveals what genre is being employed by Scripture, whether it is dialectics or rhetoric, whether it is the external form or the inner energy. The latter releases the force in the word-event that it becomes. *Ergon* or *energeia* are the terms often used to describe these two aspects of language that grammar

---

27. LW 39:181.
28. WA 6, 29, 7–8. Of course, for preaching rhetoric is the most important art to master.

discerns.[29] The universal word as *energeia* is that which effects my conviction as sinner and announces the unconditional gospel. It does what it says and says what it does. Different from this universal word are the circumstantial expressions that survive for our edification in the letter of the Scriptures. This distinction corresponds to the one Luther uses between Christ as a sacrament and as an example. The sacrament enfolds us for what it is; it is the means of grace itself. The example, on the other hand, indeed needs a translator. Foundationalists, with their liberal strategies, evade the distinction and invent a new grammar alongside with Scripture. They create an "Esperanto" that is as salutary as the actual Esperanto is in the world today: of little worth. Fundamentalists, with their legalistic strategies, conflate the distinction and idolize dialectics, legislating it as the only *lingua franca*.[30]

For Luther, the question left for theological discernment was about the distinction. Thus he writes from Coburg to Justus Jonas in June 1530: "We start with this distinction: the Decalogue is the dialectic of the gospel and the gospel the rhetoric of the Decalogue, and thus we have all of Moses in Christ, but not all of Christ in Moses."[31] In other words, Moses is enough, yet we never make it—we don't meet the standards; Christ is more than enough, and we don't need to meet the standards for they are beyond ourselves in any case.

In his commentary on the Ten Commandments in the *Small Catechism* Luther provided the example of how to translate a dialect, even one that Luther could praise so much as the Decalogue, while proclaiming himself to be a new disciple of it.[32] He turned negative statements into positive ones, making very clear what is positively for us (*Wir sollen* . . .) out of what was negatively formulated for the people of Israel (*Du sollt nicht* . . .). Even if you are not under the civil charge of murdering someone, the Fifth Commandment applies to you because you must "help and support [the neighbors] in all of life's need." He does this exemplarily in his commentary on the

---

29. See Morse, *New World Soundings*, 11–15. Also in previous chapter.

30. One might be reminded, as an illustration, that the commandments of God, dictated by God, were written by Moses and carried his handwriting, his dialect, his peculiar calligraphy, as it were. The original tablets written by God were broken when Moses saw the idolatry of the people. The message could not be more suggestive: for an idolatrous people even a text written in God's own handwriting would become an idol and, as idols do, would arrest the gaze from the One to whom the gaze should be directed. Again this would put a tag on Scripture, turning it from the interpreter into a value in itself.

31. . . . *et coepi iudicare, decalogum esse dialecticam euangelii et euangelium rhetoricam decalogi, haberque Christum omnia Mosi, sed Mosen non omnia Christi*. WA Br 5, 409, 28–30.

32. . . . *ego hic factus sum novus discipulus decalogi*. WA Br 5, 409, 26.

Third Commandment in the *Large Catechism*. There he distinguishes the outward sense that concerned only the people of the First Testament from the Christian meaning. For the latter it means having not only the duty but also the right and privilege to have time for both to hear the Word of God and for leisure (also for the common folk, who were not socially protected, he insists). Or he could go even further than that, as he did in the "Theses Concerning Faith and Law":

> 49. . . . if the adversaries press the Scriptures against Christ, we urge Christ against the Scriptures.
>
> 52. For if we have Christ, we can easily establish laws and we shall judge all things rightly.
>
> 53. Indeed, we would make new decalogues . . .
>
> 54. And these decalogues are clearer than the Decalogue of Moses.[33]

Indeed, *tempus mutat mores et leges*, time changes customs and laws.

However, with the antinomian controversy raging (1535), Luther makes it clear that not anything goes, and he continues, "58. Nevertheless, since in the meantime we are inconstant in spirit, and the flesh wars with the spirit, it is necessary, also on account of inconstant souls, to adhere to certain commands and writings of the apostles, lest the church be torn to pieces."[34] Certain commands demand an affirmative response, and not just anything. But which ones are they? The response can only be one that follows from Luther's and the Reformers' apostolic or scriptural principle: those that do not divert us from but lead us to hearing the story of God in the flesh, crucified and resurrected. Luther adds, if the question is "Christ or the law, the law would have to be let go, not Christ." In other words, any law that pretends to have universal validity except the one that declares every one of us equally totally sinner (*totus peccator*), thus leading us to Christ, is a grammatical confusion of dialectics and rhetoric. For example, any law that would prescribe works and conditions for belonging in the priesthood of all believers, for being listeners and proclaimers of the Word, must be let go, for nothing can keep us from the love of God.

The Proper Uses of the Law

Therefore, Luther distinguished between two senses or kinds of law and justice, what the later Lutheran theologians phrased as the first and the

33. LW 34:112–13.
34. LW 34:113.

second use of the law. The first use is the civil or political use of the law, the "logical" or dialectical use. The second is the theological use, the one that the rhetorical "more than enough" addresses. The civil use belongs to the dialect that addresses particular contexts and situations and that can and will change according to civil arrangements and political contracts. Why is the civil the first use and the theological use the second? Because the civil use concerns the relation to the neighbor in ever changing circumstances. Because we are all creatures, human beings in God's continuing creation, before we are believers.

The first use of the law applies to all, Christians and non-Christians alike; and it is to be found in the Scriptures and also elsewhere, because it refers to local expressions of the orders of creation. It is the set of laws framed by Moses for the Jewish people and written in the heart, finding expression in Roman law, in the civil code of Luther's Saxony (*Sachsenspiegel*[35]), in the Constitution of the United States, or in Sharia, the Koranic legislation of Islamic countries. These laws apply to all, but not all phrase it in the same way; dialects are many. Luther, for example, found the justification for polygamy given in Leviticus 25:5–6 a "very good" rule that protected a widow and kept the name and lineage of a deceased father.[36] For that context it was a good law and its example, argues Luther, should teach us that we should enforce legislation toward those same ends. These civil uses of the law, wherever they are found, need translation, for they are dialect-bound. Not only *tempus* but also *situs mutat mores et leges* (time and location change customs and laws). When the Word speaks dialect, when the first use of the law is concerned, it is for Luther still the law of God spoken to a given community or individuals; but its meaning for us needs to be translated, carried over from one place to another, from one time to another. And the means of its translation is communicative or dialogical reason. This is why Luther could sustain that "reason is the most important and the highest in rank among all things, and in comparison with other things of this life, the best and something divine."[37] This communicative reason is what can be exercised across human communities regardless of religious allegiances. And the end of reason is to prevent chaos, produce equity (*Billigkeit*), bringing about civil justice and peace for the proclamation and the hearing of the Word. This is the *telos*, goal, and end of all laws.

---

35. LW 35:167.

36. Ibid.

37. LW 34:137. The original reads: *Et sane verum est, quod ratio omnium rerum res et caput et prae caeteris rebus huius vitae optimum et divinum quiddam sit.* WA 39/I, 175, 9–10 (thesis 4).

These laws are the expression of something deeper, which for Luther, following Paul and the later natural law tradition, can be found in every human heart. The Decalogue and all the other biblical prescriptions are but an expression of natural law codified in given dialects. thus, says Luther, "I keep the commandments which Moses has given, not because Moses gave commandments, but because they have been implanted in me by nature, and Moses agrees."[38] Or even, as we have seen, insofar as Moses agrees. Luther keeps the commandments of Moses insofar as Moses agrees with natural law. "Moses" is a dialect, which even gives us language to help us in our conversation toward finding our own voice to achieve equity. And this is an ideological task, a civic and political exercise that theologians alone will not accomplish, for their proper forum is the Word proclaimed. But as members of a civil community they are called upon to testify as to the way the people of the Bible carried out such conversations, such dialectics, the contextual results they have achieved and the example it provides us.

But is Luther sponsoring a double theory of truth by which revelation stands beside a natural and perennial truth, that is, a meta-physics? Definitely not! His point is only to say that natural law sustains us like crutches in the provisional affairs of this world. This is what natural law discloses, and what is universal about it. The fact that there is so much coincidence in legislation from all over the world and through all times as to what conveys our civil and social obligations attests to this common sense of what is right and wrong. But this is also why in different societies with their different dialects there are varied amazing ways in which this natural law might be expressed and which are always subject to change. But is there one code that is immutable? No, there is none. (From all we know, the only one that ever existed was broken, and what we are left with are dialects trying to convey it [Exod 32:19].) All that we have is our hearts, which are also broken and fail in every attempt to express that image of God implanted in the heart.

Here is a simple example. We all share the sense that in our hearts there is something written, along the lines of the Fifth Commandment, like "don't kill." However, this general law is concretely rendered with many variations through time and space. Some societies think this pertains to all living creatures. Many think that it is right to kill that which threatens our human lives, including some bacteria or those labeled as terrorists. Some think that it pertains to all *human* beings, including the arch-murderer Cain (Gen 4:15). Some include the unborn; others also those who are brain-dead. Still others think that it applies to all humans except those condemned in a court of law to be executed. According to the option chosen by a local dialect, does

---

38. LW 35:168.

anything go? Certainly not, because our broken hearts reflect their brokenness in communities severed from one another precisely over these "translations." Yet, it is the same longing of the hearts to find expression of the law written in them that also forms communities. And these communities long for broader fellowship of all human race and all creatures as much as they assert their differences that are at once expressions of sin, of the injustices we create and perpetrate, and as symptoms of our yearning to live out the law written in the heart and give to it a timely and contextual expression.

We all in our stations of life need these crutches to get along, no matter what shape or form they are cast in. For Luther, they took three shapes: the household (*oeconomia*), the state (*politia*) and the church (*ecclesia*). Yes, even the church as a visible, institutional, or empirical reality is nothing but a crutch to help us in our infirmity as much as the state and the household are.

Antinomianism, or Do We Need the Law?

Natural law is only the shorthand for the universal human search to live together under the condition of utter sinfulness, which we normally call original sin. This does not imply metaphysics, a universal truth that raises our nature to an immutable status beyond nature's vicissitudes. It implies, however, reasoning through our ever changing infirmities to find institutions that address them. And these institutions always change because God is not only the creator, but the one who continuously creates; and we are not only sin-ful, but indeed sin-ners; we keep finding new ways to dodge our condition and go against it. Antinomianism is the name we give to this attitude of living without these institutions as if the crutches that carry us were only addictions from which we have been set free. This would be like believing that throwing away the crutches would by itself heal us.

The work or function of the law in its two uses or senses is finally only one, to bring us to Christ, to be the pedagogue of Christ. Theologically, it brings us to Christ because it finally accuses us, leaving us with nothing but a promise received in faith, that is, nothing but everything. Politically, it institutes systems and structures fit to times and places in which the word as law and gospel can be proclaimed. This is why justice is such a precious and overwhelming topic in the Scriptures. It is the pedagogue of justification. It teaches us what we can never accomplish: the imputation of a righteousness we can only receive as a gift. Injustice is so detrimental not only because it creates a "noise" in God's communication to us, but also because in denying the love of the neighbor, we simultaneously change the love of God into the love of an idol that suits ourselves. The laws of Moses and all the other dialects that try to render the law written in our hearts warn us of this detrimental transformation.

The two senses of the law come together only in the *eschaton*, which happens in every moment of judgment, in all and every *eschata* (plural). These are the moments that the Augsburg Confession calls the "terrors that strike the conscience when sin is recognized."[39] These are the very moments in which the law in both its uses comes to its end and fulfills its task and the rule of God reigns. This is why Luther insisted so much that the law in its civil sense must address us, must be a dialect that speaks to us so as to bring terror into our conscience. (If terror does not strike us first, what we get is terrorism.) Only then can it also be theologically useful. But it must always strike us before them, me before you, for only then can I love you before myself; only then can we love others before ourselves; only then can we love the Other before ourselves—otherwise it simply would not be love. For Luther the end of all laws is love.[40] And we reach this end only if the law fulfills its task in us in the first place. This is why the Formula of Concord, Solid Declaration, Article VI defines antinomianism as prescribing the law to others but not to ourselves since we regard ourselves the true Christians.[41] Antinomianism is as much living without the law as it is applying to others what we do not apply to ourselves. In this sense, ironically, it reverses Luther's maxim in affirming that the end of all love is the law.

So, . . .

Is Scripture alone enough to be the ground and pillar of the church? It is for Luther more than enough. More than enough in a double sense. First, it exceeds anything we can bargain for, and in fact leaves our bargaining as worthless and detrimental insofar as it inculcates Christ in us, being for us the interpreter of the absolutely unequal exchange between what we bring (brokenness) and what Christ brings (wholeness). And, second, it also exceeds in providing us with a plethora of examples, some indeed superfluous,

---

39. CA XII, "Concerning Repentance," in Kolb and Wengert, *Book of Concord*, 45.

40. *Si enim lex contra charita temest, non est lex. Se charitas est domina et magistra legis.* WA 42, 505, 11–12.

41. ". . . we reject and condemn as a harmful error . . . the teaching that the law is not to be urged . . . upon Christians and those who believe in Christ but only upon unbelievers, non-Christians, and the impenitent." Formula of Concord, Solid Declaration, VI, "Third Use of the Law," §25, in Kolb and Wengert, *Book of Concord*, 591.

that pertain to different circumstances showing how this works out in our everyday life with its challenges, limits, circumstances, and possibilities.

The church does not authorize the correct meaning of the Scriptures, nor is it the enabler of floating meanings chosen at whim. The church is the custodian of the events it attests to and the chronicler of the events that keep on happening. She is the registry of memories, of stories told and untold. "Therefore every scribe who has been trained for the kingdom of heaven is like the master of a household who brings out of his treasure what is new and what is old" (Matt 13:52).

3

Stories That Shape the Story

> Stories reveal themselves to us. The public narrative, the private narrative—they colonize us. They commission us. They insist on being told.
>
> —Arundhati Roy[1]

Luther was not a storyteller but he loved stories and storytellers. His use of language and the Scriptures is a pointer to this. This is evident in the way in which he addresses two texts—the Psalter,[2] for which he had the highest regard, and the Sermon on the Mount in the Gospel of Matthew 5–7. And the two are very different and could be said that they cover the spectrum of Luther's attitudes toward biblical texts in that one focus on the inner experience of the heart (a metaphor Luther often used in reference to the spiritual dimension in which faith is kindled) and the other the outer manifestations. Metaphorically speaking the scope goes from the heart to the hands. Luther may not have been a storyteller but he knew how stories shape the story.

The Psalter was for Luther a collection of stories about the human experience in relationship to God. And these stories collected in the book of Psalms were for the Reformer the building blocks that told the Story of the relationship of God and God's people entailing the commandments and the promises of God. The entire Bible and the tradition of the people of God is summarized in it. How is it that from the plurality of narrations and verses the Story with its singular character emerges? This is an issue that has been discussed in the Lutheran communion for quite some time. Jens Erik Skydsgaard worked on this problem in the early 1960s in connection with

---

1. Roy, *Ordinary Person's Guide to Empire*, 3.
2. LW 35:254.

ecumenical challenges the Lutheran World Federation (LWF) was facing.³ But since then the problem has become much more complex as stories have significantly multiplied. Lutheranism is migrating *en masse* from its bedrock to more fluid places around the planet. Needless to add, stories keep accumulating in reports and consultations about Lutheranism where its future is now presaged. So, how the stories tell the story has been the pressing issue for a communion that, by the stroke of fortune, never settled down and registered in stone what its identity finally is, notwithstanding many endless attempts to mine a rock big enough to inscribe it. It is instructive to look into Luther's treatment of the Psalter as it offers clues for understanding how the Reformer saw the relationship between the story and the stories and how one shapes the other. It also gives pointers on how from the many stories the Story is culled and how the Story keeps molding stories in the history of the people with their God.

The Psalter

On April 24, 1530, the day after Luther arrived at the Coburg castle to be in closer proximity to Augsburg where, at the imperial diet, Melanchthon was presenting the confession of the Reformation, Luther wrote to his friend and co-reformer: "We have come to this Sinai of ours, my dear Philip, but once out of this Sinai we will make a Zion and we will build three tabernacles: one for the Psalter, one for the prophets, and one for Aesop."⁴

That Luther regarded the ancient fabulist Aesop the author of the best literature after the Bible, and even edited and translated him into German, is no secret.⁵ But still one wonders about the religious imagery (Sinai, Zion, tabernacle, Psalter, prophets) being associated with this ancient Gentile storyteller. This calls for a careful examination, particularly regarding the reason for these three tabernacles. A tabernacle is the inhabiting place of that which is most dear and divine, the innermost space in which the heart dwells and the soul rests. A tabernacle is an enclosure for presence, i.e., a representation of that which cannot be represented. As such a tabernacle for the Psalter is where the soul and heart of the psalmist is enshrined; the same goes for the prophets, and for Aesop! Luther's high regard for the Psalter making reference to its worthiness as a tabernacle is no surprise. Also meriting it are the prophets for their harsh words necessary for curbing

---

3. See Schjørring et al., *From Federation to Communion*, 248–83.

4. *Pervenimus tandem in nostrum Sinai, carissime Philippe, sed faciamos Sion ex ista Sinai edificabumusque tria tabernacula, Psalterium unum, Prophetis unum, et Aesop unum.* WA Br 5:285, 3–6.

5. Springer, *Luther's Aesop*.

idolatry and entailing the promises pointing to Christ. But, why Aesop? The reference to the storyteller is for Luther of such importance not for who he was or what he did, but for what he said and how he said it. This seems to me the point of this reference to Aesop, whose words were truthful to the human condition, and we are not distracted by the works he did or failed to do. And it is exactly this art of laying out the human condition that, for Luther, was of decisive worth in the Psalter. It would also be a distinguishing feature of what was most dear in the prophets for Luther: they laid bare the human condition.

In his preface to the Psalter (from 1524 and the reworked final edition of 1545), Luther develops an interesting polemic against the popular legends of saints and their deeds. "Other books make much ado about the works of the saints, but they say very little about their words." The Psalter, to the contrary, is about the saints'

> words, how they spoke with God and prayed, and still speak and pray. . . . It presents not the ordinary speech of the saints, but the best of their language, that which they used when they talked with God himself in great earnestness and on the most important matters. Thus the Psalter lays before us not only their words instead of their deeds, but their very hearts and the inmost treasure of their souls . . .[6]

And Luther's praise for the Psalter goes to show the depth of joy and the profound cry of lamentations, "as into death, yes, as into hell itself."[7]

By this measure Aesop's tabernacle can be explained as stories, fables from a person who has not even been acclaimed for sanctity but who spoke about the human condition from the depth of his heart. And that for Luther counts as earnest prayer! And this is not in spite of the fact that he was not a saint (neither was he a Jew or a Christian, for that matter), but more likely because he was not (!) a "saint." Yet, for Luther, he spoke from the depth of his heart, as the psalmists and the prophets did. But there is no illusion in this endeavor. For Luther the translation of a psalm was not to convey the original meaning, or the possibility of giving meaning, but to express in the vernacular to the reader what is in her heart. In other words, a translation allowed for the heart to speak to or communicate with the head!

---

6. LW 35:254f.
7. LW 35:256.

On Translation

Translation does say what it is when it expresses the longings of the heart, and this was above all what Luther found in the Psalter. Walter Benjamin, for whom Luther was an eminent translator, made a distinction worth considering between translation "as a mode" and translatability as "an essential feature of certain works." And he continues a point that Luther would endorse:

> One might speak of an unforgettable life . . . even if all men had forgotten it. If the nature of such a life or moment required that it be unforgotten, that predicate would not imply a falsehood, but merely a claim not fulfilled by men, and probably also a reference to a realm in which it is fulfilled: God's remembrance.[8]

Benjamin makes us ponder how much translatability is not encumbered on us, a task to be fulfilled, as much as it is an unavoidable longing to give the heart a venue to express itself.

Language, for Luther, as mentioned earlier, mirrored the heart allowing for encounters with otherness but also drawing the limits of one's world. This is what Luther writes in defending his psalm translations: "Words are to serve and follow the meaning, and not the meaning the words."[9] This is indeed a very debatable statement that evokes irreproducible circumstances. For example, how am I going to establish a meaning that evokes words in my context that was not the context of the original author? How and when is a literal translation favored and when does meaning call for words that are semantically different than the original? Centuries before this became a central question in hermeneutical theory the Reformer was struggling with this question.[10]

Luther in his defense of the translation of the Psalter in fact goes both ways; at times he ventures into a freer translation for the sake of vernacular intelligibility,[11] and on other occasions he favors a literal translation, even if the meaning becomes obtuse.[12] Is this arbitrary as it seems prima facie? He offers a hint of what would be the operational criterion for deciding between the two: "I have been very careful to see that where everything

---

8. Benjamin, *Illuminations*, 70.
9. LW 35:213.
10. See Grosshans, "Lutheran Hermeneutics," 23–46.
11. See, e.g., LW 35:193: "I must let the literal words go and try to learn how the German says that which the Hebrew expresses . . ."
12. See, e.g., LW 35:194: "I preferred to do violence to the German language rather than to depart from the word."

turns on a single passage, I have kept the original quite literally and have not lightly departed from it."[13] Obviously it begs the question, how does one decide what a passage on which "everything turns" is? Arguably the best answer to this question should be found at the very core of Luther's theology, namely, his Christology within the doctrine of the Trinity. In translating and commenting on Genesis 1 he states, "Here I have considered it necessary to repeat the principle I mentioned several times above, namely, that one must accustom oneself to the Holy Spirit's way of expression."[14] And after defending the technical language of different academic disciplines, he does not surrender to them the right of an autonomous theological hermeneutic: ". . . the Holy Spirit also has His own language and way of expression, namely, that God, by speaking, created all things and worked through the Word, and all his works are some words of God, created by the uncreated Word."[15] This is in fact the key to explaining the choices he makes, particularly in translating the notoriously difficult poetic language of the Psalter, even for someone proficient in biblical Hebrew.

The Communication of Languages

Luther offered his groundwork for translation in his basic christological principle, especially in his magnificent defense of the *communicatio idiomatum*, the communication of attributes, in the Council of Chalcedon (451) as we have it in *On the Councils and the Church* of 1539.[16] The communication of attributes or even more literally, the communication of "idioms," i.e., the communication of language, becomes the question of the translatability of the Word into words. If it is the Word of and with God it needs to be made intelligible and visible in one's proper language. And for Luther, nothing was more proper than one's language; or phrasing it differently, nothing is closer to the heart than the vernacular. But can one's heart be in communion to that to which it is external, the words as uttered or written?

In the Genesis lectures that Luther began in 1535 he starts by pointing to the difference between the Hebrew words *dabar* and *amar*.[17] For Luther, the former (*dabar*) denotes the immanent coeternal distinct person of the triune God, the Word, while the latter (*amar*) describes a speech act that is created in utterance and creates reality in its pronouncement. His point is

13. LW 35:194.
14. LW 1:47.
15. LW 1:47.
16. LW 41:100.
17. LW 1:16.

a Trinitarian one, and indeed christological. He lifted up this distinction to fend the attacks of the "Neo-Arians" (Schwenkfeld and the enthusiasts in general) who were supposedly arguing that because the speech act is a creation of a subject who pronounces it and through which it is posited externally as a creation, this word cannot be coeternal. Luther's argument is that the Word as a distinct person in the Trinity is ineffable, that only through the work of the Spirit, or breath, comes into expression as an external word, as flesh, as matter, as a visible, audible, and sensuous fact.[18] And this is what we can behold, the word as an external reality, which however ensues from the Father by the Word through the Spirit, and becomes the visible reality we can observe. And this externality, this sensuous reality we call world, matter, flesh is reality itself. And this and only this can we behold. The naked God (*deus nudus*) no one can bear to behold and live (Exod 33:20), but the one in the flesh who comes from the heart of God becomes language for us, becomes text woven in the stuff of this world—texture.

This, indeed, is the crux of the matter. Luther's reading of Chalcedon (451) late in 1539 is an attempt to name all that he meant by his christological principle: the Word of God became flesh and thus was translated into human words. And these words are all there is regarding the frail human condition that God decided to join in, or in the words of Paul that Luther so loved, God became sin. God became the language of human inability to say an authentic word, a word from the heart, and restore that which God revealed.

In introducing the Psalter, the Reformer makes the revealing comparison between the Psalms and the legends of the saints. It was necessary to know where Luther was coming from in his understanding of language, of *idioma*, in order to figure out what he meant with the criticism of the "lives of the saints" with all the marvelous accounts of the works they did and miracles they performed. The works and miracles attributed to the saints had a beautiful and undeniable quality. But they were counterfeit in the following sense: the work, the objective reality produced through a miracle, for example, is indeed an expression of the word, but the produce, the work done, was an external reality that severed its connection to the heart. For the Reformer, the works are mute and only as idols do they reproduce themselves. Luther long precedes the historical-critical method and the

---

18. It is not spurious to argue that the Wittgenstein of the *Tractatus* was giving a modern philosophical frame to the same problem Luther was struggling with, namely, the conditions of possibility for the world to be named. And the conclusion drawn by both Wittgenstein and Luther is surprisingly similar.

demythologizing program, but he reached similar conclusions as to what really counts in the biblical narrative as Lessing did.[19]

The Christological Core

Luther owes his interpretation of the Psalms to the christological principle with which he was working. For someone who championed the literal sense of the text and explicitly rejected the allegorical (along with the tropological and the anagogical) interpretation it is surprising to see how much Christ he finds in the Psalter. On the Psalter (and other texts as well), Luther is allegorical through and through, although better would be to say that his exegesis is highly metonymical; he uses a literal reference as in referring to Christ by association of ideas common to the described event and Christ. His defense is precisely dependent on the christological principle applied and what it metonymically evokes in reading the Hebrew Scriptures. When the Reformer claimed to be doing a "literal" reading of Scripture, instead of a spiritual one, he was thinking in the Latin sense in which *littera*, the letter, is the outer expression of *verbum*, the Word. It was Luther's Christology, his understanding of the second person of the Trinity that controlled his translation.

Yet different from the likes of "Origen, Jerome and many other distinguished people,"[20] Luther read the Hebrew Scriptures not only as pointing to Christ, but indeed prefiguring Christ's presence and praising what Christ had already accomplished and continues to accomplish![21] This can only be explained and justified by the way the *communicatio* works as true interchange between the divine and the human, not only in the historical Jesus, not even in the sacrament, but anywhere and at any time, before, during and after the first decades of the Common Era. For this is what Luther says in his *Confession* of 1528, a text that the Reformer regarded to be the irreversible statement of his faith[22] concerning the three modes of Christ's presence. The first is the historical Jesus, the second is where he promises to

---

19. His words that became the mantra of the exegetes that followed him: "Accidental truths of history can never become the proof of necessary truths of reason." Lessing, *Lessing's Theological Writings*, 53.

20. LW 35:235.

21. See, for example, his reading of Ps 68:7, "O God when Thou didst go forth before Thy people, when Thou didst march through the wilderness." Luther paraphrases it thus: "O Christ, at the time when Thou didst go before the Israelites in their exodus from Egypt, Thou didst presage and symbolize Thy resurrection, by means of which Thou didst really precede Thy people out of the Egypt of this world to Thy Father." And so forth. LW 13:8.

22. LW 37:360–72.

be, as in the sacrament, but the third is crucial to understand how Luther reads the Psalms as the story of Christ and of Christendom. According to this "third mode," Christ is "present in all created things.... You must place this existence of Christ, which constitutes him as one person with God, far, far beyond created things, as far as God transcends them; and, on the other hand, place it as deep in and as near to all created things as God is in them."[23]

And this same point is stressed by Luther in different parts of his *Confession* (and quoted at length in the Formula of Concord).[24] To phrase it in traditional language, for the Reformer the economic Trinity tramples the immanent, at least since the creation of the world by the Word.

This is what Luther's rejection of the spiritual senses in reading the Psalter amounts to: It is not that the Psalms may hint at something not yet realized, but they are already a testimony of that which is always being actualized in any place and any time, which is made manifest in its plenitude in Jesus the Christ. The story of the earthly life of the Messiah does not change anything about God and the world in their relationship; it provides, however, a hermeneutical key with which to read the whole of Holy Writ and to read in all that is written, as it reveals in the depth of the heart that which is holy. This is the reason to build a tabernacle for Aesop.

On Being Holy and Blessed

Luther's praises for the Psalter were of such magnanimous dimension precisely because it did not speak about deeds. It was only about "empty" words, empty as the heart is to be to host the Word. That is the condition and the requirement for God to empty Godself and dwell in it. This is the *kenosis* motif of Philippians 2 looked at from the human side in which pure receptivity, *vita passiva*, is the condition for divine evacuation so that the Word can inhabit that bare place, the place of the heart, the depth of the soul, and become words. And this is what he reads in this other psalm that is not in the Psalter, the Magnificat where he compares the human being to entailing the three compartments of Moses' tabernacle (using here a trichotomist anthropology: body, soul, and spirit) in which the spirit designates the holy of holies. In it "God dwells in the darkness of faith, where there is no light."[25]

At the end of his *Confession* of 1528 Luther makes a remarkable distinction between being holy (*heilig*) and being saved or blessed (*selig*). The

---

23. LW 37:224.
24. See Kolb and Wengert, *Book of Concord*, 609–11.
25. LW 21:304.

context is his discussion of the different orders instituted by God (*ecclesia*, *oeconomia*, and *politia*):

> For to be holy and to be saved are two entirely different things. We are saved through Christ alone; but we become holy both through this faith and through these divine foundations and orders. Even the godless may have much about them that is holy without being saved thereby.[26]

The crucial point in this passage is that one can attain holiness in the external orders of the world without having it in the depth of the heart. One can be holy as one conforms to the God-intended "orders of creation." However, blessed is the one who knows by faith that whatever these spheres of promise can become they are the outer expression, the incarnation, the materialization of the Word in words through which matter comes into existence. For Luther, matter matters. His apocalyptic proclivities never led him to despise the world. It is holy because the holy of holies has been hosted by it. This is the holy, as mundane as it can and must be. Blessed is the one who knows and believes that it is made effective by the eternal Word through the Spirit.

In the *Lectures on Genesis* Luther builds an amazing defense for a sect that was condemned for anthropomorphism.[27] Out of his materialism comes his argument showing that "a wrong was done to good men . . . because they said that God has eyes, with which he beholds the poor; that He has ears, with which he hears those who pray." It is only because God has become matter through the Word in the Spirit that God says, "Look! Under this wrapper you will be sure to take hold of me."[28] Those who do not apprehend these material and visible signs "will never apprehend God."[29]

To use "postmodern" verbiage, there is no metanarrative because "The Story" is ineffable, but there are always stories coming from the indwelling of the Word that is hosted in the world. If this ineffable Story can be received in faith and "known" there is definitely a gnostic element in Luther. But if the Word has become creation, matter that decays and dies, this Luther owes to the biblical apocalyptic and the resurrection hope that matter will be restored. And both strands, the gnostic element and the apocalyptic, Luther inherited above all from Paul. This is what allowed him to read the Psalter as stories that came from the heart but did not need external

---

26. LW 37:365.
27. LW 1:14–15.
28. LW 1:15
29. Ibid.

historical evidences to speak on what life in its materiality is about. And that is what he also found in the fables of Aesop, who may or may not have been holy—we cannot know—but who we can say with certainty was blessed.

> The Astronomer used to go out at night to observe the stars. One evening, as he wandered through the suburbs with his whole attention fixed on the sky, he fell accidentally into a deep well. While he lamented and bewailed his sores and bruises, and cried loudly for help, a neighbor ran to the well, and learning what had happened said: "Hark ye, old fellow, why, in striving to pry into what is in heaven, do you not manage to see what is on earth?"[30]

---

30. Aesop, *Aesop's Fables.*

1

Faith and Love, the Space In-Between

On the Beatitudes

"These are three things, so to speak, which every good preacher should do: First, he takes his place; second, he opens his mouth and says something; third, he knows when to stop."[1]

Such are some of the words with which Luther opens his commentary on the Sermon on the Mount. And he follows his own counsel, at least up to step two! Only after some three hundred pages does he try finally to accept his third piece of advice: "Let this be sufficient on the matter,"[2] he concludes. But this text has something about it that disturbs. It lacks the craftsmanship of other Luther texts.

Luther's *Sermon on the Mount* is taken from Wednesday sermons delivered between 1530 and 1532.[3] Questions remain about the accuracy of the nuances and subtlety of the theology of the Reformer as mirrored in the published sermons, although there is no reason to assume that the transcribers were grossly untrustworthy of the source. Although the way in which the text expresses in its details Luther's thought can be and has been put into question, the topics are in general, if not in its minutiae, consistent with other works of Luther. Clumsy articulations notwithstanding, the language follows broadly his style, and the narrative bears the imprint of Luther's theology. This is further supported by the fact that the Reformer

---

1. LW 21:7.
2. LW 21:294.
3. These sermons were delivered when Luther was filling in for Johannes Bugenhagen (Luther's pastor in the city church of Wittenberg), who was out of town implementing the Reformation in Lübeck.

himself wrote with his own pen the preface to the published edition of these sermons as they are available to us, which is as good an imprimatur as any.[4]

As opposed to his treatment of the Psalter here Luther is addressing himself to a subject that does not pertain to the heart, but rather it falls on the extreme opposite of the biblical spectrum. It addresses the question of exteriority, problems of visibility, and of the fulfillment of the law and its demands. But if the beatitudes constitute the extreme opposite to the cordiality of the Psalms, they do so as if in a circle in which the extreme opposites meet each other. These two parts of the Scriptures represent the gamut of the hermeneutical challenges Luther was faced with in reading the Scriptures.

Addressing the Hermeneutical Conundrum

Since Harald Diem published his dissertation on Luther's two kingdoms,[5] the treatment of the Sermon on the Mount in Matthew was suggested as the gauge for assessing Luther's hermeneutical principle in discerning the biblical issues that concerned the distinction of régimes or "kingdoms." Without resorting to an allegorical displacement of the text, Luther finds in the Sermon on the Mount a distinction being employed between spheres of competence, or régimes of truth-speaking, which are not transferable from one sphere to the other. They are distinct, not confused or separated. This becomes all the more clear and explicit with the appositions in the sermon. The blessings bestowed to people in particular life conditions (the poor, the meek, the hungry, the peacemakers, etc.) disturb the relationship between gift and task. It does not cancel them. However, it upsets any system of causality. One is blessed for one's condition in life and not for achieving it.[6] This blessedness does not bring about love. It is not its cause, but the negative condition of possibility for love to take place, because those described as blessed are neither subjectively nor objectively in the condition of entering into a circular economy or reciprocity and bartering. This comes into sharp focus when examining the bluntest of the beatitudes—the demands that

---

4. Note the comment by Jeroslav Pelikan on LW 21:xx–xxi, and also Diem, "Luthers Lehre von den zwei Reichen," 21.

5. Not to be confused with his older brother Hermann Diem (1900–1975). Harald (1913–41) was recruited to serve in the army after he finished his dissertation and fell at the eastern front during World War II.

6. The apparent exception is the reference to the peacemakers (*eirēnopoioi*). But note that Matthew's Gospel was written after the destruction of the temple, which suggests that a peacemaker is one who loves peace and is at ease under the most adverse circumstances.

pertains to the commandment to love, but above all love of the enemy. How can this be a commandment? And how is it to be manifested externally?

The merit of Harald Diem's work was to show that the key to open up the apparent maze of Luther's thoughts on the issue was a hermeneutical one. How do we read the Scriptures, who is addressed, and to which life station does it pertain? Does it speak to us in our "nudity" when we are as we are, without pretense, exposed and utterly vulnerable? This is how the Psalms address us, exposing ourselves in the most intimate way, pouring our hearts out, naming our hate and our love, our praise and our lament without dissimulation. But other times it is not like that. The Scriptures also speak to us when we are "dressed up," wearing the garb proper to the office we occupy. In other words, how does Scripture address us when we put on a persona, the mask we are asked to carry in performing the task to which we are called and with which we are trusted? When we perform a duty, when we answer a call, we are not simply ourselves—nude, bare—but we must carry out the obligation entailed in the calling we have, the mask we wear: the soldier, the peasant, the banker, the carpenter, the mother, the clerk, the politician, the lawyer, the teacher, the priest, and so forth, in her or his station in life. Love as expressed positively in daily life conforms to the conditions of possibility in the constraints of institutional life where our calling takes place.

The Sermon on the Mount, by carrying the commandments to their extreme, represents in an exemplary manner the point in which the two extremes referred above meet each other. On the one hand the beatitude conveys the message of the gift freely given, in the other the radicalization of the law imposes obligations exceedingly demanding. One does not invalidate the other, but if the latter addresses the office, the beatitudes address the bare self, the naked self, the self that is held in secrecy as in the bareness of the heart. "And your father who is in secret and sees in secret will reward you," as the saying is repeated three times in chapter 6 (vv. 4, 6, 18). It functions as a mantra that one may know by heart as trustworthy even and because its meaning is not evident to our common earthly (rational) experience.

What humans naturally see belong to the created world that extends itself in time and space and are there given for humans to administer as public persons fulfilling a calling through labor, political action, and in keeping the Shabbat, all visible things. We find in Luther the distinction between the realm of hearing (*Hörreich*) and the realm of seeing (*Sehereich*).[7]

---

7. See Törnvall, *Geistliches un Weltliches Regiment bei Luther*, 44. A similar distinction is the one presented by Löfgren, *Die Theologieder Schöpfung bei Luther*, 203, in distinguishing between a relationship of function (*Funktionsverhältnis*) and of acceptance (*Akzeptationsverhältnis*) to God.

That faith comes by hearing is a statement that corresponds in the visible realm to love, but is distinct from it. This love, certainly, may grow out of what is heard, but as a love its vector is toward what is seen. Love needs to empty itself of the lofty assurances of faith's blessedness to become love in its concrete and tangible expression in finite existence. But to be actual love, above all, love of the enemy, it must be a secret love. To *display* the love for an enemy is always a Trojan Horse. The poison comes along with the display. The legend of the Greek gift reverses the secrecy of the Sermon in which the gift is kept secret even if in display one cannot but see contempt. The Trojan Horse represents the opposite of the command of Jesus to keep love in secret. In the former the display hides the hatred; in Jesus what is hidden may be disguised by contempt. But all this pertains to the question of sight. Not to the reign of hearing through which blessedness is bestowed.

God is the one who sees in secret, which means that God has an overview of that which in the human side belongs to that which cannot be seen. This secrecy creates a specious emptiness that eludes the sight and thus disguises a gesture of love that cannot be directly reciprocated. So is the love of the enemy. If seen it would cancel itself out. But that which is kept in secret is only apparently the empty self. In fact what God sees is that which is in fact visible, only hidden from human gaze.

Those who follow the injunctions of the Sermon on the Mount do something that has earthly positive implications; even if kept in secret, the commands belong to *vita activa*. That is not the characterization of the *makarioi*, the blessed ones, for their blessedness is due to a negative condition and is dispensed in *vita passiva*. But if not blessed, what are those who try to follow the radicalization of the law?

Here Luther finds himself in a difficult situation in addressing himself to the hermeneutical task of affirming the finitude of love in its worldly endeavors and the acknowledgement of love's infinitely enabling source. In his commentary on the Sermon, Luther is grappling for language to convey the *est*, his signature concept, without either erasing the difference or accepting a form of gradation between the finite and the infinite. Luther was particularly concerned about distancing himself from the medieval interpretation. He was rather under suspicion of caving theologically into Rome's stance. So he wants to make his position clear.

Faith and Love

What is the connection between faith and love, two of the three traditional cardinal virtues of 1 Corinthians 13—which Luther also affirmed—namely, faith, hope, and love? His task is to explain the relationship between undetermined faith that belongs to the *vita passiva* to love which is determined and active. Love shows itself and that is why it should be kept in secret (*en tō kryptō*). It is not invisible. The father who sees in secret will reward the giver. This is the point: it is kept from sight, in order for the act seen by the receiver to be authentic. Definitely there is also an economy at work, but it is not the economy of circular exchange that happens directly when the subject of the act of mercy is rewarded by displaying the act in the open as propaganda and thus receiving proportionate compensation. This reward from the "Father" who sees in secret is absolute surplus value, because the reward of publicity is sacrificed when love is kept out of sight, yet all the same visible only *in abscondito*! This is how love of the enemy needs to proceed. It is a secret love of the pure heart that dispenses mercies without necessarily ceasing hostility. Love appears here as a disruption in the circular economy of exchange. The exchange becomes asymmetric. The gift bestowed by the secret love disrupts the economy and yields no compensation, except by the One who sees in secret.

The difference between the two is not a matter of gradation, an axiological ordering between lower and higher, and vice versa. This is something that Luther accused the systems of knowledge and power of, a recurrent motif to counter the contiguity between heaven and earth. The Sermon on the Mount is not to be taken as counsels or advice for the few who want to achieve perfection, while remaining at most as a desideratum for the average Christian. Luther opens the preface that he himself wrote for the publication of his transcribed sermons attacking the difference between *praecepta legis* and *consilia evangelica* and ordering them so that the counsels are seen "merely as advice to those who want to become perfect."[8] Luther's response is an emphatic NO. The distinction is not the one between different classes or castes of people, but it is a distinction within the person itself, between the heart and the deed, to use Luther's expressions, or between one's own being in itself, *coram deo*, and one's being for others, *coram hominibus/mundo*. What bridges the two is kept off sight, is kept in secret, for the eyes only of the one who sees in secret.

Communio

One might wonder what the theology behind the Reformer's stance is, and it is twofold. First, the person is simultaneously a Christian and a worldly person, but she is one person! Here Luther's understanding of the *communicatio*

---

8. LW 21:3f.

idiomatum, as expounded particularly in *The Councils and the Church* from 1539, is of paramount importance. The person of Christ cannot be divided, neither can the Christian, in whom Christ indwells, be divided. "Wherever you place God for me, you must also place the humanity for me."[9] For him, anthropology recapitulates theology. Hence he is plain and clear that these injunctions are no advices "to be kept by anyone who pleases."[10] They are commandments given to the whole human person as Christian.[11] Loving one's enemy means what it says, demands what it asks. But, in so much as the divine is encrypted, secretly held, in the frailty of the flesh, to be the gift, so is the love of the enemy possible as long as it remains a secret gift. In short, love of the enemy is the often missing link in Luther studies between faith and love, grace and work/law.

Secondly, Luther is quite aware of the imperious character of Jesus' radicalization of the law, stretching it to the breaking point. And somehow he delights in it, for it plays along with his theological program of letting God be God and the human truly human. Yet, the two are in communion, they communicate their properties, *idiomata*, to each other in the singularity of the person. Neither the Roman canonists nor the enthusiasts understood that. The Roman canonists "obliterate" it by making it into mere advice; the enthusiasts try to organize the whole of life with these commandments as if they belong to the organization of social existence, as if infinitude could be conquered, while it is already a given.[12] "Thus the devil blows and brews on both sides so that they do not recognize any difference between the secular and the divine realm,"[13] the enthusiasts by collapsing the difference, the Papists by rationally ordering them axiologically. The whole commentary on the Sermon in Matthew hinges upon this distinction. But how do we go from here? Luther is aware of the hazards of navigating between the Charybdis of Rome and the Scylla of enthusiasm.

The injunctions of the Sermon on the Mount neither abolish the law nor substitute for it. It also does not establish a different social sphere for which it becomes valid. It is legislation neither valid for the *ecclesia*, nor for the *oeconomia* or the *politia*. It is not valid in either of these spheres or institutions. However it does actuate itself in these institutions not being a dispositive of them. So, how does it actuate itself? This is the formulation of the problem: If the radicalizing of the law exceeds the law how does it

9. LW 37:219.
10. LW 21:4.
11. Ibid.
12. LW 21:5.
13. Ibid.

encroach itself upon the law? It does it by hiding the gift under the law. The law is love's camouflage. One does not *see* this love, but faith tells the tale.

Rhetorical Device

Yes, faith tells the tale. But it is easier said than done. How can one live up to the ethical idea that is totally beyond human achievement? Diem's early work on the two régimes based on this Sermon (as narrated by Matthew) presented it as a hermeneutical proposal of Luther to avoid the intricacies of medieval semantics and the figurative rendition of difficult biblical texts. The commandment to love the enemy functions here as the touchstone to examine how Luther's hermeneutic works in discerning between what love accomplishes and what grace through faith bestows. But can this love be taken literally? Can Luther sustain the *sensus literalis*?

After all is said about the *sensus literalis*, we are here faced with the unavoidable problem of the use of figurative language. Luther's criticism of the *quadriga* with its three figurative senses (allegorical, tropological, and anagogical, added to which the literal sense was a fourth) comes up because he claims that the Sermon on the Mount applies to all Christians—not only to the monks or other particular groups of people. However, he also says that many other things do not apply. The story of the healing of lepers in Luke 17:14[14] is another example of this.

Luther insisted that even if the whole Scripture was the Word of God, not everyone was thereby addressed. It is God's Word, "that is true; we cannot deny it, but we are not the people," he insisted in the sermon *How Christians Should Regard Moses* (1525).[15] Furthermore, in addition to using the *quadriga* himself on occasion,[16] he is known for his appeal to figurative language, and praised in particular what he regarded as the most beautiful of rhetorical devices in the Scriptures, the synecdoche. A synecdoche is a figure of speech in which the whole expresses a part, or a part the whole. "Synecdoche, to be sure, is a most sweet and necessary figure of speech and a symbol of God's love and mercy . . ."[17] However, immediately after, he discusses the biblical usage of synecdoche, noting that he does not recall

---

14. See chapter 2 above for the distinction between sacrament (*sacramentum*) and example (*exemplum*).

15. LW 35:161–74.

16. See, e.g., WA 5, 644, 19 -645, 15. Even when giving priority to the literal sense he saw the merit of the other three figurative senses as well. See also WA 13, 638, 12ff.; LW 20:107f.

17. LW 32:169f.

"seeing any scriptural texts which use that form of synecdoche in which a universal expression stands for the particular."[18] Only the reverse is the case. The particular receives a universal figure. The point of this distinction in figurative use of language only when a particular speaks for the whole is exemplified as such: ". . . sometimes when He [God] is said to strike and destroy, one is not to understand that He strikes all or completely annihilates, for He touches the whole when he touches a part."[19]

Love's Labor's Limits

The Sermon on the Mount is a helpful passage in understanding what is entailed in the love of the enemy. As in all the other injunctions, it starts with an appeal to the law or customs ("You have heard that it was said . . . , but I say . . ."). Luther is quick to note that this reference to the hatred of enemies is not found anywhere in the Scriptures. Nevertheless, "scattered" references here and there infer it. Stretching such inference by assuming its legitimacy is wrong. So, in order to get the intention of the law it was stretched to reach the point of loving one's enemy. However, this law, if apodictically prescribed, would turn out to be not only impossible to fulfill but also irresponsible. And so he asks,

> What is to be said about the fact that the Scriptures often talk about holy men cursing their enemies, even about Christ and his disciples doing so? Would you call that blessing their enemies? Or how can I love the pope when every day I rebuke and curse him—and with good reasons too?[20]

This leads to two problems. First, Luther is applying these words to all Christians, for it is the Gospel, and thus it is for all.[21] He does not let us off the hook, while so many other passages he deemed not applicable. Second, he recognizes that Christians are not able to fulfill Christ's commandments, not due to moral weaknesses, but because our calling to the divinely ordained institutions would not allow us to even try fulfilling them. It is irresponsible to apply them to our calling in the household (*oeconomia*), in the government (*politia*), and even in the church (*ecclesia*).

So, how do we get out of this imbroglio? We have to remember that we are here talking mainly about the Beatitudes, about being blessed. This

18. LW 32:170.
19. Ibid.
20. LW 21:119.
21. LW 35:171.

is the framework of this chapter, which starts with the description of the blessed and continues with the contrasting "you have heard . . . but I say to you." This brings us back to the use of the synecdoche. While love of the enemy is a gesture of universalizing love, the concrete and particular form in which this love is manifested is constricted by circumstances, which makes its employment restricted to particular expressions or gestures of love. Inconspicuous as these gestures might be, particular are they in their manifestation. This particular form in which love expresses itself may be used, by means of synecdoche, as love universal, but limited to the constraints of the earthly régime.[22]

This means we are called to be holy *coram mundo* where we are entrusted with responsibilities that definitely require work and law in the service of love in sanctification. No one is exempt from this responsibility. But we are blessed *coram deo* for the faith that by grace reaches us when we relinquish any attempt of confusing blessedness and holiness, or seeing the two as stages in an ascending scale.

Régimes

Here Luther insists on another distinction that not only discerns or discriminates among the orders[23] but distinguishes *régimes* that are not symmetrical alternatives, which are named as the earthly and the spiritual régimes, that Luther can also call kingdoms or regiments, *inter alia*.[24] The amount of literature on the so-called two kingdoms doctrine produced between the 1930s and the 1960s is immense. While an explication of this doctrine is not necessary here, a brief excursion can be a helpful guide in interpreting the Beatitudes. For clarifying the challenge of interpreting the Beatitudes, sufficient is to indicate some guiding marks. Firstly, although it relates to the three realms, or instituted orders, the distinction of régimes belongs to a different order of discourse. The institutions belong to a form of discourse that is not properly or uniquely and exclusively theological, because it intersects with philosophy *lato sensu* (to include politics, economy, sociology, anthropology, etc.) while the distinction of régimes is strictly theological. Here

---

22. Nowhere is this use of synecdoche more evident than in Luther's commentaries on the Song of Solomon.

23. *Vult Deus esse discrimina ordinum* (WA 44, 440, 25).

24. The terms to refer to these two realms are not consistently used by Luther. While in German *Reiche* and *Regimente* suggest a clear distinction between conceptual schemes, in Latin the term used for both is only *regnum*. See Duchrow, *Christenheit und Weltverantwortung*.

Luther's Christology is the overdetermining factor. It pertains to Luther's understanding of the relationship without separation or mixture of the two natures, his understanding of the *communicatio idiomatum* as referred to above. As Christ, so are Christians, as "little Christs," simultaneously and totally in the flesh, in matter, as well as, by virtue of grace, partakers of the divine. The reality is one, as the finite is capable of the infinite, but the perspective by which we look at it is different. It is as different it is to look at the same crystal from different facets, yet it is the same crystal, to use Luther's simile.[25]

The beatitudes describe those whose situation is one that goes against the ways of the world or resists its ways by not following them. The poor, the weak, those who mourn a loss, those who hunger, those who are merciful, those pure of heart, the peaceful, the persecuted all those characterized by negative characteristics, by adverse features. These characteristics do not apply to the orders of creation characterized by positive features. The household or the economy has to feed the people and not let them hunger, the government has to defend the weak even into engagement of war, and the church's calling is to enrich the people spiritually by preserving the dignity of the Shabbat and educating them.

Holy Orders

In his *Confession Concerning Christ's Supper* (1528), as already mentioned, Luther makes the distinction between being holy (*heilig*) and being saved (*selig*) as two entirely different things. That the beatitudes go against the grain finds its ally in this distinction of Luther's. This distinction applies precisely to the problem we are trying to resolve: "We are saved through Christ alone; but we become holy both through this faith and through these divine foundations and orders."[26] As a Christian one is not excused from participating in any or all the divinely instituted orders, as Luther states in the *Confession* of 1528: "But the holy orders and true religious institutions established by God are these three: the office of priest, the estate of marriage, the civil government. All who are engaged in . . . these are engaged in works which are altogether holy in God's sight."[27]

---

25. Luther loved this image of the crystal and played with the sound of the word to speak about Christ-All, the omnipresence of Christ that we perceive in only one of its dimensions or facets at a time. See LW 37:224; WA 26, 337, 9–31.

26. LW 37:365.

27. Ibid.

This brings us back to the question about the connection between the two. Simply put, can one be blessed and saved without being holy or a saint? Or the reverse, can one be holy without being blessed? Luther admitted that there was a lot of holiness among the pagans, without being blessed thereby. There is some form of causal relationship implied here. But if there is holiness without confessing the faith in Christ, this would break down the union of natures (*unio hypostatica*). The same would be the case if there were the possibility of being blessed without yielding holy works. There is enough in Luther's writings to corroborate these possibilities as the emphasis in the *sola fide* and the invectives against work and law. These seem indeed to corroborate this breaking down of the union, which is only mildly assuaged by the metaphor of the tree and the fruits. But even this analogy breaks down when one might conceive of a tree without a fruit, but never the fruit without a tree.

We may resolve the dilemma not by finding some expressions in the Luther corpus symptoms of vitality in expressions of concerns for justice and good works as sort of exceptions, or afterthoughts. Instead, we need to take Luther at the root of his theology, radicalizing him therefore, drawing the consequences that he should have drawn.

Love's Labor's Won

Luther makes a surprising move right after assigning the orders as the spaces to exercise holiness. Instead of remaining close to the expression of love as it is shown within the instituted orders or hierarchies, he added to them a vague reference to the "order of Christian love." This "order" is not a hierarchy or institution, similar to the attributes Luther used to describe the three classical orders.[28] What is this order that is not covered by the established institutions in which holiness inscribes itself?

> Above these three institutions and orders is the common order of Christian love, in which one serves not only the three orders, but also serves every needy person in general with all kinds of benevolent deeds, such as feeding the hungry, giving drink to the thirsty, forgiving enemies, praying for all men on earth, suffering all kinds of evil on earth, etc. Behold, all of those are called good and holy works. However, none of these orders is a means of salvation.[29]

---

28. Luther inherited this from medieval times and ultimately from Aristotle's distinction of human faculties in the *Metaphysics*. See chapters 21 and 22 below.

29. LW 37:366.

In medieval theology there were "seven acts of mercy," consisting of those listed in Matthew 25:35f., plus the burying of the dead. But forgiving one's enemy or suffering all kind of evil were not among them. Luther does not use these acts as an addition to improve our chances of salvation, but as an excess in the sanctifying régime. Faith remains as the unconditional gift. Tenuous as it might seem, there is a link that connects faith and love, blessedness and holiness, which the eyes cannot behold, yet the ears hear. And that is the tale of a secret love, the love of the enemy. That was God's love, secret, *absconditus*. It is the small act of forgiving an enemy in an inconspicuous merciful gesture toward a foe, above all if it is kept secret. It is this frail gesture that is in synecdoche universalized, and literally expressed by the incarnation. One extraordinary gesture of kindness, be it almost insignificant, fulfills the commandment of universal love. A meek gesture of love covers a multitude of sins (1 Pet 4:8). The synecdoche gives expression to this while respecting the limits of the flesh.

What the Reformer was trying to express is akin to the reminder by Carl Schmitt that modern languages (German or English) notwithstanding, *exthrous* (as in Matthew) is not *polemios* in Greek; neither is *inimicus, hostis* in Latin.[30] Following Matthew, the reference here is to enemies in a private and not political sense. For Luther, however, the distinction that Schmitt makes so adamantly is blurred in the fluidity of the rhetorical use of figurative language. One's vocation calls for political craftiness. The enemy is not reduced to an adversary that can be "loved" in a phlegmatic detachment that for Schmitt would make politics possible. The enemy remains as enemy, while a gesture of love disturbs the logic of hatred without legislating itself as a new politics.

The excess in the realm of holiness does not add to the realm of blessedness. In fact, the procedure is one of subtraction. This is the genius of the Reformer and the novelty of the proposal. By the simple fact of not enforcing the means to carry out hatred, reacting to persecution, love makes its meager appearance an opening space for blessings to blossom. This is why love of the enemy comes together with prayer for those who persecute.

Blessedness belongs to the one who loves, forgives, the enemy at heart, even if the foe remains in the temporal sphere. It is through the synecdoche that the two acceptations of enmity are connected. So, the pope, the Turks, the enthusiasts, the usurers could be met with the fantastic accusation of being the devil, and all the filthy language that Luther could think of (and not much did he miss from the scatological lexicon) keeping with his use of the synecdoche. But in the earthly régime they were secular adversaries to

---

30. Schmitt, *Concept of the Political* (chapter 3).

be met according to the rules of the ecclesio-politico-economic régime, and exceeding their demands. This excess is the decisive element in Luther's "political theology." The love of the enemy is the cipher of this excess which is its victory even if no bigger than a mustard seed. Even if there is no positive causality between love and faith, love of the enemy releases, *via negativa*, a space of peacefulness for the word to be heard in the chambers of faith. This is love's labor's won.

The Reformer, it has been often repeated, was a child of his time, but his theological "DNA" passed on produces fruits kept in secret from his own sight and of many of his custodians. And what is kept secret must be accepted in faith—such is love of the enemy, the link between faith and love.

Part Two

Theology Matters

5

On the Playground of God

*Justification as Event
and Representation*

The Gift of Death

THE "'ARTICLE' OF JUSTIFICATION is both quite simple and at the same time highly complicated. It is as simple as Christ saying, 'Stay close to me, I am your rock and castle . . .' And it is more complicated than a learned dogmatics of several volumes . . ." These words of Klaus Schwarzwäller from the foreword to a comprehensive study on the role of justification in major contemporary theologians say it all.[1] In other words, this article is as simple as receiving a gift out of sheer generosity of the giver, but as complex as the phenomenon of the gift is, its workings, and operations.[2] Can we really evade the inescapable logic of the economic principle of *do ut des*, I give so that you give (in return)? The complexity of it is that the simplicity of purely receiving a gift cannot even be *expressed* if not in the very denial of what it is supposed to entail, which is: pure receptivity. The moment of acknowledgement is simultaneously the moment of its destruction because it enters into an economy of reciprocity. Jacques Derrida phrased it sharply: "If the gift appears or signifies itself, if it exists or if it is presently *as gift*, as what it is, then it is not, it annuls itself. Let us go to the limit: The truth of the gift . . . suffices to annul the gift."[3] In other words, if the gift is *represented* it is no longer (a) gift.

---

1. Mattes, *The Role of Justification in Contemporary Theology*.
2. See Holm, "Luther's Theology of the Gift." Holm gives also a good overview of the subject and its complexity in recent theology, anthropology, and philosophy.
3. Derrida, *Given Time*, 26f.

Yet justification is about an "exchange" (and a happy one at that) which is radically one-sided all for nothing, nothing for all. But how can this nothing be maintained as an element in the exchange. It would mean the cessation of all barter, even the attempt to acknowledge it. Even a discourse about it is in itself a contravention of what it stands for. In other words, can there be an explanation, a "justification" offered as an "exchange" for the justifying gift? Nothing could be more paradoxical or aporetic. How are we to actively present that which is given without annulling the gift and inserting into an economic transaction? How can a gift not produce a debt by which it is annulled?

How can we understand this incongruousness? An analogy that best describes this predicament is the attempt to describe leisure or playfulness. Such enterprise is no play and no leisure. In other words, the discourse and practice of playfulness becomes a self-contradiction in the moment it becomes a serious business. The discourse of describing playfulness or the practice of playing for a prize engages in the very negation of leisure itself; it becomes a negotiation: *nec-otium*, as the Latin etymology of negotiation has it, is the very denial (*nec-*) of leisure (*otium*). Purposeless playfulness itself eventually calls for toil, in competition, and in the commercialization of sports and thus it enters the commercial cycle that rule the industry of entertainment. What might be an enjoyable leisure time for those entertained is toil for the athletes and actors producing it. Even for the individual that does engage in play for fun a certain amount of mental and physical deftness is required. Leisure itself is often not an end in itself, but a means to restore mind and body from fatigue, for the sake of returning afresh and rejuvenated for the work at hand. This is then the core of the conundrum: leisure (*otium*) requires its opposite (*nec-otium*); playfulness needs a body as a playground. The same with the gift of grace, which paradoxically is costly in order to be a gift; the body that plays toils. The pure gift, the unconditional gift, the consummate leisure, would be death itself,[4] as any playfulness is always a rendezvous of a lively body with death, because aiming at respite it courts radical rest; it courts death.

Only a god in its mythical or philosophical impassibility can be otiose, radically idle, a god without creation, without passion. In his reflections on the "end of philosophy," the Russian immigrant Alexander Kojève, with poignant wit, remarked thus:

> It is true that philosophical discourse, like history, is closed. That idea irritates. That is perhaps why the *sages*—those who succeed the philosophers and of whom Hegel is the first—are so rare, not

---

4. This is the daring statement that underscores Derrida's *Gift of Death*.

to say nonexistent. It is true that you may not adhere to wisdom unless you are able to believe in your divinity. Well, people with a healthy *esprit* are very rare. To be divine: what does that mean? It might be Stoic wisdom or even play. Who plays? The gods: they have no need to react, and so they play. They are the do-nothing gods.... I am a do-nothing.... Yes, I am a do-nothing and I like to play . . . at this moment, for example.[5]

Kojève's droll description sets the terms of the paradox; if justification has to be taken as the pure gift, it would have to be as in radical playfulness, but this implies "nothingness" as the only possibility. And this is death itself. And any attempt of describing or comprehending it discursively is already its very betrayal. So the option for engaging the "doctrine" of justification seems to be an unqualified apophatic, silent withdrawal from discourse itself; kataphasis, discourse, destroys the gift. Yet the very philosopher who announced the end of philosophy continued to philosophize and likely got something in return for the interview he gave, books he published or seminars he held. Kojève played with the gift, but the play was no different than the one of Sisyphus, who, by fooling the gods, imprisoned Death. In the version that Homer presents of the myth, Pluto, seeing the underworld, his domain, deserted, frees Death who, in turn, seizes Sisyphus and condemns him to the underworld to carry a rock uphill that rolls back in an unceasing toil. Sisyphus has no rest because he was not put to rest. In the Greek myth, before being seized by Death, Sisyphus made his wife promise not to bury him, but to leave his body in public display. As long as the body is present no pure gift can be realized. Albert Camus, in his rendition of this myth, concludes with this playful remark: "Sisyphus teaches a higher fidelity that denies the gods and carries rocks. . . . We must imagine Sisyphus happy."[6] The myth is about the denial of gift in a sort of celebration of its incoming triumph. Death, the radical idleness, is the objective of play, but also its end and termination. Therefore we have the dodging of it in its luring proximity. A classic example is when Goethe's Faust, at the approach of death, brought to him by Mephistopheles, attempts one last bargain: "*Verweile doch, du bist so schön!*" (Stay a while, you are so beautiful!).[7]

The language of justification by which the church stands or falls entails such paradox. This is the reason for Luther's seemingly hyperbolic language in which justification can only be received in *vita passiva*, "destroying," "annihilating," "killing," all the presumptuousness of *vita activa*, which does not

5. Cited by Rosen, *Hermeneutics as Politics*, 106.
6. Camus, *Myth of Sisyphus*, 88–91.
7. Goethe, *Faust*, 335.

bring about any hope.[8] And this hope is a "hoping against hope," as Paul described the justifying faith of Abraham in Romans 4—not the least because it required the killing of Isaac, the only hope he had of inheriting the promise of being a great nation. For his faith Abraham surrendered perennial survival through his descendants by sacrificing the promise. And that "was reckoned to him as righteousness" (Rom 4:3).

Justification kills, and this is the only unconditional act of ultimate mercy; it kills the presumptuous self of the *vita activa*, kills the modes by which one pretends to create an enduring presence that is nothing but the lifeless leftovers of a gift not received, but somehow transacted, negotiated. Yet, even for that to be asserted, life *counts*; life calculates, negotiates and hustles. In the case of Abraham, ironically, the sacrifice was saved, Isaac lived on. In any case, life plays and frolics, and in this playing the paradox is embraced and the toiling body is engaged. Justification thus expresses itself in finitude and frailty, with its immeasurable dimensions which only a joyful heart can indeed have a glimpse of, and experience.[9]

The Shabbat

In his exposition of the creation story in the Genesis Lectures,[10] Luther offers us a frame for engaging this conundrum. Contrary to the do-nothing gods of Kojève, the God of the biblical narrative is engaged, not impassible. This God is the "author" of the world[11] or the "'poet' of heaven and earth" (*poiētēn ouranou kai gēs*) as the Nicene Creed has it in the original Greek. It is only after the work of creation that God rests, and in this resting the Shabbat is instituted.

However, while God rested at the end of creative labor, humans by virtue of having just been created, begin their existence on the Shabbat. On their first day they join God in resting. Humans don't have a pre-existence of toil from which they have to rest. They begin their existence by doing nothing. And this is the experience of pure reception; this is the *vita passiva* that precedes *vita activa*. And if this rest was a radical rest, the pathos of passivity was death itself. Humans begin their existence in dying.

---

8. "*Activa sane vita, in qua multi satis temere confidunt, quam intelligent quoque per merita non producit nec operator spem, sed presumptionem . . . Ideo addenda est vita passiva, quae mortificet et destruat totam vitam activam . . .*" WA 5, 165, 33–37.

9. See Stolt, "Luther's Faith of 'the Heart': Experience, Emotion, and Reason."

10. See the first volume of LW.

11. The expression is from Bayer, *Gott als Autor*.

For Luther, the Shabbat was not a day of creation but of instituting the first estate, the *ecclesia*, the state of communion of humans among themselves and with their God. This is the church radically universal, for it is the church of Adam and all his children. But calling it "church" is inappropriate here, because nothing of human doing and making structured or shaped this, not even were sacraments administered, nor a sermon delivered for proclamation; it was pure event instituted by God for nothing: an apophatic church! For Luther, that church was the tree God planted in paradise, which was "Adam's church, altar and pulpit."[12] So there was nothing of human doing, nothing instituted by *ius humanum* when the "church" God instituted happened.

On May 12, 1530, when Melanchthon was at the imperial diet in Augsburg presenting the confession of the reformers, Luther counsels him in a letter with this elegy of leisure: "God is indeed served by leisure [*otio*]. There is nothing greater than pure leisure. This is why he wanted the Shabbat to be most rigidly observed."[13] In the beginning of biblical narrative, human experience in the world starts in a radical otiosity. This means that it starts by dying and it is in that death that God's work is finally accomplished and God also becomes otiose.[14]

This is the first of the only two times in the narrative of the Scriptures that radical leisure and emptiness is registered with such sharp resolution. The other will be on the Friday afternoon, after the work of redemption had been done and God dies on a cross to be mourned in a Shabbat of idle lament, prayer and rest. That Friday God totally rests, the duty roster is cleaned and no activity is left; creation is set free from law, work and obligation because it dies with God, and comes to rest in God. This is what justification means: to be at rest with and in God when God is definitely at rest. This is how the "work" of redemption is consummated and why we die with Christ, in God lying in a tomb, as Paul so emphatically formulated it: "Therefore we have been buried with him by baptism into death" (Rom 6:4). Luther's affirmation of Christ's third mode of presence by which he is "as deep in and as near to all created things as God is in them"[15] is an attestation

12. LW 1:95. See Westhelle, *Church Event*, 6–9.

13. "*Deo etiam servitur otio, imo nulla re magis quam otio. Ideo enim sabbathum voluit tam rigide prae caetaris servari.*" WA Br 5, 317, 40f. (Nr. 1516).

14. But this paradoxical statement of beginning existence in death is curiously assuaged by Luther himself when he suggests that the human being conceivably "fell on the seventh day," which leads to a curious attenuation of the paradox. If original sin implies disobeying the third commandment, then it makes sense that *vita activa* is an inevitable condition of existence. LW 1:81.

15. LW 37:223.

of the paradoxical nature of justification. It is a radical confirmation of the fact that the God who brings us and all that exists into life does it by joining us, by being present there where we cannot but receive the gift without even a gesture of returning it, without even pretending any presence, which means death. To express it in the words of Luther's commentary on the Magnificat, "God dwells in the darkness of faith, where no light is."[16]

Justification can be therefore conceived only as an eschatological event; it meets us at the "end." The end—death itself—meets us at the beginning, at the end, and in the very middle of our existence, wherever and whenever there is an impossibility of pretending a presence. This is the promise of the Shabbat.

Søren Kierkegaard's claim that "the work of love in remembering one who is dead is a work of the most unselfish love" because it "eliminates every possibility of repayment"[17] is equally true in its reverse. The gift the dead receives in remembrance is a pure gift, because it cannot be repaid. This is the deeper meaning of the Shabbat, both in the first account of creation in Genesis and at the end of the gospels. God is at rest both times, following the work of creation, and the work of redemption. Both are symmetrically presented within the same template. The book of Genesis only tells us that God rested (2:2–3), closing the P account of creation. From the Gospels we know almost as little. Luke cryptically refers to the practice of the women after having witnessed the body of the beloved being laid to rest as "on the Sabbath they rested according to the commandment" (23:56b).[18] So, as much as the old Adam starts in pure rest, the first day of his existence, the new Adam starts the first day as the eternal Christ with and for us resting in a tomb. That is the work of justification that God does to us and to God's own self; it is to declare that all has been accomplished. If in Genesis we find that "God rested . . . from all the work that he had done" (2:2), in the gospel it is proclaimed in a single word, *tetelestai*, "It is finished" (John 19:30). Justification is at the end, and at the very beginning of life itself. And because it is the end, it is also the beginning, and vice versa. But this "end-beginning" meets us in the middle of our existence in the dark abyss of faith. Faith can say what reason cannot grasp: death is at the beginning as much as creation is at the end, and in and through the two God abides.

---

16. LW 21:304.

17. Kierkegaard, *Works of Love*, 320.

18. The only other reference to that Shabbat, Matt 27:62–66, tells the story of the religious and political leaders working to secure the tomb so that the body would not be stolen and claimed to have been resurrected.

The Wrappings of the Gift in Law and Work

The template that is symmetrically reproduced in the beginning of Genesis and at the end of the gospels has the Shabbat at the center. In Genesis it is between God's new creation (*ex nihilo*) and human activity, which Luther called human cooperation (*cooperatio*) with God.[19] In the gospels it is between human activity of the truly human God and new creation (resurrection).[20] This Shabbat in which we rest in and with God is the point of contact between the heavenly and the earthly in reverse order. This is the experience of immediacy, what happens without mediation, without discourse and negotiation. Yet to express this, even if in a single word (as in *tetelestai*), already implies mediation. It is to make present something that is absent, to re-present something. The present, the gift, is concealed by its wrappings, the body needs protection (Gen 3:21), and the tomb is sealed (Matt 27:66). This wrapping and this clothing are masks[21] that display existence (from *ex-sistere*, to stand outside). This is what we call life, which is an artful disguise of the gift. Yet this disguise entails promises, as the wrapping of a present entails the gift hidden by it.

In the meantime there is mediation, life lingers and is a play, a rendezvous with justification, a dodging of death in its presence. Justification is already accomplished, we just don't get used to it. Instead, we play around it trying to show and pretend that we have not been put to death, or feign that we are not dead yet. Thus we live in this pretense of being present when we are not and we dodge the consummate fact by this posturing of presence. We play this game in trying to get used to what already is the case. In other words, we *re-present* ourselves, by regulating our existence through the "law," and by striving presence through "work." It is pretending presence.

However the efforts to pretend presence, through "law" and "work," entail two promises in and through which we are invited and inducted by God to the playground of creation. Our freedom can lead us to live a life of acceptance of the gift or one of denial of it and pretend to construe a life that lasts. This is why the Abraham story is so central to the monotheistic faiths. He forfeited the pretense of being present, *re-presented*, by his lineage, and that was reckoned to him as righteousness. He accepted the consequences of the play, surrendering the gain.

---

19. LW 33:241–45.

20. The affirmation of the *ex nihilo*, both in 2 Macc 7:28, where the expression comes from, and in Paul, is affirmed in the context of resurrection faith.

21. Luther used these three notions—*involucrum* (wrapping), *vestitus* (clothing), and *larva* (mask)—to speak about creation in general. See chapter 8 below.

What has been said so far can easily be misconstrued as flirting with Gnosticism if it were not the case that this earthly existence is God's creation, the mask, the clothing, and the wrapping of God's own doing. Irenaeus' response to the Gnostics lies at the core of creation theology: "The glory of God is a living human being."[22] But the genitive in the expression is double. The human being, fully alive, not only is God's glory but also manifests who God is. And this can only be apprehended indirectly, in the flesh, in the masks, in the transience of life. What was described as the experience (*ex-pati*, out of pure receptivity) of justification, that which is immediate, can only be apprehended in its hidden and masked form, for no one can see the glory of God and live (Exod 33:17–23).[23] That is, no one can be justified except by dying. But life shall be lived to render glory to whom glory is due, not only because we wait for its manifestation, but also because we have been and are being born out of its depth. Meanwhile, whilst life endures in this playground of God's glory we live by the promise, in the double sense of *pro-missio*: that from which we have been ousted and that to which we are being sent.

Playground of Promises

The promises by which we live are housed in the orders of creation instituted by God. To explain this Luther uses medieval categories that operate with the Aristotelian distinction between human production or *poiēsis* and human communicative interaction or *praxis*. *Poiēsis* pertains to the human metabolic relation to nature (including human nature, as in sexuality and reproduction) and belongs to the sphere called the household or economy (*oeconomia*). *Praxis* pertains to intersubjective relations through which social relations are construed and regulated and belonged to the sphere of political and civil government and legal regulations (*politia*).[24]

These two are the playgrounds of God to which we are invited to exercise in freedom the glorifying of the one to whom all glory is due. This is the point about sanctification: amusing ourselves in the playgrounds of God in the firm conviction that all is well, that we are sanctified and redeemed. However, such play (due to what is called original sin originated) turns into a dead-serious game of our own pretense (original sin originating) in which

---

22. *Against Heresies* 4.20.7 (ANF 1:490).

23. Immediately after the quoted passage in *Against Heresies*, Irenaeus discusses precisely this text of Exodus, of which Luther also offered insightful commentaries.

24. The church (*ecclesia*) as an empirical institution is a hybrid reality that borrows from the other two for its formation. See Westhelle, *Church Event*, 9.

the economy of the game and the rules that legislates it become ends in themselves. The work demanded by the game, or its regulations, turns the play into a ploy and the playing becomes a means to achieve it. The play is spoiled when competition and success at the expense of others ensues. When work toils its way to inequality and oppression, when law is used to alienate and discriminate, playfulness ends, and justification is forgotten. Injustice, prejudice, and oppression are not the result of the failure of our efforts to *achieve* justice and live fairly with one another. It happens, instead, precisely because we strive so much in being the best at the game and thus destroy the gift that is freely given, forgetting that which we come from and denying that to which we are destined. This is the reason Luther in shocking candidness calls "good works" mortal sins, the end of playfulness. But we need to examine this further, lest we condemn the world, the playground of God, in a Manichean or Gnostic fashion.

At work in these two spheres of promise where we are invited to playfully re-present ourselves, the *oeconomia* and the *politia*, are different human drives or wills. One is impelled by *desire*, while the other is ruled by *interest*. Guided by these, human beings come to re-present themselves, children are born, the land is cultivated, artifacts are produced, codes for behavior are devised, laws are made, theological books are written, constitutions are drawn, habits and mores are acquired, and so forth. Patterns for living are created and guided by the twin pairings of desire and labor at the home front or the *oeconomia*, on the one hand, and by interest and human interaction in the civil or political arena, in the other. Let us briefly examine these two mechanisms, always aware that they are conspicuously embedded in each other, creating a myriad of hybrid forms of representation. However, their distinction is important for analytical reasons even as they overlap, which makes the recognition of the distinction at times elusive. But losing awareness of the distinction is part and parcel of the reason why we forget that we are not whole in our existence, but pretend to be; we forget that it is in the depth of death that we are whole and justified.

Desire and Interest

In the *oeconomia* one represents oneself; one posits reality that one shapes, reshapes, consumes, and in the process surrenders one's own self to it. However, what one wants is always immediate satisfaction, a fullness of the self, unencumbered by the claim of otherness. And this is the role and lure of *desire*.

Hegel (who incidentally regarded himself as a Lutheran and who would "ever remain as such"²⁵), in his celebrated elucidation of the relation of "Lordship and Bondage" in *Phenomenology*, avidly describes the role of desire and its relationship to labor.

> Desire [*Begierde*] has reserved to itself the pure negating of the object and thereby its unalloyed feeling of self. But that is the reason why this satisfaction is itself only a fleeting one, for it lacks the side of objectivity and permanence. Work [*Arbeit*], on the other hand, is desire held in check, fleetingness staved off; in other words, work forms and shapes the thing.²⁶

This relationship between desire and labor is what Luther's use of *oeconomia* refers to. This is not to be understood in the modern sense of "economy," but in the sense of what is "domestic," the playground of the *dominus*, the lord, but also the primary place where labor was performed and endured. This is one dimension through which we pretend presence, where work and labor are in a tense-ridden relation with desire for immediate enjoyment; this describes a dialectics between sacrifice and satisfaction. Labor is triggered by desire, and sacrifice is endured by the expectation and deferment of enjoyment.

Desire is one way of negotiating justification. Desire consumes, enjoys that which kills. It is the logic of the anthropophagic lure, the yearning to have the other for oneself. And this can encompass a loving relationship dominated by erotic passion or by annihilation. The words of God to Cain insightfully suggest it: "Desire is for you, but you must master it" (Gen 4:7).

In the *politia*, the civil dimension of cultural formation, cultural representation unfolds a different dynamics. In Luther's reading of Genesis the political play is introduced thus: Cain is a wanderer, and in his wandering he becomes the first builder of a city. He was not murdered (as wanderers often were) because the first piece of "written" legislation for life together that the Bible presents us with, the first policy for *politia*, was engraved on Cain's forehead. ("And the LORD put a mark on Cain, so that no one who came upon him would kill him," Gen 4:15.) Reason, which grounds legislation, curbs the crude and instinctive interest of annihilating the other, as long as reason plays. Otherwise, *homo homini lupus* ("man is the wolf of man"), as the old Romans (after Plautus) decried it. The use of reason for the sake of equity (*Billigkeit*) was Luther's criterion for a fair government, as much as generosity for the sake of justice was for the household. However, interest always trumps equity. In the section on "Reason" (which closely follows the

---

25. Hegel, *Werke*, 18:94.
26. Hegel, *Phenomenology of Spirit*, 118; *Phänomenologie des Geistes*, 153f.

"Lordship and Bondage" in Hegel's *Phenomenology*) he addresses interest, saying that reason is lured by interest in much the same way that labor is enticed by desire:

> Reason now has, therefore, a universal *interest* [*Interesse*] in the world, because it is certain of its presence in the world, or that the world present to it is rational. It seeks its "other" [*ihr Anderes*], knowing that therein it possesses nothing else but itself [*nichts anderes als sich selbst*]: it seeks only its own infinitude.[27]

As much as desire triggers labor in human play of re-presentation, interest performs a similar function. Its negotiation with justification, unlike desire, is not an assumption, but a trade. It does not aim at canceling it but deferring it by careful calculation and projections. If desire is to bring the other into the domain of the self, interest is to regulate it.

Desire is to labor what interest is to reasonable intersubjective relations. What was incipient already in the Heidelberg Disputation's parallel use of "work" and "law," as metonymies for the two spheres of representation, became explicitly elaborated in Luther's writings from the 1530s onwards, particularly in the Genesis lectures. Neither one of these two dimensions— "work" represented by the *oeconomia*, and "law" by the *politia*—can bring us to justification. In fact, they are ways by which we dodge the awareness of its immediacy, because they are infested by desire and interest, respectively. Nevertheless both spheres, along with *ecclesia*, were divinely instituted so that labor may hold desire in check, and reason will curb interest's infinite ambitions. However, there is also no frolicking and divinely sanctioned amusement in the playgrounds of God and for God's glory without the endowed human drives of desire and interest.

Desire and interest, though God-given drives, are also conduits through which sin manifests itself. While desire through its pretense of suspending death consumes justification, interest, by negotiating with death, legislates justification into a well-behaved doctrine among an array of others. These are then two basic manifestations of sin. Desire, in striving for satisfaction, leads to the human labor of producing idols, fetishes of human confection through which death is denied and justification forgotten. The sacrifice is made in the urge to possess, dominate, and produce a god of our own making and design. Interest, on the other hand, in its striving for gain turns human relationships into a dispute for recognition. It becomes the way in and through which we shape the others in our image, impose our language and legislate ourselves into immortality. As desire can lead

---

27. Hegel, *Phenomenology of Spirit*, 145–46; *Phänomenologie des Geistes*, 186 (emphasis in the original).

to idolatry, interest steers headlong toward the demonic.[28] Idolatry and demonry are the expressions of our incessant attempt at forgetting and denying the reality of justification and thus are the instruments by which we condemn ourselves.

Justification—End of Doctrine

Justification is not a doctrine among others. It is not even a doctrine. It is not a teaching that we engage in our theological endeavors, either in construing systems to ground the church or devise policies to legislate and administer it. It is the habit of learning, of receiving what has already been given, it is an event grounded in sheer conviction and trust (*fiducia*). But this sheer conviction, its event that is received by us with the unconditional features that correspond to receiving death, takes place in the midst of life itself. The end and the beginning are in the midst of our existence, in the playground we are inducted into. This existence is at the same time the joyful display or expression of this conviction as much as its evasion.

God's creation as it takes place displays and plays with the drives of desire and interest, grounding the conviction of having been made right. What remains is in the left hand of God where desire can be for enjoyment and interest for the welfare of the neighbor. Creation, which is simultaneously from nothing (*ex nihilo*), continuous (*continua*) and consummated (*consummata*), can only be known and enjoyed because it takes place. And what takes place is a reenactment, a re-presentation of what is pure presence, the present, the gift.

"Justification" should be addressed as one would in writing an obituary to oneself saying that it is neither what one wanted or desired, nor what one's interest bargained for. Justification is what only a single word would convey, and yet would already be a word too long to account for justification: *tetelestai*, finished.

---

28. See my article "Idols and Demons: On Discerning the Spirits."

6

Beholding the Core

Reading Chalcedon

The Hybrid

"If we try to speak of God in abstraction and of humanity in abstraction, we distort both God's and humankind's being."[1] This is the core of Lutheran theology out of which all the other distinctions (law and gospel, two régimes, etc.) and the exclusionary *solas* (*solus Christus, sola gratia, sola fide*) ensue and on this christological core alone are they grounded. What is being explored here is this very core: The significance of Luther's reading and interpretation of Chalcedon, beginning with a discussion of a topic not often found in theological pages. I would like to present the significance of the reading of Luther and his interpretation of Chalcedon and the question of the two natures as decisive to theologically address a problem of extreme significance in discussions that range from biology to post-colonial studies. The issue is the question of what a hybrid is and how it helps to understand the core of Luther's theology. What is a hybrid identity? This then is the first problem, which I just enunciated as an oxymoron: hybrid identities.

Hybridity is a transgressive phenomenon. It is precisely the transgression of identities, of *idios*, of that which is *proper* to oneself and does not belong to another. Hybridity crosses the line between purity and pollution. Therefore it is neither the Hegelian identity nor the nonidentity. Is it the *Aufhebung*, sublation, of identity and difference, or is it as Hegel most concisely defined the absolute: the identity of identity and nonidentity?[2] The very word "identity" in this context would have to be placed in quotation

---

1. Widmann, "'Reformation' as Common Faith," 247.
2. This definition appears consistently from his early writings to his last. See Hegel, *Werke*, 2:96; 5:28; 9:277; etc.

marks, for that is really not what it is. It is not a synthesis, as the vulgarized and inaccurate reading of Hegel would have it. Hybrids essentially do not have identities. Their "identities" are "impure"; they have been "corrupted," polluted, and displaced.

Hybrids are impure because they defy the either/or of propositional logic, the great maxim of Western thinking: *sic aut non et tertius non daretur* (yes or no and the third is excluded), as they settle not for a *tertium datur*. They are neither one nor the other, yet both, without yielding to a synthesis. They cannot reproduce themselves, they only spawn further impurity. They are degenerative. Identity is to purity what hybridity is to pus (Pus: white cells and exuded necrotized bio-debris and tissue).

Hybridity has migrated from its original use in genetics to ethno-cultural studies. In fact this is not new. In Latin antiquity it was used not only to describe an offspring of different animal species, but also children begotten by a Roman man and a foreign woman, or by a freeman and a slave. In theology it is only of late that it has become a significant issue of discussion. In fact, since after the great syncretism of the first four centuries of Christian endurance, when the Constantinian era of the church received definite contours, until the twentieth century, Christianity, at least in the West, only solidified its own sameness and avoided anything hybrid and impure like a plague. Examples abound, but let me draw on a modern and familiar one. In *Die Glaubenslehre*, the monumental document that opens the history of modern Protestant theology, Schleiermacher offers the most telling account of Western Christian doctrinal purity. For him, "new heresies no longer arise, now that the church recruits itself out of its own resources; and the influence of alien faiths on the frontier and in the mission-field of the Church must be reckoned at zero." And then the great Berliner adds condescendingly: ". . . there may long remain in the piety of the new converts a great deal which has crept in from their religious affections of former times, and which, if it came to clear consciousness and were expressed as doctrine, would be recognized as heretical."[3]

However times have changed for Christianity since Schleiermacher. North Atlantic Christianity concentrated on the vast majority of Christians from the Constantinian age throughout the beginning of the twentieth century. One hundred years later, by the end of the millennium, the majority of Christians (roughly sixty percent) were to be found in the Third World.[4] This shift is not only demographically significant. Contrary to Schleierm-

---

3. Schleiermacher, *Christian Faith*, 1:128.
4. Lutherans are an exception (about 45 percent in the Third World), but it is changing rapidly.

acher's colonial view of mission, Christianity is not only growing in the South, but, most importantly, growing precisely in areas in which it often is not a hegemonic religion, disputing spiritual territory with other faiths. The "majority" has become "minorities." The onus of this to the self-understanding of Christian theology is still to be seen. Different religious affections are bound to come and are coming into consciousness[5] and it is doubtful that Schleiermacher is going to be consulted to check whether they are heresies. This is significant, but not unique in the history of Christianity, which from its very inception is soiled. In this lies its *dis-tinctiveness*, that which has either lost or has a different coloration (*dis-tinctum*). Therefore instead of the oxymoron, hybrid identities, it should be hybrid *distinctiveness*.

The Reformation and a cascade of other ecclesial schisms are nothing more but caste affairs, an inside group-selection. H. Richard Niebuhr's chastising of denominationalism notwithstanding,[6] it ensued from multiple schisms in the Western church. But this is not really a major theological issue in itself. It is just a symptom of a malady at the very core of Christianity itself. This symptom evades the embarrassing hybrid impurity that lies at the heart of Christianity.[7] To use an expression coined by Jacques Derrida, this evasion is an archival malady (*mal d'archive*): the feverish recruitment of the past to justify the present.[8] It is the search for a genealogy to establish a lineage. I harbor no illusion that my revisiting of Luther and then of Chalcedon is anything but the symptomatic expression of the same malady. Actually, this search for pure origins has an illustrious place in the history of Christianity, which is called the Eusebian Hypothesis. Eusebius, the church historian and theologian at the beginning of the Constantinian age, defended (in a time in which the Roman Empire was trying to unify the church with so many disputing parties) that there was an uninterrupted line of true Catholic faith. We now know it to be a fallacy. One can only find a red-line by imposing it retrospectively. That means the past we take as our heritage is in fact a construal.

This zeal for the archival search in order to justify the present has often afflicted Lutherans. One need not look farther than Matthias Flacius Illyricus who in the name of true and pure Lutheranism, gnesio-Lutheranism, published the *Magdeburg Centuria*, a collection of volumes throughout the centuries of Christian history up to the Reformation, which attempted to

5. See Jenkins, *The New Christendom*.

6. See his *Social Sources of Denominationalism*, 6.

7. This is arguably the case in any religion, but I am concerned here in defining its theological roots in Christianity.

8. Derrida, *Mal d'archive*.

show that Lutheranism was the true and pure expression of the unadulterated and unbroken Christian faith throughout the ages. However, archives do conceal surprises. And this is what I am trying to unravel here in my own fervent pursuit. We might find dead ends rendering an irretrievable genealogy or else discover that the search for a pristine wellspring will find only a polluted puddle, later sanitized by orthodoxy's segregation of the deviant past as heretical.[9]

Origins can be very embarrassing. And the embarrassment comes not only because of debasement and impurity but more so in their failure to justify the present. While Genesis 3 has been inscribed by Augustine as the master narrative for the human condition for Western Christianity, for some scholars of rabbinic theology it is Genesis 6 that accounts for human wickedness due to the intermingling of the sons of God with the daughters of humanity, who bore children to them. Noteworthy is that this narrative is the actual template for the account of Mary's pregnancy in the Gospels of Matthew and Luke. In these accounts Jesus is not the Pauline second Adam, the eternal logos made flesh of John's Gospel, or the anointed Galilean man of Mark. Here Jesus is, what we hear as the second instance in the Jewish-Christian tradition, the offspring of divinities impregnating women. Nietzsche hailed the death of God as "Christianity's stroke of genius."[10] Ernst Käsemann remarked that if there was a historical proof of Christianity, it was that no one would have thought about grounding a religion in the shameful and scandalous crucifixion of its founder.[11] Mary's bearing of God (*theotokos*) set against this background of impurity is as much disturbing, puzzling, and a/mazing.

By way of a preamble I therefore suggest that hybrid transgression of purity is at the very root of Christian "identity" which has been dissimulated in the search for genealogies and pristine origins but was never successfully evaded in the history of Christianity. Hybridity is at the very core of a distinctive Christian doctrine of incarnation. In recent theology attempts have been made to conceptualize it, as did Luther, or the early Fathers in their own contexts. I herewith present a brief review.

---

9. Cf. Bauer, *Rechtgläubigkeit und Ketzerei im ältesten Christentum*. Bauer's thesis has produced significant results in more recent research. See, e.g., Pagels, *Adam, Eve, and the Serpent*.

10. Nietzsche, *Werke*, 2:123.

11. Käsemann, *Jesus Means Freedom*.

Mestizaje, Syncretism, and Hybridity

In 1925 the Mexican philosopher and writer, José Vasconcelos, published one of the most celebrated, criticized, and controversial books produced in the Americas within the past hundred years: *La raza cósmica,* the "Cosmic Race." He introduced a concept that only in the last couple of decades has been reclaimed and owned by theology: *mestizaje,* the mixture of races that was fashioning the cosmic race. In theology the notion has been widened to include also social and cultural intermingling. Some have even conjectured that Jesus himself was a *mestizo,* having as a father a Roman soldier who had raped his mother Mary. There is obviously no concrete indications for this, but the social analysis of the times and place makes it at least plausible. But the problem with *mestizage* theory is that it suggests a blending of difference into a new unity, a new race. This has not been the case. Intermingling of races produces not a synthesis, but even a greater diversity than before.

To avert this problem the notion of syncretism was brought up. It aimed to address the intellectual effort in accounting for this observable fact in which there is intercultural overlapping, while still retaining difference.[12] Syncretism was thus rescued from its infamous association with sacral impurity and pollution, thereby challenging the pejorative connotations implied by "impurity" when used in ethnic, cultural, or religious contexts. Syncretism thus came to represent a qualitative step beyond *mestizaje* by providing christological grounding in the doctrine of the incarnation, particularly in its emergence at the time of "the great Christian syncretism" (of the fourth to fifth century) when the Chalcedonian dogma of the two natures and one person was conceived. Two transcending dissimilar or incongruent entities are not only related to each other, but are united and yet maintain the difference in the union: *vere deus et vere homo.*

If the theory of *mestizaje* lifted up the cultural significance of ethnic miscegenation, syncretism was able to highlight a broader context that gave prominence to the social and religious dimensions of intercultural phenomena. However, categories are always haunted by their etymology that lingers on as a specter or a ghost, long after they are consciously remembered. And this is also the case with syncretism. For example, s*yn-cretism,* as had been accepted, meant to do it *like* or *along with* (*syn-*) the Cretans. But there were differing views about what it really meant. What was it that characterized the Cretans? One explanation resorts to Homer who in the *Odyssey* makes mention of the supposed fact that the many towns on the island of Crete,

---

12. This was first suggested more than a century ago by Hermann Gunkel but made popular by Rudolf Bultmann. See the latter's *Das Urchristentum im Rahmen der antiken Religionen.*

often in strife with each other, would overlook their differences and unite when threatened by a foreign enemy (hence the prefix *syn*). In this sense syncretism means a tactical and temporary move in order to defend a cause in the face of a greater enemy. Far from the embodiment of true difference, syncretism would only mean an occasional truce, but neither a true yoking, nor an organic unity (in Christology this would end up in Nestorianism).

The other interpretation, probably more widespread, moves in the opposite direction. It suggests that the island in the middle of the Mediterranean (which was the conceived center of the earth, as the name of the sea implies: *medius terrae*) was a place where people from everywhere (Africa, Asia, Europe) would meet, creating a culture that blended elements as different as they were known in Mediterranean civilization of the classical era. In this sense, syncretism would be an indiscreet, or careless amalgamation of differences. This is probably the sense that has equated syncretism, in its common acceptation, with the fusion of cultures and religious systems—an anything-goes sort of approach (christologically this would take the form of a sort of monophysitism). The problem with these two etymologies is that one never really unites that which is different, while the other (as it was the case with *mestizaje*) fuses all difference. The challenge is to find a concept that can simultaneously affirm union while not forfeiting difference.

This impasse paved the way for the introduction of *hybridity*. It is an attempt to simultaneously affirm union and assert difference. Building on the foundations of the insights from cultural, anthropological, and theological re-appropriations of *mestizaje* and of syncretism, concerns have been raised and theoretical efforts developed to attend to issues that have not yet been addressed explicitly either by the *mestizaje* or by the syncretistic approach. In addition to the ethnic miscegenation that *mestizaje* tackled and the cultural and religious intermingling that syncretism was able to address, theories of hybridity encompass other dimensions also. The blurring of the line that divides the natural from the artificial is one among them. What follows offers an insightful example of this particular dimension.

Donna Haraway, a historian of science at the University of California at Santa Cruz, trained as a molecular biologist and self-proclaimed theologian, wrote an article in 1985 known as the "Cyborg Manifesto." Cyborgs are organisms that have physiological and mental processes aided or controlled by mechanical and/or electronic devices. What was already common in science fiction, at least since Frankenstein, she turns into a strong philosophical claim, namely, that humans as well as other organisms have been so conditioned and shaped by technology and artificial apparatuses that it is impossible and utterly idealistic to speak of human nature apart from technical, artificial, and cybernetic devices that are part and parcel of our existence and survival. "It is not clear who makes and who is made in the relation between human and machine. . . . Insofar as we know ourselves, . . . we find ourselves to be cyborgs, hybrids, mosaics, chimeras. Biological organisms have become biotic systems. . . . There is no fundamental ontological separation in our formal knowledge of machine and organism, of technical and organic."[13]

Cybernetic devices operate both indirectly and directly. Indirectly and externally they work through cultural and environmental means from which we cannot dissociate ourselves, like the tools we depend on, electrical gadgets, transportation devices, cyberspace communication, and so forth. Internally and directly they operate in a strict biological sense. Our dependence on technologically enhanced drugs, surgeries, implants, prostheses, artificial organs, pacemakers, joint replacements, prophylactics, in vitro fertilization, cloning, etc. are examples. We are cyborgs, claims Haraway; we have crossed the boundary, transgressed and blurred the line that divides a presumed pristine nature from technology, the natural from the artificial. By overcoming this basic anthropological binarism other binary structures crumble, as in gender differentiation, for instance. We are cyborgs and have been so for a long time. It is only now it has reached such proportions that we can name it.

Various theological arguments for this cyborgian form of hybridization have come to the fore in the area of science and religion. One such discourse that reclaims and "updates" contemporary theology is the notion of the *imago Dei* in the tradition that can be traced back to Irenaeus' understanding of the human in the process of growing up to full maturity. The capability to grow up in God's providence is what *imago Dei* ultimately means, even if our maturity, our likeness (*similitudo*) to God, has been originally lost. And this capability of growing up in God's providence is the endowment of God's *imago* to humanity. This would account for the emergence of the Cyborg. Hence the Cyborg is the intended prospective image of God. The *imago* concept is de-essentialized, it is not some*thing* we have inherited (our rational capacity, our bodily appearance, our moral disposition, etc.), but the capability of life self-generating itself in the process of transgressing boundaries between the humans and machine, and also between humans and other creatures. This particular transgressive hybridity is what we will delve into next.

In spite of this positive anthropology, it does not mean that there is a necessary evolution towards an increasing goodness and perfection. As Haraway put it, ". . . a cyborg world might be about lived social and bodily

13. Haraway, *Simians, Cyborgs, and Women*, 177f.

realities in which people are not afraid of their joint kinship with animals and machines."[14] But, she continues, from another "perspective, a cyborg world is about the final imposition of a grid of control on the planet, about the final abstraction embodied in a Star War apocalypse waged in the name of defense . . . in a masculinist orgy of war . . . [the point] is to see from both perspectives at once because each reveals both dominations and possibilities . . ."[15] "Dangerous possibilities" is how she names it elsewhere.

There is indeed always the demonic, or the "many-headed monsters," as Haraway names it. The demonic, in the line of Tillich's interpretation of demonry, is the good turned upon itself (it echoes Luther's *incurvatus in se ipsum*).[16] But it is also the case that technology, in this perspective, is not essentially demonized. The point is to recognize in the cyborgs the magnification of the options between promise and disaster. Such interpretation of the *imago Dei* lends a theological grounding for this mode of hybridization in which the divide between the natural and the artificial is transgressed without romanticizing pristine nature or demonizing technology.

Another dimension of hybridity questions the divide between humans and the rest of the animal kingdom. More and more of their interconnectedness are coming to the forefront, as exemplified by the "genome project." It reveals the small amount of difference in the genetic mapping of humans in comparison to some other creatures, who are not only strikingly similar to us but often hold the key to our survival. If the Cyborg transgresses the line between the natural and the artificial, the "OncoMouse" questions the presumed divide between humans and nonhuman nature, and in a very radical way.[17] OncoMouse is the name given to laboratory mice that undergo transgenic operations and are infected with an activated oncogene that will induce carcinogenesis, turning them into guinea pigs in the attempt to find treatment for different sorts of human cancer. The OncoMouse has become a symbol for the human immersion in the rest of nature to the point that a rodent that we trap and kill in our homes might hold the key for the survival of many humans if not eventually of the species. As a symbol it just heightens the growing awareness, not only of our interdependence with the rest of nature, but our utter immersion in and dependence on it. Nature carries our genes; it is us. Nature not only provides for our maintenance (like in food,

---

14. Ibid., 176.
15. Ibid.
16. See his essay "The Demonic," 77–122.
17. The word "OncoMouse" is in itself already an orthographic hybrid that mixes the Greek prefix *onko-*, which means mass or tumor, and the Old English word *mūs*, which possibly comes from the Latin *mus*, meaning rat or mouse.

water and shelter), but even more, provides for our survival and regeneration insofar as we are *in* it, in the strongest, even genetic sense of it.

The theological implications of what the OncoMouse symbolizes are thus quite evident. Consider what in the fourth century Athanasius attested to by reverting the way we now conceive the chain of being that sets the humans at the top of natural evolution. In his work *On the Incarnation of the Word* he says,

> Now, if they ask, Why, then, did [God] not appear by means of other and noble parts of creation, and use some nobler instruments, as the sun, or moon, or stars, or fire, or air [and we may add: or a mouse], instead of a [human] merely? Let them know that the Lord came not to make a display, but to heal and teach those who were suffering . . . nothing in creation had gone astray with regards to their notions of God, save the [humans] only.[18]

This form of hybridity represents God's presence in a human that goes to such low depths into depravity as to encompass the whole of creation, the cosmos, from the galaxies to mice, and even way down to humans for, as Gregory Nazianzen phrased it, "what is not assumed is not redeemed." Or in the words of the fifth-century Christian poet Cajus Caelius Sedulius of Achaia, *carne carnem liberans* . . . The flesh is liberated through and by the flesh.[19] *Cum grano salis*, mice save humans.

All of these dimensions of hybridity have profound theological implications. But here I would like to lift up a further dimension that not only has implications for theology but is theologically foundational in its very non-foundational hybridity. I am referring to the postcolonial consciousness's criticism of the assumption that a clear dividing line can be drawn between high and low culture, between accepted or hegemonic régimes of truth and those that do not meet the standards of the former, and are thus excluded and marginalized but which have the power of "insurrection" (Foucault), disturbing those régimes. As Homi Bhabha formulated it,

> Hybridity is not a *problem* of genealogy or identity between two *different* cultures which can then be resolved as an issue of cultural relativism. Hybridity is a problematic of colonial representation and individuation that reverses the effects of the colonialist disavowal, so that other "denied" knowledges enter upon the dominant discourse and estrange the basis of its authority.[20]

---

18. Athanasius, *On the Incarnation of the Word*, 97.
19. A hymn quoted and translated by Martin Luther in WA 35, 150.
20. Bhabha, *Location of Culture*, 114.

Here the distinctiveness of hybridity lies in the crossing and displacing of different cultural, semantic, economic ethnic or social spheres. What is crucial for hybridity is the act of transgressing these domains and not the unifying, blending, binary coupling, or assemblage of different entities. Anyone can be a hybrid as it does not depend on any essential endowment, be it racial, cultural, ethnic, social or any other. Hybrids transgress. They are not beholden to any exclusive constituency. However, they don't surrender their own selves in the transgressive roles they play. If they would so do, they would egress existence as such and be only accessible in the tradition of the memory of the victims, of which we have plenty. They can pretend an identity that is not false but is intentionally and deceptively always something else, *dis-tinct*.

There is no example that can be matched to the one offered by Luke in Acts 17. It gives an account of Paul's speech at the Areopagus proclaiming to know the unknown god of their worship to be the one who became a man that was killed, that is, the identity of the unknown is "revealed" only to be in the same act displaced. Karl Barth, in a rare praise of Luther, says that the genius of his understanding of revelation is not only that it is indirect, taking the form of a creature instead of the creator herself, but that it is doubly so in that it expresses itself under utter sinfulness, Christ as the *maximus peccator*.[21]

Reading Chalcedon

This particular dimension of hybridity that transgresses the line that divides the high and the low, wisdom and madness, power and weakness (1 Cor 1), the outer and the inner (Derrida called it "insideoutness") offers the most compelling reason for the hybrid character of Christian "identity."

And it is only proper that I go to the roots of the Christian "identity," the Jewish-Christian narrative tradition, in my exponential endeavor. In *Mimesis*, the monumental commentary on the development of Western literature from Greek antiquity to Virginia Woolf, Erich Auerbach presents the distinctiveness of the biblical literature (either the one written in Hebrew or in Greek) as truly a unique hybrid product:

> [The] mingling of styles [is] inconceivable [in classic Greek literature]. . . . It was rooted from the beginning in the character of Jewish-Christian literature . . . The principle of mixed styles makes its way into the writings of the Fathers from the

---

21. Barth, *Die kirchliche Dogmatik* I/1, 171–80.

Judaeo-Christian tradition. . . . In antique theory, the sublime and elevated style was called *sermo gravis* or *sublimis*; the low style was *sermo remissus* or *humilis*; the two had to be kept strictly separated. In the world of Christianity, on the other hand, the two are merged, especially in Christ's Incarnation and Passion, which realize and combine *sublimitas* and *humilitas* in overwhelming measure.[22]

According to Auerbach, this conflation of *humilitas* and *sublimitas* that first distinguished biblical literature has been described by the early twentieth-century scholar Martin Dibelius as little or low literature (*Kleinliteratur*),[23] which, Christians say, conveys nothing less than divine revelation. That the lowest can be the vessel of the highest is not a strong enough statement of what we are witnessing. A more accurate substantiation would be to say that only the lowest can encompass the highest as the highest encompasses the lowest.

That the highest gives itself to the lowest and is with it inseparable is properly called a gift, for it cannot enter an economy of exchange or return, which is always a negotiation between two values (*do, ut des*). This *divine* economy is the transgression of all rules of *our* economy, even as we try to define divine economy.[24]

The Lutheran reading of Chalcedon finds in Luther himself many anecdotal expressions. But the *locus classicus* for the definition of what came to be known in Lutheran Orthodoxy as the Lutheran fourfold definition of the *communicatio idiomatum*, the communication of identities or attributes, has its basis in the Reformer's *Confession Concerning Christ's Supper* of 1528,[25] extensively quoted (more than ten paragraphs) by the authors of the Formula of Concord.[26] In this previously quoted text (part I, chapter 3) Luther distinguishes "three modes of [Christ] being at any given place" according to his human nature. The first is the corporeal mode of presence, namely the historical Jesus of Nazareth. The second is the "incomprehensible, spiritual mode of presence" which is exemplified by Christ's presence in the Lord's Supper, in, with, and under the bread and the cup. But this mode

---

22. Auerbach, *Mimesis*, 72, 151.

23. Dibelius, *Die Formgeschichte des Evangeliums*, 1–2.

24. See Holm, "Luther's Theology of the Gift," 86: "Consequently, it is possible to concentrate the economic structure of Luther's doctrine of justification in the twofold sentence '*Deus dat ut dem, et do ut des*' (God gives that I may give, and I give that you may give)."

25. WA 26, 335, 29–336, 27; LW 37:222.

26. Formula of Concord, Solid Declaration, VII, 93–103, in Kolb and Wengert, *Book of Concord*, 609–11.

of presence is still located in a recognizable "place," which is the eucharistic community. Then Luther adds a distinct third mode of presence "according to which all created things are indeed much more permeable and present to him than they are according to the second mode." And he continues: "You must place this existence of Christ, which constitutes him as one person with God, far, far beyond things created, as far as God transcends them; and, on the other hand, place it as deep in and as near to all created things as God is in them." This includes even the dead, in whom Christ can also be present according to his human nature.[27]

It is this third mode of presence that allowed for the confection of the peculiarly Lutheran understanding of the *communicatio idiomatum*, the communication of attributes or identities between the divine and the created. The generally accepted interpretation of the *communicatio idiomatum* asserts two genres of discourse that in Lutheranism are called the *genus idiomaticum* and the *genus apotelesmaticum*. The *genus idiomaticum* asserts that what can be said about one nature or the other can be ascribed to the whole person (Christ is the son of Mary—Christ is the son of God). The *genus apotelesmaticum* allows for what is brought into effect by one nature to be brought into effect by the other in the same person (Jesus saves—we are atoned by the son of God).

These two genres of communication refer to the relationship of the *natures to the person*. They are forms of hybridity analogous to the ones I discussed with the examples of the Cyborg and of the OncoMouse. In the case of the Cyborg we have a case of the *genus idiomaticum* in which both machine and natural organism can interchangeably be ascribed to the Cyborg. The Cyborg is truly a machine and is truly an organism. Both propositions are true and yet each is incomplete. As in the example I gave about Jesus being the son of Mary and the son of God, both propositions are valid, but they are also each incomplete. The OncoMouse, on the other hand, illustrates the case of the *genus apotelesmaticum* in which both human and rodent natures cooperate in the same organism either to produce or to cure cancer. Again, as we can say that the blood of Jesus saves us or that the sacrifice of God is our redemption. Both are theologically valid but still they are propositions that pertain to the relationship between the identities of the natures and the persons to which they are ascribed.

The Lutheran reading of Chalcedon, while maintaining the communication between the natures and the person, insisted that the communication is not only about ascribing attributes and operations of either of the natures

---

27. See Anthony, *Cross Narratives*; Nilsson, *Simul: Das Miteinander von Göttlichem und Menschlichen in Luthers Theologie* .

to the person, but to be true communication it also needs to be a communication from the person to the natures, or more precisely, it needs to be a communication between the natures in the person. This communication between the natures was later in the confessional debates called the *genus majestaticum* (according to divine majesty) and the *genus tapeinoticum* (according to human humility). They are, in fact, not two different genres referring to different procedures in *union* of the natures, but only the mutual sides of the same communication between the natures, the double transit from the majestic to the humble and vice versa. By this mode of communication both the divine attributes can be ascribed to created reality (*finitum capax infiniti*) as much as attributes of creation can also be ascribed to the divine reality (*infinitus ferat finem*—the infinite bears the finite). They are thus not different genres but, to be precise, reciprocal sides of the same communication.

The Lutheran insistence that God died according to the human nature is the final expression of the consequences of this third *genus* (actually it is traditionally listed as the "second"). The consequence is that wherever God is present there is also Christ according to the *human* nature. The Lutheran *est* affirms this in Luther's second mode of presence in the bread and cup. But the third mode of presence carries this to its logical and radical end, for the Spirit (that is the energy working the *communio et unio*) blows wherever it wills and the person cannot be divided. This is the reason for the creedal affirmation that the "seated at right hand of God" means everywhere. Or to phrase it more rhetorically, using Luther's words: "Thus it is right and truthfully said that God is born, appeased or breast-fed, lays in a crib, feels cold, walks, stays, falls, wanders, awakes, eats, drinks, suffers, dies, etc."[28] Luther's insistence that one cannot divide the person or confuse the natures is a definite affirmation of hybridity in the very core of his Christology. And this is not only a theoretical point for Luther. This admixture or rhetorical conflation, the transgression of genres of the highest and the lowest that Auerbach found in biblical literature, abound in Luther's own rhetorical style in which the sublime and the burlesque are so often joined.[29] Jesus is God, the hybrid.

In his most detailed study of Chalcedon, *On the Councils and the Church* (1539), Luther argues that the problem with Nestorius is not, as it is commonly assumed, that he divides the person of Christ, but that he does not allow for the *idiomata* of the human nature to be communicated to the divine. Euthyches' problem, in turn, is not that he denies the human nature of Christ, but that he denies the communication of the divine

---

28. WA TR 6, 68, 37–40.
29. See chapter 1 above.

to the human.³⁰ For Luther, the problem surrounding the interpretations of Chalcedon was not the one that pertains to the relationship between the natures and the person, but of the undivided person in whom the natures are perichoretically related.

Here Luther echoes the eighth-century theologian John of Damascus who when faced with the same problems in the post-Chalcedonian disputes developed the notion of *enhypostasis*. *Enhypostasis* sharply distinguishes between nature (*physis*) and subsistence (*hypostasis*) by which the natures can only have a "being" if they subsist in the hypostasis, which makes the divine-human union not a derivation from two self-sustaining essences, a divine and a human, but what the essences receive can be spoken about only because of the union. In the words of the Damascene,

> Through the union it is made clear what either [nature] has obtained from the intimate junction with and permeation through the other. For through the union in subsistence [*enhypostasis*] the flesh is said to be deified and to become God and to be equally God with the Word; and God the Word is said to be made flesh, and to become man, and is called creature . . . for instance, His birth from a virgin, His growth and progress with age, His hunger, thirst, weariness, fear, sleep, piercing with nails, death and all such like natural and innocent passions.³¹

What John of Damascus does is to turn the doctrine of the incarnation into an epistemological principle for theology. Only from the standpoint of the admixture of the natures from the mutual indwelling (*perichoresis*) can we even think about the attributes of the natures. As Luther would say, we could not be more wrong if we start from the purity (aseity) of the divine or of the human nature as such. These can only be *obtained* from them being in the hypostasis.

The "admixture" or "mutual indwelling" through which we obtain the very notion of a nature is the hybrid. Only because of hybridity can we even think about the divine attributes or else what nature, and *human* nature, is. The notion of purity, of aseity, is always a deduced abstraction from the only thing we really know, namely the conflation of the lower and the higher.

---

30. WA 50, 595, 2–7: "Euthyches meinung is auch (wie des Nestorij) uber den jdiomaten jrre, doch auff eine andere weise, Nestorius wil die jdiomata der menscheit nicht geben der Gottheit in Christo, ob es wol fest stehet, das Christus Gott und Mensch sey, Widerumb Euthyches wil die jdiomata der Gottheit nich geben der menscheit, ob er gleich auch festhelt, das Christus warer Gott und Mensch ist."

31. John of Damascus, "Exposition of the Orthodox Faith," 91.

The dispute within Lutheranism as to the interpretation of the *genus majestaticum* along the lines of the cryptic (Tübingen) and the kenotic (Giessen) schools is still the echo of the more "rational" constructions of Nestorius and Eutyches. The former follows the *tertium non daretur* propositional logic. The latter settles for the closure of the *tertium datur*. Historically the dispute found its resolution after the 30 Years' War (1648) in favor of the kenotic school. In consequence, the emphasis on transcendence and difference that the Tübingen school emphasized was downplayed—thus the problem with monophysitism that is often the charge against Lutheran Christology. The kenotic school affirmed identity but could not elude the problem of monophysistic "synthesis"; cryptic constructions succeeded in raising the protest cry of difference, but failed to keep the Nestorian diastasis at bay. Keeping the difference with conflation of opposites without a resolution or a closure is always so challenging because it is a pneumatological problem. The spirit is this paradoxical energy that keeps the transcendent divide between the creator and the creature and yet unites them; it simultaneously multiplies difference and creates communion. It is much easier to settle either for a theology of the Word that stresses the difference, or for a mystical solution that sustains identity. It is in this sense that the *communicatio*, the *co-munus*, the reciprocal sharing of the gift[32] is indeed a two-way process in which transcendence and immanence are mutually affirmed.

Both and Neither

Hybridity is a helpful construction that might serve theology in its elusive search for a language to convey that which, ultimately, cannot be reduced to words. I conclude with the literary genre that most struggles with this quest for language. In his long poem called "The Book of Monastic Life," Rainer Maria Rilke approaches the hybrid irresolution between identity and nonidentity with these words:

> YOUR very first word was: Light:
>
> Thus made was time. Then silent you were
> > long.
>
> Your second word became flesh
> > and distress
>
> (darkly we are submerged in his growling)

---

32. On the different etymologies of communion, see Saarinen, "Communicating the Grace of God in Pluralistic Society," 67–77.

and again your face is pondering.

Yet your third

    I want not.[33]

The Word that creates, the Word that communicates, entails the premonition of a third that does not come, that the poet does not want, but it is here in our midst as precisely the silence he fears and desires (*Ich aber will dein drittes nicht*). The third the poet averts, but has it in the moment he denies it, is the hybrid *tertium datur*, yet in the polluted *sub contraria specie* of the *non daretur*. It is the word that creates and it is simultaneously also the word in flesh, the third that is both and neither.

---

33. Rilke, *Gedichte*, 227: "Dein allererstes Wort war: Licht: / da ward die Zeit. Dann schwiegst du lange. / Dein zweites Wort ward Mensch und bange / (wir dunkeln noch in seinem Klange) / und wieder sinnkt dein Angesicht. / Ich aber will dein drittes nicht."

7

Enduring the Scandal

theologia crucis

Theology of the Cross: An Ironic Epistemic Move

CRUX SOLA EST NOSTRA *theologia*, "the cross alone is our theology" wrote Luther in *Operationes in Psalmos* of 1519–21.[1] This short definition comes in the aftermath of his Heidelberg Disputation of 1518. In the Heidelberg Disputation, Luther, with alacrity and precision, presents the much celebrated distinction between the *theologia gloriae* and *theologia crucis*, or as Luther most often preferred to phrase it, the distinction between the *theologian* of glory (*theologus gloriae*) and the *theologian* of the cross (*theologus crucis*): "A theologian of glory calls evil good and good evil. A theologian of the cross calls the thing what it actually is."[2] Gerhard Forde called attention to Luther's preferred choice of words and points to the subject of doing theology instead of being the object of the discourse: "Luther does not talk about theology in the abstract but rather about the different kinds of theologians and what they do, and the way they operate."[3] This distinction becomes the sharpest expression of Luther's rejection of the dominant canons of rationality that have been accepted as ancillary partners of theology (*ancillae theologiae*) guiding and ordering the theological discourse.[4] Such a rupture with dominant ways of thinking or speculation was kindled by Luther's discovery of the epistemological implications of the scandal of

1. WA 5, 176.32–33.
2. *Theologus gloriae dicit malum bonum et bonum malum, Theologus crucis dicit id quod res est* (thesis 21), WA 1, 354, 21f.; LW 31:40.
3. Forde, *On Being a Theologian of the Cross*, 11.
4. See Bayer, *Theology the Lutheran Way*, 16–32.

having a crucified God. Naming the thing for what it is takes away from theology the pretense of saving God from death and humiliation. This epistemological gesture of Luther, eclipsed during Protestant Orthodoxy, resurfaced with the emergence of pietism and its emphasis on *praxis* and not *theōria*.[5] Later came the devastating effects of the Enlightenment and its criticism of the traditional pillars that supposedly sustained the Christian church rationally.[6] For the theologian of the cross, reason does not sustain that which faith alone maintains, which again raised the question of the relationship between theology and the philosophy of science.[7] A window for reconsideration of the importance of Luther's insights was open, but the opportunity was not seized.

The theses of the Heidelberg Disputation, the *locus classicus* for the *theologia crucis,* conclude with an often overlooked section on philosophy, which would explain what those accepted canons were for the present-day reader. The frequent polemical references to Aristotle (in all but three of the 12 theses) are figurative expressions or metonymies for speculative and rational theological constructs in general. Medieval standards for theology would start with general philosophical assumptions—most often appealing to Aristotle—to establish the premises of natural revelation before special revelation could be presented. However, Luther is sardonic in these philosophical theses. If the present-day reader were to take them up first, it would be clear that the philosophical theses provide the background for his basic argument in the theological theses. And the fact that he places them at the end is an ironic subversion on the part of the Reformer.

The Disputation opens with two seminal concepts that would inform Luther's theology throughout his life: law and work. These categories also function in the later Luther as synecdoches for two of the earthly spheres, or orders of creation, for which humans are responsible and "cooperators with God" (as he eloquently phrased it earlier in the *Bondage of the Will*[8]): *oeconomia* and *politia*. In these orders, philosophy and science—even Aristotle's—have precious contributions to make. Luther would agree that the

---

5. See, e.g., Spener, *Pia Desideria*, 95: "It is by no means enough to have knowledge of the Christian faith, for Christianity consists rather of practice." Luther is quoted more than any other author and always with reverence and affection, even if it certainly misses Luther's worldliness and the recognition of the *vita passiva* for the reception of faith.

6. See the classic essay by Gotthold Ephraim Lessing, "On the Proof of the Spirit and of Power," 53, with his famous thesis: "Accidental truths of history can never become the proof of necessary truths of reason."

7. See Bayer, *Theology the Lutheran Way*, 74–82.

8. WA 18, 754, 14–16; LW 33:243.

hegemonic modes of rationality are not necessarily opposed to theology but definitely are distinct fora (*sunt diversa non contraria*[9]). However, his earlier work of radically distinguishing them was the necessary and opportune move to bring an epistemic change to the way theology was being done. Luther's theological manifesto was indeed "only the cross is our theology" even as it did not exhaust the scope of what he had to say.

It was Martin Heidegger, in *Being and Time*, who brought Luther's novel epistemological approach into the limelight. In the introduction of his opus, he writes,

> *Theology* is seeking a more primordial interpretation of man's Being toward God, prescribed by the meaning of faith itself and remaining within it. It is slowly beginning to understand once more Luther's insight that the "foundation" on which its system of dogma rests has not arisen from an inquiry in which faith is primary, and that conceptually this "foundation" not only is inadequate for the problematic of theology, but conceals and distorts it.[10]

For Luther the concealment and distortion were manifest in the ways in which the cross and the contradictions it entails were veiled and domesticated. The theology of the cross is a *habitus*, a way of accepting contradictions. The very expression the*ology* of the cross is thus an oxymoron, for the cross does not fit into a logical scheme, a "foundation." It implies an ironic epistemic move.[11]

Two Interpretative Tendencies

Luther uses the expression "theology of the cross" (*theologia crucis*) for the first time in his *Lectures on the Epistle to the Hebrews* of 1517–18. The context in which it emerged is precisely the one that stresses the unresolvable paradoxes. In this lecture he writes,

> Frequently in the Scriptures there are two opposite ideas side by side. For example, judgment and righteousness, wrath and grace, death and life, evil and good. This is what is referred to

---

9. WA 39/II, 26, 31; LW 38:259.

10. Heidegger, *Being and Time*, 30.

11. See Solberg, *Compelling Knowledge*, 95–139; Kolb, *Bound Choice*, 3, and also 148, where he discusses a passage in the *Bondage of the Will* regarding the necessary weakness of human knowledge to the understanding of the word of God. WA 18, 659, 28–33; LW 33:99f.

in the phrase . . . "And alien work is done by him so that he might affect his proper work" [Isa 28:21] . . . Here we find the Theology of the Cross, or, as the apostle expresses it: "The word of the cross is a stumbling block to the Jews, and foolishness to the Gentiles" [1 Cor 1:18, 23], because it is utterly hidden from their eyes.[12]

Luther's resolve to keep the irresolution that the cross entails is directed to the two dominant "solutions" he inherited from the models of atonement developed in medieval theology. These are represented by Anselm's "satisfaction" model and by the "moral influence" theory suggested by Abelard. Both options—one emphasizing the objective dimension of the cross event as working out the redemptive work of Christ and the other the subjective affection of a radically loving gesture—worked out the contradiction into a resolution. One tends toward a sacramental emphasis, working *ex opere operato*, while the other emphasizes the cross as an exemplary token. Neither is to be excluded, *exemplum et sacramentum*,[13] the favor and the gift. Luther's retention of the paradox, his decisive avoidance of "closure," keeps the focus on a cross that we simultaneously behold and endure.

Danish theologian Regin Prenter put this very sharply when discussing Luther's theology of the cross in relation to the two dominant schools of theology in Germany, at the time the hegemonic center of Protestant theology. These schools were easily recognized by the names of Rudolf Bultmann and Karl Barth. Prenter's evaluation of these two main theological currents when he originally wrote his essay (1959[14]) is worth looking into. The first was a theology of the cross without the word, while the latter was a theology of the word without the cross. And he concludes his essay with these words, referring to Barth and Bultmann respectively:

> But a cross which is either only objective (outside of us) or only subjective (personal to us) is not the cross of Christ which is the means of our salvation. The deep truth of Luther's theology of the cross is that it views the cross on Golgotha and the cross which is laid upon us as *one* and the same. Is there no wisdom in this old truth for our own teaching and life?[15]

---

12. WA 57/III, 79, 2–80, 11; cited in Prenter, *Luther's Theology of the Cross*, 1f.

13. WA 5, 639, 32–34; WA 2, 501, 34–37; LW 27:238. See also Bayer, *Promissio*, 78–100; Blaumeiser, *Martin Luther's Kreuzestheologie*, 368–82.

14. Prenter, "Zur Theologie des Kreuzes bei Luther," 270–83.

15. Prenter, *Luther's Theology of the Cross*, 18. The italics are in the original but not in the English translation.

For Prenter "the cross we are called to bear is in a mysterious way identical with the cross of Christ."[16] This brings to the fore a pertinent point in Luther's use of the cross-motif. The Reformer normally equated the cross of Christ and (human) suffering and often used cross and (human) suffering interchangeably. However, even as this equation avoids the pitfalls of the objective Anselmian or the subjective Abelardian types it can easily equalize suffering across the board, which Luther himself could be accused of, particularly in the crucial year of 1525 with the tragic events that culminated in the Peasant Revolt.[17] However, the suffering he equates with the cross is not a state of mind but a physical and concrete condition in which not all participate in the same way. In the commentary on the Magnificat (1521), he becomes very explicit:

> You must feel the pinch of poverty in the midst of your hunger and learn by experience what hunger and poverty are, with no provision on hand and no help in yourself or any other man, but in God only; so that the work may be God's alone and impossible to be done by any other. You must not only think and speak of a low estate but actually come to be in a low estate and caught in it.[18]

Prenter is the first to acknowledge that "Luther is not speaking here about spiritual hunger and thirst, but about actual physical hunger and thirst."[19] But then he immediately asks the pertinent question that a sensitive, privileged person would ask: "Can we go along with this at all? And if not, must we then not admit that Luther's theology of the cross is not relevant for us? I will not go so far as to say that Luther's theology of the cross is completely irrelevant to us."[20] And why is it not *completely* irrelevant? Because we still experience "the reality of guilt and death." The Dane at the end of his otherwise enlightening analysis still leans back into a sacramental interpretation of the vicarious suffering of Christ.

Another attempt of avoiding the objective-subjective pitfall in discussing the theology of the cross can be found, for example, in the work of Jon Sobrino, a Jesuit theologian from El Salvador. He is a Spaniard who followed Luther's counsel to feel himself "the pinch of poverty" and went to work in Central America. He confesses his preference for the "Lutheran" option for a theology of the cross that is not caught in metaphysical theodicies, or in

16. Ibid., 13.
17. Ruge-Jones, *Cross in Tensions*, 152–59.
18. WA 7, 593, 30–594, 3; LW 21:347–48.
19. Prenter, *Luther's Theology of the Cross*, 17.
20. Ibid.

atonement theories.[21] As Prenter does he too combines the particularity of the cross of Jesus with the suffering of daily life, but he does not equate them. Rather Sobrino speaks of an "analogous" relation between the cross that Christ endured and the "crucified people . . . the ones who most abundantly and cruelly 'fill up in their flesh what is lacking in Christ's passion.' They are the Suffering Servant and they are the Crucified Christ today."[22] Sobrino's merit is to recognize the particularities of sufferings and their social locations. They cannot be equated but only analogically related. He avoids the sacramentally vicarious interpretation and says that "the only suffering that has meaning is the suffering for the sake of struggling against suffering."[23] And here is where the cross of Christ becomes an exemplary case. And the one who so suffers becomes also a redemptive agent. But how can the victim's struggle become redeeming for herself if it brings her end? Here we have a case in which Christ, and the imitation of him, becomes exemplary in a similar way as Prenter's proclivity leaned toward a sacramental view.

These two options in the interpretation of the theology of the cross have been already detected in a different context by the influential work of Walther von Loewenich, *Luther's Theology of the Cross*.[24] But von Loewenich's theological frame is more related to the doctrine of justification than to atonement theories. The first German edition of this book was published in 1929; in the introduction von Loewenich gives the reason for the stance then taken:

> In current research it is generally regarded as settled that Luther's theology of the cross must be understood as his pre-Reformation theology. . . . Otto Ritschl gave the clearest expression to this view. . . . Ritschl claims that the theology of the cross bears a typically monkish stamp and thereby proves to be only a preliminary stage of the real Luther.[25]

Von Loewenich's interpretation of the theology of the cross severs any relation between the theology of the cross and mysticism, and locates it as the core of Luther's Reformation theology; it was not a relic of ingrained monkish life. But with this he also reveals that his programmatic move was predicated on a particular contextual cleavage in post–World War I Germany and the strong emergence of the "neo-orthodox" movement that rejected all but the supremacy of the *verbum externum*, the word that does not

21. Sobrino, *Jesus the Liberator*, 235.
22. Ibid., 271.
23. Ibid., 241. He attributes this approach to Dorothee Sölle. See her *Suffering*.
24. Loewenich, *Luther's Theology of the Cross*.
25. Ibid., 12.

indwell in creation, it is *extra nos*. In his "Addendum" to the fourth edition some three decades later, he offers a careful yet candid acknowledgment:

> I continue to maintain that Luther's theology of the cross and the German mysticism of the Middle Ages are basic conceptions that diverge. But I have made this difference too pointed in a systematic way, and turned it into an absolute antithesis for the sake of the conclusion. With that I paid my tribute to the dominant theological view of the time.[26]

This discussion and the ensuing tendencies are indeed very contextually bound. Consequently present Luther research is plowing its way to some implication of how to read the theology of the cross in the context of the debate over Luther's understanding of justification. The debate ranges from a *forensic* understanding of it that emphasizes the priority of the external word, received in faith, as an act of imputation of a benefit (*favor*) in declaring the sinner righteous, and the *indwelling* of Christ through faith (*theosis*) in which Christ is received as gift (*donum*).[27]

The emergence of the cross-motif in Luther's early theology and his interpretation of the righteousness of God, the Reformation's breakthrough, go hand in hand. The distinction between *theologia gloriae* and *theologia crucis* is connected with the "new definition of justice",[28] as the Reformer enticingly phrased it. And it is so because it distinguishes *active* speculation from the purely "pathic experience," a simple and utterly *receptive* disposition (*vita passiva*) that alone makes a theologian.[29] In this context, the attempt to frame Luther's theology in general, and his theology of the cross in particular, regardless of its merits, might be misguided if the paradigms offered and employed are the ones that have dominated the Western academic world since the nineteenth century, or as von Loewenich aptly phrased it in his "confession," in "the dominant theological view of the time."

A New Definition of Justice

The doctrine of justification and the theology of the cross are distinct but symmetrically complementary perspectives through which Luther unfolds

---

26. Ibid., 221f.

27. For a summary of the indwelling of Christ in Luther's theology with critical responses, see Braaten and Jenson, *Union with Christ*; for the specific relationship of *theosis* to Luther's theology of the cross, see Peura, *Mehr als ein Mensch?*, 175–294.

28. LW 17:230; WA 31/II, 439, 19f.

29. LW 54:7; WA TR I, 16, 13 (Nr. 46): *Sola experentia facit theologum.*

all the further aspects of his theological work, as the two focal points of an ellipsis. Already for the early Luther, *iustitia dei* required a rupture with human rationality defined by the *economic* principle of fair exchange, "I give so that you give back" (*do ut des*) and the *juridical* retributive principle of giving to each his due (*suum cuique*).³⁰ These principles found their way into Anselm's celebrated question, *Cur Deus homo?* (Wherefore God became human?). Not long after Anselm's argument became public, Abelard responded carrying the premises of Anselm to its logical absurdity. If God's son had to die to pay for human sin, who is to pay for killing the son of God? Abelard abandoned the question of justice altogether and gave prominence to God's love that does not need to comply with juridical principles. But for Luther the question of justice could not be evaded. What tormented him was the classical and hegemonic definition of it as controlled by human reason. And that was his theological struggle in the years that led to the inception of the theology of the cross as it was explicitly named between 1517 and 1518.³¹

A decade later, Luther carefully elaborates the meaning and magnitude of this discovery. In his 1528 lectures on Isaiah, he provides this definition: "Behold the new definition of justice [*definitionem novam iusticiae*]: justice is the knowledge of Christ [*iusticia est cognitio Christi*]." The expression *cognitio Christi* must be understood as a double genitive: We need to know about Christ, but equally have the mind of Christ in us. In other words, this knowledge is not only historical but also existential, Christ in our stead and we in the stead of Christ in his relationship to the Father.

Luther uses Isaiah 53, the song of the Suffering Servant, as the springboard for his explication and employs the expression "wonderful exchange" (*mirabilem mutationem*). Such exchange is marvelous in that it nullifies human reason's definition of justice at its best: *suum cuique*. And he goes on to explicitly state, "The sophists say that righteousness is the fixed will to render to each his own."³²

The Hiddenness of God

Jesus on the cross was not the Anselmian settling of accounts. He was God as a gift in a sacrificial act of revelation that at the same time discloses the

---

30. WA 31/II, 439, 5ff.; LW 17:229.

31. For a careful debate about this development and the emergence of a new awareness of what *iustitia dei* means, see McGrath, *Luther's Theology of the Cross*, particularly 95–147.

32. LW 17:229; WA 31/II, 439, 5–6: *Iusticia est constans voluntas renddenti cuique, quod suum est*.

human condition and God's hidden identification with it. Both entail an ironic severance with the predominant mode of rationality based on analogical reasoning, in ordered discourses, and systems of speculative accomplishments. In the early Luther these ordered discourses fall into two broad categories, law and work, which are metonymies for the two estates (*Stände*), *politia* and *oeconomia*, that he develops positively as orders of creation alongside *ecclesia*.[33] They are good and necessary but not of the essence for the theological endeavor *stricto sensu*. They are God's masks (*larvae*). God is only revealed there where the word became flesh and took the decisive consequences of embodiment: death, and death on a cross as an executed criminal. In this *revelatio sub contrariis*, "under its opposite," God is ultimately revealed as the Word incarnate, taking the ultimate consequences of creation, sin, decay, and death. For that very reason it defies the *logos* of this world and its régimes of acceptable truth.[34] But it begs the question of how this could be revelation. This led Luther to make a sharp distinction between God in God-self, God's aseity, and the God revealed in the Word, the "preached God." [35]

What needs to be kept in mind is that when Luther speaks of the hiddenness of God two senses are implied. One says that God is hidden *sub contraria specie* as in the cross, in suffering, and death. Yet another sense implied is of a God hidden even behind the Word. Von Loewenich and Paul Althaus early in the twentieth century already detected this double sense, which is elucidated in "To the Unknown God," an essay by Brian Gerrish.[36] God is both hidden *in* and *behind* the cross.[37] The crucial passage in Luther comes from *The Bondage of the Will* where he has a lengthy discussion on the "distinction between the Word of God and God himself" who "is not to be inquired into, but reverently adored, as by far the most awe-inspiring secret of Divine Majesty, reserved for himself alone and forbidden to us."[38] To use the expression of Rudolf Otto, the divine is at the same time *fascinans*

33. The unique status of *ecclesia* will be addressed later in this chapter.

34. Dietrich Bonhoeffer, in his early lectures on Christology, captured Luther's point: "Christ is the Counter-Logos. Classification is no longer a possibility, because the existence of this logos spells the end of the human logos" (*Christ the Center*, 30).

35. Cf. WA 18, 685, 10f.; LW 33:139f.: "God must be left to himself in his own majesty. . . . It is no business of ours. . . . [We must make] the distinction between God preached and God hidden, that is, between the word of God and God himself."

36. Gerrish, "To the Unknown God," 263–92; Loewenich, *Luther's Theology of the Cross*, 221, which appears in the "Addendum" to the fourth edition (1954) correcting his earlier underestimation of the significance of mysticism for Luther (217–23).

37. A criticism of this "ambivalence" can be found in McGrath, *Luther's Theology of the Cross*, 164f.

38. WA 18, 285, 25–31; LW 33:139f.

and *tremendum*; it makes us wonder in devotion and tremble at what may come. David Tracy offers a pertinent comment:

> All Christian theology today needs to read Luther again for rethinking both Hiddenness I and II in God: Hiddenness I for facing the central christological insight that God is understood in Christ *sub contrariis* in and through Christ's cross and, in the light of that cross, in and through the suffering caused by all violence throughout history; and Hiddenness II to allow one to admit the fearsomeness of God that Luther, in his volcanic religious experiences as well as in his commentaries on Genesis and Isaiah, makes available to all serious readers of the complexity and ambiguity of the full biblical portrait of God. It is Luther (here quite different from even Augustine and Pascal) who will not hesitate to reflect on what the ancient Greek tragedians named "fate."[39]

Again in his argument against Erasmus in *The Bondage of the Will*, Luther, in defending the clarity of the Scriptures (*claritatis scripturae*), says that whatever is not revealed in them and pointing to Christ belongs to a mystery that we cannot explain or dare to speculate about; the Scriptures are enough (*sola scriptura*); not that by them we will be appeased and satisfied, but because with them we will be nourished to continue to wonder the mystery.[40] He refuses to venture into the territory that explores God's intent or election and predestination. This territory remains uncharted. "Let God be God" is a daunting affirmation of this.[41] But it is better to admit that there is an inscrutable shadow-side to God than the other options available. It would be simply a descriptive statement of our finite experience, and of the very finitude of our reason. If it is blasphemy, it is the one of Job; this is the one God is great enough to take. In Luther's words, it is "to flee from and find refuge in God against God."[42]

Theology is properly done *in usu passionis*, at the foot of the cross. It demands a suspension of all human endeavors and, particularly, those that pertain to theological and systematic constructions. Therefore, Luther never adopted or developed the models of atonement competing at his time, but pointed to the cross rather as an epistemological cipher that destabilizes all theological discourse and theoretical, or speculative achievements so that

---

39. Tracy, "Hidden God," 11.
40. WA 18, 631, 37–632,2; LW 33:60.
41. WA 10/I, 24, 4–11; LW 7:117. See Kolb, *Bound Choice*, 32–34.
42. WA 5, 204, 26f.: *ad deum contra deum confungere*.

the word of God can be heard.[43] Luther widely used the expression, "theologian of the cross," and less frequently referred to "theology of the cross." This is a pointer to his resistance to reify the theological discourse, but have it as *usus*, an experience, an attitude (*animus*), or a disposition (*habitus*) toward the reception of God's free grace. When the expression *theologia crucis* is used it should be primarily understood as a *genitivus subiectivus*; it is from the standpoint of the cross that theology itself is possible.

The theology of the cross is the doctrine of justification and vice versa. As justification accomplishes its work by killing all that pertains to human efforts and accomplishments (*vita activa*),[44] the cross represents the reality of Jesus' passion in surrendering to God, and is also the symbol[45] for all human suffering insofar as it is an experience of the human participation in the same pathos where God, as *deus absconditus*, ubiquitously meets us. Cross and suffering as pathos becomes the key to divine revelation under its opposite (*sub contraria specie*). In consequence, revelation under its opposite entails the double meaning referred to earlier: it denotes the cross of Christ as God's solidarity with humanity and is conveyed by the word of God (revelation hidden in the cross), but it also denotes the human suffering that the word does not decode or explain (revelation hidden behind the cross). God's hidden revelation appears not only in the word of the cross but also beyond and behind it. In biblical terms the difference between the two encompasses the spectrum of the passion narrative of Mark's Gospel and the book of Job.

Developing Further Theological Consequences

Although Luther's most celebrated works on *theologia crucis* are dated from the early reformation through 1525 the basic theme receives renewed treatment in various later works, both in continuity with the early work, but also in applying it to other theological loci. If explicit references to the theology

---

43. Aulén, *Christus Victor*, 101–22, argues that although atonement was not a central topic for the early Reformation, Luther, contrary to many of his followers and interpreters, aligned himself at least implicitly with the "classical type" used during the Patristic period, departing decisively from the Anselmian ("Latin") type.

44. WA 5, 165, 33–37. See Bayer, *Theology the Lutheran Way*, 106–14; see also chapter 5 above.

45. Symbol is here used in its strong Tillichian sense as that which points to a reality in which it *participates*. See Tillich, *Systematic Theology*, 1:177: "The concept of participation has many functions. A symbol participates in the reality it symbolizes; the knower participates in the known; . . . the Christian participates in the New Being as it is manifest in Jesus the Christ."

of the cross dwindle, what the Reformer does is to elaborate some of the theological consequences and hermeneutical implications of the insights evoked by the theology of the cross.

As we have seen earlier, in the *Confession Concerning Christ's Supper* of 1528,[46] Luther presents three modes of Christ's presence. He stresses the third mode of Christ as one person with God, beyond and far and at the same time deep in and as near as God is in them. And this presence needs to be material, enfleshed in the finitude of matter to its most radical consequences and depth, even in death itself, "otherwise our faith is false."[47] Dying is the ultimate form of pathos, of radical receptivity that excludes any juridical (law) or economic (work) negotiation. This explains why, for Luther, the theology of the cross essentially links the passion of Christ with human suffering as we saw above.[48] All suffering is an experience of *passio*, of receptivity that makes any human effort to administer it a failure. The cross of Jesus and suffering are essentially identical because the cross of the historical Jesus is identified with the human situation as the condition for the reception of grace and the annulment of law and work. In the cross death and gift coincide. And implicit in this "third mode" is something that still needs further development.[49] What is the implication of this to all things created, including the whole planetary environment, if God is in Christ there in the depth of all suffering, immersed in what Luther once called "the majesty of matter"?

If in the *Confession* of 1528 Luther takes the insight of the theology of the cross and applies it to Christology and in particular to his interpretation of Chalcedon,[50] in the preface to the publication of his German texts from 1539 he takes the methodological consequences of doing theology at the foot of the cross. There he describes what makes a preacher and a theologian. During the middle ages theologizing was largely accepted as comprising three steps: *lectio, oratio,* and *contemplatio*. Luther changes the order of the first two. He starts with *oratio*, and then moves to *meditatio* (which includes *lectio*). But what is more significant and relevant for our topic, is that he totally changes the last step from *contemplatio* to *tentatio*. His choice of inserting these terms in Latin in the midst of a German text underscores his intention of making clear where the difference lay between his way of doing

---

46. WA 26, 261–498; LW 37:161–372. Also quoted at length in Formula of Concord, Solid Declaration, VII, 94–103, which corresponds to WA 26, 335, 29–336, 37; LW 37:223. See Kolb and Wengert, *Book of Concord*, 609–11.

47. WA 26, 336, 19; LW 37:223. See Anthony, *Cross Narratives*.

48. See Prenter, *Luther's Theology of the Cross*, 4.

49. But see Gregersen, "Deep Incarnation: The Logos Became Flesh."

50. For more on this, see my chapter "Hybridity and Luther's Reading of Chalcedon."

theology and the dominant one in the Middle Ages. The radical difference finds itself in the explanation where he presents his choice for a German translation: "Third, there is *tentatio, Anfechtung*. This is the touchstone that teaches you not only to know and understand, but also to experience how right, how true, how sweet, how lovely, how mighty, how comforting God's Word is, wisdom beyond all wisdom."[51] *Anfechtung* means being in trial, probation, and tribulation, spiritual or otherwise. This is the "touchstone" because you cannot do theology without *experiencing* cross and suffering and persecution. Prayer and meditation ought to lead to *Anfechtung* only so we may know that the Devil and his minions are indeed being confronted.

In the later Luther cross and suffering made its appearance very explicitly in his discussion of the church in *On the Councils and the Church* (1539).[52] In this text he expanded his earlier minimalist definition of the church comprising alone the gathering around word and sacrament.[53] In this latter text there are seven marks or holy possessions. The first four are encompassed in Word and Sacrament (Word, Baptism, Eucharist, Confession and Forgiveness, which is the daily return to Baptism). Then he adds two, Ministry and Public Worship, which are indirectly implied in the church being a community gathered around Word and Sacrament. A seventh mark is yet added: cross and suffering, which is his application of the consequences of the theology of the cross to ecclesiology. This is significant insofar as not only the individual Christian, but the social collectivity of the community is in itself, as community, suffering affliction and persecution (*tentatio, Anfechtung*), which therefore also makes the church a space for a revelatory event. Hence regardless of whether it is the individual, the theologian in her vocation, the church, or the world, the cross remains as the theological criterion *sine qua non: crux probat omnia*.[54]

---

51. WA 50, 659, 3-660, 16; LW 34:287. A good commentary on these "three rules" can be found in Bayer, *Theology the Lutheran Way*, 42-65.

52. WA 50, 628, 35-643, 52; LW 34:148-66.

53. Luther had defined these as necessary and sufficient marks of the church as early as 1519. WA 2, 754, 9-16; LW 35:67. This is the definition celebrated in article VII of the Augsburg Confession, which Melanchthon presented in 1530. Calvin (*Institutes* IV, I.9) and other reformers also follow the same definition.

54. WA 5:179. 31.

8

Cross and Creation

WHEN IN 1967 LYNN White Jr., in his article "The Historical Roots of Our Ecological Crisis," charged the Judeo-Christian tradition with the attitude developed in the West toward nature, he set fire to a theological circus overly concerned with keeping the christological performance on the central stage. Even if he did not point directly to Christocentrism as the fertilizer feeding the roots of the ecological crisis (as others following his steps would), the message was well understood: theology, too focused on the *homo perditus et Deus salvator*, has, in its relationship to God, lost a more incisive view of nature (human included).

A theocentric perspective in theology followed the criticism of the so-called unitarianism of the second article (H. Richard Niebuhr). Consequently, theologies of creation began to exercise the muscles of the atrophied classical dogmatic locus. Proposals went from renewals of Thomist infrastructural approaches to *quasi* pantheistic views of nature and creation as an "original blessing" (Matthew Fox) or as mother earth incestuously raped by her own children.

The prominence of the theology of the Word in Protestant theology caused the resurgence of a theology of creation with some peculiar characteristics. As opposed to the Roman Catholic tendency to regard nature as a somehow positive epistemological *datum* for the construction of the knowledge of the relationship between Creator and creature, Protestants tended to favor a negative epistemological view. Even if there was some resistance to a radical rejection of natural revelation (the case of Emil Brunner vs. Karl Barth), the significance of creation was focused on salvation history: creation as the first act of salvation.

Until very recently the suspicion that a theology of creation seeped away the energies of theologians who were failing to take seriously enough the political challenges in the history of suffering prevailed in the political and liberation theologies. A "green" theology would not blend with a "red" theology, until the peoples of the Amazon rain forest and other indigenous peoples of the world vindicated the urgency of having what could be called a "brown" theology, a theology maroon, a *distinct* blending of red and green *tinctures.*

Despite the strong emphasis of the Reformer on the theology of creation, there has been a clear embarrassment in the Lutheran tradition in dealing with this issue. With the exception of some major works in the last three or four decades (e.g., Heinrich Bornkamm, Philip Watson, Regin Prenter, Joseph Sittler, David Löfgren) Luther's emphasis on creation has been much filtered through the *Ordnungstheologie,* whose heritage is a static view of nature allied to some political and ideological uneasiness. Lutheran theology attempted to regain credibility and relevance with the works built on the theology of the cross. Luther's concern with creation was largely dismissed as a well intended, even insightful inventory of theological motifs, but not systematized enough to serve as a foundational theological argument.

The difficulty of linking Luther's theology of the cross (with its assertion that "God is not to be encountered but in suffering and in the cross"[1]) with the theology of creation (with Luther's affirmation of the double knowledge of God[2]) is a point of conflict and dispute. The distinction between special and general revelation as a way of interpreting Luther's *duplex est cognitio Dei* has been regarded with suspicion by those who consider the cross as the radical Christian *specificum,* constituting both the identity of God and God's relevance for the definition of God's immanence and divine economy.

On the other hand, questions have been raised by those who see the restriction of God's revelation to a Christian *specificum* as a hindrance to the growing awareness of ethnic, cultural, and anthropological relativism, or to the ecological sensitivities eager to read the divine hieroglyphics in the book of nature. Are these two incompatible ways of organizing a Lutheran theology?

The Audible and the Visible

The basic difficulty here concerns the conceptual distinction and articulation between the visible and the Word, between creature and Creator, the outer and the inner, between what the senses register and reason draws together, and what grace reveals to the heart. These sets of categories instead of the common approach situate the issue in the relation between the First and the

---

1. *At Deum non inveniri nisi in passionibus et cruce.* WA 1, 362, 28f.
2. *Duplex est cognitio Dei.* WA 40/I, 607, 28.

Second Article of the Creed because, before it becomes a dogmatic problem as such, it is an epistemological one. It refers to the mode of cognition of, and the constraints for, the knowledge of God. Therefore, the correct *locus* for this discussion is revelation and not primarily creation or redemption.

In Luther there is a paradoxical and asymmetrical relation between the two sets of categories within which Luther operates to formulate his understanding of the *duplex cognitio Dei*. It is paradoxical in that one (the visible) points to the other (the Word) but is in it simultaneously negated or contradicted. It implies the rejection of analogical reasoning with apparent analogical correspondence, i.e., its mode of argumentation is ironic. It is asymmetrical in that what appears to be the case in one set of categories is not simply reflected in the other, but is shaped in the other in unexpected ways.

A look into Luther's well-known imagery, particularly in his commentaries on the Psalms, provides a good explication. In it we find affirmations that nature is full of parables, metaphors, and signs. He will deny nevertheless that through them the Creator can be known. In fact even what is seen is debased if not seen through faith. Only faith can see creation.[3] That means that the view we have of nature is simultaneously our blindness to creation. Between one and the other there is no analogical leap. The "mechanism" through which we link creation and Creator cannot be grasped externally.

The famous metaphor of nature as a mask (*larva*) or wrapping (*involucrum*) of God points to the same ironic mode of reasoning. This can be understood better if we go to the origin of the mask metaphor. It is worth remembering that Luther adopted the motif of the mask from the medieval carnival. Here the mask served as a means of caricaturing reality, revealing it but, at the same time, concealing it in its reverse. The mask presented popular projections of social and political life with burlesque resources within the space of the festival. Nevertheless, restricted to that space, it also concealed the true social relations in everyday life: it provided a glimpse of the "unseen" and intentionally distorted it. Nature is the carnival of creation.

The same goes for the wrapping motif: it reveals a presence while denying to sight any evidence of its content or even of its existence. The wrapping is all to sight, but it also blinds one to the essential. The one who receives a wrapped present is convinced, if at all, of the existence of an unseen content by trust alone in the giver.

The visible things (*visibilia*) do not allow for any direct or indirect access to revelation, but they are what simultaneously makes it directly and indirectly present. In the visible God's presence is a "mediated immediacy"

---

3. WA 38, 53, 24f.

(John Bailie). Still, this very affirmation attests only to God's utter absence. To rely on natural reason for evidence or indications of God's presence will reveal only the idol of the heart (*idolum cordis*),[4] The visible becomes an idol if it is seen as a directly reflected image of the unseen so that the gaze of the beholder is captivated by it. Yet, at the same time, it can become a "picture" of the unseen when the gaze does not stop at, nor is frozen in, what is presented to sight, even if it cannot go beyond it to have a direct vision of the unseen. An oxymoron, like "mirroring transparency," is required here to convey the intended meaning. What is reflected is not the visible presence as such, like in the reflection of a mirror, but it is an absence manifested in the reflection.

Nevertheless, this does not mean that the visible is indifferent or neutral with regard to the knowledge of God. The *Deus vestitus*—the potential idol—is simultaneously that which protects us from the *Deus nudus*—the irresistible abyss of being.[5] The clothed God is the representation of that which cannot be represented. By affirming its very absence it simultaneously offers the experience of a presence. The clothed God is the God of religious experiences by which humans open themselves up to whatever transcends real existence, while at the same time closing themselves off to the radical experience of otherness.

Such is the importance of the "majesty of matter" (*maiestate materiae*):[6] it prevents our knowledge to convince us of the need for God's self-revelation through the Word. In this sense the double knowledge of God is affirmed, even though in paradoxical and asymmetric terms. What Luther said about the efficacy of the liturgical elements is exactly what could be said about the visible in general: not because of them but never without them.[7] God, as Luther would state it in the Heidelberg Theses,[8] is neither to be seen nor sought behind creation, nor to be inferred from it, but only to be recognized in and through it. However, this "in and through" would again be misleading were we not to understand that that which creation "reveals" is the concealment, the absence of God or, our blindness to the divine reality.

Behind the notion of the *Deus absconditus* lies the conviction that the visible in general presents us a clothed God who, as such, remains a mystery. The *Deus absconditus is* not to be taken as an axiological statement

---

4. WA 14, 587, 30.

5. WA 31/I, 250, 24f.: *"der Teuffel wird und ist kein Teuffel, er sey denn zuvor Gott gewest."*

6. WA 39/II, 4, 32f.

7. See Luther's preface to the German Mass. WA 19, 72–78; LW 53:61–67.

8. Theses 19 and 20, in LW 32:40; WA 1, 354, 17ff.

alone that accounts for the presence and the role of evil by manifesting God's strange work (*opus alienum*). For Luther this is also an ontological statement. God is not only hidden in wrath, but in fact hidden in the external things in general! The reason that the concealment of God is realized in God's wrath through the *opus alienum* is because it is through evil, in particular, that one comes to realize the failure to know God through the visible. This means that God is hidden in the beauty and goodness of nature, and also in ugliness and evil. The point is that it is tempting to find evidence of the divine in goodness and beauty whilst simultaneously rejecting evil as a pedagogue. This amounts to idolatry. Not because beauty and goodness are false instructors, but because they become false projections of the heart when separated from evil and ugliness. The goodness I see outwards conceals the evil that lies *absconditus,* inwards. And the reverse is also true: the evil I see outwards reveals the goodness that lies inwards.

For Luther evil is not beyond God's infinity. Hence, there is only an epistemological primacy of the *opus alienum* in the knowledge of God. God should not be praised for the greatness of creation in spite of evil; God should be praised in the midst of evil where God's continuous creation works out of the annihilating force of evil. Because of this force—the nihility of evil—God's creativity is manifest in and through it. It is this creativity, then, and not evil itself, that makes the knowledge of God possible. This is the fundamental thesis for supporting theologically the *creatio ex nihilo* within the negative Augustinian view of evil as the sole absence of goodness (*privatio boni*).

A call for responsibility grows out of the awareness of our sinful condition. For Luther, nature did not fall but suffered the curse of evil because of human failure. "Not only in the churches, therefore, do we hear ourselves charged with sin. All the fields, yes, almost the entire creation is full of such sermons, reminding us of our sin."[9] Therefore, the point in Luther's use of the mask motif is not so much to stress that God is hidden, as to underscore that we are hiding ourselves by not recognizing this mask for what it is, either by trying to get a glimpse of the face behind it or simply by ignoring it.

The hidden God raises a mask in which humans recognize themselves as in a deceptive mirror, for it reveals the other side of the goodness creation has been endowed with. Humans are called to recognize themselves in it, in its beauty, and from its sinister side. The *Deus absconditus* is then also the *Deus revelatus* because God's concealment, once recognized as such, prompts the emergence of the *homo revelatus*. Therefore, the Reformation's outcry for letting God be God corresponds to the motto "let nature (human

---

9. WA 42, 156, 24ff.

included) be nature." Auschwitz, Hiroshima, or the hole in the ozone layer are the masks of God raised for our self-recognition, in which we measure ourselves as much as in the lilies in the fields. The nature we see is the mirror image of what we have made it, or have allowed it, to become. Nevertheless, in the experience of evil we do not have the mask as such, but a fissured mask in whose clefts we have the terrible sight of the abyss of being. This is why evil, as a cracked mask, becomes a pedagogue: by its cracks we know that we are not looking at a face, and through them we know that there is no pretty face behind it.

Cross and Suffering

If the visible is the projected side of our own inner beauty and hideousness, the Word is always the word of the other. If I can possess what I see (because I can reduce it conceptually to my own sameness), the Word comes always from beyond the limits of my possible domain. Without the Word, reality loses all focus and *telos,* for the visible does not allow for transcendence. It is by definition the immanent. What it reveals is not the other but, rather, only what we have made ourselves to be. The Word is the creative force in God's continuous work of creation; this is a transcendent force capable of bringing reality out of nonexisting things (*creatio ex nihilo*).[10] If reality becomes aimless without the Word, it is the presence of the Word that attributes finality to reality, because, in the presence of the Word, reality itself is being constituted, restored, and created.

It is the epiphanic presence of the Word, as transcendence in immanence, that attributes to reality a sacramental character. It is in this sense that we can affirm God's ubiquity in creation itself. This affirmation is not deduced from a capability of "seeing" beyond the visible, but, precisely, because the visible becomes transparent. In being transparent it does not, strictly speaking, have a beyond! The visible does not, by its sacramental character, gain a magic force. The transparency of nature is in fact its own mirroring effect through which we are sent back to the depths of our own existence, which in Luther's "eccentric" anthropology is outside us. Nature loses, therefore, its own pretensions of otherness. And this is the same as saying that we lose our illusion of being strange to nature in recognizing ourselves as strange to God. This lies at the core of the *finitum capax infiniti,*

---

10. It is important to remember that the origin of this concept, in 2 Macc 7, is the experience of evil; it is a response to the theodicy question and not a cosmogonic argument.

for the infinite is never attainable, but always present in the mirroring transparency of the visible.

Luther, once again, defines this sacramental or mysterious character of God's ubiquitous presence through Christ in the context of his discussion of the three modes of Christ's presence[11] of which the third mode presents him "as near in all creatures as God is immanent in them." Precisely this argument of Luther's is quoted in the Formula of Concord to support the position that affirms at once the real presence of Christ in the Eucharist, and the distinction between a sacrament *stricto sensu* and the affirmation that all of creation entails God's masked presence.[12] What distinguishes the sacramental or mysterious character of God's presence in creation from the proper sacraments for the authors of the Formula of Concord is not the combination of element and Word, but its use (*usus*) in the ritual tradition instituted by Christ.[13] Nature entails the continuous interrelatedness of Word and creature.

The word can only be the way in which otherness comes to me if I have accepted to take the visible for what it is. The theologian, said Luther in reference to the theology of the cross, "calls the thing what it actually is."[14] To ignore the visible or to flee from it in the search for the pure Word is to take the cross out of this world (something like the satirical paintings of the crucified Jesus in the paintings of Salvador Dalí). This is but another version of the theology of glory with the difference that the one Luther criticized took the visible as a mediation to the invisible, while here there is a direct or immediate leap into the invisible, not realizing that the invisible—encompassed in the visible—is the very transparency of the visible.

Suffering (the unbearable sight of the visible), makes this visible transparent when the suffering seen is the suffering of which the human, *qua* human, knows itself to be an active agent. In Luther there is no ontological distinction between natural evil and human evil. The cross of Christ—the archetypical shape suffering takes in the Christian story (the suffering of God's own self)—manifests the *Deus revelatus* when it is known to be caused by the evil powers engendered in the human heart without appeal (*non posse non peccare*). The confession of the centurion in Mark 15 is of such theological significance not because he knew the deeds or the teachings of Jesus but because he knew himself to be part of those who directly

---

11. LW 37:222–24; WA 26, 335f.
12. Kolb and Wengert, *Book of Concord*, 609–11.
13. I owe to Philip Hefner this insight for distinguishing a sacramental/mysterious character from a sacrament proper.
14. LW 31:40. *Theologus crucis dicit id, quod res est.* WA 1.354, 21f.

imposed suffering. Seeing himself in that mask became for him that "mirroring transparency" into his own condition.

In the cross of Christ, general and particular revelation meet each other, for God's creativity is witnessed in its annihilating force. Therefore, the cross is the material criterion by which the visible becomes constitutive for the knowledge of God, as much as the theology of creation (creation out of nothing/evil) establishes the formal criterion for the recognition of the visibility of the cross and the suffering in the world. Through the theology of creation the cross becomes "essentially identical" (Regin Prenter) with the suffering in and of the world. Through the theology of the cross the suffering in and of the world is recognized as the *locus* of God's creative work.

The suffering of nature (human included) assumes a privileged sacramental character not in and of itself, but because in it and through it, divine creativity manifests itself. The primacy of the word in God's creative redemption is for humans only a passive primacy that allows them to stand and behold suffering for what it is. On the human side, the response is one of action, the practice of giving glory to whom glory is due. The work is not meritorious precisely when and because it assumes this doxological character.[15] This practice is not done by the redemptive merit of the work accomplished, but because it is the only way to express our confession of sin, the human sin through which evil insinuates itself into nature (human nature included).

Balance

From here we can understand that for Luther the care and concern for nature are the response to the belief that God is the cause and source of all creatures. Humans are the poets of a medieval carnival creating masks through which we protect ourselves from the terrible sight of the abyss, the vision of the *Deus nudus*, the *horror vacui*. Therefore, ecological responsibility is neither a mystical nor a romantic response to the positive goodness of creation, nor conformity to a natural law, but a doxological act of repentance and renewal out of the depth and the void that emerges from the clefts of a broken mask. It is not the artificiality of nature (Karl Marx) that we should fear but the view of nature, bucolic or scientific, which protects us from the experience of suffering and of the cross. Far from a naive view of nature or from the modern divorce between *homo* and *natura*, Luther's theology provides for

---

15. See CA XX: "It is taught that good works should and must be done, not that a person relies on them to earn grace, but for God's sake and God's praise." See Kolb and Wengert, *Book of Concord*, 56 (§27).

criteria to face evil in nature and society. In other words, the visibility of suffering in the silence of the innocent is what opens the space in which the creative Word resonates, evoking our practical response. Every vocation is a stewardship in and through (and not for and to) God's creation. The focus of ecological responsibility is not in the preservation or protection of nature, but in the knowledge we have for the power we exert in and through it.

The problem of Luther's theology for contemporary appropriation is not linked to the supposed incoherence in relating special and general revelation. The problem lies in the fact that, while Luther advanced far beyond the medieval understanding of nature, he remained medieval in his understanding of social institutions (*ecclesia, politia, oeconomia*). The anthropological reductionism in Luther's equation of sin and redemption fails to comprehend sin and evil in their structural dimensions. *Addito salis grano*, nature was for him artificial, but the institutions were natural. The nature we see is not the creation we believe but the production of our own knowledge and power. The inability to recognize that this knowledge and power consubstantiates itself in institutions and social structures, and is not only a direct expression of our individual sin, is the missing connection in Luther's theology. In this sense Ernst Troeltsch was right to recognize the medieval character of Luther's social thinking, even if he has gone far beyond medieval constraints in his concept of revelation where the theology of the cross and creation theology meet.

9

The Groaning Mask

Ecojustice and the Human Place in Nature

The Asymmetric Face of Ecological Consciousness

TIMES OF CRISIS ARE frequently also times of birth. Yet a birth is always also an experience of fear and death. In the case of the ecological crisis the relation between the hope for a rebirth and the experience of fear and death is marked by an enormous asymmetry. Hope, however slim, is nurtured by very relative and dim signs, while the fears and manifestations of death remain absolute and bright in their evidences. One species is granted some guarantee of continued life; a reservation is created that will preserve an environment; a river shows a falling rate of pollution, or successful negotiation diminishes by percentage points the production of a chemical polluter. However, the specter of a total collapse of the ecosystem that sustains life as we know it still haunts hearts and minds. Such is the pessimistic diagnosis of the crisis. We mend in retail what we destroy in wholesale.

It is no surprise that in such a context the discipline of eschatology no longer appears the exclusive domain of theology or religious studies. Calculations of the outside limit for the existence of the earth before it is engulfed by an expanding sun—four to five billion years—foster a sense of relativity as to the ontological status of the earth. Based on this scientific data, are we to schedule this as the plausible apocalypse on our agendas?

The asymmetry between the small signs of hope and the terrifying visions raised by the imminence of an ecological collapse has revealed to us that there is another crisis behind the ecological one. The problem lies not only in what could be called the ontological character of the crisis, i.e., what the crisis really is, but also in its symbolic character. We lack a creative vision, an imagination that creates a cognitive dissonance into imagining nature and redefining our relations within the environment in a different way.

R. G. Collingwood[1] has described the evolution from the Greek organic view of nature to the Western mechanistic understanding that came with the Renaissance. In its modern version the meaning of nature has been dissolved finally into the idea of history. Such development is an accumulation of losses, the most important of which is the disappearance of space as a category that cannot be reduced to extension—extension understood as a simple medium that once possessed becomes an exchangeable value. In the name of the relativity of time and space, we have sacrificed this notion of irreducible space in favor of a quasi-absolute notion of history.[2] Our lack of understanding of existence as being conditioned by the place that occupies us has exiled us from pre-modern or ancient views, in which the detachment of a people from its place is a rupture that amounts to death. This manner of thinking is expressed powerfully in the words of Job who says of those who go down to Sheol that from there they will not return "nor do their places know them any more" (Job 7:10). The symbolic character of the crisis has turned the ecological problem into a riddle that will not be solved either by oblivion or by a quantitative increase of technical solutions.

The Crisis of Legitimacy

The very word *ecology* appeared in our vocabulary only at the end of the last century, used then to designate that branch of biology which deals with the relations of living organisms to their environment. Only in the middle of this century has the term begun to be applied also to human communities and to receive the common meaning of a science that studies the structure and development of human communities and the effects of their processes of adaptation to the environment.

Thus we are dealing with a relatively new term that refers to a problem linked to Western societies. It is one of those problems that humanity poses for itself in order to solve it. It is certainly the case that the very fact of raising the problem allows for some optimism, if we agree with Karl Marx's observation that humanity poses for itself only the problems it can solve. But as soon as we start to deal with such problems, we are left with the impression of trying to cover ourselves with a short blanket. For example, the implementation of the grand projects in the Amazon region will certainly increase the gross national product and the average income of Brazilians,

---

1. Collingwood, *Idea of Nature*.
2. See Westhelle, *Eschatology and Space*, 1–36.

which might offer the opportunity to bring great portions of the population out of absolute poverty. For these and other reasons huge dams were built for the generation of electricity and thousands of hectares of rain forest were destroyed. Still other dams are planned. To avoid the flooding of the Amazon region that these dams would necessitate, the building of nuclear plants was proposed. Thermoelectric plants would accomplish the same purpose. We are still left with difficult choices: either we continue deforestation, which expends great amounts of nonrenewable fuel and also aggravates the greenhouse effect, or we face the problem of disposing of atomic waste—not to mention the risk of accidents.

Obviously, the presupposition is that we will need ever-increasing amounts of electrical energy for development. Environmentalists will immediately say that the model of development must be questioned, that we need a sustainable development using alternative sources of energy. But the complex technology involved has made such proposals more of a problem than a solution for the two-thirds of the world's population who live on the other side of development. This is the reason why, when such solutions arrive south of the equator with a Nordic accent, it is as if the winner wants to stop the game before the score starts to shift.

It is indeed the case that we are all in this vessel together and that national or regional interests cannot override the chances of life for the whole of humanity. However, the problem is who decides the measures that will be taken to save the earth? Gerald Barney illustrates this problem rather well:

> Consider the hole in the ozone layer. The hole was caused in large part by CFC [chlorofluorocarbon] chemicals produced and used in the industrialized nations. One of the most damaging is the refrigerant CFC-12. It is used in virtually all refrigerators and air-conditioners. Refrigeration of food is one of the key ways to reduce diarrheal disease, which is a major cause of infant mortality in developing countries. Are 4 billion poor people to be allowed to put as much CFC-12 per capita into the ozone layer as we in the industrialized countries already have? Are 4 billion poor people to be told they can't have refrigeration unless they buy more expensive refrigerators that don't use CFC-12?[3]

The reduction in the production of CFCs by 35 percent by 1999 has been already approved by the Montreal Protocol of 1987, subscribed to by twenty-four industrialized nations. The problem seems to lie not so much in

---

3. Gerald Barney in an open letter to bishops, executives, chairs, and leaders of the Evangelical Lutheran Church in America, presented at the "Year 2000 and Beyond" conference (March 30–April 2, 1989).

the diagnosis nor even in some of the basic measures that must be adopted, but rather in who decides where and when they ought to be implemented. Furthermore, there is a lack of legitimacy—or even will—in those who currently hold the power to make some decisions. Hypocritical situations are created. A highway project in the state of Acre in the heart of the Amazon region, which should link Brazil to Peru and thus to the Pacific Ocean, has been politically and financially supported by Japan, which has aluminum plants in the region. The United States, however, has opposed the project, giving ideological and financial support to the organizations of the peoples of the forest. But, simultaneously, the United States is supporting the militarization of the Amazon region, which is regarded as a major threat to both the forest and the indigenous population. The ostensibly pro-environment action of the United States against the Acre highway is in fact only a geopolitical and economic action against the growing Japanese influence in the area.

In his book on Simón Bolívar, Gabriel García Márquez reports a conversation of the general with a Frenchman who was trying to teach him how to organize a politically advanced system. At the end of a lengthy argument, Bolívar remarks, "Don't try to teach us how we shall be, don't try to make us like yourselves, don't expect us to do well in twenty years what you have so badly done in two thousand. . . . Damn you! Please, let us by ourselves make our own Middle Ages."[4]

Repentance and Revision

Gone are the days in which ecological problems were regarded as a North Atlantic issue. It is no longer feasible to separate economic and social justice from environmental concerns, as the case of Chico Mendes so well illustrates. But neither is there any reason for accepting the proposal to begin ecological action as if the political and economic actions of the past could be totally forgotten. Brazil got its name from a reddish wood—Brazil wood—which practically disappeared in the first centuries after the conquest. It was all transported to Europe in caravels, whose construction contributed to the deforestation of Europe. "The forests of Europe were sacrificed so that the forests of America, Africa, and India with their coveted noble woods could be exploited."[5] It is not by chance that Luther saw a sign of the coming of the end to be the disappearance of wild forests. This past history cannot be used to deny the gravity of the environmental problems we face. Nevertheless, it argues for an unavoidable suspicion regarding the integrity of the

4. Márquez, *O general em seu labirinto*, 129.
5. Schütze, "Waldgeschichte und Weltgeschichte," 8.

sympathetic proposals coming from those who not long ago established the pattern for what progress meant and how our relation with nature should be framed.

If it is so that an efficacious approach to the ecological crisis requires a qualitative leap, a symbolic shift, that will allow for a new paradigm for framing our view of nature, then we should not wait for a solution from those who historically represent the very attitude that lies at the root of the crisis. Humans have turned their best creative efforts against nature and the environment, but not all have done so to the same degree. For a rebirth to come, for the new vision to be formed, repentance is presupposed. To borrow the words of Bernard of Clairvaux, it will come only through the gift of tears (*dona lacrimarum*). But who carries the enormous guilt of such sin? To universalize it, as some modern Marcionites do, would not only render any corrective effort senseless, but would also compromise the intended original goodness of all creation by dualistically dissociating grace from nature. It is important to recover the theology of creation in this effort to recognize the dignity of nature and our particular responsibility for its depletion.

Discussion of the ecological problem in theological terms is compelled by consciousness of a need for a point of departure that transcends the predicaments of anthropocentrism. A theological approach to nature is, by definition, theocentric. This means that nature is not something merely given, but it is creation; its main reference point is God. Ontologically, humans stand on the same level as the rest of nature; their difference is only an analytical one.

Dominion and Subjection

Within the Christian tradition, however, we face some problems when addressing ecological issues or when trying to find relevant images to redress the issue. There is very little in the Bible or in history that can be regarded as somehow directly related to the issue. Indeed, the wrath of Jesus against a fig tree (Mark 11:12–14, 20) or the folkloric narrative of Saint Boniface cutting a sacred oak in order to demonstrate the power of the Christian faith against paganism certainly will not be the best images in support of the ecological movement. But the difficulties go further, and question even creation theology as a ground for an ecological consciousness or as a possible contribution to overcome the symbolic character of the crisis.

In the well-known article "The Historical Roots of Our Ecological Crisis," mentioned in the previous chapter, Lynn White Jr. made an immense impact and received equal support for his affirmation that "our science and technology have grown out of Christian attitudes toward man's relation to nature."[6] He saw such attitudes to be the result of the foundational axiom of the Judeo-Christian tradition, according to which nature has no other reason for existing except to serve the human. The Priestly account of creation (Gen 1:1—2:4a) conveys this peculiar viewpoint: the human is the last act of Creation from whom all the rest of creation receives meaning, being placed at the human's disposal. For White, Christianity inherits and radicalizes this view, becoming the most anthropocentric of the religions that the world has seen. Herein lies the contradiction with which we live. It is the crown of all creation (Psalm 8) that turns itself against its own biological support. White argues in conclusion that the Judeo-Christian teleology, by which everything is understood from the perspective of human redemption, is the only frame within which it is possible to conceive of the development of human sciences. Still, it is White himself who turns to Eastern Christian mysticism and to the piety of Francis of Assisi in search of the religious antidote to the West's mistakes, even suggesting Saint Francis as a "patron saint of ecology." On this point his article was not forgotten. Thirteen years later Pope John Paul II proclaimed Francis of Assisi the "patron saint of ecology."

The argument of White rests on two pillars. First, he affirms that the relation *homo-natura* constitutes the fundamental opposition in the Judeo-Christian tradition. Second, he maintains that this opposition, which favors the human at the expense of the rest of nature, is the foundation upon which Western science and technology grew.

As to the first point, White's interpretation depends upon his reading of Gen 1:1—2:4a. In fact, the affirmations that the human is given the dominion and the right to subdue nature (vv. 26 and 28) and that the appearance of the creature of earth (*adam* formed from *adamah*) is in the image of God seem to give prima facie support to White, if taken outside of their context. Although White's position is well-argued, some observations must be made in response.

The Priestly account of creation does not culminate in the creation of the human being, but with the Sabbath of God, in which all creation rests, and which serves also as the justification for the Jubilee of Leviticus 25. Doxology is the goal toward which all creation is directed. The text itself has its setting in the cultic life of the community; it is a liturgy. Doxology is the *telos* toward which the text itself was composed.[7] That the text was composed during the Babylonian captivity gives even more relevance to its radical affirmation of the day of rest and worship. The pattern used to

---

6. White, "Historical Roots," 1206.
7. Schwantes, *Projetos de esperança*, 32–35.

frame the narrative is influenced by the Babylonian myth of creation. But in comparison to the latter, it shows an interesting rupture. The Babylonian myth locates the establishment of the monarchy and of the official cult right after the creation of the human being.[8] Furthermore, the affirmation that the human is made in the image of God differs significantly from contemporary Mesopotamian and Egyptian myths, where it is only the king who is described as being made in the image of the creator.[9]

It is in such a context that the problematic statement about dominion over nature must be framed. While that dominion is generally referred to the whole earth, only animals are specifically mentioned. The main point to be noted about this affirmation is its negative tone. What is stressed is not what humans can do toward nature, but that all human beings are equal in the face of God. It is an affirmation of democracy. Besides, when dominion is asserted in the naming of the animals, they are simultaneously excluded from the human diet (Gen 1:29). What would be the point of asserting such dominion?

To dominate the animals can be interpreted as a mandate for peaceful coexistence. At least until the Neolithic Age (ca. 3000 BC), animals represented a threat to the very survival of the human race, whose numbers are estimated at no more than 100 million. It is even probable that the great steppes of Europe and Asia were a result of the method of hunting with fire during the Pleistocene Age. In this context, the imago, besides affirming that humans should not dominate over other human beings, reflects as well the fear that the animal world represented. The ecological problem appears here only in its reverse side. The human communities are still the weak link in the environmental chain. It is, therefore, not the opposition between humans and nature that characterizes this text. On the contrary, what is seen is the recognition of the human frailness within creation. The implication of such recognition is even strengthened when we observe that it is a people in captivity who used it to affirm its faith. The spirit of the text should now maintain the concern for the new weak link in creation—the animal world. Milan Kundera is right when he suggests that the true moral test for humanity is its relationship with those who are subject to us—the animals.

White's argument is correct in that the ecological crisis is intimately linked with Western science and technology. Although the history and origin of science and technology are a matter of great dispute, particularly as to possible Christian influence, this debate need not concern us here. For our purpose, it is only important to establish how nature came to be viewed not

---

8. Westermann, *Creation*, 51.
9. Kilpp, *Teologia do Antigo Testamento*.

only as a reality to be subdued, but as merely having use-value for humans without any dignity in itself. Such dignity the Priestly account maintains by affirming liturgically the goodness of the acts of Creation in each and every day. The Christian tradition reaffirmed this dignity by its vigorous rejection of gnosticism. It does not seem plausible to deduce from this tradition the reduction of nature to a source of value to be accumulated.

Rather, the first step toward seeing nature's value only in its use takes place with the astronomic revolution of Copernicus in the sixteenth century. His heliocentric system "consisted not so much in displacing the world's centre from the earth to the sun as in implicitly denying that the world has a centre at all."[10] Matter had been homogenized; the world had no objective reference of its own. From this point it was not far to the new Baconian understanding of reason as an organ for the examination, prediction, and control of natural processes. The Cartesian dualism between mind and body, the thinking thing and the extended thing, was the first philosophical formulation of a view of nature as a machine at the disposal of the thinking "points" that explore and manipulate it.[11] Even the overcoming of this view, with history being the paradigm to frame nature, has not restored what Scheller called the psychic drives of matter, in spite of the efforts of a Hegel, a Whitehead, or the one-sidedness of the vitalists.

The Wrappings of the Sacred

However, this is more than an ideological problem. The current ecological crisis emerged in the midst of a social, economic, and political system that affirms a model of social organization and economic development to which the crisis is endemic; it is not restricted to a side-effect that could be corrected with some minor adjustments. However, an alternative economic or socio-political model of society will not suffice by itself to address environmental issues. The problem is a global one; it requires the reshaping of the very cultural values that have oriented the present hegemonic civilizations of the world. It is therefore a cultural problem in its broadest etymological sense. It implies the recognition of what we have done with the mandate to cultivate the earth. It goes to the source of this mandate, to its religious substance. The required reorientation implies, therefore, a religious act of repentance that will need to break with three fundamental myths that modernity has cherished. The first is the myth of the atomic individual; the

---

10. Collingwood, *Idea of Nature*, 97.
11. Scheler, *Man's Place in Nature*, 72.

second is the myth of progress through accumulation; and the third is the myth of private piety.

The Myth of the Individual

The individual has been the irreducible component of the social matrix since Hobbes, and extending through Leibniz to recent neopositivists. Nietzsche described this well when he said that the individual is the most recent creation. Collectivity, civil society, is a compound of contractual arrangements among individuals in the affirmation of their interests. Such arrangements are an expression of a rationality that, as Max Weber has shown, gives to modern capitalist societies the shape of an efficient bureaucratic machine.

What disappears with modernity is community as a center of decision, of power, and of the identity of the individual. The divorce of individuals from their vocations has reduced social interaction to function and role. Organic solidarity is lost with the separation of reason from passion, of the group from its constitutive place, of social function from individual identity, and, finally, of mind from body. The recovery of a sense of community might represent the relinquishment of some important values of bourgeois civilization, like that of individual freedom, but it might be the price we will have to pay in order to have an organic understanding of the use of power, in which justice will be not only distributive and retributive, but also fundamentally contributive for the sake of the community in the context in which it is constituted.

The Myth of Accumulation as Progress

The second myth to be fought demands a reconsideration of our understanding of labor. The understanding of labor as the individual or corporative appropriation of nature not only for human ends but for the sake of further accumulation is the basis for the triumph of the spirit of capitalism. Karl Marx called this process "originary accumulation," pointing out that proper to the capitalist economy is the transformation of money into capital by the inversion of the traditional relation between commodity and money. Accordingly, commodities become the means to the end of accumulating money; that is, money, instead of functioning as a universal mediation of value, becomes, as capital, a value in itself. Consequently, nature loses its proper and independent dignity and the product extracted from it, defined by its use, establishes its value. The accumulation of such value determines the rhythm of progress.

Intrinsic to the use-value of a commodity we will find also its abuse, an abuse that does not refer exclusively to nature outside of human existence. The very nature that constitutes the body of the worker is treated in the same way and viewed as a means for the accumulation of value. Considerations of value depends on production and always begin from the results of productive effort. Value is not derived/considered from the organic relation of the human within nature. Marx saw original accumulation as playing the same role in political economy as original sin in theology. He suggested using the notion of metabolism (*Stoffwechsel*) as a concept to reinterpret labor from the standpoint of the organic interrelationship of the human within nature, instead of approaching labor from the standpoint of human intervention in nature for the sake of accumulation of value. This notion of metabolism brings us closer to the Jahwist account of Creation, according to which the mandate to keep and cultivate the garden (Gen 2:15) is addressed to the living creature (*adam*) shaped from the very humus (*adamah*) toward which the efforts of labor are directed.

Such a metabolic comprehension of labor offers the possibility of approaching the problem of justice in such a way that human interests are not separated from the intrinsic rights of nature, including human nature. This organic link is what Martin Luther called the "majesty of matter." Metabolism opposes a separation between mind and matter that must rightfully be regarded as a "diabolism" characteristic of our sinful condition. The culmination of human use of science and technology for the sake of defending disputed interests is represented in the use of the atomic bomb. Robert Oppenheimer, reflecting about the involvement of scientists in the so-called value-free development of science and technology, rightly said in 1948 that "scientists have known sin." He was referring to this dramatic case of diabolism. We had arrived at the point of knowing that sin, as the separation from God as the ground of life, can be rendered concretely as the undermining of the very possibility of biological survival.

The Myth of Private Piety

The third problem that requires repentance and revision is piety itself insofar as it expresses our relationship to the ground of all creation. The great movements of spiritual renewal that have marked Western Christianity since the seventeenth century (Pietism, Methodism, Puritanism) partake of the same "diabolic" characteristics of modernity in their clear-cut separation between subject and object, grace and nature. The Cartesian dualism is transfigured but not surpassed. Although it is no longer reason but feelings which are the basic criterion for the recognition of grace and truth, it is still the atomized individual that floats over this world by the power of a supernatural faith.

Luther's understanding of the mystical tradition lends legitimacy to a more organic wholistic view than the pietists would ascribe to. Absent in pietism is the view of nature that some mystics like Hildegard of Bingen, Francis of Assisi, Mechtild of Magdeburg, Meister Eckhart, Julian of Norwich, and others have. What distinguishes them from pietism, relevant in the context of the ecological crisis, is the appreciation of nature as a place of divine epiphany, as the place God creates to manifest God's glory. This is not the natural theology of scholasticism trying to find the logic of God engraved in the laws of nature. In medieval mysticism the point is to approach divine mystery, qua mystery, in the creation that surrounds us and envelops its own ground.

The comprehension of nature as the expression of divine mystery, which simultaneously reveals and conceals it, opens up new possibilities for the representation of God. Meister Eckhart, for example, answers Augustine's classical question, What was God doing before creation? without the philosophical anguishes of the bishop of Hippo: God is from all eternity giving birth. It is the attempt to reformulate the problem of revelation, using metaphors instead of concepts, that distinguishes mysticism from scholasticism. Mysticism finds through nature the reason of the Creator behind the creation. Aside from any difficulties mysticism might present in its asceticism, its importance lies in this insight that nature manifests to reason, in the form of a mystery, the glory of the Creator.

Luther, whose respect for the *theologia germanica* is well known, kept precisely this insight when, in the Heidelberg debate, he distinguished the theologian of the cross from the theologian of glory. According to him, God is not to be sought as the invisible reality behind creation and then defined by the arguments of reason. But God is in creation without being creation. Creation is the envelope, the wrapping or the mask (*involucrum* or *larva*) of a God we do not see face to face, but who is communicated in the paradox of contrariness. This notion of the mask or the wrapping of God in which God is—without nature itself being God—lends to nature a sacred dignity without falling into pantheism.

The richness of this image is that it allows us to face nature not as a source of utility, while at the same time not taking it as a direct source of revelation. God remains hidden but definitely present in the opposite. This is a God that paradoxically offers Godself without mediations, but, simultaneously always along with the mediations, though indirect. This revelation is the mediated immediacy. It is not given because of the mediations, but never without them. This conception is linked to the mystical comprehension of knowledge by participation in the mystery and distinguishes itself from a subjectivist piety, in which there is no mediation for grace—except faith itself, that is, *fides qua*—as well as from ecclesial orthodoxies where the institutions and the rites are the mediating conditions for grace.

God's Weeping Mask

Nature qua creation is not in itself divine. It is only a mask. But we see now that this mask is weeping and groaning in travail. We don't know where the tears come from, but we know we are responsible for them. The respect due to nature does not follow from its merits, but from the intrinsic right of its being, which ultimately sustains human life. Above all it sustains the life of those who are on the edge of existence, beholding an eroding mask that will reveal only the terrifying vision of a naked God. The impulse to redress our ecological consciousness will have to come from those who in powerlessness make community solidarity the only option for survival, who in dispossession experience labor as a metabolism, and who outside of the walls of official religion experience God revealed in the mask of creation.

There is no need to stress that natural processes are normally violent, that the struggle of the species is real, and that survival of the fittest operates at the expense of the weakest. We have learned so much from Darwin. The point that needs to be made addresses the new situation created in this century. In three or four billion years of evolution and natural tragedies it has never been the case that any species acquired the capability to destroy life as such. We have this power now. This truth is so forceful because the destruction of nature begins with the destruction of the body of the exploited person. Ecce homo! Hence we might gain a better insight in the mystery of the Incarnation. The self-emptying of God could not be more radical than the affirmation that God has become a human being in the great variety of the works of creation. Or else, consider the lilies of the field!

10

The Church in Eden

On the Priesthood of the Faithful

> Be still, my heart, these great trees are prayers.
>
> —Tagore

A Double Captivity

Days are among us, and they have been around with a decisive penchant for almost a century, in which church-talk has been held captive, captive again, yet not specifically to the church in Rome. New installments of the Babylonian captivity, to appeal to a historical template, are double-sided, holding entrapped all conversation about church either to its inner institutional formation or to its assimilation into the politico-cultural order of the day. Most denominations—Roman Catholicism with its robust magisterium, Eastern Orthodoxy with its elaborate liturgy, Pentecostalism with its charismatic spontaneity, financial, and organizational strength, and mainline Protestantism with its congregationalism and ecumenical endeavors—articulate their teachings about the church and its ministry either out of its own resources, being its own public, or else draw it from the public arena in which it finds itself immersed and adjusted. With few protests, church-talk has been a territorial dispute shifting from fighting over borders to signing truce treatises.

The challenge to the church calls for liberation from this double captivity, one of being obsessed by its own home economics—keeping the house in order and its accounts solvent—and the other of adjusting itself to the whims of the régime of the day. The two options may seem to be alternatives but occasionally the two assail the church simultaneously. While home economics is necessary for the church, the political order also needs to be a critical companion. But if it loses its identity to either or both of these adjacent ambits, the church displays its captivity either as idolatry or as demonry. Idolatry results from an obsessive preoccupation with its own house, while refraining from having a public voice is a manifestation of the symptoms of demonic possession, which has as one characteristic the one of being mute, incapable of having a public voice. The litmus test to see if the church retains its own integrity and fulfills its calling is expressed through a uniquely distinct practice that ensures its authenticity and freedom.

Priesthood of All Believers: The Reformatory Signature

Luther's words in his *Open Letter to the Christian Nobility* of 1520 has the signature of a major teaching of the Reformation, the priesthood of all believers:

> If a little group of pious Christian laymen were taken captive and set down in a wilderness, and had among them no priest consecrated by a bishop, and if there in the wilderness they were to agree in choosing one of themselves, married or unmarried, and were to charge him with the office of baptizing, saying mass, absolving and preaching, such a man would be as truly a priest as though all bishops and popes had consecrated him.[1]

The implications of this for ecclesiology are immense and quite noticeable, though the political impact has not been so obvious. Regardless of the fraudulent "Donation of Constantine,"[2] the Roman Church still amassed enormous political power. An attack on the chain of power in the church was nothing short of a revolutionary political gesture that is at the origin of modern democracy. Needless to say, this attack on the most organized and hierarchical estate in medieval Europe had a trickle-down effect with extraordinary consequences for the political realm, and also for the household and the emerging financial capitalism.

Luther was more radical than what today is conveyed by the idea of "reforming" the church. First because he was dealing not with one institution among others, but with the institution whose power could not be

---

1. LW 44:128.
2. Lorenzo Valla, the Italian humanist, revealed the fraud of the "Donation of Constantine," which Luther was not only aware of but which he also helped disseminate.

rivaled by any other institution. Second, because he universalized the institutions, it also made its truth contingent upon a subjective experience without a necessary causal relationship to a particular institution. Church meant for Luther something like what could be called religion, arguably a universal phenomenon, but then also that which designated the singularity of an event whose truthfulness precedes any demonstration. This is the succeeding character of church as event, its singularity and non-reproducibility. However, as an institution, as *ecclesia* it endures, has some permanence, and is always relative and relational.

In his *Lectures on Genesis* he explains the establishment of the day of Sabbath as "intended for the worship of God. . . . [in] which God speaks with us through His Word and we, in turn, speak with Him through prayer and faith." The human, says Luther, "was specially created for the knowledge and worship of God." "This is the real purpose of the seventh day: that the Word of God be preached and heard."[3] And in addition God build for Adam, "as it were, a temple: . . . the tree of the knowledge of good and evil was Adam's church, altar and pulpit . . . somewhat like a chapel in which there were many trees of the same variety, namely, the trees of the knowledge of good and evil."[4] In Luther's view the "church was established first."[5] This is indeed a radically catholic view of the church, it includes all humans insofar as all are descendants of Adam "who would have gathered on the Sabbath day . . . where trees were planted in large number."[6]

The Reformer's interpretation that there were several trees of life and also of the knowledge of good and evil "does not appear at all preposterous," as he insists, is indeed intriguing yet very revealing. Henceforth it is sensible to postulate that it is equally not preposterous to imply that this multiplicity portends, consciously or not in Luther's mind, the diversity of religions and their different forms of worship and the diversity of their organizations. It is at least consistent with Luther's and the Reformation's conception of the multi-center character of the church. This conception entails quite a radical view of what "catholic" means; every tree of life offers sustenance and a vital space for different communities. Every tree of the knowledge of good and evil, which for Luther was also the tree of life, is a place of worship and discernment, and there are many of them: to each tree its creed; to each creed its prayer, its piety.

---

3. LW 1:80f.
4. LW 1:95.
5. LW 1:104; but cf. LW 1:94f.
6. LW 1:105.

The tree or trees as the figure of the church that Luther dwells on for so many pages of his *Lectures on Genesis* is exceedingly rich in its imagery. Nevertheless we can only understand the role it plays in Luther's theology, and the suggestive plays with the metaphor, by looking at the way he places it in relation to two other institutions mandated by God, which flank the church. Here Luther is not talking about the church-community as event, but as *ecclesia*, church as institution that entails endurance and guards as its treasures the traces of the event that occasioned it.

The Church between Economics and Politics

Luther was working with the popular tripartite division of estates in the Middle Ages, which finds its roots in classical antiquity, more specifically in Plato and Aristotle. It is impossible to simply translate these social strata or estates to a modern society as ours. For example, the American and the French revolutions did away with the nobility's entitlement of being the guardian of civil affairs. The economy, since the emergence of industrial capitalism and the industrial revolution, is no longer lodged primarily in the space of the household. Nevertheless there is a fundamental core procedure that distinguishes each of these instituted mandates, an operational principle at the nucleus of each that still remains the same. These operational principles at work in each institutional sphere can be recognized as discrete human faculties. In the case of the church it is the word of God, audible and visible that operates, addresses humans in their *vita passiva* and elicits human response in form of doxological praise or lament. In the case of the household or the economy it is human biological reproduction and labor, the production of the means for the sustenance of life and its reproduction. Finally, as far as civil government is concerned it is about human intercommunication for the sake of building a reasonable, equitable, and peaceful order in the earthly city with positive laws to foster and regulate it. Now the church is this reality that stands squarely in the in-between spaces where life is produced and reproduced, and the space of political life, of human communication, policy making, and mores-forming activities and legislations. Between these two spaces the church stands, in a way, as a tree in the garden stands between the house and the public space represented by streets and buildings where civil life is lived out, negotiated, and administered. While we are active in the *oeconomia* and in the *politia*, we are totally passive as the church event takes place.

This "third space," to borrow an expression of Homi Bhabha, the space between spaces, distinguishes itself from the other two, not as a demarcated territory in the sense that it is not the result of the human active drives, creating an institution sui generis and non-representable.[7] However, the church borrows its institutional life both from the economic realm and its legitimacy as an institution from the political régime. Hence it is a hybrid space, or rather a hybrid territory. In one sense it is an ordinary space as the etymology suggests: a grounded space (*terra*). But, in another sense, it is also that which evokes what Rudolph Otto called the *tremendum et fascinans*. This territory is the one that also frightens (*terrere*). In the first sense of its hybrid character, territory as *terra*, the church (*ecclesia*) borrows from the earthly institutional neighbors (*oeconomia* and *politia*) sustenance and legitimacy. In the words of Luther: "The home must produce, whereas the city must guard, protect and defend.[8] Then follows the third, God's own home and city, that is the church, which must obtain people from the home and protection and defense from the city."[9] Yet often it loses itself in these neighboring fields, falling thus into idolatry or is possessed unable to find its voice.

The first, the space of the *oikos*, is represented by the human interaction with nature that provides for the sustenance of life and the reproduction of the species. The other, the space of the *polis*, is represented by human intersubjective relations that provide normative or legal ways or the administration of government preventing a war of all against all. In *Bondage of the Will* Luther makes a distinction between these two spaces insisting that in and through these spaces God "does not work without us."[10] Equally important in the "third space" of the church, God works through our preaching, consoling, admonishing, but there is something distinct. In politics and economy, even if God has the efficient and final agency it is the human who is the subject of the relation to its object. In case of the economy, it is the relationship to nature; in case of politics it is the relationship to the other as a subject with whom we interact. In these two cases—economy and politics—the human achieves a *representation* of herself through which she constructs an identity. In one case the representation is a material object extracted from nature through labor or present in an offspring being biologically generated. In the other case the representation is done by one recognizing oneself in the encounter with the other.

This is the reason why, strictly speaking, we cannot define the church as such. As long as we define it, however, we can only do it by pointing

7. Bhabha, *Location of Culture*, 37–39.
8. Please see also chapter 22, "Power and Politics."
9. LW 41:177f.
10. LW 33:243

to external characteristics, vestiges of the event that founds it. Essentially, however, it is not left up to us. We can only refer to it as this elusive "third space" determined by God's enunciation of the Word and the promise to be present materially in the elements of the sacrament. What we "do" is not our action, but only our *re-action*. This is why properly speaking we can say that the church happens as God speaks; Luther called it *creatura evangelii*,[11] the creature not of our doing and making, but of God's good word, even as it comes through our mouth. Church happens![12]

Already in the Hebrew Scriptures the Tent of the Tabernacle provides such an image for the Christian church precisely by being a "house" of sorts on the way. It was a tent; neither the intimate and stable space of the household, nor the utter exposure to the world outside, yet both at the same time: the presence of the divine, yet in dynamic transition. To phrase it differently, according to its earthly nature, the church is always a relative reality. Never is the church absolute. Such is the case because it is always in this tension between the politics and homestead, being in and out at the same time. Whenever one says "church" a conjunction must follow to qualify it as to where the church finds itself in this polarity that comprises its hybrid identity, constituted by its interface with politics and the economy. Thus, earthly speaking, there are these three overlapping spheres with distinct functions. This is why the Reformer is so adamant in keeping the relative character of the church. If now, in our times, we need to protect its relativity from falling into idolatry and demonry, at that time, Luther's time, the church was attempting to subsume all under itself: "Now why should we have the blasphemous, bogus law or government of the pope over and above these three high divine governments . . . of God? It presumes to be everything, yet is nothing."[13]

The evangelist Luke, in the book of Acts, often refers to the Christian community in a paradoxical way. He defines it, or describes it, as those of the "Way" (*hodos*: road, way, street, path; cf. Acts 9:2; 19:23; 22:4; 24:22). But then he refers to it as the church in the "house [*oikos*] of . . . ," suggesting a place of refuge and safety. Luke also uses the same double complementary, if asymmetrical, tasks of the church in rendering a speech of Paul in Ephesus referring to himself as performing the church's public role and its domestic one (*oikos*): "I did not shrink from doing anything helpful, proclaiming the message to you and teaching you in public [*demosía*] and from house to

11. WA 2:43, 6f.

12. In the *Lecture on Galatians* where Luther called the church a creature of the gospel he refers to Paul's letter to the Corinthians (1 Cor 4:15) in which Paul claims to have generated the community through the gospel.

13. LW 41:177.

house [*kat' oíkous*]."¹⁴ Refuge and displacement are complementary images that in tension suggest a simultaneous movement and exposure and at the same time also a sense of security, of calm and ease. Exposure and also haven, solace and risk, ease and dis-ease, wanderlust and refuge are often the biblical notions attached to the church, which, as opposed as they are, also complement each other lending to it an unstable image to account for its own happening.

This was Luther's very early characterization of the earthly church as he formulated it already in 1522: "The necessary signs of the church we have are baptism, the bread [Lord's Supper] and the all-powerful Gospel."¹⁵ But it was Melanchthon in the 1530 Augsburg Confession (art. VII) who provided the classical wording: "The church is the assembly of saints in which the gospel is taught purely and the sacraments are administered rightly."¹⁶ These external signs, also called symbols by Luther, point to the two secular realities adjacent to the church. The sacraments symbolize the church as a place of nourishment and sustenance, the "house" function of the church, while the proclaimed word point to its public character, its "street" function where public announcements are made through loud speakers either by people on foot or atop motor vehicles. But when either of them snares the church into their proper domains, *oeconomia* or *politia*, the church falls prey to idolatry and to demonry, respectively. This is why late in *The Councils and the Church* of 1539 Luther lists seven external signs of the church, apparently parting company with the traditional definition that restricts it to the assembly in which there is the administration of the sacraments and the proclamation of the word. As mentioned earlier, the first six marks only unfold the classic definition, entailing word and sacrament in a gathered assembly (Word, Baptism, Eucharist, Absolution [return to baptism], Ministry, Worship). However, Luther then adds another external sign, the cross, yet not as a relic, but as the endurance of suffering in the midst of trial (*Anfechtung*). What this addition infers is that without risking its safety by aligning itself to the dominant politics, and without risking its sustenance by amassing economic resources, it cannot proclaim the word that disturbs the political

14. Acts 20:20. Giorgio Agamben has made a persuasive case for *oikos* and *polis* to provide the two root concepts for the formation of the classical paradigms for social thought in the West, including its theology. See Agamben, *The Kingdom and the Glory*. But his zeal in distinguishing the two paradigms and the merit of acknowledging the "economic" dimension resulted in a somehow one-sided result in which Paul is "portraying the *ekklēsia* in domestic rather than political terms." Ibid., 25.

15. WA 7, 720, 34–36: *Signum necessarium est, quod habemus, Baptisma scilicet, panem et omnium potissimum Evangelium: tria haec sunt Christianorum symbola, tesserae et caracteres.*

16. Calvin followed this literally. *Institutes*, IV, I, 10.

order and legality; it cannot administer the sacrament that nourishes and renews the life of faith. The cross is the mark of the earthly church, its ordeal faced in faithfulness to the gospel that brought it into being.

Adjacency: Exposure and Shelter

The reality of the "third space" I am attempting to convey is best explained by the Greek word *chōra*. *Chōra* designates a liminal space, a boundary space that is not more than a space between spaces. An example of such a space is Golgotha. It is located outside of the walls of the city of Jerusalem; hence it is not *in* Jerusalem as such. But neither is it in another village or in the countryside; hence it is in Jerusalem. To be more exact it is in Jerusalem's adjacency. The word *adjacency* comes from the Latin (*ad-iacere*) and means "lying by"—lying by what we call home, as well as by the political world of the other.

This notion of adjacency that designates the limit of the familiar and the exposure to the outer spaces infused with danger and promises is a way to approach the reality of the church. The church finds its existence in this limit between what is ours—our language, our culture, our values—and that which is foreign to us, the strange world out there of danger and promises. As such it is the space of belonging and of transit and displacement. Adjacency is the threshold. As a threshold it is the gateway through which we are sent out to become guests of others as much as it is the opening through which we host those who are strangers and not like us.

In Sermon XLV of the "Homilies on the Acts"[17] Chrysostom, the great preacher of the fifth century, raises his voice against his fellow Christians who have accommodated themselves to the now rich Constantinian church, which (says Chrysostom) has plenty of "money and revenues." Institutions for the care of the poor and strangers were created as the church tried to address its diaconal task. *Xenodoxeion,* as they were called, were places for the care of the foreigner, the homeless, the sick, and the poor. It seems strange that the great preacher would attack what apparently was a good effort of stewardship. With his thundering golden mouth, Chrysostom launches an attack on the *Xenodoxeion,* for they were being used by the now well-off Christians to avoid the face of the poor themselves. These institutions served as a veil that protected them from being exposed directly to the reality that was nearby now. The church by virtue of its wealth was able to shield itself from the unpleasant reality of the other. The incisiveness of Chrysostom's argument reveals someone who was ashamed of his fellow Christians for he

17. *NPNF*[1] 11:272–77.

knew that the church should be adjacent to the pain and the wounds of the world, instead of protecting itself from it. The church as adjacency happens by allowing the other, the poor, and the stranger to emerge, to have a voice, to have a face. Luther's words convey the same sentiment of his own church and of the theologies of his day looking for glory and power gazing at the heavenly splendor of doctrine. He said, "The world is full of God. In every alley, at your door you find Christ; stare not at heavens."[18]

However, adjacency is not only about exposure. Paradoxically it is also about sheltering, refuge, and protection. In situations of minority communities threatened to lose their own self-identity the sheltering function of the church, its sanctuary character, needs to be lifted up. In dominant or hegemonic communities, exposure needs to be preached and practiced, as Chrysostom did. Between the two functions the word takes in the church—of being a shelter and of practicing exposure—the end result will be different. It leads to the two phenomena mentioned earlier. Exposure without sheltering leads to despair. It is the "despair of weakness" that Kierkegaard talks about, which is the loss of the self, the defused self, described by demonry, or demonic possession. In this despair we are lost in the polis incapable of being ourselves, of having a voice of our own. This is the sin of politics when the church is assimilated and acculturated muting the word that calls for another world. But refuge without vulnerability and exposure is idolatrous segregation. It is idolatrous because it is navel gazing as Luther defined idolatry in his famous expression *incurvatus in se ipso* (bent onto oneself). This is the sin of the economy, or of the household into which the church is tempted to insulate itself caring only about its own institutional self-preservation. These two ailments are indicative of the church's double captivity.

Blessed Difference

What is it in Luther's mind that grants the freedom of the Christian and its simultaneous dutifulness in the three spheres that Luther sees as necessary and sufficient? In referring to these spheres, which he also calls hierarchies, orders, estates, etc., he writes, "These are the three hierarchies ordained by God, and we need no more; indeed, we have enough and more than enough . . . in these three."[19] In and through them we are sanctified. The Household or *oeconomia* must provide for nourishment, sustenance and procreation;

---

18. *Also ist die welt vol vol Gott. In allen gassen, fur deiner thur findest du Christum. Gaff nicht ynn himel.* WA 20, 514, 27f.

19. LW 41:177.

civil life, secular government or *politia* must protect and enforce equity; and the church must be the hour and the space of Shabbat for the word of God to be proclaimed and dispensed.

Church happens, and it happens to be in the conjunctive reality of shelter and simultaneous exposure. It finds itself called upon by the establishment of the Shabbat, the time and place in which neither the chores of home-keeping nor the political demands define its existence. It exists by the unilateral Word of God. But it does not subsist apart from the adjacency of politics and economy, being thus a word that calls for another world and a balm for the weary soul of all of us who find ourselves so often homeless. But all of this pertains to the church in its earthly and secular calling. But the church event is something else as well. It points to another reality that is not controlled by the coordinates of time and space, yet it manifests itself in these coordinates leaving traces and vestiges that the *ecclesia* is called to administer and celebrate.

Keeping in mind Luther's distinction between being holy (or saint-*heilig*) and being blessed (or saved-*selig*), the priesthood of all saints is to practice this holiness in all and any of the earthly orders, but with particular reference being made to the ecclesial sphere. This attribution of holiness to every member of the church applies in equal measure to the *oeconomia* and *politia*. The holiness is an attribute of every person who is entitled as anybody else to decide, delegate, dispute, and legislate in matters political as it is equally the entitlement of every woman or man to participate and make appropriate decision for the nourishment and sustenance of the household and the economy. The criteria of reasonableness and equity supply the underlying principle of democracy. While this is good and salutary, it is not the same as blessedness. That we get by Christ alone is the event in our midst, the presence among us, adjacent to us in its infinitude, neither dogmatically nor confessionally controlled. But by introducing the seventh holy possession of the church—cross and suffering—Luther is offering a suggestive hint. The cross is the only one of the seven marks of the church that is not only a sanctifying mark as the others were in yielding earthly holiness. It is the sole mark by which "the Holy Spirit not only sanctifies his people, but also blesses them."[20] And this is the cross we carry for being between the house and the street, risking exposure by speaking publicly and offering sanctuary as expression of holy love. As Luther says, citing Romans 5:1–5, we are bound to face trouble, trial, and suffering that "produces hope."

---

20. LW 41:164.

11

Apocalypse

Yet-Time and Not-Yet

Apocalyptic was the mother of all Christian theology.

—Ernst Käsemann

Eschatology and the Apocalyptic

"Apocalyptic was the mother of all Christian theology" was a claim made by the Lutheran New Testament scholar Ernst Käsemann in the early 1950s.[1] Rudolph Bultmann, his former mentor in Marburg, rejected the thesis, but conceded that it could be said that eschatology is the mother of Christian theology, keeping in line with his existentialist proclivities.[2] Then came along Gerhard Ebeling, another student of Bultmann, and one of the great names in Luther research in the twentieth century, who wrote a reply to Käsemann criticizing him for never defining what apocalyptic meant. An undaunted Käsemann wrote a second article on the subject, reinforcing his case and cause. He does not take direct issue with his mentor or colleague in the text of the argument, but in a long footnote (a page long and in small font) he acknowledges Ebeling's criticism.[3] His response to Ebeling was a sharp but precise assertion that to render revelation, that is, *apokalypsys*, in a reasonable and disciplined form would be the very denial of its significance. It means that it is that which cannot be controlled or reasoned about insofar as it is an incision into reason itself. By this it is not meant that it is

---

1. Käsemann, *New Testament Questions of Today*, 102.
2. Bultmann, *Presence of Eternity*, 31f.
3. Käsemann, *New Testament Questions of Today*, 107–10 nn. *, 1, 2.

irrational but that it defies the well behaved patterns by which rationality is regimented. To explain the apocalyptic would be tantamount to revealing the revelation, which would be the undoing of revelation as such, showing it to be no revelation but a predictable outcome. To explain revelation in a book (or in a movie) is to undo it by surrendering presence and imposing a re-presentation. There was more than a Lutheran penchant in Käsemann when he writes what is not off the mark if applied to Luther himself:

> Jesus is obviously speaking of the coming of the *basileia* in a sense different than that of the Baptist and of contemporary Judaism; his reference is not only or primarily to an end of the world which can in principle be dated within chronological time. This means, however, that the alternative—so useful in other contexts—of a present or future eschatology becomes, ultimately in the strict sense, useless when applied to the message of Jesus.[4]

As it happens in the apocalyptic literature, the apocalyptic as such cannot be framed. The apocalypse is not scheduled in any calendar or located somewhere. It is an event that happens, and this verb must be rendered in the present tense. It is something near and not distant, but not quite present, and yet close enough for its reality not to be represented.

To speak or to write about the apocalypse can only be done by using hyperboles, something that is out of the ordinary that insinuates itself as a grotesque dissonance, a cacophony in the course of a suave melody. The hyperbolic language and imagery of apocalypticism is the recourse to a figurative language that borders the nonsensical in order to somehow insinuate an event extraordinaire. In the words of Luther, it is like faith in Christ, which is "the most arduous of all things, for it is a being taken away (*raptus et translacio*) from all things of sense, within and without, into the invisible, the most high and incomprehensible God."[5] *Translacio* and *raptus* cannot be represented. They belong to experience. To something that has to be lived through. So, this is the problem with texts that express the apocalyptic event. By definition they are self-referential.

Apocalyptics was an antique genre that disturbed a well-organized cosmos that through the time of the Reformation was paradigmatically accepted. Apocalypse was something out of the ordinary that broke with well-established patterns of how events should take place. This completely changes by the time of the Reformation in which neither was the science of the day on the firm grounds of the pillars of the cosmos, nor were the

---

4. Ibid., 112.
5. WA 57/III, 144, 10–12.

dogmas of the church in stable and unshakeable grounds. Much was happening of significant apocalyptic import.

By the middle of the last century, Jacob Taubes wrote a dissertation titled *Occidental Eschatology*[6] in which he argued that Western eschatology was brewed in the slow distillery of its history that blended the philosophical tradition of classical Greek antiquity with its gnostic persuasion and the Jewish apocalyptic as developed in the inter-testament period. However, this process was arrested by old mythological cosmologies and Ptolemaic geocentric astronomy. According to these influences that were dominant through the medieval period, eschatology as in the end of the world was conceived as the earthly conformity to the heavens above. It was with Copernicus' *De Revolutionibus* published in 1543 (under the sponsorship of the Lutheran theologian Andreas Osiander) that a new way of understanding the cosmos came to fruition. It is not a coincidence that the Copernican revolution is contemporaneous with Reformation. However, what Copernicus came to demonstrate with his work was already in gestation, giving rise to an eschatology that no longer harmonized with the old cosmology. An active God working in and through history brought about a change in the understanding of eschatology. It was no longer an imitation of immutable celestial spheres but as divine intervention in time and space. As the heavenly spheres found themselves in revolution so the paradigm for thinking of God's intervention in the world went through a revolution of its own. Heavens became unstable.

The "Yet-Time"

Luther's apocalyptic is born of this conviction that God intrudes, and this intervention is not only the reversion of things in a symmetrical order as the apocalyptic is often portrayed. It is much more and something radically different. The reversion undoes symmetry. It is unstable. It is not an inversion of the order of things, but an incision. In a way it is what is called a "rapture" of the ways of the world. It is not about the "metrics" we can control.

Astrological speculations abounded at the time of Luther with the increasing awareness of influences of stars and their surprising locations in the constellations that were anomalous in the Ptolemaic worldview. Calculations about times and eras as well as their end were practiced in circles close to Luther. Known are the legends about his mocking comments in regard to Melanchthon's astrological speculations.[7]

6. Taubes, *Occidental Eschatology*.
7. Ludolphy, "Luther und die Astrologie."

Luther himself indulged on speculations about the time of the end. In 1541 he wrote a text called *Supputatio annorum mundi* (which received an enlarged edition in 1545) offering a calculation of the ages of the world and its supposed termination. In a Patristic chronological style he figured that 1540 corresponded to the year 5500, leaving another five hundred years before the eternal Shabbat.[8] But then he dismisses it also as a vain calculation, for God shortens (and lengthens) time at will. What matters is the now-time, or even better said the yet-time (*jtzt zeyt*), which is not even time or hour, but an all eternal moment (*ewiger Augenblick*) in which hell and heaven are decided by the presence or the absence of the Word.[9] The presence of the Word is eternity itself breaking into time as a now, but a now that is in time, and yet cannot be timed! It breaks through time. This apocalyptic intimation has a dialectical character if ever the word "dialectics" was etymologically rendered. It is the slanting word, the oblique incision into the lexicon (*dia-legō*).

This obliqueness cannot be dissociated from Luther's understanding of the modes of Christ's real presence, the incarnation, enfleshment, as we have it in his *Confession Concerning Christ's Supper* (1528). The *Confession* was Luther's own theological testimony written when he thought that his life was coming to a close. As I have articulated in earlier chapters, the first mode of presence refers to the historical Jesus, which was not a matter of contention by any party at the time of the Reformation (it would only become such after Reimarus and Lessing more than two centuries later laid the foundations for the historical-critical examination of the Scriptures). The second mode of presence was the one that prompted Luther's *Confession*. It is about Christ's real presence in the bread and the cup, instead of "representation" functioning as a symbolic remembering.[10] This was the point of dispute with the likes of Karlstadt, Zwingli, and Oecolampadius, each with his own way of circumventing the fantastic implications of "real presence." Besides it carried with itself a Roman Catholic flavor and metaphysical speculations ("transubstantiation") that the Reformers abhorred.

But the third mode of presence is the one that comes as a truly theologically unexpected move, but logically coherent with the argument hitherto developed. If Jesus is truly God according to his humanity, being one with God, and God is everywhere, then Christ Jesus is present everywhere (as in Luther's interpretation of the creedal placing of Christ at the "right

---

8. WA 53, 1–182; see also Torrance, *Kingdom and Church*, 21.

9. WA 10/III, 192, 20f.; cf. WA 33, 404ff. for the recurrent use of *stündlin* in his sixth sermon on John 7.

10. A figure of speech technically characterized eruditely by Zwingli as *alloiōsis*.

hand" of God as being everywhere). What is particular in what he wrote one year before his dispute with Zwingli in Marburg is about Christ's presence everywhere "even according to his humanity."[11] "Even according to his humanity" is the crucial point here. There is no presence without materiality, without something that has mass and body, taking up time and space, having thus some permanence and resilience.

This "third mode of presence" follows logically from what precedes. However, the interesting point is that it did not need to be there. It was superfluous, gratuitous, for Luther had taken care of the argument of his antagonists within the Reformation with the "second mode" for over two hundred pages. But it is this "third more of presence" that reveals Luther's own apocalyptic view of things and how it crystalizes in his entire Christology. Christ is everywhere, not spiritually as would be easy to assume (and it was by many of Luther's "radical" opponents in the Reformation movement), but according to his humanity. This is of decisive importance for according to his humanity means according to matter. The embodied, enfleshed humanity and that, finally for Luther, is what matters. There, where the world's crucible is, God is in the flesh, in the rock, in the tree in a way that borders pantheism, except that there is ambivalence in this presence. And this is Luther's signature. The God one may hold as Mary's babe can also be the one whose phantom will haunt us as a ghost. Luther's materialism cuts both ways. The masked God, the embodied, incarnate God holds this promise of all matter. What it reveals is all there is, the mask itself. This divine pantomime, a dancing of masks conveying the word that is never uttered, is all that there is.

Wherever pain and death are at stake and the resurrection is a promise, a new creation happens by the incision of the word in the yet-time. Or in the words of the Reformer himself: "No, comrade, wherever you place God for me, you must also place the humanity for me."[12] This was Luther's conviction that he grounded in his reading of Chalcedon, as he carefully discussed in *On the Councils and the Church* from 1539.

In his polemics with the Jews Luther insists that Christ the Messiah is not to be awaited, but that he has come. This sort of affirmation can be carried to anti-Semitic proportions if Luther is not read along the lines of Paul, the Jewish Pharisee for whom also presence is in history, even if not historically measurable. It is in history even when it is not of history. That the Messiah has come is not a passive participle. The Messiah, who brings history to

---

11. The fuller quote is: "Since he is a man . . . and apart from this man there is no God, it must follow that . . . everything is full of Christ through and through, even according to his humanity." LW 37:218.

12. LW 37:219.

an end is really present in word and sacrament which manifest itself in the midst of cross and suffering, that means in death, which is the only way to the resurrection. *Crux sola est nostra theologia*, the celebrated phrase of the early Luther (1518), has been explored and expanded to countless books on Luther's theology of the cross. This cross of Christ is identical to the cross we carry, as Regin Prenter argued persuasively.[13] What is being lifted up is not only its individual importance to our own condition but its social and ecological significance as well. God is there identified with the suffering of the human and of the earth, and indeed with death itself. There is one cross and it is plural.[14] There is one incision that crossed through the world's "schemes" (*schema*, 1 Cor 7:31; cf. Rom 12:2), its lexicon. It crosses through anything, anywhere as a "yet-event."

The apocalyptic is not a result of a derailed mind of the old Luther that resorted to a "vulgar and abusive" language.[15] It is also not the way in which his rhetoric resorted even to scatological, filthy language to underscore his argument, as Melanchthon already had vaguely suggested in his funeral oration at Luther's burial. The apocalyptic is at the beginning. To use Karl Kraus' known aphorism, "origin is the goal" (*Ursprung ist das Ziel*), the apocalyptic takes place at the beginning whenever creation and recreation happen. That is, when the Word becomes flesh, creation, humans and nature. For Luther, God is in matter or else God does not matter, to paraphrase Catherine Keller.[16]

The question that must be raised, however, is: what was the reason for Luther's embittered, obscene, and even scatological language? The approach to an answer needs to reverse the assumption that this kind of language was a testimony to his apocalyptic and idiosyncratic proclivities. The apocalyptic bent to the Reformer's work grew out of the fact that the proclaimed word conjured the appearance of figures, divine and demonic. The work of the devil, the *Teufelstreck*, was to oppose God's revelation. God's apocalypse is in the flesh, in matter, now, in the present, in *parousia*, which is in Greek and is precisely what presence means in Latin (*para-ousia/prae-esse*). The devil's work is that which veils God's Word, it is simultaneously *apousia*, the obfuscation of that which counts, of the essential by which we stand (*prae-esse*).

---

13. Prenter, *Luther's Theology of the Cross*.
14. I am indebted to Neal Anthony for this expression.
15. See, e.g., Edwards, *Luther's Last Battles*, 208.
16. "If God is immaterial, God doesn't matter." Keller, "Flesh of God," 91.

The Hiddenness of God

However, this dialectical move is at the root of what is properly apocalyptic, for in the inter-testament period, Jewish apocalyptic held the belief that the coming of the Messiah coincided with the arrival also of the naysayer, the detractor, the Antichrist. These "Jewish insights acquired down the centuries," writes Schillebeeckx, "are something [that] is impossible to dismiss. On the contrary, these already existing ideas helped the Jew, now become a Christian, to place in context and understand the life and destiny of the Master he already venerated and worshipped; they were not the cause of that veneration."[17] The disputes in the Gospels, particularly in Matthew, whether Jesus was the true Messiah or the detractor, impressed Luther very much. The indisposition of Luther to decide, in principle (and "in principle" here is decisive), what is divine and what is devilish is strictly connected to what Luther called the *deus absconditus*. In the hiddenness of God there is a shadow over shadow that theoretically points to the undecidability of whether it is God or the devil. "God cannot be God unless He first becomes a devil."[18]

Brian Gerrish, following a lead by Paul Althaus, has shown that the use of *"absconditus"* entails two irreducibly different meanings in Luther. One is the God hidden in the cross, the revealed God in its opposite, and the other the one that is hidden behind the cross, the terrifying *deus nudus*.[19] To use the expression of Gerhard Forde, this is the "God not preached,"[20] the terrifying image of the abyss. In keeping with the spirit of Luther, this is expressed with precision and eloquence by well-known Roman Catholic theologian David Tracy:

> The central dilemma for Christian self-understanding is that Luther *does* speak . . . of a second sense of hiddenness . . . as behind or even "beyond" the Word. At the very least, this literally awful, ambivalent sense of God's hiddenness can be so overwhelming that God is sometimes experienced as purely frightening, not tender, sometimes even as an impersonal reality—"it"—of sheer power and energy signified by such metaphors . . . as abyss, chasm, horror. . . . This hiddenness allows for a new theological recovery of apocalyptic as a fragmenting form of our own period. Indeed, to "let God be God again" is

---

17. Schillebeeckx, *Jesus: An Experiment in Christology*, 287–88.
18. See his commentary on Psalm 117, LW 14:31; WA 31/I, 249, 25f.
19. Gerrish, "'To the Unknown God': Luther and Calvin on the Hiddenness of God."
20. Forde, *Theology Is for Proclamation*, 13–37.

also to let that awesome and numinous strand of our common Christian heritage be heard again with the kind of clarity and courage that Luther found in his apocalyptic visions of history and nature alike, and in his willingness to dare to speak of God's hiddenness in the full sense.[21]

If apocalypse is rendered in English as "revelation," Luther's "apocalyptic" is really his sense of a *kalýptō*, a veiling of God's presence, of God's *parousia* in a terrifying *apousia*. This is what Tracy might have meant with "fragmenting": God's revelation as a cubist painting. Luther's fascination with the narrative of the revelation episode of Exodus 33 is telling. When Moses in Mount Sinai, frustrated with the unfaithfulness of his people and his own leadership, asks for God's own identity, i.e., God's glory or the divine face, God places him in a cleft of a rock and passed by preventing Moses from seeing him, except when he had passed by, and then Moses could see his "back" (NRSV). Luther, much less sensitive to politeness and correctness, translated this as God's behind (*hintennach*). The two meanings of *deus absconditus* correspond to the two meanings entailed in Luther's understanding of the *larvae dei*, the masks of God in and through which God's glory is hidden, accessible only through faith. The disparaged Luther's apocalyptic is really the result of the apocalypse being eclipsed while present; the revelation being veiled in its appearance.

As in the early apocalyptic of the inter-testament period, the opposites coincide, the Messiah comes along with the blasphemer, and so was it with Luther in his struggle between revelation and veiling. The very word revelation (as the Greek *apokalypsis*) entails these contradictory meanings. It may denote disclosure, but it can also mean to veil something again that had been disclosed or even laying another veil over what is already veiled. This is where the typical Lutheran expression of the *coincidentia oppositorum* is at play. And that is not an idiosyncrasy of the older Luther, but it is there from early on when cross and suffering became the navigating guide throughout his entire starry theological constellation.

In the so-called Second Wittenberg Sermon Luther acknowledges that what conjures God and demons is the word when proclaimed. "We should give free course to the Word and not add our works to it. We have the *ius verbi*, but not the *execution*. We should preach the Word, but the results must be left solely to God's good pleasure."[22] The right to speak is not a step

---

21. Tracy, "Form and Fragment," cited in Westhelle, *Scandalous God*, 57.
22. WA 10/3: 15; LW 51:76.

shorter of the deed, but precisely that which invokes the deed, a deed not hampered by our intended doing of it.[23]

And the consequences of just saying the Word alone reached some apocalyptic dimensions. Such were Luther's times. The Word did the work that the work could not do. And the same dynamics or "logic" is used in the distinction between Gospel and Law. The Gospel has already done what the Law still demands. Works and Law are the two concepts that Luther sought to dismantle theologically without surrendering their enduring importance. The apocalyptic in Luther is this incision breaking through work and law showing that in its fissures apocalypse takes place. Apocalyptic is therefore not eschatology "in heat," but eschatology being lived out in the awesome and awful stratification between heaven and earth, revealing what comes out when the Word happens and goodness is proclaimed. Appealing to the Copernican revolution, heaven and earth are in collision. And this is indeed a disaster (dis-aster to mean "no-star"), the disappearance of a guiding star that however brings about a miracle to behold.

The apocalyptic in Luther's theology is always this struggle between the light that reveals darkness and simultaneously veils it. And one does not exist without the other as long as the pilgrimage continues in the midst of the apocalypse. Or to use the words of Walter Benjamin, "The Messiah comes not only as the redeemer, he comes as the subduer of Antichrist. Only that historian [theologian] will have the gift of fanning the spark of hope in the past who is firmly convinced that *even the dead* will not be safe from the enemy if he wins." But then in a somber tone that unavoidably reminds one of Luther he adds, "And this enemy has not ceased to be victorious."[24]

---

23. Asendorf, *Eschatologie bei Luther*, 224ff., lifts up the church as being the *discrimen*, the decisive factor in Luther's apocalyptic. This is true as long as church is understood not as *Kirche* but as a community event.

24. Benjamin, "Theses on the Philosophy of History," VI, in *Illuminations*, 255.

Part Three

The Planet Luther: Transfigurations

12

Globalization and Fragmentation

Lutheran World Federation

> Turning and turning in the widening gyre
> The falcon cannot hear the falconer;
> Things fall apart; the centre cannot hold;
>
> . . . .
>
> Surely some revelation is at hand ...
>
> —William Butler Yeats[1]

If the myth of the Tower of Babel represents the antipode of the Pentecost, the story of the siege and destruction of Jericho is the counter-narrative of the building up of the walls of Jerusalem. In the first case we have the symbolic expression of the dialectics of dissemination and communication, in the second of deconstruction and totalizing. The simultaneity or the rapid oscillation between the two poles of both dialectical movements is a prevailing feature of late modern society. In the words of Anthony Giddens,

> It has become a commonplace to claim that modernity fragments, dissociates. Some have even presumed that such fragmentation marks the emergence of a novel phase of social development beyond modernity—a postmodern era. Yet the unifying features of modern institutions are just as central to

---

1. Yeats, "The Second Coming," in *Collected Poems*, 187.

modernity—especially in the phase of high modernity—as the disaggregating ones.²

At the theoretical level, moments of diastasis and of synthesis have been brought so close together that systems are erected almost as fast as they disintegrate. The legitimacy of systems of referentiality is both, and at the same time, the highest and the most contested value in late modernity.

Theologically this same movement reproduces itself in the continuing efforts of finding a universal foundation for religion or Christianity, and the equally militant attempt at eschewing any foundation. Also in theology the global village with its new missiological promises—as expressed in a Parliament of World Religions or in proposals for a global ethics—finds its counterpart in the old and renewed adage "to every tribe a scribe"—now phrased as the incommensurability of language-games.

Globalization and Fragmentation among Lutherans

For a particular confessional family or communion such as Lutheranism the same phenomenon can also be observed. After reaching a global expression as a result of massive European emigration and of the missionary efforts of the nineteenth century, Lutheranism first felt the impact of fragmentation with the breakdown of political colonialism. Does fragmentation follow globalization, or is it the other way around?

In the case of a confessional family, such as Lutheranism, there is a complicating factor. It supposes by definition a tightly defined common ground, the confessional writings that sustain a common language; or so we were led to believe. Does this sanction by its historical confessions exempt Lutheranism from the vicissitudes of this age? Examples to the contrary are legion, but one is emblematic. In the Helsinki Assembly of the Lutheran World Federation (LWF) in 1963, one of the main purposes was to discuss and approve a common statement on the meaning of "justification" for today—as the article by which the church stands or falls. However, the efforts at reaching a consensus ended in a major collapse. The assembly failed to adopt the document prepared by the Commission on Theology, even after it was redrafted. In response to the frustrated delegates, the chair of the said session assured all that, despite no agreement having been reached as to what justification meant, no one had challenged the "Unaltered Augsburg

---

2. Giddens, *Modernity and Self-Identity*, 27.

Confession."[3] Nonetheless, delegates from India and Tanganyika (now part of Tanzania) went on record asking why they should adhere to a confession issued in Germany in the sixteenth century if no agreement could be reached about its present meaning for the communion.[4] A common symbol of faith assumed to be of universal relevance and the fragmentation of its meaning subsisted side by side. In a sense, the appeal to the past rescued the present, but in another sense it obviated itself.

The LWF completes, on July 1, 2017, seventy years of existence. It was founded on this day in 1947 (at 12:25 p.m., the report tells us) in Lund, Sweden,[5] as the successor to the Lutheran World Convention, an almost exclusively North Atlantic organization. What are some shifts in the theological self-understanding of the LWF since its creation in the middle of the last century? The assemblies' proceedings indicate emphases and new trends in theological discussions. This does not mean, however, that theology in the Lutheran communion is done only or even mainly in and through assemblies. They are not the Lutheran magisterium, but they have been markers in the history of the role of theology in the Lutheran communion, defining emphases and magnifying trends. Since the assemblies are the privileged places where policies are drawn and strategic priorities are conceived, these are regarded as main events to diagnose the discontinuities in the theological self-understanding of the LWF in its attempt to be the expression of a global communion of churches.

Perusing the assemblies' reports a number of questions emerged as to the self-understanding of the communion. Who is the subject of the theological discourse? On which grounds is this subject constituted? What is the relationship between ecclesial, confessional, academic, and social factors in the definition of the theological agenda? What is the relation between the shifts in theological orientation and cultural changes in society? A genealogical approach instead of a historical or systematic one laying emphasis on types of attitudes and characteristic features of some periods is apt for this examination of the communion. A typology does not impart logic to history, but it reveals trends inherent to it.

Theology and Culture

The transformations the LWF went through since its inception reflect a general movement observable in the late modern culture in the West after

3. *Proceedings of the Fourth Assembly of the LWF, Helsinki,* 365.

4. Ibid., 294.

5. *Proceedings of the LWF Assembly, Lund, Sweden,* 21.

the Second World War. This is not an attempt at characterization of modern culture in general, except to define the post-WWII period as belonging to late modernity as a phase marked by a tremendous acceleration of the unifying and the disaggregating trends observable in modern societies. Four basic periods can be identified linking theological changes to cultural drifts.

The fifteen years that followed the Second World War were viewed as a period for building a sense of identity in world Lutheranism based on strong theoretical and confessional foundations. During this time the master narrative was the European Lutheran confessional heritage as expressed in academia. In Lund (1947), Anders Nygren expressed it with the motto that would symbolize the creation of the LWF: "Always forward toward Luther."[6] In his catch phrase the Swedish theologian was able to characterize both the confessional anchor and the sense of a progressive movement toward a common identity.

Building a sense of identity and finding a ground for legitimacy was by and large also the general mood in post-WWII Western culture. The reconstruction of the world order, the foundation of the United Nations, the large consensus that there were universal human rights, the Cold War with its implicit assumption that the world had to opt between competitive political systems (both entailing universal claims), the Third World being compelled to join an option for development and/or a socialist revolution that would usher its countries to the assumed universal status of the developed nations, the creation of the World Council of Churches in 1948—all of these features mark an era in which there was a certain ground for legitimacy. Legitimacy had a referentiality by which universal claims could be made; and even when contested, it was in the name of another referentiality. There were master narratives competing for the allegiance of humankind.

From the 1960s on this confidence in a referential basis for legitimacy was considerably corroded. There was a demise of master narratives that would grant legitimacy. Globalization is a name given to the phenomenon that marks simultaneously the dissolution of privileged spaces, of a geographical hierarchy, and the consciousness of an irreducible pluralism. Economic systems, financial structures, and communication networks are now crossing cyberspace at the speed of light and bringing the world closer; but this phenomenon will also cause a profound sense of a pervasive relativism and of increasing local basis (instead of universal foundations) for knowledge. Similarly, during this second period the LWF experienced the withering of a professorial type of theological orientation, matching the general cultural trend of holding as suspicious any theoretical system

6. Ibid., 140.

claiming universal validity. "Praxis," then "alterity" and "difference," are terms that gained currency. Students and not professors (or administrators) became the ones to reshape the university. Not by coincidence, in the Fifth Assembly of the LWF in Evian, 1970, a militant student outvoted an established European professor of theology in the dispute for a position in the Executive Committee.[7]

But if the 1960s and 1970s were marked by the paroxysmal hope that walls would fall down, it is in the 1980s that, paradoxically, the Cold War ends, and walls fall, but a new sense of conformism, of neoconservatism, makes its debut on the stage that earlier had displayed an enraged prophetic optimism. Neo-tribalism affirms the autochthonous values of cultures while national states are downsized in favor of a global market. A global market is mobile, and ever more strongly detached from national allegiances. It was thus the time for technicians, for experts in and consultants for microspheres where competence and effectiveness in administering the knowhow take the lead and seize the place once occupied first by academic professionalism and, in the subsequent phase, by social prophecy. Subsequently, in the 1990s through the current century, comes the awareness that the voices of the other need to be heard. This elicited a renewed sense of mission and witness to Lutheran theological inflections, followed by diaconal work.

From Dogmatic Argument to Contextual Reflection

In the history of the LWF since its inception, the role of theology changed in considerable ways emulating general cultural patterns. The trend goes from confessional unity to contextual pluralism. Any examination of the procedures of the assemblies and inter-assembly reports reveals that classical theological argumentation and dogmatic formulae have progressively disappeared from the documentation. Contextual reflections on a diverse set of issues have gained theological relevance. The semantic field of the theological discourse drifted away from its traditional center. Questions related to social justice, ecology, peace, ecumenism, racism, sexism, ageism, technology, and so forth have been substituted for the classical loci of Lutheran theology that dominated the language of the LWF until the middle of the 1960s. The attempts at defining Lutheran identity, which were prevalent in the first assemblies, are not absent from the later period, but their semantic value is different. In the Lund Assembly of 1947 or in Hannover in 1952, confessional Lutheran theological loci functioned in apologetic and

---

7. Lutheran World Fellowship Assembly, *Sent Into the World*, 138–39, 146.

foundational ways. When they appear in more recent documents or statements they are used frequently in a rhetorical and non-foundational sense.

Methodologically also there have been significant changes. The movement is from deductive procedures to inductive ones, and then more recently to a basic uncertainty about what a methodological procedure really is. To a large extent, methodological issues are themselves issues in dispute. While in Lund (1947) and Hannover (1952) the structure of the reports moved from confessional principles into theological definitions and then into particular recommendations, Evian (1970) and Dar-es-Salaam (1977) started from the contextual realities of the churches and economic, social, racial, gender, and age issues. Budapest (1984) and Curitiba (1990) were pressing the issue of globalization dealing mainly with the challenge of world religions and ecology, respectively. From the Assembly of Hong Kong (1997) followed by the ones in Winnipeg (2003) and Stuttgart (2010) changes from the preceding methodological and epistemological implication of the process of globalization in an attempt to reach out in mission and diaconal work is seen. In Hong Kong the theme was "In Christ Called to Witness." In Winnipeg it was "For the Healing of the World," while in Stuttgart the theme was "Give Us Our Daily Bread." This continued the move beyond the walls of identity and distinctiveness marked by significant ecumenical agreements: the signing of the "Joint Declaration on the Doctrine of Justification," (1999) and the moving reconciliation with the Mennonites in Stuttgart (2010), which theologically implied an acknowledgement of the abuses incurred by Lutheranism on Anabaptists and peace-churches.

Building Up and Breaking Down Walls

Transformations in the theological self-understanding of Lutheranism as expressed by the LWF are far from erratic. In these changes the same periods, marked by the assemblies, can be identified: the first goes from Lund (1947) to Helsinki (1963), the second from Helsinki to Dar-es-Salaam (1977), and the third from Dar-es-Salaam to Hong Kong (1997). The fourth period is from Hong Kong to Stuttgart (2010). The crucial moment in this development is the Evian Assembly in 1970 and its surrounding events.

From Lund (1947) to Helsinki (1963) there is the initial development of a crisis in theological conception. In Lund the theological self-understanding and identity was so evidently at the core of everything that theology was not even one of the five departments then created. (It would be created five years later in Hannover.) That theological identity was at the center could not have been more obvious with the creation of the other departments as planets, so to speak, whose orbits were by it determined. The metaphor used in Lund for the theological task was the all-encompassing need to rebuild the "ruined walls of Jerusalem" (cf. Neh 2). The wall metaphor gave expression to what the concerns really were. "Unity of faith [is] reflected in the common body of doctrine."[8] In Hannover (1952) this is still the dominant approach (the image of building or rebuilding is still kept), but tentative questions start to emerge as to the importance of the relation between theory and practice, between doctrine and existence.[9] In Minneapolis (1957) this becomes structurally formulated by the recommendation of both the Commission on Theology and on Liturgy that the latter be integrated into the former.[10] But still the doctrinal emphasis is dominant. The building of walls was still the theme. And the wall was to separate Lutheranism both from secularism and from an irresponsible ecumenism (the target being the Roman Catholic Church and, to a lesser extent, the Reformed tradition).

The crisis surfaced in Helsinki (1963) where the assembly put forth a statement on the doctrine of justification and its relevance for the contemporary world. In dispute were two views of the human condition. A hitherto uncontested fundamental biblical and confessional anthropology was challenged by a contextual anthropology ("circumstance" language is introduced, implying that context and experience had a role to play in theological reflection). A disputed diagnosis of the human condition led to the disagreement on the meaning of justification and brought the failure of the Commission on Theology to have its document on "justification" adopted by the assembly. This is in itself revealing: the discussion was not about the doctrine of justification as such, but the relation between justification and the human condition. The impasse happened at the methodological level implying the acknowledgement of an epistemological displacement. The time in which professional theologians of high reputation were able to lead and shape the theological identity of the LWF was withering and along with it went the strong sense of a defined confessional nucleus. Without direct reference to Lund, the wall metaphor was inverted: Christ "has broken down the wall of hostility" (cf. Eph 2:14).[11] The expression entails a double entendre: it not only makes a christological assertion but it also reveals the incapability of sustaining the building of the walls called for in Lund. Exit Jerusalem, enter Jericho.

---

8. *Proceedings, Lund*, 96, 99, 71.
9. *Proceedings of the Second Assembly of the LWF, Hannover, Germany*, 32, 143.
10. *Proceedings of the Third Assembly of the LWF, Minneapolis, Minnesota*, 102.
11. *Proceedings Helsinki*, 442–43.

Make Love, Not Theology

The second period, leading from Helsinki to Dar-es-Salaam (1977), marked a transitional stage, at the center of which was the controversial Evian Assembly in 1970. Much is known and debated about this assembly. Theology was conceived in a new way. If the meaning of theology were to be restricted to the sense it had in Lund, the Evian students' motto, "Make love, not theology!" was indicative of a fundamental shift. But it was not theology as such that would fade away. It was a new methodological approach signaling its advent. The new emphasis started to manifest itself in the anthropological emphasis observable in Helsinki (1963). Helsinki's introduction of anthropology as a critical and unsettled issue would then be radicalized in Evian's emphasis on sociology and politics. The increase of "two-thirds world" (a concept introduced at Evian) representation (which had been already called for in Helsinki) and the polemical decision to change the venue from the host country Porto Alegre, Brazil (due to the suppression of human rights in the country) brought to the agenda questions like human rights, poverty, racism, sexism, and so forth. The unifying center for theological reasoning drifts to new locations.

Two of the world's leading theologians present at the Evian assembly—Heinz Eduard Tödt from Germany and Gustaf Wingren from Sweden—changed the nature of the theological contribution as it was known in the LWF until then. A new tone with respect to the confessional heritage was introduced. In Tödt's keynote address Luther was criticized for having the very motivating quest of his theology: How can I find a gracious God? Tödt's argument was that Luther's quest for a gracious God was conceived within a sordid monastic context by an "isolated monk" with a "deeply anxious conscience" and should not be "used, therefore, as the leading motif either for theology or for preaching."[12]

Wingren, in turn, took a drastic hermeneutical stance and proposed that article VII of the Augsburg Confession offered the freedom for "more than merely 'unity of churches.'"[13] He then made a significant and debated proposal for the LWF to support the nomination of the Brazilian Roman Catholic Archbishop and human rights activist Helder Câmara for the Nobel Prize (the proposal was later adopted as a resolution by the Council[14]). A socio-politically informed theology was to dominate the Department of Studies in the following period, exemplified by the multi-volume

---

12. Lutheran World Fellowship Assembly, *Sent Into the World*, 32.
13. Quoted in Scaer, *Lutheran World Federation Today*, 23.
14. Lutheran World Fellowship Assembly, *Sent Into the World*, 145–146.

study on "The Identity of the Church and Its Service to the Whole Human Being," published by the Department of Studies in the middle 1970s. The understanding of mission as service to the world reverted definitely to the wall metaphor of Lund.

This trend culminates in Dar-es-Salaam's discussion on *status confessionis* in relation to apartheid in South Africa.[15] The best illustration for the new tone in the discussions and the culmination of this period was given in Dar-es-Salaam by Dr. Manas Buthelezi. The South African called for new confessional barriers, now being drawn along social, political, and racial divisions: "The drawing of a new confession is a matter of a redefinition of boundaries within which the unity of the church is possible."[16] The cycle is completed: the Lund motif, the wall metaphor, returns in Dar-es-Salaam. The role of theology returned to the ecclesiological concentration. But if at Lund confessional and doctrinal unity was conceived to strengthen the identity of Lutheranism, in the 1970s this identity had to be reinvented from the concrete social, economic, political, and ecclesial experiences of the churches worldwide, going, on the one hand, beyond the institutional churches—as Wingren suggested. Yet, on the other hand, it redefined boundaries that traditional theological discussions did not detect—as the resolution on *status confessionis* exemplified. The significant critical confrontations that had to be faced in the first period—secularism and a hasty ecumenism—were now the significant positive and welcomed challenges.

In the period leading to Curitiba (1990) the contextual concern of the theological task is brought to fruition in a department that addresses questions that go from worship to social systems, passing through education, women's issues, youth, ecumenism, and encounter with other faiths and ideologies. If this seems to be a theological inflation, it represents also a significant fragmentation in the theological agenda. Normative and confessional issues give place to a pluralistic conversation where voices of the Third World start to emerge with more consistency. If in the first period foundational confessional questions were dominant, the second provocatively led to a methodological shift and a relocation of the semantic field of the theological discourse. In the third period, which started with the predominance of an inductive methodology, the question was again largely on substantial issues—still related to social, political, racial, and gender issues, but much more focused on the concrete ecclesial experiences of the different churches.

---

15. Lutheran World Fellowship Assembly, *In Christ, a New Community*, 180.
16. Ibid., 93.

The Sage, the Prophet, and the Other

A review of history, moving from unity to fragmentation, is called for here. The *first* period can be defined by its emphasis on doctrinal unity. It can be characterized as having the role of theology interpreted in terms of providing a dogmatic foundation for the unity and the mission of the Lutheran family. A look at the methodological structure of the proceedings in Lund makes this clear. By and large, the argumentation is professional and academic. It moves from principles to definitions and then to practical (missiological) applications. The spokespersons (who were actually spokesmen!) for theological affirmations, were for the most part professors from Germany or Scandinavia who brought their academic approach and credentials into the theological practice of the LWF. Theological professional competence in the tradition of established European universities was a requirement to enter into the conversation. The Luther Congress founded in 1956 gathered the theological academic resources to lend its support to the LWF's theological identity and offered to buttress the confessional walls. The subjects of the theological discourse are the "sages." The sages are those who speak the truth as foundation, the ground for what is. With a look from the outside, the sage describes what the case is and suggests the answers that will convey identity and foster unity. The sage defines.

The *second* period is marked by prophetic denunciation and signals the crisis of the model dominant in the first period. The crisis announced itself when European theologians were no longer able to accept a common statement even on the doctrinal core of Lutheranism, the doctrine of justification. Helsinki could be seen as a premonition of the dramatic events that would shake Europe, and so also the LWF, in the 1960s, with the Evian assembly in 1970 as its culmination. There, the still dominant Europeans, joined to a certain extent by the "third block" (the United States), would raise their prophetic voices in denouncing injustices in the world. The change of the assembly venue in the last minute is highly emblematic. It was the North Atlantic world from outside that was raising the prophetic voice of denunciation threatening to boycott the Fifth Assembly if it were to be held, as planned, in Brazil. The prophet takes the place of the sage— standing, however, still outside of an alienated condition. Prophets are able to discern better what is taking place inside. They are the seers in a world in which even the victims don't realize the fate that besets them. Contrary to the sage, the prophet is not an enunciator of what is, but of denouncing the *status quo* and announcing what ought to be. The new definitions of *status confessionis*, as they came to be discussed in Evian and defined in Dar-es-Salaam,[17] emerge precisely after no agreement on the *articulus stantis aut cadentis* (the doctrine of justification by which all teachings stand or fall) had been reached in the 1963 Helsinki assembly! While the sage pontificates, the prophet proclaims.

The *third* period can be defined as a moment of global fragmentation. What distinguishes the third period from the second is again a change in the subject of the theological discourse. Theological voices from the Third World start to appear with more consistency in the conversation. I believe that this shift was already announced in the context of the Resolution on Human Rights at Evian. The text originally submitted had a clear prophetic tone. It looked at the world in which human rights were being violated from outside and denounced it. The Brazilian situation was used as the exemplary case. A heated debate followed until a compromise was reached by the so-called Marshall Resolution (named after Robert Marshall, then president of the Lutheran Church in America) that redrafted the document to include a confession that no one has the right to point the finger at another, for "the hands of oppression in any country receive their support from many sources, so that the blame must be shared by virtually all of us."[18] This started a shift in the prevailing prophetic tone surrounding Evian by overtly admitting that, if the responsibility must be shared by all, the right to enter the theological conversation also had to be for all.

Obviously, this brought along a new sense of democratic participation and representation, as it also signified the eclipse of the hegemony of the professional academicians as well as a fragmentation in the theological conversation. This new trend was announced in Curitiba (1990) by both the self-understanding of the LWF as a communion and the restructuring of the organization which downsized the Department of Studies to four desks. The latter move can be interpreted in one sense as a return to a more traditional view of the task of theology. But, as worldwide representation increased, the new Department for Theology and Studies had less of a teaching and overseeing role (as it would have had in Lund or Hannover) and more of a catalystic function, gathering the pluralistic expressions of Lutheran churches in the world.

If the third period may be represented as a centripetal movement in which voices from the peripheries of the world began to manifest themselves, the *fourth* phase represents a centrifugal process. No longer was it listening to the "cry of my people," but reaching them where they are in mission and diaconal service. It was no longer a question of reforming theology

---

17. Ibid., 180.
18. Lutheran World Fellowship Assembly, *Sent Into the World*, 148.

but transforming the life of people, in particular the most vulnerable. The recognition that Lutheranism is migrating *en masse* to the South means not only that the majority of Lutherans in the world are about to be found in latitudes that do not have a long Lutheran tradition as in Europe or even the United States.[19] What is more important is that this majority that is coming into being live in places where they are in the minority, tiny minorities in fact, confronted by other denominations and religions. Subjacent to this situation is an understanding of the church more along the simile of the yeast in the dough or the salt of the earth—something completely different from the folk-churches' challenges of European Lutheranism. Thus we have the themes of "healing" in Winnipeg (2003) and "feeding the poor" in Stuttgart (2010). The restructured LWF after the assembly at Curitiba rendered theology as the poor department receiving only a fraction of the funds previously assigned. Later, theology even lost its condition of being a department to become a committee within the newly formed Department for Theology and Public Witness. The whole department, of which theology is a commission, receives about 1.3 percent of the total funds allotted to the three departments.

Kenosis and *Communio*

What has been described has also been seen as a sort of theological *kenosis*. But the lamented demise of any historical reality is often the result of a view that takes the historical definition of the past and protects it into the future, failing to realize that what seems to have disappeared has only moved outside of the past's field of vision. This can be exemplified by an observer's remark at Evian that the sanction given to the so-called union negotiations (allowing united churches, i.e., those that bring together the Lutheran and the Reformed traditions, to affiliate with the LWF), which passed in plenary on July 22, 1970 (at 4:15 p.m. on that day, as reported by the observer), represented at that very minute the death of Lutheranism on a worldwide basis.[20] Obviously, this observation is easily understandable if one is restricted to the theological self-understanding of Lund. The important thing is to try to define the new ways a theological self-understanding is

---

19. There were massive waves of Lutheran immigrants from Germany and Scandinavia beginning in the seventeenth century, but particularly from the nineteenth century through the middle of the twentieth.

20. Scaer, *Lutheran World Federation Today*, 41. Scaer was a theological observer of the Lutheran Church-Missouri Synod, a nonmember church.

taking shape. World Lutheranism did not disappear but continued, exactly by owning the new dimensions theology took.

In a sense, since the Curitiba restructuring, the LWF has conceived the role of theology as requiring again the foundationalism that characterized theological endeavors at its inception. But the presuppositions are no longer given. This has resulted in a certain ambiguity that was conceptualized by the former Commission on Studies as a necessary complementary task: (*a*) to provoke a spiral effect in all the work of the LWF, guiding and monitoring its programs and the theologies of the *communio*, and (*b*) to serve as a catalyst and coordinator for theological discussions in and among the diverse churches.[21] These two tasks, clearly meant as complementary charges, are in fact not so easy to put together. They even undermine each other at least in methodological terms. But it is exactly this contradictory coexistence that characterizes the present theological situation. While the second task (being a catalyst) represents a continuation from the previous agenda, the one born in the 1970s and affirmed in the 1980s, the first one (the centrifugal effect) attempts to retrieve the foundational agenda of the first period. In fact the new title of the Department for "Theology and Studies" (as it was named after Curitiba) reveals the concern of merging the first period's Department on "Theology" with the second period's Department of "Studies."

In its 1995 meeting in Windhoek, Namibia, the Executive Council of the LWF received a document titled "Ten Theses on the Role of Theology in the LWF," prepared by the Program Committee for Theology and Studies. Theses 6 and 7 set the tone for the way theology should be defined and practiced:

> 6. In the history of the LWF as a communion of churches, the awareness of the tension between the gospel that holds us together, and the diversity by which we express it, grew as creative challenge for both the self-understanding of the LWF as a communion and its theological practice.
>
> 7. This challenge offers new opportunities for the exercise of theology in the LWF through which the communion will be promoted if, and only if, these characteristics of theological practice are followed: a) the LWF offers itself as a place for different articulations of diverse experiences; b) as a catalyst for innovation within theologies in different contexts; and c) as a guarantor of both the diversity and of the necessity of expressing commonalities.

---

21. *Theology in the LWF: Legacy Document of the Commission on Studies.*

With this theological charter the LWF moved into its assembly in Hong Kong. With still greater pluralism in the conversation within global Lutheranism, and a deeper pursuance of identity now challenged by other religions, the assembly of 1997 moved outwards, which was expressed in its theme "In Christ Called to Witness." That the polar opposites of greater pluralism and deeper pursuance of identity appear simultaneously is what links Lutheran theology to our late modern condition. The diaconal emphasis of the subsequent assemblies (Winnipeg in 2003, and Stuttgart in 2010), together with the celebrations of ecumenical agreements seem to suggest that the tension between pluralism and identity is going to be addressed as a practical issue in outreach and service.

Whether this is a captivity to a form of assistentialism or a promise of overcoming the theory-praxis divide depends now on how communion is understood. The *communio* ecclesiology has joined Lutheranism to other traditional confessional families. The question is whether it will also be expressed as a *communio* theology, a theology that incorporates in its practice the awareness that it is done neither before nor after Pentecost, neither before nor after Babel, but in the midst of the fragile balance of the Spirit that scatters and draws together. If something is to be learned it is that we don't have the right to despise the present, either in the name of an honorable past or for the sake of utopian dreams. Between the discourses of the sage and of the prophet a semantic field is open to those inspired to speak the truth with boldness. And this is the plight of those who understand that fragmentation and globalization can also be simultaneous gifts of the Spirit.

13

Transfiguring Lutheranism

Displacing Tradition

The Displacement of Tradition: New Contexts

"NEW CONTEXTS" DESCRIBE THE places to which Lutheranism is moving. They are not traditionally Lutheran contexts, and definitely not the context in which Martin Luther lived and theologized five hundred years ago. "New contexts" are those in which Lutheranism and Luther himself were adopted centuries after the birth of the Reformer and in distant lands south and east of his homeland. Luther was a German from Saxony, which at the time could be described as a rather "backward," underdeveloped corner of Europe. As already reviewed above in Part One, the Reformer himself was aware of his social location and used to brag about being "an ignorant German" who was made fun of for not writing the tomes recognized as the standard of high theological scholarship. Above all, he was a pamphleteer, a man firmly rooted in his time, geography, and environment, and an occasional theologian, even as the occasion engulfed almost the entirety of his life. From these circumstances, some distinctive Lutheran theology and pastoral practices emerged. Even if these rapidly spread throughout northern Europe and developed a body of normative orthodoxy with its universal pretentions, comparable in its rigor to the erudite scholasticism that Luther abhorred and left behind, they were still bound to a particular and relatively homogenous context.

It took more or less three centuries until Lutheran theology and pastoral practices started to speak languages other than the central and Nordic European ones. This happened first on a minor scale, through the work of missionaries, and secondly, more massively, through the waves of immigration from northern and central Europe reaching the shores of the Americas.

Four centuries after the Reformation, at the turn of the twentieth century, just over a hundred years ago, the vast majority of Lutherans (more than 90 percent) were still to be found on the North Atlantic axis, namely, Germany, Scandinavia, and the United States. This was still very much the situation half a century later when the Lutheran World Federation (LWF) was founded in Lund, Sweden (1947). For the next two decades, LWF documents still referred to the "three blocks" that made up the visible constituency of the Federation: Germany, Scandinavia, and the United States.

So what about the new contexts, those places where the majority of Lutherans will soon be found? They were largely invisible, particularly with regard to their claim of being Lutheran. The "three blocks" still have the hegemony of defining and adjudicating what Lutheranism is. "Hegemony"[1] is a term used in the social sciences to describe a social formation in which a given group has the hold on power and the intellectual influence to provide leadership without having to resort to overt use of force to sustain its dominion. Those kept under the dominion of hegemony are the subalterns. Subalterns are those who are deprived of power and unable or prevented from exercising leadership.[2] In the case of the Lutheran communion, power was the money with which the "three blocks" financed LWF's operations, from World Service to Church Cooperation (precursor of the Department of Mission and Development) to Studies (precursor of the Department of Theology and Studies, and now subsumed under the Department of Theology and Public Witness). Intellectual leadership was provided by the unquestioned supremacy of the Western Enlightenment tradition and its influence on the sciences in general and theology in particular. Outside the "three blocks," there was no money to purchase a ticket for the fancy Lutheran cruise, nor did these "new contexts" master the etiquette deemed necessary to behave theologically in a "proper" manner. Etiquette here is the command of certain languages, familiarity with the concepts operating in the hegemonic discourse, agile dominion of the "Robert's Rules of Order" for effective participation in the parliamentary decision-making process, access to the huge amount of literature produced in the centers of Reformation studies, the critical edition of primary sources, and so on and so forth.

The "new contexts" lacked power and felt inadequate to provide intellectual leadership that could challenge Western academics and, worse,

---

1. The concept was introduced by Italian philosopher Antonio Gramsci. See *Gramsci Reader*, 422–24, and 249.

2. "Subaltern" is likewise a term coined by Gramsci. Cf. ibid., 210, and 351.

they constituted a tiny minority. Hegemony always presents itself as having universal validity, the rest is the rest, and the rest is at best heresy, or does not even reach the status of a heresy.

In his seminal work that opens the history of modern Protestant theology, *Glaubenslehre*, Friedrich Schleiermacher, reflecting on the missionary work in distant lands, discusses the impossibility of new heresies appearing in Christianity. As mentioned in part I, he condescendingly gives room for "religious affections of former times" in the new converts[3] but swiftly he dismisses any serious threat coming from that. Was he in for a surprise!

Schleiermacher was not a Lutheran, of course. In the eighteenth and nineteenth centuries, the situation in Lutheran circles was even more flippant. The debate was whether Jesus' Great Commission (Matt 28:19-20) was meant only for the first apostles (the position of Lutheran orthodoxy) or whether it extended to every generation of Christians (the position held by Pietism). If it were the former, it preempted any need for mission work in the traditional sense of reaching out to the Gentiles. But the latter would require missionary work. Nonetheless, unlike Schleiermacher, they did not even entertain the question of possible heresies creeping into the new converts' faith.

The situation in the LWF was thus a stalemate till the 1960s, when for the first time, through its Department of Studies, the LWF started to take an intentional look at the interface between Lutheran churches and societies around the globe, creating, unsurprisingly, a crisis within the hegemony. The crisis was still manageable, but heralded things to come.

Today, the LWF, which assembles some 95 percent of all those who claim the Lutheran heritage, comprises nearly 150 member churches, the majority of which are from the planetary South. In other words, Lutheranism is moving outside the North Atlantic axis. Most of these are small churches, but their membership makes up almost half of world Lutherans. They are now more than 45 percent and growing, while the "three blocks" remain at best stagnant, and in several places are registering declines in membership. Soon the planetary South will be home to the majority of Lutherans in the world.

This is only one aspect of this rapid transformation. Probably even more significant is the fact that unlike the contextual circumstances that set the agenda for the churches of the North, the planetary South has minority churches that are facing challenges not only from the traditional opponents of Lutheranism in the North Atlantic world (namely, the Roman Catholics and the Reformed), but from a number of other religions next to whom these

---

3. Schleiermacher, *Christian Faith*, 1:128.

Southern Lutherans exist. Additionally, they are witnessing the emergence of robust new forms of Christian piety expressed by the Pentecostal and Charismatic movements often within the ranks of the Lutheran churches.

These two factors—the growing number of Lutherans in the South, and the challenge they face from nontraditional neighbors, other faith traditions, and new emergent pieties—have implications for Lutheran theology and pastoral practice the breadth and depth of which we are only beginning to realize. To paraphrase Paul, "O hegemony, where is thy sting? O universal theology, where is thy victory?" Or, in the ironic words of a Brazilian poet, Vinicius de Moraes, "Ninguém é universal fora de seu quintal" (no one is universal outside their backyards).

This change, so radical and still far from having completed its entire revolution, significantly influences theology and is redrawing the face of Lutheranism (giving it a lift down, or a lift south, as it were). The changes to come are inevitable, as we shall see. This is not a triumphal paean: responsibility is increased, leadership needs to be provided and resources will have to be found from new sources. But meanwhile, who are those redefining the landscape of Lutheran theology? What is the claim to legitimacy that "new contexts" have? Which is the Lutheran badge? And these are very good questions for more than one reason.

Representation

A fifth-century theologian, Prosper of Aquitaine, proposed a rule for theologizing that has been influential as it is simply descriptive of what happens with good theology. He is often quoted as having said that "theology follows the liturgical practice" (*lex orandi, lex credendi*). Actually what he said is even more pertinent: "The prayer of the supplicant shall be the measuring stick of theological doctrine" (*ut legem credendi lex statuat supplicandi*).[4] The supplicant is the one who is under the weight of oppression, persecution, sin and trial. Although liberation theologies have reminded us of this, it was not their invention; it is an old church tradition. So what is this plea of the faithful supplicants in "new contexts" that presumably sets the agenda for theology? And why would that have to be cast in Lutheran lingo? Do we need to "import" Lutheran theological conceptions to express what is autochthonous, proper to these "new contexts"?

This is a complex problem because it first begs the questions of who is presenting or representing this agenda and how. One thing is the supplicants' plea; another is who speaks for them, who represents them. As we

---

4. Migne, *Patrologiae Cursus Completus*, 51:209.

have seen, the hegemonic theology of the North Atlantic world spoke on behalf of the supplicants and articulated their pleas. Consequently, the agenda was set in different variations of Luther's own well-known plea: "How do I find a merciful God?" But who says what this means, whose voice represents the plea from these "new contexts"? Hence, there are a set of questions pertaining to this specific issue that are left for us to examine first, namely: Who speaks for Lutheranism today? Who represents Lutheran theology and pastoral practice? What is its face, its ethnicity, its nationality, its class and caste? What languages and accents carry it? Who are the authorized spokespersons? Do we need to immerse ourselves in Luther's own context, his language, European history from the Middle Ages through the Enlightenment and beyond in order to represent Lutheranism or to be Lutheran in "new contexts"? What is its identity, what is proper to Lutheranism? Let us be blunt. Do we need the doctrine of justification and how it responded to medieval theories of atonement explained, and then incorporate it into our theological work? What will set our agenda, the agenda emerging from these "new contexts"?

These are not merely rhetorical questions, and finding an answer relevant to these "new contexts" is an awesome and humbling task. Awesome and humbling, because talking about context is in itself a treacherous enterprise! In her now classical essay "Can the Subaltern Speak?"[5] and in her in later works, the Indian philosopher and literary critic Gayatri Chakravorty Spivak develops a fascinating, albeit complex, argument discussing precisely this question of defining one's context, of producing a representation, an image of a context, of an experience. She begins by engaging some of the literature on the Hindu practice of *sati*, in which a recently widowed woman would immolate herself on her husband's funeral pyre. She probes the unexamined assumption of those that presume to know what the widow's context is, either in shunning the pyre or submitting to it. Spivak shows that there is a fundamental and irreconcilable distinction between that woman's experience, her actual context, the construction she makes of her identity, on the one hand, and the *representation* of the *sati* ritual when made by others in describing the woman and her place in the ritual. This representation by others, either when done by orthodox Hindus or by Western anthropologists and other colonial agents, inscribe the ritual into a discourse fraught with moral, religious, and political presuppositions. The one justifying the ritual will etch it within the traditional religious interpretation, while the one describing for a Western audience will likely cast it in

---

5. Spivak, "Can the Subaltern Speak?," 271–313. Cf. also her reevaluation of the article, in Spivak, *Critique of Postcolonial Reason*, 306–11.

terms of individual rights and inalienable freedom of the individual. But where is the woman in these discourses that reduce her to a gesture within a ritual that is either defended or decried?

Spivak's point is that when the widow is represented by a proxy, when someone wants to speak for her, or stage her context, paradoxically she loses her own voice and what remains is only a picture, or a gesture that defies translation and interpretation. In fact, we are not dealing with contexts as such, for they are unstable realities, in constant fluidity. From the time people inhabited caves, the act of representing is human. Otherwise, communication would not be possible. Nonetheless, when we represent something or someone, when we speak on behalf of a context, we are stabilizing that which is very unstable and fluid, we are producing an image that can be passed on as a commodity and communicated to other contexts. This is similar to a photo one takes of a landscape or a street market. It is never the same the moment after the flash goes off and it comes to us in another context always demarcated by a frame that the photographer chooses. And the choice is not only what to portray, but always also what to exclude from the frame of the picture, what is deemed irrelevant for what one wants to present.[6] One's communication to friends about a vacation trip, for instance, comes with a filter that brackets out innumerable other factors that are part of the experience, but will never enter the picture or be fully conveyed by it. Some contextual experiences, such as for instance speaking in tongues, invoking of spirits, apparitions or manifestations of the dead, are difficult or impossible to communicate because they have no correspondence or analogies in other contexts. What happens to them? They are filtered out, kept outside of the frame or, then, psychologized or dismissed as exotic fancy. This happens to every context, including these "new contexts."

Why is this important for us in "new contexts"? Because these have not only been defined by others, but have also been colonized by political, economic, ecclesial, and military powers, including also their symbolic and religious systems, which the colonial subjects, the subalterns, had no choice but to buy into, to adjust to, and negotiate with. Symbols, images, figures, concepts, and doctrine circulating on the market of representations became the tools available for the construction of identities in "new contexts"; they have thus been defined, codified, and filed.

---

6. This is exemplarily studied in Walter Benjamin, "The Work of Art in the Age of Mechanical Reproduction." Addressing film he phrases this reversal thus: "The audience's identification with the actor [*Darsteller*] is really an identification with the camera. Consequently the audience takes the position of the camera; its approach is that of testing. This is not the approach to which cult values [*Kultwerte*] may be exposed" (228f.).

So, what can we who have been colonized do? Should we not get rid of the symbolic system, with its imposed models of "democracy," "communism," or a given religion and instead use only autochthonous images, representations, rituals, and forms of governance? Why not get rid of a spurious legacy and imposed heritage and return to our roots, the aboriginal ground of our symbolic systems? Most "new contexts" were formerly under colonial rule. A postcolonial condition is one in which the colonial power no longer has direct military and/or political dominion but whose symbolic systems and institutions linger as a specter fed and nurtured by a global imperial economy. Once symbols and representations of a certain reality have been implanted in a given context, it is virtually impossible to extricate them. The question is how to make use of them. What is important is not so much how a context is being represented, or what images and symbols are being used, but who does the representation.

Transfiguration

If postcolonial theory has taught us anything then it is that it is a reflection on a practice, a practice of dealing with these haunting ghosts that we have grown accustomed to, for they have been with us for centuries. Such practice is the one of taking a symbolic figure that was part of a colonial project and investing it with new contextual meaning. In the words of Oswald de Andrade's *Anthropophagous Manifesto*, published in Brazil in 1928, "We made Christ be born in Bahia [a state known for representing Brazilian syncretic culture at its best] or in Belém of Pará [a city in the Amazon that is Portuguese for Bethlehem]."[7] The point is not to dismiss Christ because he came with the colonial powers, but to turn him into a figure that can be indigenized. The word *figure* (*figura*) is used to describe emblematic characters or events that—unlike concepts, symbols, and doctrines—are rooted, grounded in concrete historical circumstances. Figures have a genealogy, a place and a time to which they belong. In addition, figures are capable of migrating across time and space and to find roots in other characters or events. In the words of Erich Auerbach, figures establish "a connection between two events or persons, the first of which signifies not only itself but also the second, while the second encompasses or fulfills the first. The two poles of the figure are separate in time, but both, being real events or figures, are within time, within the stream of historical life."[8] When figures perform their migration

---

7. Andrade, "Manifesto Antropófago," 388.
8. Auerbach, *Scenes from Drama of European Literature*, 53.

they produce what Edward Said called a "contrapunctual"[9] dissonance. The figure becomes the host of contextual experiences different from the ones it was originally invested with but in a certain way is also consonant with. A figure is the catalyst of different experiences at different times and in different places. We can call this the practice of transfiguration. A figure that was part of a given context reemerges in another and in it is trans-figured.

Take the story of Jesus' transfiguration (Matt 17:1–13). The passage needs to be read in the context of the preceding one in which Jesus foretells his coming passion and Peter rebukes him. Unlike what the people said of Jesus being Elijah or one of the prophets—even the greatest one, Moses— Peter had just confessed him as the son of God. Right confession? Yes! It is the right confession but the wrong context! Jesus' retort, "Get behind me, Satan!" (Matt 16:23) was like saying, "Peter, don't flee from your context, here is Elijah, here is Moses, it is also about them, they are also in me and with me." That is precisely what happens in the narrative of the transfiguration. The figures of Moses and Elijah emerge from different times and contexts, and their own mantle, which charged them with historical and popular repute, is laid upon Jesus. Their figures were transmuted (*metemorphōthe* is the Greek word) to Jesus, and in him they again became alive and present. When the disciples remind him that the scribes said that Elijah must come before the Messiah, Jesus tells them that Elijah had already come and was not recognized. They realize that he was talking about John the Baptist. Now Jesus was also the new Moses, the liberator of the people. Here is this marginal Galilean claiming the staff of Moses when the high priests were those who sat in Moses' chair. This is contrapunctual, yet the melody was the same: liberation like in the Exodus. For the disciples, it was at that moment that Jesus became contextualized and his figure became the host of all the relevant and cherished experiences of that Jewish context. Jesus was not the "son of God" out of this world above the ambiguities of history. In that context, Jesus, the son of God, was rooted in the history of his people; he was not the pristine "son of God" as Peter believed. Jesus embodied the ambiguous and frail history of the context into which he was immersed.

Transfiguration is what postcolonial practice does. Consider these few examples from the history of Christianity. Christ, the mighty conqueror of the Crusades, of the Conquest, is transfigured into Jesus, our brother, the liberator, the companion on our journey and our struggle; he becomes our contemporary. The narrative of the exodus, used as a symbol by the Afrikaners in South Africa and by the US government in the southern United States to legitimize the expropriation of land from the Africans and the Mexicans,

---

9. See Said, *Culture and Imperialism*, 51, 259, passim.

is transfigured into a narrative that gives expression to struggle and longing for liberation from oppression and slavery. The Franciscan spirituality of the *via crucis* with its fourteen stations, each telling the story from Jesus in Gethsemane, his condemnation by Pilate, to his body being laid in the tomb, is transfigured from an exercise that often borders masochism into a liberating reflection on the present condition of the people when even a fifteenth station, depicting the Resurrection, is added.[10] Sometimes the transfiguration is so thorough that we even forget its hybrid origin.

Hic Rhodus, hic salta

In the fable from Aesop we have the legend of a boastful athlete who brags that he once achieved a stupendous long jump while in competition on the island of Rhodes. A bystander challenges him to dispense with the reports and simply repeat his accomplishment on the spot. This is the origin of the maxim *hic Rhodus, hic salta*, "Here is Rhodes, jump here!" Transfiguration issues a similar call: spare the report, forfeit the information and all alleged documentation; make it happen!

Confessionalisms boast similar claims and profess allegiance to Moses, Jesus, Paul, Augustine, or Luther, or else to the tradition that has been conveyed and preserved by the German, Scandinavian, or North American readings of them. Transfiguration calls for their words and deeds to be enacted in different contexts. It is important to honor tradition indeed, but in a similar way as Jesus took the mantel of Moses or Elijah upon himself or Luther regarded the Scriptures distinguishing what pertains to a context and what does not, between precepts that belong to other contexts and the gospel that makes itself present, that is *parousia*.[11]

Luther acknowledges the importance of reports and representations. We "read Moses for the beautiful examples of faith, of love, and of the cross, as shown in the fathers, Adam, Abel, Noah, Abraham, Isaac, Moses, and all the rest. From them we should learn to trust in God and love him. In turn there are also examples of the godless . . ."[12] These are figures;[13] they describe emblematic characters, as the ones Luther mentioned, or events, which unlike concepts and doctrines are rooted and belong to a context. Additionally, figures migrate and find roots in other characters or events. As mentioned earlier, the Exodus of the Israelites from Egypt is the figure of

---

10. See Westhelle, *Scandalous God*, 160–76.
11. LW 35:161–74.
12. LW 35:173.
13. Auerbach, "Figura," in *Scenes from Drama of European Literature*, 11–76.

many contemporary liberation struggles. Pharaoh is the figure for many oppressive and authoritarian rulers. Moses is the figure for revolutionary leaders. Peter is the figure for the papacy, Luther is a figure for resolute leadership, as in "here I stand," and so forth. But decisive is that figures cannot be left as reports from Rhodus, Sinai, Bethlehem, or Wittenberg, it must be reenacted here, in the new context.

Transfiguration is this procedure by which a figure from a given context has the potential for being a catalyst of experiences for other contexts, or when a figure from a given context embodies the spirit of figures from another context. This is the reason why we say that these contexts are hybrid. They inject autochthonous materials in what used to be an alien figure. Another example for transfiguration is that of Harriet Tubman. She was called the Moses of the abolitionist struggle due to her transformative role in the abolitionist movement and in bringing slaves from the South to the North along what was called the Underground Railroad. Transfiguration tells the history of how the past comes alive, is metamorphosed into the present contexts. The malady of the archive does precisely the opposite—dissolves the present into a dead past. In Luther, Paul and Augustine were indeed transfigured, but he did not *repeat* them; he took upon himself their mantle, but on his own skin, in his own context, in order to preach Christ for the people of his time. That is what he meant by the term "apostolic." In his own words: "Whatever does not teach Christ is not apostolic, even though St. Peter or St. Paul does the teaching. Again, whatever preaches Christ would be apostolic, even if Judas, Annas, Pilate, and Herod were doing it."[14] And the same that Luther said about the Scriptures must also be said about Luther. Luther's example, his figure can be emulated insofar as he preached the precious good news, the words of novelty, even when some of his teachings given to his "dear German people" are not for us, even as the example is useful.

Postcolonial theory suggests that there is nothing pure and pristine, we are all hybrids. "The universal word speaks only dialect," as Brazilian Roman Catholic Bishop Pedro Casaldáliga so often insisted.[15] The art of postcolonial resistance is really to trans-figure that which came as part of the colonial enterprise, and use it as a weapon of resistance, disavowing hegemony the monopoly over the discourse. Even the "Lutheran" discourse (and the corresponding missionary enterprise) was a colonial discourse which defined and represented the subaltern's plea. It went like this: "You are sinners under the threat of God's wrath, but I bring you the gospel of

---

14. LW 35:396.
15. The expression is from Pedro Casaldáliga, *Creio na justiça*, 211.

justification of the ungodly!" Now the postcolonial consciousness retorts: "You have misrepresented my plea," and the subaltern adds defiantly: "You don't even know what you are saying when you use the word 'Lutheran' in these contexts." Indeed!

On Being a Lutheran

I have already suggested that "Luther" or "Lutheranism" functions as a figure that was brought to colonial contexts as part of the missionary work and of the colonial enterprise as such. The question is whether this figure can be transfigured and, thus, catalyze experiences far removed in time and space from those that originally gave rise to it. For a figure to inspire such new experiences, it must have intrinsic features that make it attractive as a host in the process of transfiguration, as Elijah was to give a profile to John the Baptist, or Moses to Jesus.

As far as Luther is concerned, there are a number of motives that lend themselves to this purpose. Luther's rich but under-studied creation theology can become a catalyst to address the ecological crisis (creation as the living mask of God). Luther's harsh criticism of emerging financial capitalism is as pertinent in the time of the global market as it was in the sixteenth century. His recognition of the cross of Christ in the suffering of a crucified world is strikingly similar to the arguments of liberation theologians. Luther's emphasis on the vernacular as the means for theological communication is similar to the case of Latin during Luther's time and is as relevant today when English has become the lingua franca. Luther also saw the church (*ecclesia*) as an "order of creation" established by the institution of the Shabbat, belonging therefore to all humankind, not only to Christians.[16] *Ecclesia* stands roughly for what we call religion. This is what it means to be catholic, and radically so: Islam is also "church," Judaism is also "church," Hinduism is also "church," Shamanism is also "church," and so forth (the Christian church is a community of believers who gather around the word made flesh and the sacraments—that is its particular shape). Luther's argument for Christ's presence not only in the person of Jesus or in the sacrament of the altar but in the whole of creation, *according to the flesh*, closer to anything than anything is to itself,[17] is a surprisingly neglected issue in Luther studies done in the North Atlantic world, but is something already known by the aboriginal people in Australia.

---

16. See LW 1:80f.

17. WA 26, 335f.; LW 37:222f. Also quoted in Kolb and Wengert, *Book of Concord*, 610 (art. VII).

There are a number of issues in Luther that need to be rephrased if not rejected altogether, including his last stance on the peasant's revolt, his doubled-edged pronouncements on Jews and Muslims, his disregard for the Epistle of James. But this always happens in transfigurations. To take the example of Moses and Jesus, it was Luther himself who said that we need to have all of Moses in Jesus, but not all of Jesus in Moses.[18] Moses, as a metonymy for the text of the law, is the frame, the casing into which Christ is poured to be the living word.[19] In the process of transfiguration, the host figure is always enlarged and expanded. The original figure becomes *quasi* larger than life.

But what about the sacred cows of Lutheranism, such as the doctrine of justification of the ungodly, or the law–gospel dialectic, or even the two kingdoms doctrine? The problem here is that, contrary to the positive and the negative examples referred to above, these "doctrines" have become so reified that their contexts can hardly be detected; they are doctrines and no longer figures, no longer attached to their contexts, and thus also incapable of migrating to other contexts.

This brings me back to Proper of Aquitaine's rule for doing theology: the plea of the supplicant is the measuring stick for theological teaching. Luther's doctrine of justification, to take the most prominent example, can only be properly understood against the background of Luther's own afflictions and despair in knowing that he was not pleasing God to merit grace. His "discovery" of God's unmerited grace is the key that opened the deadlocked condition in which he found himself. When he succinctly described his theological method, he followed a common three step process, popular in medieval theology.[20] The two first steps that he described were prayer and meditation, making clear, however, that prayer included talking to and about God, while meditation was not a solitary pondering of things divine but reading and engaging books and other people in reflection. However, while in medieval theology the third step was blissful contemplation of the divine mystery (*contemplatio*), Luther made a radical change. The final and decisive step in becoming a theologian was not peaceful and idyllic contemplation, but on the contrary; it was struggle and being on trial (*tentatio, Anfechtung*). His own experience as an outcast, persecuted by religious and political powers, driven almost to madness by the occasional doubt that

---

18. "... habere Christum omnia Mosi, sed Mosen non omnia Christi . . ." WA Br 5, 409, 28.

19. The same quote above begins with this distinction that for Luther was the one between the art of "dialectics" and of "rhetoric": ". . . est coepi judicare, decalogum esse dialecticam euengelii, et euengelium rhetoricam decalogi . . ."

20. LW 34:283–88.

maybe he could be wrong, that is what he said made him the theologian he became. Experience, he said, is what makes a theologian,[21] and not any existential experience of angst! He was talking about undergoing concrete persecution and trial, being afflicted. This was the deadlock to which justification became the key that released him. Only having the key, without knowing the type of lock it fits, becomes an exercise in irrelevancy.

So, what does it mean to be a Lutheran in the new contexts which are not traditionally Lutheran, and being in the neighborhood of other faith traditions? How can we understand this relationship between the church being Lutheran and the contexts that are no longer of yore? Being a Lutheran cannot be seen as something that is separate or over against these new contexts. Being a Lutheran and for that matter the church itself can be understood only as a reality that is at the same time at ease and in tension between and amidst the new, diverge contexts. This is especially urgent considering the fact that we inhabit a world that is increasingly becoming religiously pluralistic and globalized. Adjacency becomes then a constitutive feature of the church as historically intended. The church cannot be an entity in and of itself and has never been. Not being of the world, it is still in the world. One cannot be a Lutheran apart from the multidimensional contexts—religious, political, economic, or cultural—that border and even inhabit one's own. We live in a world that is broken and damaged, but it is so in ways that need to be defined locally. And our identity as Lutherans does not lie in the laudatory proficiency in reciting articles from the Augsburg Confession but in our willingness to be vulnerable so that while being immersed in the traditions of the church our theologizing is one that allows the cries of the broken, the forsaken and the frail to interrupt our traditional listening so that God's voice might be heard.

Today, when talk of justification is bandied about lightly, I am reminded of a parable.[22] A man was given a key. A very special key, he was told, that would open the lock to the greatest treasure anyone could find, and pure joy and happiness would be unleashed. He believed in the assurance that the key was indeed the secret to the most beautiful life one could imagine. He tried the key in all the locks that were imprisoning his life, and the key did not fit any of them. But the key, he surmised, was so precious that he decided to construct a lock that would fit the key, and so the key would finally be of use. Indeed, the key unlocked the custom-made lock, but it did not open anything. When "justification" language is bandied about, it is like

---

21. LW 54:7.

22. I first heard this parable from my friend and colleague Professor Reinhard Hütter.

the key in the parable and people receive it only to construct locks to fit the key, which do not open anything other than the lock itself. In Luther's case, the key was so important because it opened a real lock that kept his life in fear and despair. Prosper's rule applies; it opens the gates of joy and peace. The key is a real gift if, and only if, it opens the lock that holds us captive. The doctrine of justification, or any other doctrine of the Lutheran church, is irrelevant if it does not fit the plea of the supplicant heart, the broken soul and the damaged life.

14

Lutheranism and Culture in the Americas

A Comparative Study

Prologue

LAKE WOBEGON, A FICTIONAL town in the northern Midwest of the United States, could be seen as the cultural symbol for American Lutheranism in the United States. It is a figment of imagination of the radio-show host, Garrison Keillor. In Keillor's sardonic words, Lake Wobegon is where "all the women are strong, all the men are good-looking, and all the children are above average," which is nothing but an ironic description of the overestimation of one's capabilities and accomplishments in comparison to others. Humorous and witty as Keillor's observations are, they are by and large a caricature of the core of the American Midwest, the place where many Scandinavian immigrants settled in the nineteenth century. But anywhere else in America people would roll their eyes if asked whether that was the Lutheranism they actually knew. Keillor mocks, with quite some gentle deference to it, conservative and pietistic Lutheranism. Only through the eyes of a stranger living in Minnesota or the Dakotas will one realize that Keillor's depiction of Lutheranism in the Midwest is not only a caricature, but that at times it becomes a realistic portrayal. The local culture of Lake Wobegon shaped the Lutheran community as much as the reverse is also the case.

Otherwise, however, the embracing of a cultural formation has evoked only a tepid response from the Lutherans. Interestingly, this cultural insecurity has its own theological grounding. Lutheranism has not shaped a cultural ethos in North America as, say, Baptists, Presbyterians, Evangelicals, Catholics, or Anglicans have done. And to this day, in the United States, the distinct mark to identify Lutherans is not by their confession but how they claim an identity for themselves by ethnic-national origins, namely,

Norwegians, Danes, Swedes, Finns, and Germans, even as they have been in North America for generations. Lutherans are halfhearted in their role of shaping a *sui generis* cultural ethos in these latitudes; and there is a significant theological reason for that, which I propose to examine.

In the case of Latin America, the situation is even more pathetic. Although the theological and academic influence of Lutheranism and of Lutherans is widely recognized, the popular perception is all but elusive. In the largest Lutheran churches in Latin America, which are the Evangelical Church of the Lutheran Confession in Brazil (IECLB) and the Evangelical Lutheran Church of Brazil (IELB) its presence in the southern part of Brazil has been prominent. But in the 2010 Brazilian national census neither of these churches is acknowledged among the religious options offered in the census questionnaire. Instead there are more than half a hundred options for one to choose and among them "Lutheran Pentecostal," "Evangelical Lutheran Guarani," and "Episcopal Lutheran," which do not represent any sizeable group or denomination. But the sizeable official churches are nowhere to be found. Engaging in this comparative analysis will allow me to better explain the halfhearted attitude of Lutheranism toward culture in the continents, south and north, with their different expressions.

The Lutheran Cipher

The use of the "Lutheran" epithet to describe an ecclesial formation that became common since the protest at the Diet of Speyer in 1529 has become a debated issue. Luther's famous disavowal in 1522 of the followers of the Reformation for calling themselves Lutherans is a position that he increasingly abandons to the point of completely owning the epithet to describe the movement launched by him.[1] However, outside of northern Europe the epithet was used not in the way Luther and his followers had hoped it would be; it carried pejorative connotations.

By the middle of the sixteenth century, even before Luther's death, his name became the established trope for heresy, particularly in Spain and Portugal, the first countries to launch the maritime explorations to reach the Americas, as well as other colonies on three continents. In the newly found continent, when the *autos-da-fé* were read (throughout much of the sixteenth century) at the condemnation and eventual execution of infidels, these very words were included in reference to the heretics: ". . . and they left this kingdom to become Lutherans."[2] No significant knowledge of Lutheran

---

1. See Kittelson, "Luther on Being 'Lutheran,'" 99–110.
2. Bastian, *Protestantismo y sociedad en Mexico*, 23. Later, the word *Calvinistic* was

writings and teachings has ever been evident until the waves of migrations reached the coasts of the newly found continent, starting in the seventeenth century and reaching its climax in the nineteenth and twentieth centuries. "Luther" and its derivatives ("Lutheran," "Lutheranism") were not proper names, but figures of speech that conveyed and denoted dissent, transgression . . . and freedom.[3] Even after the eventual acknowledgment of Luther as a denser historical figure and recognition of the movement named after him as an objective historical force to be dealt with—which, incidentally, was effectively undertaken by the Iberian Counter-Reformation—these terms did not stand for any confessional position; they were signifiers for rebellion and liberation.[4] And there is a reason for tracing its genealogy to the very theology of Luther and its initial impact.

In Europe, this initial impact was halted or at least masked by the Augsburg Religious Peace of 1555, which was epitomized by its motto, *cuius regio, eius religio* ("whose the realm, his the religion"). The religious peace did not bring back the moribund *corpus christianum* of the Middle Ages; instead it multiplied it by what we would nowadays call cloning; the Augsburg agreement reinstated the *corpus christianum*, only now in multiple midget copies of the original.

In what follows I argue that in the Americas Luther's understanding of the relation between religion and culture is more readily recognizable than on the continent that gave birth to the Reformation, even as this impact overseas was more indirect than direct. But what was the reason for this? In a region four times the size of Europe, religiously the colonial powers, both north and south, were so overwhelmingly homogenous—Protestantism in North America and Roman Catholicism in Latin America—that there was no need for (à la Augsburg) religious peace. However, by the same token, dissidence was possible in both north and south, because the idea of a cohesive body, and integrated kingdom ruled by Church and Empire, was very tenuous at best. From the time of early colonialism the political interests of the conquistadores, the Crown, and Rome often went in different and conflictive directions, yielding a common saying: "The King is in Spain, the Pope in Rome, and here we rule."

---

also added in the hyphenated form: "Lutheran-Calvinistic." See Bastian, *Protestantismo y modernidad latinoamericana*, 41–67.

3. Luther himself made his name into a trope by signing early letters as *Eleutherius*. Buchwald, "Martinus Eleutherius," 421–24. See Kittelson, "Luther on Being 'Lutheran.'"

4. Although, to my knowledge, the first theological response to Luther's diatribe against Erasmus, *The Bondage of the Will* (1525), was written by the infamous Ginés de Sepúlveda, *De fato et libero arbitrio* (1527). Sepúlveda defended the just war against and slavery of the Indians against Las Casas in the debate of Valladolid in 1550–51.

The words of the *autos-da-fé* ("they left this kingdom to become Lutherans") are indicative of at least the impact the Lutheran-led Reformation would have in the Americas. Just as Luther was not a fix-it man, Lutheranism was no repair shop to mend the wrongdoings in the "kingdom," but it was a cipher pointing to the fact that another world is possible, to quote the motto of the World Social Forum. Initially, it was not the doctrinal body of Lutheranism but its spirit that fed the imagination of Americans from south to north in striving for their independence and shaping a different ethos from the one the Iberian crowns—and later the French, the British, the Dutch, and, on a smaller scale, the Danes—had devised through their colonial enterprises. There is a spirit of Lutheranism that wrought the cultures in the Americas. But the procession of this spirit is twofold. It came with the Puritans seeking a land of religious freedom and prosperity in North America, while in Latin America it inspired movements of insurrection for independence from within, most of which was finally won in the nineteenth century. In the words of historian Richard Morse:

> It is not outlandish to suggest that we might find a fitting analogue to the Spanish American wars of independence in the Protestant Reformation. Both movements occurred within a far-flung, venerable Catholic institutional order that betrayed decadence at its upper levels. Both movements developed an uncoordinated pattern of dispersed and disparate revolt. Neither was heralded by a coherent body of revolutionary doctrine, and each improvised a wide range of "ideologies" under pressure of events.[5]

In North America the situation is not identical, as we shall see later, but has similar features, as Kenneth Burke argued long ago:

> In contrast with the [Roman Catholic] church's "organic theory," whereby one puts a growing social concern together with the toleration of *differences*, the Protestant sects [denominations] stressed the value of complete uniformity. Each time this uniformity was impaired, the sect [denomination] itself tended to split, with a new "uncompromising" offshoot reaffirming the need for a homogenous community, all members alike in status.[6]

And this peculiar Protestant "innovation" can be traced back to Luther's rejection of the medieval concept of the *corpus christianum*, the understanding that society is an organism that in its higher levels is grounded

---

5. Morse, *New World Soundings*, 108.
6. Burke, *Attitudes toward History*, 1:176.

in supernatural claims, while the lower belong to nature, being organically integrated and membership granted by the visible and public act of baptism. This conception of the *corpus christianum* attributed to worldly institutions, though finite, the presumption of being a direct representation of the spiritual head.[7] Anything or body that rebelled against this, any institutional dissent, meant leaving this orderly cosmos, this world, this "kingdom."

The End of the *Corpus Christianum*: Reframing the Three Estates

The use of the trope "Lutheran" happened to capture what the historical Luther was about in his criticism of the medieval order, removing the guarantees of the integrity of its body, offered by the verifiable sacrament of baptism, and substituting it by faith. Exit *corpus christianum*, enter *corpus fidelium*! There was no *jus divinum* guaranteeing the visible cohesiveness of this body. In earthly matters, namely, the social institutions, it was about *jus humanum*. This was consistently sustained by the Reformer's doctrine of vocation, the priesthood of all believers, and his teachings regarding the instituted divine mandates or orders (*Stände*) of the earthly régime, *ecclesia, oeconomia*, and *politia*. Thus the modern understanding of society was born—which, incidentally, is not the translation of the medieval *societas* that was still grounded in the idea of the *corpus christianum*.

Certainly Luther inherited the three estates classification from the Aristotelian-medieval conception, but reshaped their medieval frame by leveling these institutional orders, attributing to each a relative autonomy. Even in modern times, since the Industrial Revolution, when the household was split from modern economy—the domain of human sexual reproduction and sustenance severed from the real of economic production—the modern household and the economy still share the same essential relation to nature in what Hannah Arendt defined as the "urgency of life" in laboring, sexual reproduction, and consumption.[8] In *politia*, however, as in modern politics, what defines it is communicative action. "Only activity," argues Arendt, "goes on directly between [humans] without the intermediary of things or matter, [and this] corresponds to the human condition of plurality . . . This plurality is specifically the condition . . . of all political life."[9] And this includes all that

---

7. Küppers, "Luthers Dreihierarchienlehre," 361–74.

8. Arendt, *Human Condition*, 30, 99. Aware of the different time, Arendt, however, distinguishes labor from work. In an analogous way, Bonhoeffer distinguishes between marriage and labor; see his *Ethics*, 207–13.

9. Arendt, *Human Condition*, 7.

pertains to intersubjective relations, from formal politics, to civil society, through the web of modern electronic information networking.

Luther's use of the three instituted orders (with his simultaneous suspension of the notion of a *corpus christianum* holding them supernaturally and organically by the combined divine right of the church and empire) offers a view of the different possibilities of how a culture represents its own society. The difference lies in the fact that we are able to discern that there are distinct principles through which society can be represented and thus understand how it works. Under the scholastic idea of the *corpus christianum* there was no alternative for cultural representation; there is only one possible cosmic order as it was clear who held the power and divine right of representation, even if there were tensions between church and empire over this right. Dissent meant leaving this world, the orderly cosmos it purported, as the *autos-de-fé* had it.

Paul Tillich in his lectures on theology of culture offers some help in explaining that there are different principles at work in the two models, the medieval *corpus christianum* and early modern society. He distinguishes between meeting a *stranger*, on one hand, and an *estranged* one, on the other.[10] Tillich is discussing two different types of philosophy of religion, one being grounded in the Aristotelian cosmological argument as developed in Christianity by Thomas Aquinas, and the other on the basis of the ontological argument as presented by Augustine and the Franciscan school of the thirteenth century (Alexander of Hales, Bonaventure, and Matthew of Aquasparta).

Tillich's argument is elegant but complex. While his interest was in developing an explanation for two different forms of philosophy of religion, the discussion, however, applies also to cultural formations in general, where we meet others as *strangers* or *estranged* ones. In the case of the cosmological method, the other has to be deduced by visible evidence and then through abstraction and speculation one tries to reach that which lies behind and beyond perception. In this sense they are strangers.

The ontological approach, on the other hand, relies on the other as a priori given. It supposes that somehow we knew the strangers were us even before we met them, and so we encounter them as estranged from an ontological union that allows us to recognize them. Distinct from the ontological argument developed by Anselm, Augustine's is "neither an argument, nor does it deal with the existence of God."[11] "The divine substance is known in such a way that it cannot be thought not to be," Tillich quotes Alexander of

---

10. Tillich, *Theology of Culture*, 10–29.
11. Ibid., 15.

Hales.[12] And he adds, "And this Being (which is not *a* being) is pure actuality and therefore divine. We always see it but we do not always notice it; as we see everything in the light without always noticing the light as such."[13]

One of the most outstanding examples of these two approaches is the celebrated debate between Bartolomé de Las Casas and Juan Ginés de Sepúlveda, held in Valladolid in 1550. The issue was the human status of the natives the Iberians encountered upon their landfall in the New World. Las Casas assumed that the native habitants of the Americas were in principle "humans made in the image of God," a postulation that he did not care or need to prove; it was for him ontologically self-evident, as the being of God was for Augustine. In other words, for Las Casas the indigenous other was estranged from a basic ontological belonging. Sepúlveda, searching for the natives' stature in the cosmic order he presupposed, declared them strangers, as animals are to humans, in need of being "tamed and subjected to the empire of man."[14] It was not so much a question of who was right and who was wrong as it was a question of the different principles from which they departed to lay out their arguments. Given the presupposition, each argument could be sustained internally with certain coherence. The difference between meeting the other as God, the *primum esse*, or as a subaltern human is only the direction of the vector either argument takes. The logic is the same regardless of whether it moves upward or downward, for every other is the wholly other.[15]

Luther's doctrine of justification broke with the cosmological approach to otherness and grounded the knowledge of God in pure reception, in *vita passiva*, not in perception. This opened the possibility of developing alternative ways to engage the *vita activa*. There were different possibilities represented by the institutional orders. Each of them had to justify itself by the criteria that applied to it, but neither one could be justified *ex nihilo*. Justification was not granted by the operations in these institutions. It was left to repentant sinners, who are unable to justify themselves, even as they work, by divine mandate, to make just, reasonable, and equitable the stations of life in which their vocation is cast. This is the verve of Luther's understanding of justification by grace through faith; it did not belong to the visible *corpus christianum*, but to the *corpus fidelium*. The body of the faithful interlaces the institutional orders, but it is not reduced or caused by them, not even by the institution called *ecclesia*.

12. Ibid.
13. Ibid., 14.
14. Quoted in Romano, *Mecanismos da conquista colonial*, 84–85.
15. "Tout autre est tout autre." See Derrida, *Gift of Death*, particularly 82–88.

Commanding Paradigms: North and South

In these three estates or instituted orders we can frame Luther's understanding of culture. Culture is the human representation of itself and of its interrelations expressed in these three institutional orders. The true spiritual community, the hidden church, however, does not represent itself since it lives by the gift of grace alone; it is not active, but purely receptive. But the church as *ecclesia*, an earthly institutional and visible reality in its formation and constitution, borrows from the other two institutions, the *oeconomia* and the *politia*. As we shall examine in the following pages, it borrows from the *oeconomia* its structure and rationale for the administration of the sacraments; from *politia* it solicits the means necessary for the teaching and proclamation of the Word. In other words, *ecclesia* is a hybrid institution. These latter two, *oeconomia* and *politia*, are formative for the way Lutheranism relates to culture, contributes to it and is shaped by it in the Americas. The operative principle in each, by which representation is defined, is labor (*poiēsis*) for the *oeconomia* and interaction (*praxis*) for the *politia*.[16]

In Luther's *Lectures on Genesis* (1535-36) he distinctively isolates these three orders. Take, for example, his comments on Genesis 4:11-12, where he discusses the curses Cain receives. The first cuts his spiritual relation with God's glory. And then he continues: "In the second place, the earth is cursed, and this is the punishment that affects his [Cain's] domestic establishment [*poena oeconomica*]. The third punishment—that he is to be a wanderer . . . involves civil government [*poena politica*]."[17] These latter two dimensions refer, first, to our metabolic relationship with nature where we produce and reproduce ourselves through labor, and second, the relationship to one another in intersubjective communicative praxis or activity (to use Arendt's terminology). These form the two paradigms that since Western classical antiquity determined the framing of the procedures in managing worldly responsibilities.[18]

In the "economic" paradigm culture *represents* by offering a portrayal of what society actually is, without, obviously, being ontologically identical to it. It would be like when one says: "This is a Picasso," referring to one of his paintings. Cultures that operate with this sense of representation as the dominant way of presenting themselves work with what Richard Morse

---

16. See Part Four, chapter 22 for an elaboration of this. See also Westhelle, "Power and Politics," 284-300.

17. LW 1:294; WA 42: 127, 13-18.

18. For the formation and the role played by these paradigms in biblical literature and early Christian theology, see Agamben, *Kingdom and the Glory*, 1-16.

calls an "architectonic" principle in which the "house" (*oikos, domus*) is the given, an *edifice déjà construit*, a ready-made building.[19] The question is only to know in which quarters the inhabitants are lodged. There is room for all to belong, as long as they do not abandon the house, or "leave this kingdom," as the *autos-da-fé* phrased it. This is the ground of what Kenneth Burke called the capability for the "toleration of differences." But here is also where desire lurks. And it is driven by coveting a space that is not one's own, a room in the house, as it were, that does not belong to one by right, or remodeling the house to fit new needs. Freedom is defined positively as the choice to be bound to the place one is assigned to, as it were, by nature.

In the "political" paradigm culture *represents* itself not by offering its objective portrayal, but by proxy, by a standing in the stead of (*Stellvertreter*), or speaking for, as in politics where representation is won by delegation, where unity is achieved in flexible processes of democratic procedures. There is no one presentation of culture that stands for the whole by itself. It depends on the conditional agreement that a circumstantial enactment holds sway by a tenuous agreement. Unity is forged out of an unstable plurality. As the US coins declare—*e pluribus unum*, "from the many, one"—in the "economic" paradigm the opposite is true—*ex uno plures*, "from one, the many."[20] For example, no US president would be able to say what is attributed to Napoleon: *je suis l'état*, "I am the state"; nor would any artist in the north of the continent say what the Brazilian composer Heitor Villa-Lobos said: *o folclore sou eu*, "I am the folklore."

This is the religious and philosophical basis of what I have called the "political" paradigm. In the other case, it is inversed; unity is the presupposition. The goal is to bring back or reunite those who have been estranged from the "household" (the *oikos*) in which all should naturally belong. Those who have stranded away need to be reincorporated or else be extirpated. Democracy is not the point, but acceptance of one's place in the pre-existing construction. This is the basis of the "economic" paradigm. Yet the two modes of cultural formation, since the decapitation of the *corpus christianum*, operate ultimately with an ontological argument.

These two paradigms for culture in society largely overlap and it has become distinctively difficult to set them apart. However, in a broad generalization, even if it were for analytical reasons, one can say that in Latin America, from Mexico to the southern tip of Chile, there has been a predominance of the "economic" paradigm, while in North America the "political" paradigm has been prevalent. And this difference—even when

---

19. Morse, *New World Soundings*, 104.
20. See ibid., 110.

enlightened by Luther's understanding of the three institutional orders—molds Lutheranism, while Lutheran theology and ecclesiology take different shapes and also influence culture depending on the dominant paradigm under which they operate.

The "political" representational principle that accounts for much of what happens in North American Lutheranism in its search to find a unity and forge a compromise over different factions and traditions (often resulting in splintering ecclesial formations) betrays an ecclesiology and theology that has yielded to the "political" paradigm, and is often held captive to it.[21] However this does not describe Lutheranism that grows out of defying the authority of political régimes (i.e., reorganizing the household) or uncritically adjusting to them (accepting the rules of the house as it stands). And this is a characteristic mark that has shaped Lutheranism and its cultural impact south of the Rio Grande where the "economic" paradigm is dominant.[22]

What has been attempted so far is to frame the relationship between Lutheranism and culture in the Americas that define otherness, aided by Luther's own way of describing institutional shapes. The genius of Lutheranism provides a frame to understand these two types of cultural formation without attaching ultimate value to either.

The Elusive Lure of Lutheranism

Mark Noll in his essay on American Lutherans[23] points out three contributions of Lutheranism to American society: First, Luther's Augustinian approach to human nature that counters North American optimism; second, the objectivity of salvation that goes against the rampant subjectivism; and, finally, the "gift of ambiguity." The first contribution is the one that offers impetus to the "political" paradigm. Interest needs to be kept in check. The second, that salvation is an objective reality, lends its support toward the "economic" paradigm with its emphasis on the objective results of the gift

---

21. See Niebuhr, *Social Sources of Denominationalism*, 130. However, a stronger investment in the episcopal office in significant segments of the ELCA betrays a tendency toward the economic paradigm.

22. The glaring exception is the majority of lay Lutherans in Chile under the Pinochet régime. However, nearly all of the pastors, under the leadership of Bishop Helmut Frenz, resisted, resulting in the majority, under lay leadership, forming a new Lutheran body. But unable to get Lutheran pastors to serve them, they got independent evangelical pastors from Switzerland to serve them. See Frenz, *Mi vida chilena: Soliadriedad con los oprimidos*.

23. Noll, "American Lutherans Yesterday and Today," 337–47.

of grace. Here language becomes revealing. The preference for "freedom" or "liberty" defined in an interpersonal and subjective sense in North American Lutheranism is countered by the more objective language of "liberation" and "emancipation" with strong economic overtones. The third, the "gift of ambiguity," is the crucial point because neither of the two—economic or political—provides ground for ultimate certainty. This is the reason for the ecclesiological weakness of Lutheranism with its original rejection of founding itself unambiguously either in an irresistible experience or else in an infallible church or Scripture. The true and hidden church remains an evasive reality that, even when borrowing its institutional formation from either paradigm, neither offers an ultimate ground for certainty.[24] The true church is present and it can never be re-presented.

The veritable Lutheran gift to the cultural formation is that it is never ultimately at home in either paradigm; even when one dominates the other looms as an alternative. Although North American Lutheranism gravitates toward the "political" one, it knows that it will never have its niche unambiguously there. The same is the case in Latin American Lutheranism's proclivity toward the "economic" paradigm where it is never at ease in going all the way to the ultimate consequences of the commanding patrimonial model. Yet the difference is still visible in the way Lutheranism interacts with culture in the different Americas. Even with regional and denominational variations[25] the tendencies prevail and with them the temptations of falling prey to the hegemonic cultural paradigm.

In conclusion, the recognition of the different modes of cultural representations and their relative autonomy accounts for different emphases Lutheranism takes and both can claim Luther's support. Nonetheless, by missing Luther's point about the validity of both and their relativity, what results or follows is a miscommunication between the two camps. Here are some examples. While Lutheranism in North America has laid emphasis on the "two kingdoms" theology, which has normally been framed within church-state relations and polity interests, in Latin America the emphasis has been on Luther's economic thought, his criticism of usury and the greedy desire that lead the rich to exploit the poor.[26] While Luther's political

---

24. See the instructive essay by Peter Berger, "On Lutheran Identity in America."

25. In Latin America the two largest regional church bodies that are members of the LWF (IERP in Argentina and IECLB in Brazil) might count as exceptions. However, historically these churches are united churches combining in their confessional stances Lutheran and Reformed elements, the latter being highly influenced by the "political" paradigm.

26. Rieth, "Luther on Greed," 336–51

texts receive special selective editions in North America,[27] Latin American theologians have focused on Luther's economic thought, and particularly on texts that have not received English translation as yet.[28] While Latin Americans go to the Marx of the *Capital* to guide them in reading society, in North America are those of the liberal tradition with emphasis on political relations, in which questions of gender and race set the agenda, and not the labor movement. Ecumenism in the North follows suit among Lutherans in which policies and doctrinal agreements for visible unity are emphasized and the lack of attention to, say, the Joint Declaration on the Doctrine of Justification by the part of the South is decried. In the South, ecumenical relations are driven by socioeconomic realities (the plight of the poor) and when consultants and representatives from the South are included in Faith and Order ("politically" driven) dialogues it is often for token motifs.

One interesting area of observation would be the outlook on environmental concerns. Until now the South has taken an "economic" slant while it is a "political" one in the North. But since the environment is about our relationship to the earth, the "economic" paradigm offers more analytical sources than the political one. It is not hard to see the need for more attention in the North to Cain's second curse that, according to Luther, is the punishment that affects Cain's *oeconomia*.

Meanwhile the church draws from both. It is a hybrid institution (as is the case of hospitals, prisons, airports, or shopping malls). It needs the "economic" paradigm to structure its theology and practice of the sacraments, that is, that God is encountered in relationship to the external stuff of the world, to water, the universal communicant among earth's ecosystems, bread and wine, gifts from nature and products of human labor. It needs also the "political" paradigm to frame its task of communicating the gospel in a world accursed by the law. But more importantly, it needs to remember that in midst of these realities it comes into being as an event prompted only by the sheer gift and favor of God's promise. The church is an event.[29] But it only happens in, with, and under *oeconomia* and *politia*, in, with, and under sacrament and the Word, yet not because of them. When and where this happens, there the Lutheran spirit is at work, even as the "Lutheran" trope is no longer the source of the scandal it once was.

27. For example *Luther—Selected Political Writings*, edited by J. M. Porter.

28. See Rieth, *"Habsucht" bei Martin Luther*; Altmann, *Luther and Liberation*, 101–12; and Westhelle, "Luther and Liberation." A case in point is a text that has not been translated into English but that has received extensive treatment by Latin Americans: "Admonition to Pastors to Preach against Usury" (1540). This text, which Karl Marx quoted at length in the first volume of *Kapital*, led Marx to call the Reformer "the first national economist."

29. Westhelle, *The Church Event*.

15

Contextual Hermeneutics

THEOLOGIANS WEAVE A SPECIAL kind of tapestry called "theology" and each is distinct, each has a unique tint. Weaving is done by interconnecting warps and wefts; warps are the longitudinal threads and wefts are the transverse threads. Out of this weaving, the recurring intersections, comes the tapestry. Our tapestries take shape depending on what we throw across. A tapestry weaves a text, a texture within the context in which it is being woven.

Etymologically, context is that which is woven together, braced along, interconnected (*con-text*). In the literary field, a text is the product of something that has been woven, the weaver being the writer, author, or the composer of the text. What comes together are the surrounding circumstances that affect and allow for the weaving to take place; hence its importance for hermeneutics. In biblical exegesis, context referred first to the relationship of a pericope to the broader literary work in which it is inserted. It was then expanded to include other, extrabiblical literary works of the time of composition, and finally also the historic-cultural circumstances that might have influenced the composition, that is, the sociopolitical and economic setting. In other words, contexts are made of a set of commonly shared experiences that offer lenses through which the reception of given information is filtered and conveyed. This is the critical task that probes the texture and thus changes the interpretation that can be given to a text. The task of hermeneutics is manifold. Learning the patterns of the weaving of a text by dissembling it is complex and demands dexterity. The task does not end in the work of negation. The text calls to be woven again with warps and wefts suitable to other environments and as beautiful as the old intended to be for times and places inaccessible and unfamiliar to the artisans that have been in the onetime occupied with it and oblivious to uses it would be employed in times and places the imagination could not fathom.

Context and Hermeneutics

Since Friedrich Schleiermacher, at the beginning of the nineteenth century, modern hermeneutics recognized the distinction between the grammatical sense of a text and that which he called the psychological sense achieved by a reader's insight or divination into the meaning of a text. The psychological sense tried to establish the nongrammatical features accounting for peculiarities that allow for the understanding of a text, which are embedded in it but not evident to the occasional reader. Texts bear the mark of the environment in which they were woven, which is required for the understanding of it; texts have an ecology, an environment with which they interact.

Since the last century, after the work of Martin Heidegger, Hans-Georg Gadamer, and, particularly, Paul Ricouer, it became clear that it is not only the environment of the "weaver" of a text that matters for the understanding of a text but also the environment of the reader. This is so because the meaning of the text is not only in the text and behind it, but always also ahead of the text itself, that is, in the milieu of a future reader who encounters it with a pre-understanding that tints its apprehension as if colored by spectacles when looking at a texture.

In dealing with a text theologically, it is the context of the writer and the context of the reader, in addition to the grammatical features that need to be probed for meaning to be evinced. The development of the historical-critical method in biblical studies, to use an example of a hermeneutical technique, can be traced back to the fifteenth century when Italian humanist Lorenzo Valla demonstrated that the "Donation of Constantine" was a forgery. This discovery was very important for Luther and the Reformation insofar as it established the text as a product, as a result of God-given human ingenuity and craft and thus also susceptible to corruption. But textual criticism became a controversial issue in Protestantism when it was applied particularly to biblical interpretation. Since the eighteenth century, starting with Reimarus and Lessing, rules for textual and exegetical studies taking its original context into consideration were established and continued to be developed through the next couple of centuries. However the concern was mostly focused on the original context in the formation of the text.

The present context of the reader was important insofar as it established the limits of toleration for alien materials and their potential for triggering allergic reactions. Making the text relevant often meant making it more palatable for a contemporary audience. It was mostly due to the emergence of liberation theologies in the second half of the last century that the context of the reader became decisive for determining the theological meaning of a text not by distilling the text to fit new sensitivities, or by bringing the text alive in a new context. On the contrary, the question is how the new context comes alive in the text! This is a process of transfiguration, reading the context into the text. What follows are some examples of contextual impact and criticisms to the contextual approaches in the hermeneutical endeavor, and finally a text of Luther as a case study in contextual theology.

The Setting of the Author: First we shall consider an example of an original context and how it shapes the message and then look into the significance of the receiving context as the context to be invested in the text, to make the text its own habitat. Let's take the Gospel of John as the exegetical text. Written late in the first century CE, when the Christian message made inroads into the surrounding pagan culture, it adopts from the new enveloping environment language and concepts used therein, thus contextually relevant. And one of the most influential popular philosophies of the day, shaping the language and culture encircling the Christian incursion in the pagan world, was Gnosticism. The Gospel of John was developed in such an environment that encased its message. Yet even with the adoption of elements of a philosophical system that by the second half of the second century was deemed inimical to the main claims of the Christian gospel, as Irenaeus fiercely argued,[1] John was able to be a witness to the gospel.[2]

Circumstances of the Reader: Let's consider an example of the importance of the receiving context. For many liberation theologians, particularly from Latin America, the text of Exodus, from the deliverance from Egypt to the possession of the Promised Land in the book of Joshua, became paradigmatic for a whole generation of theologians. But the same texts that promise a land for displaced people and ensure its occupation is read very differently by black South Africans, by Dravidians in India, or by Native Americans and Mexicans whose land has been taken by Boers, Arians, and the US, respectively, who, not surprisingly, often appealed to the same biblical promise of land to be conquered in the name of God. Indeed, the receiving context matters; it matters as it assesses how the text can offer a breathing space to be inhabited.

Selective Readings: Readings are always selected not only because they are appropriate for certain circumstances, but because circumstances live and thrive differently in different texts. Howard Thurman, the dean of early black theology in the US established academia, and mentor to Martin Luther King, Jr., remembers his mother who grew up on a farm. A preacher would

---

1. Irenaeus, *Against Heresy*.
2. Käsemann, "Ketzer und Zeuge," 292–311.

come regularly for worship services where he heard the Bible read and the sermons preached. And every day, at night, Howard's mother would read him biblical stories. He grew up thinking that there were two bibles, because he never heard the same stories from the preacher and from his mother. Only later did he come to realize that the preacher only read to the black farm laborers from the letters of Paul, while his mother was always reading to him from the Gospels. The ideological implications are quite suggestive, if not disturbing, but the decisive element in this memoir is to show that selection implies also exclusion. As in a picture, what the camera captures is a scene intentionally abstracted from other surrounding features. Howard Thurman's mother and her context wove themselves into and came alive in gospel stories in a way they did not in the Pauline epistles. But this was not because of the theological content of the gospel narratives as opposed to the letters of Paul, but because the former became the conduit for the transfiguration of her context.

Criticisms of Contextual Theologies

However, we should not forget that the contextuality of all theology has often been criticized. Three of these criticisms are worth mentioning, most notable of them being the *fundamentalists*. The fundamentalists would reject the importance of any sense of context: the grammar and placement within the work, the circumstances surrounding the author, and definitely the context of the receiving end were decried. The letter, the written word, is to be maintained in its assumed pristine purity. This theological posture has often been out-rightly dismissed by academic theology with nonchalance. Yet its relative sociological importance needs to be addressed for it is itself part of many a context. The predicament of fundamentalism as a sociological and cultural phenomenon is not its literalism, but the fact that it suffocates the life of one's own context. This is not unlike Peter's wanting to build a tent for Moses and for Elijah.

Some theological and philosophical developments, not without reason, have led to the criticism by the *neo-orthodox* movement in the twentieth century. With its stress on God's revelation as unfettered by any human circumstance, history and context are regarded as only pointers to a dogmatic content, as in the creedal expression ". . . under Pontius Pilate." Pilate's reference in the creed is only to attest to the full humanity of Christ, but substantially the prefect's name is an accident in the philosophical sense of the term; it is not essential, bearing no dogmatic weight. Yet this stance shoulders the marks of a context in which forms of existentialism were a response to a situation in which the message of the gospel could not be distinguished from the context itself. This criticism of a contextual approach describes a hermeneutical procedure akin to transfiguration, but in its reverse. It brings the text to a spurious life in which the figurae are defaced. Disfiguration properly describes the process through which a text comes alive in a new context, while transfiguration describes the procedure through which the new context comes alive in the text. The former defines acculturation that adjusts the text to a hegemonic régime; the latter turns the text into a breathing space.

Other critics point to a more complex issue that plagues contextual approaches to a text. In this *third* criticism, context is too spongy a word. What are the limits of a context? When is something out of context? How porous are the boundaries of a context? How far can they be expanded, or how strict are they? Which are the social parameters that serve as a criterion to define a context? Here issues such as race, gender, geographic location, economic stratum, nationality, language and so forth create unmanageable variables that defy a working definition.

Contexts are made of shared experiences. But experiences are themselves an ensemble of stimuli in an individual that are not reproduced exactly the same in any other. This means that if a strict definition were to be adopted the result would be a form of solipsism, for, my context, in a *reductio ad absurdum*, is only my own solipsistic self. And that is the end of communication, because meaning, bound to context can only be assessed by me and nobody else, because this alone is the "context" to decipher meaning, since no one else shares exactly the same experience as I. This is self-contradictory because meaning that cannot be communicated is no meaning at all, since it cannot be mediated.

The Representation of Context

Over against the impasse of the importance of context and its reduction to absurdity, postcolonial theory has offered some help.[3] Context as such is not the issue to be abstractly defined and transcendentally used. The point is to recognize how a context is produced and conveyed as such to others, and thus the importance of weaving. How does a context present itself as a context, and who does this "presenting"?[4] In other words, the issue that

---

3. Westhelle, *After Heresy*, 121–42.

4. See chapter 13 above in connection with the discussion of the sati ritual and how it was portrayed in colonial India by Spivak, "Can the Subaltern Speak?"

concerns us is not the context as an abstract category, but the mechanisms through which a given context is *represented* and who does the representation. So this moves the discussion from the classical hermeneutical question of meaning to who defines what a context entails, what are the variables that define its contours, and to what end the definition is employed. Phrasing it differently: Who is the stool pigeon? Whose is the representation, and whose is the reading of the text? For postcolonial writers the representation of a given context when done from outside, independent of the moral intent of the one doing the representation, is already cast in the cultural presupposition of the context of the one who does the representation; and this, again, independent of the moral intent, is an act of violence, because violence is precisely to deprive the other of the possibility of self-expression, of having the other's representation recognized.[5]

However, this is not exactly an either/or logic. There is always an asymmetry between the representation of a context and the event that triggers the representation. For example, there is a difference in how a burqa is represented by a Westerner and an Afghan woman actually wearing it. For the Afghani it might be a liberating mode of presenting herself, of making herself uniquely present, while for the Westerner, say, a journalist or politician, it is turned into a representation, say of oppression and gender discrimination. The difference between the two is the one that marks the dividing line between the hegemonic context and the subaltern one. The former, the hegemonic context, enjoys the pretense of holding the accuracy of the representation, its "scientific" status because it also controls the régime of truth and the canons to which it is accountable. The other is denigrated insofar as it does not operate within the environment of the hegemonic epistemology or the reigning régime of truth. Yet the act that endows subjectivity with presence is never fully rendered in the frozen rendition of the representation.

The subaltern's gesture of presencing is neglected. However, the subaltern in presenting herself aims also to offer an alternative representation, but this representation is always "contaminated" by elements imported from the external contexts that do the casting of the representation from the outside, or the hegemonic side. The reason for this is the following: The context that claims the right to represent itself does it in such a way as to intervene in the field controlled by the dominant context. For this it needs to use concepts and categories that are imported. This process in postcolonial theory

---

5. In the story of Cain and Abel, the first act of human violence recorded in the biblical narrative, this is well illustrated. Abel's offering was recognized and Cain's was not; thus violence ensued. See Westhelle, "'The Noble Tribe of Truth': Etchings on Myth, Language, and Truth Speaking."

is called hybridity.⁶ Hybridity in postcolonial studies is the ability to make incursions into other contextual and conceptual territories and employ for one's own purposes notions familiar to the hegemonic context. This process is in play, for example, when Franz Fanon uses Freud, when Paulo Freire employs Hegel, when Gayatri Chakravarthy Spivak uses Jacques Derrida, when Edward Said employs Michel Foucault, or any one of them uses Marx. They employ critically progressive elements coming from the very context that has always defined them from outside and imposed on them an identity that is not *proper*. The postcolonial response is to represent the subaltern from inside out but always also making *improper* incursions into the hegemonic context. This is called resistance or counter-violence.

Luther: A Case Study

What is the point of this discussion on representation of context? The point is best laid out in a sermon that Luther delivered in August of the turbulent year of 1525, as part of a series of seventy-seven sermons on Exodus.⁷ Contemporary postcolonial theorists have explained the problem regarding the role of representation in interpretation or hermeneutics. However, Luther, much before these explanations/instructions, was practicing it. Luther's text *How Christians Should Regard Moses*,⁸ which I have quoted greatly, is exemplary of this hybrid practice. Luther was struggling with the influence of some enthusiast preachers who, not unlike fundamentalists today, would take the laws of the Pentateuch (then still attributed to Moses, and thus Moses becoming the metonymy for the law and promises in the Pentateuch) and impose them on the people under the admonition: "Dear people, this is the word of God." Luther's response, which has been quoted before, is a terse lesson in contextual hermeneutics: "That is true; we cannot deny it. But we are not the people." And further: "It is not enough to look and see whether this is God's word, whether God said it; rather we must look to whom it has been spoken, whether it fits us."⁹

---

6. For the use of this concept, see Part One, chapter 6; cf. Westhelle, *After Heresy*, 129f.

7. The text of the sermon was reworked for a publication as a pamphlet a year later, and in 1527 was used as a fitting introduction to the publication of Luther's sermons. This translation is from the reworked pamphlet of 1526, as found in WA 16, 363–93.

8. LW 35:161–74. The German title is "Ein Unterrichtung, wie sich die Christen in Moses sollen schicken." WA 16, 363.

9. LW 35:170.

Luther's sermon and the essay as published tell us three things about contextualization, or three criteria by which it should be normed. The first is about *pertinence*. A text is valid to you insofar as it addresses your situation, your context, and offers a language to give expression to it. If it does not, it does not pertain to you. The law is helpful insofar as it addresses a particular condition. The second criterion is about *innovation*. Moses is of universal validity not because of the particular laws addressed to a particular people but because of "the promises and pledges of God about Christ."[10] This newness, this gospel, speaks to and delivers promises to Jews and Gentiles alike, and it is for all nations and addresses all, indeed, "also to angels, wood, fish, birds, and animals, and all creatures," but we are neither one of those.[11] Moses becomes an example, as many of the other prophets, to be emulated in one's own context, and serves as the hermeneutical locus to the task of transfiguration.[12] These criteria define the norming task of hermeneutics. Such a task is not done to find a pristine Luther but to apply to Luther's own text the same contextual hermeneutic principles he applied to the biblical text. Transfiguration calls for its own examination through pertinence and innovation.

Pertinence

The first task and criterion takes into consideration the germaneness of a text for a given people, how it resonates with the experience of a people. Here Luther distinguishes between the universal ground "implanted in me by nature," or "natural law," and its codified form, positive law, that is contextually bound. The Decalogue, for example, is the codified form for a given people. We don't follow the Decalogue because God gave it to Moses and Moses gave it to us, but because "Moses agrees with nature."[13] But from natural law to its codification in positive law requires adaptation, even insofar as the Ten Commandments are considered. On encounter with new and different circumstances/contexts, be it time, place, or experience, they are renewed; "these [new] Decalogues are clearer than the Decalogue of Moses," boasted Luther on the basis of this hermeneutical principle.[14] "Clearer" (on other occasion he said "better") is to be understood in the sense of being more suitable to the context different from the one of the Israelites camping by Mount Sinai.

10. LW 35:168.
11. LW 35:171f.
12. See chapter 13 above.
13. LW 35:168.
14. LW 34:112–13.

Yet we often long for an indisputable external word that we can rely upon independent of our own circumstances. Why? So we don't need to argue, and we don't need to think, just obey; we need only to be sure that the unquestionable word is maintained. We suffer from what Derrida called "the malady of the archive" (*mal d'archive*), that is, to use the past to authenticate the present, to find a pristine origin, a pure and authentic source.[15] But this implies always a disregard for the present and the places this present occupies (and the present always takes place, or it is not a present, a gift). This is what we do when we use other categories, ideas, and concepts (biblical or not) that other contexts honor as crucial to their experience, and repeat them, parroting them, in complete abstraction of our present and where it is situated. What might have been good in one context will not necessarily be good in another. Luther uses examples of Old Testament ordinances—as the one of a widowed been taken as a wife by the brother-in-law, or the practice of tithing, and the jubilee year—as good practices. But they do not "pertain to the Gentiles, such as tithing and other equally fine" ordinances.[16] So how do other contexts become important for us in our context? They help us to devise strategies and tactics to enlighten the present. It is necessary to recognize how the word of God is addressed to a given people so that we might also discern how it is relevant for our context. This is what Pedro Casaldáliga meant when he said that the universal Word speaks only dialect.

So this is the first task: to discover what resonates in the text. Resonance is a term that has for long been used in physics and chemistry and has been applied by social psychology to describe the fact that our nervous system is not self-contained, but reacts to stimuli from the social environment in which an individual is inserted, i.e., their context. Resonance implies responsibility. In this sense one can say that a text resonates not because one individual relates empathically to it, but because it feels right and responsibly fits the context offering vistas to move along. Resonance in socio-psychology is the opposite of dissonance, the experience of something not expected, and disturbing assumptions.

An illustration that exemplifies the task of resonance is pertinent here. Flávio Koutzii is a Brazilian militant of the sixties and seventies (today he is a politician). He went into exile in Argentina after the military coup d'état took place in Brazil in 1964. When the same happened in Argentina some ten years later (1975–76), he was arrested and jailed with other political prisoners. In prison they had no access to outside information and the conversation among them was monitored and any mention of politics did not go unpunished. Yet the military jailers allowed them to have a Bible.

15. See Part Two, chapter 6 above.
16. LW 35:168.

Instead of the political jargon they were used to and was off-limits, they started to have conversations using biblical stories and concepts to describe the political situation they were living through, and thus fooling the censors. Koutzii, himself a secular Jew, tells, in his memoire entitled *Pieces of Death in the Heart*,[17] of a surprising phenomenon. Biblical stories of exile, oppression, liberation, the healings of the New Testament, the Cross and Resurrection provided them with a language that amazingly was adroitly pertinent to describe the context and pointed to rays of hope in a way that the socio-political language they mastered so well was not able to do with the same incisiveness. This is a story that can also be heard from many annals documenting the early experience of Base Christian Communities as they morphed into an ecclesial context from outlawed political groupings in Latin America, which originally were not connected to the church or religion in general. This is resonance: the text speaks to my situation.

Now, the critical issue that emerges with this criterion of pertinence and the hermeneutical principle of resonance is the risk of *acculturating* Christian theology and proclamation. *Inculturation*, instead, has been the goal of the criterion of resonance, but when difference is hampered, inculturation turns into acculturation. Difference and otherness are dimmed by adjustment to a cultural ethos. This has been the warning issued in the twentieth century by neo-orthodoxy, particularly against Lutheranism's alleged tendency to acculturate the message of the gospel. But this is what Luther says in his text: "In this manner, therefore, I should accept Moses, and not sweep him under the rug: first because he provides fine examples of laws, from which excerpts may be taken. Second, in Moses there are promises of God which sustain faith."[18]

This brings us to the second criterion, and this is a criterion that a culture cannot provide, out of its own resources; it needs to come from outside!

Innovation

Luther introduces this criterion with these words: "In the second place I find something in Moses that I do not have from nature: the promises and pledges of God about Christ. This is the best thing. It is not something that is written naturally into the heart, but comes from heaven."[19]

If the law needs to be cast contextually, the gospel says: now that you understand where you are (which is the function of the law), it is time for a

---

17. Koutzii, *Pedaços de morte no coração*.
18. LW 35:169.
19. LW 35:168f. This is one of many examples in which Luther asserts the presence of the gospel in the Hebrew Scriptures.

transformation, change; it is time for innovation. It is time for the book of the law—and every "book" is about the law—to be closed so that the living word of the gospel can be opened. Even as we respect our cultural bearings and are faithful to them, transformation comes from the outside, comes from the other, and the other is the one who announces, "I have come not to abolish the law, but to fulfill it. . . . You have heard that it was said . . . but I say to you" (Matt 5). Paraphrasing: "I have come not to disregard your context, but to make it whole. . . . You have learned to accept what resonates with you . . . but I am daring you to do something new." This is Luther's hermeneutical *discrimen*, the critical and decisive moment that sets the limit to pertinence. While pertinence looks for resonance of a text in relation to a situation, innovation is attuned to the moment of dissonance in which novelty brings about transformation. This double task that entails both resonance and dissonance is biblically presented with perspicuity in a short parable closing the collection of parables in the Gospel of Matthew, the gospel that most evinces the concern for contextuality and pertinence. "And he [Jesus] said to them, 'Therefore every scribe who has been trained for the kingdom of heaven is like the master of a household who brings out of his treasure what is new and what is old'" (Mattt 13:52). And what is new is gospel, the good news, that which has not been there; it breaks in, it renews and disturbs.

Novelty brings people out of their comfort zone and calls for boundaries of contextuality to be transgressed. Again I offer a biblical example. In the Gospel of John, chapter 20, we have the story about the disciples gathering in the upper room, with the doors shut for fear of the Judeans. It is the Sunday of Resurrection. Suddenly Jesus stands among them and says, "Peace be with you," and the disciples rejoice. All is cozy and everything is in order as long as they stay in the upper room with Jesus in their midst, as long as they stay in their reliable context. Now something interesting happens. Jesus has already wished them peace. But he says to them again: "Peace be with you." It is a salutation not much different than saying "good morning," or so the disciples thought. And you don't repeat a salutation unless for some reason the person to whom it was directed did not hear it. The repetition was necessary because they did not get it! The disciples were clueless as to what "peace" meant. So Jesus repeats it—"peace be with you"—and, to make it clearer, he paraphrases it: "As the Father sent me, so I send you." That meant, get out of here, face your fear, and dare to go for the new. In fact, novelty is always a source of anxiety and fear, because it exposes us and disrupts that which we learn to administer in ordinary contexts. The oldest of the Gospels, Mark, in its probable original ending, has the women at the tomb of Jesus on Easter Sunday being told that Jesus had been resurrected; the final words of the Gospel are these: "Terror and amazement had seized them; and they said nothing to anyone, for they were afraid"(Mark 16:8). We even know and are trained to administer grief, but a surprise, even if wonderful, scares us because it is out of our control.

Cultures seek to represent their context. In theological language this representation is called the law, the frozen image that purports to exhibit the way things are. But the reality represented is dynamic, unstable, and ever-changing. So the moment a representation is displayed it is no longer faithful to the context it presumes to portray; it is no longer *presence* but *representation*. Novelty, the gospel, cannot be represented because it is presence; to use Paul's image, it is not the letter that is dead in its frozen state. It is the living word, *viva vox*. This presence is of Jesus himself by the power of the Spirit that breaks in and breaks out, as the spirit is the breath that inhales and exhales.

In Greek, and so in the New Testament also, the word for "presence" is *parousia*. But this word has a vitiated and often false connotation referring to an eventual future return of Jesus, a "second coming," a *deutera parousia*, which is an expression never used in the New Testament.[20] *Parousia* is the presence of the gospel, that is, of Christ. This has an eschatological character to it. But it is an eschatology that is undistinguishable from the experience of the Christ breaking in and convoking us out of the familiar places we inhabit and learn to control by the mechanisms of representation described above.

This is then the tension between pertinence and innovation. One defines our context and the other calls us out or brings about a transformation inside. Pertinence without innovation is blind legalism, but innovation without pertinence is empty spiritualism. Pertinence and innovation meet in transfiguration, the space in which a context finds itself alive in a text. There is where it takes place.

---

20. It was probably used for the first time by Justin Martyr in the middle of the second century. See Westhelle, *Eschatology and Space*, 26f.

16

A Communion of Teaching and Learning

The Experience That Makes a Theologian

FOR OVER THIRTY YEARS I have been working with theological education and how its impact in the Lutheran communion is felt.[1] During this time and even earlier I have also been involved in more informal theological education with biblical literacy for university students (University Biblical Alliance [ABU]), with grassroot movements, base ecclesial communities (through the Ecumenical Center for Biblical Studies [CEBI]) and with landless peasants and native Brazilian communities (through the Indigenist Missionary Council [COMIN] and the Pastoral Commission on Land [CPT] and its work with the Landless Peasant Movement [MTS]). During the 1990s I was also on the Program Committee of the Department for Theology and Studies (DTS) of the Lutheran World Federation, when we submitted to the Nairobi meeting of the Executive Council in 1995 "Ten Theses on the Role of Theology" in the DTS, which redirected the department in emphasizing the task of facilitating networking to replace the dominant model up to that time of direct theological production for dissemination.[2]

One's experience is the least important thing to be said; but things experiential are still of import. It is only the least important because it is based on one's experience, not necessarily of anybody else. This brings me to the question of experience. One of Luther's mantras is well known: "Experience alone makes a theologian."[3] Two things are to be remarked concerning this quote. *First*, for Luther the experience that makes a theologian makes *one* theologian. That is, one theologian among many theologians, her or his theology does not establish the normative theology for the church. This

---

1. See Westhelle, "Theological Education: *Quo Vadis?*," 273-85.
2. See chapter 12 above.
3. *Sola experiencia facit theologus*. WA TR I, 16, 13 (nr. 46).

distinction between a theologian and theology is often employed by Luther.[4] Luther's mantra means that the experience that makes one a theologian only qualifies one to be in the circle of those doing theology: Jane, Kevin, Miguel, Stacia, Kitagawa, Moses, Miriam, Isaiah, Paul, Esther, Ruth, John, Jacob, and why not, Buddha, Mohamed, Kardec, and the list becomes innumerable, all the way to include the anonymous Syrio-Phoenician woman, or the landless peasant Donalina, who barely literate was a brilliant theologian. In such an open circle, or an expandable round table, is where *theology* is done when the experiences of the participants become channels through which information is received and shared.

The *second* point about Luther's quote is that Luther knew his Latin and therefore knew that *experientia* means trial, testing, ordeal, tribulation, temptation. In other words, "experience" is not a word as in, e.g., "I had a good experience buying in such or such store." Or, "I did not like my experience going to that game." "Experience," for Luther, happens in the midst of and includes *Anfechtung, tentatio*, being taken over by trial and tribulation, cross and suffering. This is experience. The rest are perceptions, opinions, appraisals, sensations, or affections, but not experiences in the sense that Luther used the term.

Obviously there are many who have experiences similar to one's own; therefore they share resemblances. Others might have had experiences at times and places very different, but which resonate with my own and then we speak figuratively about "our" Damascus Road experience, the experience of carrying the cross, the experience of going through hell, etc. But no one has the exact same experience, for that makes the individual unique. This is the reason why experience has been held with suspicion of being but subjective projection incapable of reaching theoretical reason. Such was the opinion of Kant, who, in opposing reason to experience, said, "Nothing, indeed, can be more injurious, or unworthy of a philosophy, than the vulgar appeal to so-called adverse experience."[5] It is now acknowledged that it was feminist theology in tandem with feminist theory that by and large recovered the epistemological credibility of experience.[6] Once the point was made and

---

4. In this sense, Tillich represents a Lutheran stance when for him "experience" is not a source but a medium through which we read the sources. Tillich, *Systematic Theology*, 1:40–46.

5. And the quotation continues, "Such experience would never have existed at all, if at the proper time these institutions had been established in accordance with ideas." Kant, *Critique of Pure Reason*, Book 1, Section 1.

6. In the 1960s, in the context of emerging contextual theologies, the still proscribed "biographical" theology began to appear with audacity. Cf. Metz, "Theology as Biography."

the evidence-of-experience became admissible in the epistemological court, it expanded itself as an epistemological principle for different groups (gay, people of color, women of color, third-world peoples, natives, tribals, Dalits, Latinas, and so forth adding as well those derived from combinations or transactional admixtures of groups). It was again from the feminist front that voices pointed to the inevitable *reductio ad absurdum* of such theoretical stratagems of relying on experience alone, because it tended toward essentialism by naturalizing social groups, and thus missing the fluid character of historical and contextual identity formation.[7] In other words, the insurgence of experiences as irreducible events soon were reduced to frozen representations. But more importantly it fails to account for the fact that the experiences that shape the interests of one group (say, Western middle-class white women) can be in contradiction with the experience of another (say, Asian sweat-shop working women), a point that has been championed by the likes of Chandra Mohanty.[8] Finally we have the contributions of Gayatri Spivak who has shown that experiences are irreducible to their representations (as in a "narrative" or "theory"), implying always a betrayal, unavoidable as it is.[9] The point is that experience ultimately ends up in solipsism without an intervention of an informing theory that is agreed upon to offer parameters for epistemic claims. But what qualifies as such? The venerable magisterium comes back reinvigorated, the old metaphysics regenerated or with a new face lift in process theology that has made significant advances. Marxism has been, in its many shades, a century-long competitive candidate. Deconstructionism with its anti-metaphysical proclivities has made inroads. And what about Lutheranism?

Peculiar to Lutheranism is that there is no agreed-upon canon. Experience is important or even decisive. Nonetheless, the question remains: When experiences are represented in narrative or theoretical form as presenting an objective reality, how are they to be received as such? In other words, how are the narratives born of different experiences communicable? This is a question of communication and its pedagogical impact. But communication has two complementary meanings derived from its etymology.[10] It can come from *co-unio*, (*koinonia* in Greek), which means coming together to share our narratives as a union of different voices in communion. This we have done quite a lot, but it is not enough; narratives need to be credible and accessible to others that don't share the root experience. The task ahead,

---

7. See Scott, "The Evidence of Experience," 79–99.
8. See Mohanty, "Women Workers and Capitalist Scripts," 362–88.
9. Spivak, *Critique of Postcolonial Reason*, 256–65.
10. For this distinction, see Saarinen, "Communicating the Grace of God," 67.

then, is to develop the other sense of communication, communication as *co-munus*, how we pass on the *munus*, the *donum*, the gift or the task. It is a question of how we pass on the information that experiences sediment, before we fall back into the old cliché in which we dismiss something with the words: "this is not my experience." Pedagogically speaking: How do we pass on information that might be relevant to others who cannot harvest them from the gardens of their own experiences? Or else, how do we receive the communication of a gift that will enrich me even as it does not resonate with my experience? Sharing experiences in communion is one thing, receiving them as gifts is another!

This seems to be the greatest challenge because it runs against two of the fixed ideas we have, which Francis Bacon singled out as two of the four idols that distort human understanding. One type is the "Idols of the Cave" (*idola specus*), the other the "Idols of the Theatre" (*idola theatri*).[11] The first refers to the tendency humans have to cherish experiences that speak to them despite other ways of understanding, and keeping the story only to themselves. Caves are places that protect experiences, hiding them from public scrutiny. That is the legitimate fear of being re-presented, obviating presence. This is a legitimate concern, but without representation what we have is only pure immediacy and solipsism. The "idol of the theater," on the other hand, describes the way we take for granted orthodoxies and dogmatisms and stigmatize everything that does not cohere with canonic codes and venerable traditions. Here the problem is precisely the opposite: there is only representation and no presence, only the establishment counts and experiences are sacrificed on the altar of "true" historical and "scientific" objectivity. This brings us back to the other question intimately related to the query about experience: contextuality.

Contextuality and Universality

Contextuality is experienced zoomed out. A context is the ensemble of experiences shared by a given group, race, class, cast in a given social location (geographical, politico-economic, or "ideological"), which is demarcated by the gamut of experiences shared. So contexts are overlapping and all of us participate in different contexts simultaneously. But no one participates in all contexts. Contextuality militates against universalism, and any universalism (as in naturalism, positivism, humanism and so forth), if at all defensible, surrenders irreducible particularity and contextual relevance.

---

11. See Bacon, *Novum Organum*, part I, aphorisms XXXIX–XLIV. The other two types of idols pertain to the tribe and to the marketplace.

There is a story told by Anatole France about a metaphysician defending the universality of metaphysics to his skeptic friend. The friend offers an illustration of what he understands metaphysics to be. It is like if a knife-grinder would take copper coins with the lettering attesting its value and symbolizing the state it represents. By putting the coins to the grinder he effaces all the identifying marks of the coin. It is not any longer redeemable by the value stated by the kingdom, or the republic that secures its value. Now indeed they become universal. Their exchange value can be traded anywhere by the weight of copper they carry and are delivered from their particular attachment to a state. And the friend concludes: "It is obvious what they lose in the process; what they gain by it is not so immediately apparent."[12]

Lutherans are about 1 percent of the world's population; but pretensions of universality are not alien to it. Take for example the doctrine of justification, supposedly universally valid in explaining the human condition and God's redeeming mercifulness. The episode concerning the acclaimed universality was discussed above[13] but merits another reminder. For the Lutheran World Federation General Assembly of Helsinki in 1963 the Commission on Theology appointed a group of celebrated theologians to draft a statement to be adopted as normative for the communion. Even after some redrafting during the assembly itself, the text was not adopted. Among the different issues the major one was of the doctrine of justification. The drafting committee worked with the presupposition of rendering the doctrine intelligible for a secularized world, while minority representatives of the Third World could not understand its relevance for a world that had too much, instead of too little, religion. The drafters were blinded by Bacon's "idol of the theater" in believing that their interpretation of development of societies in the civilizatory process reaching its apex in the Western world was valid already or would soon be for the rest of the world. At that time the vast majority of Lutherans was still in the north-Atlantic axis. Now we are approaching an even divide between Europe plus North America, on the one side, and, on the other, the Third World where the questions about the human condition are radically changed, thus affecting how doctrines are articulated.

However, the more the "idol of the theater" arrests the gaze of the beholder (the more the dominance of orthodox canons), the more it evokes in the other, who does not feel included in the "canonic" narrative, the manifestation of the "idol of the cave." That means, those who don't *feel* (and it is

---

12. France, *Garden of Epicurus*, 194f.

13. See chapter 12 on how the critical question of identity surfaced in the Helsinki Assembly of 1963.

a question of feeling) included in the official "universal" narrative have their experiences confined to their small context in which they can be shared, articulated, and recognized because it resonates. How many a time have we heard in international meetings comments along these lines: "I cannot tell my experience with [here one can fill in: healing, demonic possession, communication from or with the death, not to mention classical "heresies" prevalent in popular religiosity] for people would laugh or just roll their eyes, or at best have a condescending look." Or, if one wants empirical evidence we could just compare the heated debate that accompanied the lengthy process of adopting the JDDJ (Joint Declaration on the Doctrine of Justification) that took place in Europe and to a lesser degree in the USA with the meager, if not negligible, response that it received from Third World churches in the Lutheran communion.

The raising of one of the "idols" calls upon the other on the other side of the spectrum. In other words, the more universalizing the discourse of experts becomes, the more pocketed are contextual expressions of the experience that brings to faith. To return to the monetary parable of Anatole France, we have both the effacement of the inscription in the name of universal currency and the simultaneous restriction of locally issued mints. The effort at universalization is at the same time a limitation. It restricts the mints to enclaves in which the inscription is recognized and honored, but with no exchange value outside the "cave," except for the insignificant prize of the metal out of which it is made.

This brings me to the challenge ahead for theological education, which if addressed may be our offering to be brought to the celebration of the five-hundredth anniversary of the Reformation. And what is this offering? For the fiftieth anniversary of the LWF in 1997 the previous assembly in Curitiba (1990) launched a plan to establish its programs, system of representation, and structure as a *communio* in the Greek sense of *koinonia*, or in one of the senses of the Latin *communio*, i.e., as *co-unio*. Much has been accomplished to this end, and it should be applauded. There have been round tables and a conscious effort of networking to bring people in the communion to a common ground. But this ground is still unleveled! There are those at the table who teach and those who learn and are instructed to learn the grammar of Lutheranism. The communion is the *communio docens*, the teaching communion.

In early Christianity there was a tension (see Gal 2:1–10; Acts 15) between the mother community of Jerusalem and the Gentiles whose plea was articulated mostly by Paul and the circle around him. The tension was between the teaching church of Jerusalem that kept the "orthodoxy" of their faith according to Mosaic precepts, and the church that learned from the

Gentiles to accept the grace of Christ (and thus not needing to keep those precepts). This would become a gift even for the staunchest leaders of the mother community, as in the case of the Apostle Peter (see Acts 10). And this gift was revealed to Peter in a dream! This is how the church came to understand that communion had also the sense of *co-munus*, of receiving the gift in the task of mission. In reaching out to Gentiles the community received a gift; it thus became also a learning community, a *communio discens*.

With all the differences of time and space that separate the Lutheran communion today from the early Christian communion of Jews and Gentiles we are in a comparable situation. We are also between celebrating what we have in common in listening to each other and the reception of the gift. Those gifts come from places and knowledges, contexts and experiences, not yet familiar to the old bastions of the Lutheran tradition. The task ahead is to level the ground of the *koinonia* so that those gifts can be shared around in this spirit: what was given to me and rooted in my experience and context I also give to you. This is me and I give it to you. It is in this giving and accepting that we know that we are at the leveled table of Christ.

17

Luther Yet Incomplete

A Global Inquiry

Introducing

> Nothing that has ever happened should be regarded as lost for history. To be sure, only a redeemed mankind receives the fullness of its past—which is to say, only for a redeemed mankind has its past become citable in all its moments. . . . The true picture of the past flits by. The past can be seized only as an image which flashes up at the instant when it can be recognized and never seen again. . . . For every image of the past that is not recognized by the present as one of its own concerns threatens to disappear irretrievably. . . . To articulate the past historically does not mean to recognize it "the way it really was" (Ranke). It means to seize hold of a memory as it flashes up at a moment of danger. . . . In every era the attempt must be made anew to wrest tradition away from a conformism that is about to overpower it.[1]

WALTER BENJAMIN'S WORDS ARE evocative here for two reasons. First, every past occurrence that is not remembered as an event that has an incision in the present is a loss that keeps us away from "happiness," that is, from redemption. And this is a past of those victimized by the brutalities of a history accommodated to silence. For some reason, Martin Luther, persecuted as he was, escaped this obliviousness and continues to enrich humanity. The second reason is that in this remembrance the Reformer inserts himself into our own present on the side of those who, like him, have been and are persecuted. But it is a remembrance not as a monumental figure to be studied,

---

1. Benjamin, *Illuminations*, 254f.

as one would study an archive to establish what "really happened," but as an enquiring in the midst of our own torments.

I am speaking here of Martin Luther as a representative case of many women and men who were reformers not only in religion but in society, who in different ways share similar experiences. The remembering, or even celebration of Luther is or should be the tribute to all those who, in their tribulations, have contributed to this reformation movement with faith and uncertainties in the midst of danger and anguish.

The Reformation assumed different contours in the places where it took root. Faces and voices vary, be it of the continent they came from or the issues they brought to the fore. Some of them enjoy international reputation and have even triggered revolutionary movements, while others were ill-fated and fatal, as was the case with the peasants' revolt at the time of Luther himself. One such specific case is that of Latin America, in which since the late 1960s this movement is most commonly referred to as "liberation theology" and sometimes simply as "Latin American theology."

Connections

What is it that ties together the protestant Reformation and liberation theology? This would mean a probe into the relation between colonizing Europe and colonized Latin America in theological terms. These distinct theologies, shaped in different points of the planetary compass, had their modest origins separated by almost five centuries. Tentative and experimental as they were, they entailed vigorous polemics born out of the people's cry. These prophetic theological voices that dared to speak the truth with audacity are being heard in their embryonic formulations.

In the New Testament this boldness and nerve is called *parrhesia*, in Greek. And this is more than prophesy. This word, *parrhesia*, describes with precision the transition from the prophet to the apostle. The latter is not only denouncing a situation and pronouncing a promise, but is the one who is captive to the word revealed by the Messiah and enunciates it at any cost, indeed at the cost of martyrdom. Apostles most often became martyrs, a fate not shared by most of the prophets. While the prophet denounces the present and announces the future, the apostle comes to attest that this future has taken place and is waiting for us to join it. *Parrhesia*, to speak boldly without reserve, comes with the apocalyptic urgency to proclaim not the end of time, but the time of the end, the time that reveals the present (*apokalypsis*) and how distant it has grown from the past of promise and the promises of the past. This apocalyptic urgency is found both in the content and in the style that sets up the conditions for the emergence of the Reformation as well as of liberation theology.

A retrospective look at the immense volumes produced and compiled of a Luther, or a Zwingli, Melanchthon, Bucer, Calvin, etc., often distract us from the fact that they were not produced as a monographic opus and were not even intended to be so. They emerged from parrhesaic acts, of confronting structures and powers that made a monk, at the cost of his own life to say in front of the emperor:

> Unless I am convicted by scripture and plain reason—I do not accept the authority of the popes and councils, for they have contradicted each other—my conscience is captive to the Word of God. I cannot and I will not recant anything, for to go against conscience is neither right nor safe. God help me. Amen.[2]

Those who know the internationally renowned publications of Juan Luis Segundo, Gustavo Gutiérrez, Hugo Assmann, Joseph Comblin, Enrique Dussel, Rubem Alves, Jon Sobrino, Leonardo Boff, and Ivone Gebara often miss the point that they are built upon an apocalyptic movement that began by saying, "God set God's tent among us," "God heard the cry of the people."

Luther was above all an occasional theologian and pamphleteer, in the decisive period of the Reformation, that is, in the decade that followed the posting of the Ninety-Five Theses. This means that he was a contextual theologian. In his own words, "experience alone makes a theologian"[3] in the midst of her or his trials (*Anfechtungen*). As Melanchthon reminds the audience at his friend's funeral, the Reformer had a hot temper that went along with an unshackled and invective tongue, which admittedly was not always proper.[4] Luther himself mentions the fact that his writings were considered by the literati of the time as boorish, unsophisticated, and pamphleteering in nature and did not have the greatness of the summae and dogmatic compendiums. And he would take this with humor. Melanchthon, who was an erudite humanist with systematic proclivities, comments on the style of his colleague: "When the disease is so severe, God in these last times [note the apocalyptic motif] gave us a harsh doctor."[5]

The beginnings of liberation theology were not that different when countless numbers of publications were produced locally. Examples include

2. LW 2:112f.

3. WA TR I, 16, 13 (nr. 46).

4. Melanchthon attributes the citation to Erasmus; it was pronounced in the funeral oration at Luther's burial. *Melanchthon deutsch*, 2:161.

5. Ibid.

mimeographed leaflets for occasional use in grassroots communities, flyers of protest of the militant student movement, and posters affixed in public places or carried as banners in protest marches. And, as with the Reformation, when lithograph engravings offered sarcastic drawings of the circumstances in Europe in the early sixteenth century, the proliferation of drawings and humor-filled caricatures sarcastically describing the Latin American reality were not a minor factor in fomenting liberation theology. These graphic resources served not only to elicit laughter that reflected the sordid state of affairs but also as pedagogical resources for people who were not keen readers, if not illiterate, which was the case in Saxony during the Reformation as well as in Latin America. Hence, it is this pamphleteering culture, often derided by the literati, that signals a connection between the Reformation and liberation theology and that needs to be emphasized.

In the case of the Reformation the exploding of the vast production of pamphlets by 1518 is well documented,[6] and this proliferation encompassed not only pamphlets written by religious people, but by common folk (*gemeine Mann*), manual workers who were militants of artisans' leagues (*Zünften*) who thus contributed to the cause of the Protestant Reformation.[7] In Latin America a similar process ensued. There, a form of theological literature emerged and was called "small literature"[8] that step by step received more systematic elaborations and full book forms, which then were labeled as "liberation theologies." As it occurred in the Reformation's evolution of the seminal pamphleteering and disputations into more extensive treatises, so also in the theological literature of Latin America—the progression from pamphlets to journals, from extensive essays to full length books that enjoy an international market, and various translations can be seen. The tendency is that from occasional and punctual fragments a consistent unity is slowly formed; in other words, from a popular literature, contextually rooted in particularities, more abstract and systematic treatises with universal aspirations shape themselves, always at the cost of becoming elitist and severing its ties to its roots.

In this respect one should not miss the catalyst factor in turn of which the theological discourse regimented itself: the Bible. The allure to the Bible comes from two related motives. First, the Scriptures represent in Western literature the moment in which subaltern classes (nomads, migrants, slaves, fisher folk, carpenters, etc.) become main protagonists in a literature that

---

6. See Arnold, *Handwerker*, particularly the statistics in 38–41.

7. Ibid., 10–14.

8. Brandt, *Gottes Gegenwart*, 94–98, uses the expression *Kleinliteratur*, borrowed from Martin Dibelius' depiction of New Testament literature.

entered the class of great literary works.[9] It is no surprise that these socially marginal voices found resonance in the conscience of subalterns both at the time of the Reformation with its *sola scriptura* as well as the Ecumenical Centers for Biblical Studies (CEBI) that proliferated throughout Latin America and beyond. The second factor is that the Bible and its reading empowered the poor to have a voice that irrupted through the protective ideological crust created by those, religious and secular alike, who reserved for themselves the right to decide over human fate. The ensuing result was similar to what happened at the time of the Reformation. It created the ambience for the individual right to constitute himself or herself accountable to conscience guided by the word of God and plain use of reason. In other words, the freedom of the person is affirmed. This is the importance of the criticism of the Roman Magisterium at the time of the Reformation and the central point of the *sola scriptura*. An analogous criticism was issued in Latin America toward the control of the media by the old oligarchies and the newer bourgeoisie, supported decisively by ecclesiastical hierarchies (mainly Roman Catholic, but sometimes even more viciously in Protestant churches[10]).

The use of the notion of "freedom" or "liberty" in fact gets close to the notion of "liberation" in Latin American theologies exactly because both focus on the constitution of the subjectivity of agents. The difficulty in seeing the proximity of Luther's "liberty" and "liberation" is due to the modern understanding of freedom as a negative concept that emerges only with the Scottish enlightenment of the eighteenth century: to be free is *not* to have the private space of an individual transgressed by another. Luther's early assertion given in On the Freedom of a Christian ("A Christian is a perfectly free lord of all, subject to none. A Christian is a perfectly dutiful servant, subject to all.") does not presuppose the liberalism of the eighteenth century, which turns that assertion into a paradox. But this paradox is made comprehensible considering the estament structure of medieval societies, where there was no class mobility. One is born into a given social estament and the only option out would be to join a religious order or the priesthood. In this context freedom was defined as a right one has toward lower ranking estaments, while obligation was due to the ones ranking above. Thus the paradox is solved by this simple statement: The Christian is free in relation to those who traditionally demanded servitude, and dutiful toward those who were socially servants in the societal structure. If the first part implies also the negative concept of freedom (freedom from), the second implies

---

9. Auerbach, *Mimesis*, 72, 151.

10. See Alves, *Protestantismo e repressão*; Westhelle, "Considerações sobre o Etno-Luteranismo Latino-Americano."

the positive implication of freedom (freedom for). Hence the concept of liberation also implies that the oppressor may be free to serve the oppressed, as the latter "restore to the oppressor the humanity they had lost in the exercise of oppression."[11] Thus there is proximity between the two notions of freedom and liberty with the concept of liberation, because for Luther freedom also implies a positive action. Yet a difference still remains in the fact that liberation is understood as a collective process, while for the Reformer it is still seen primarily in individual terms.

Compatibility and Challenges

The parallels and mirroring between the Reformation of the sixteenth century and the theology of liberation today seem to belong not only to the theological domain but also beyond it.[12] The attempt here is to present axial and foundational moments of these agreements and compatibilities. Subjacent is what Hegel dubbed the "Protestant spirit," which Tillich rendered in a similar way as the "Protestant principle." This spirit or principle implies, explicitly or implicitly, that no positive institution, secular or ecclesial, is founded on divine right (*ius divinum*), but solely on human right (*ius humanum*), and thus is subject to its adjudication by reason in light of the gospel. From this insight many theological *loci* were reread in new light. The doctrine of revelation as exclusively tied to the word, creation not as a valley of tears, but as entailing spheres of promise, sin as an ailment that has incrusted the whole human being, incarnation and cross as central to the evangelical narrative, ecclesiology grounded on the priesthood of all believers, spirituality as the presence of the spirit in the flesh accepting even syncretism are some examples. All these are shared by most expressions of liberation theology, even if differences in emphases are recognizable.

Nonetheless worth mentioning are some contributions of the Reformation that remain a challenge for many a liberation theologian and represent a promise yet to be fulfilled. On the other hand there are some queries raised by liberation theology that are pertinently asked to European theologies, also, if not particularly, to the Lutheran variants. These present themselves as questions for European theology to engage and embrace with honesty and humility. There are some challenges from Reformation theology that ought to be seriously taken up by liberation theology. And then are also some queries that liberation theology is daring European Protestant

---

11. Freire, *Pedagogy of the Oppressed*, 42.
12. See, e.g., Morse, *New World Soundings*, 108.

theology, particularly Lutheran, to engage. Pertinent are three challenges to liberation theology, and three queries or contests to European theology.

Challenges from the Reformation

Sin, Penance, and Justification. Ernst Troeltsch in his *Glaubenslehre* described, not without sarcasm, the doctrine of original sin as the greatest treasure of theology.[13] He was representing the position of a critical heir of the Lutheran Reformation. This doctrine comes from Augustine, and is not shared ecumenically. It does not exist, for example, in the oriental churches of orthodox rite. But to a large extent it is a common heritage in the Western churches. However, since the Reformation the understanding of universal concupiscence hailing from Adam and Eve was a decisive mark in the rupture between the Reformation and the Roman Church. This is still the case even after the signing of the "Joint Declaration on the Doctrine of Justification" by Rome and the Lutheran World Federation in 1999.[14] For the Reformers concupiscence is not only a proclivity toward sin (the Roman Church's position), but it is sin itself. This led to the understanding that the Reformation, and particularly Luther, sustained too negative an anthropology. But the problem, in fact, can be traced back to the dispute over indulgences. If sin is only reckoned if it is a positive act to be acknowledged, confessed, and given absolution with penance, then there must be an instance that defines the divide that separates the actual sin that condemns and the "virtual" concupiscence that can be curbed so as not to incur in sin. This was Luther's problem. If this distinction remains, this "instance" has the power to decide and administer the question of salvation and condemnation, that is to say, the issue of liberation. Thus if this distinction between actual sin and the inclination toward it is maintained, then this instance that administers the distinction cannot be criticized as to its nature (but only as to its abuses and deviations). Hence only the radicalization of sin to encompass concupiscence allows for the radicalization of grace. So if grace is radicalized as pure gift that cannot entail a negotiation, the administrative instance, in this case the magisterium that disciplines it is rendered obsolete. Even if Luther regarded the private confessional as good piety, by stripping

---

13. Troeltsch, *Glaubenslehre*, 300ff.

14. Annex "B" states, "The concept of 'concupiscence' is used in different senses on the Catholic and Lutheran sides. In the Lutheran Confessional writings 'concupiscence' is understood as the self-seeking desire of the human being, which in light of the Law, spiritually understood, is regarded as sin. In the Catholic understanding concupiscence is an inclination, remaining in human beings even after baptism, which comes from sin and presses towards sin."

it from its sacramental mediating function he set in motion the theological ground for the abolition of it in the churches of the Reformation.

Among the Latin American Roman Catholic theologians only Juan Luis Segundo and, to a certain extent, Leonardo Boff, have publically lifted this problem. If this problem fails to be addressed, there will be always the spectrum of this authoritative instance that will decide *de jure* and *de facto* what is salvation and liberation and not the people of God fed by the liberating Word. The church is asked to proclaim this word to which it remains a servant. The controversial discussion regarding the appointment of "conservative" bishops to replace "progressive" ones during the papacy of John Paul II is a symptom of this problem (something similar can be observed in the Protestant churches, but with their parliamentary procedures this problem is more dissimulated). Here the problem is not the ecclesial structure as such, for all earthly institutions are equally affected by sin. The predicament is the attributions assigned to it. In the earthly régime, including the church, what counts is *ius humanum*. Hence the nomination of a "progressive" bishop does not change the fact that to this person is given the jurisdiction over condemnation or salvation/liberation as if by *ius divinum*.

Ecclesiology. The ecclesiological challenge has already been introduced. The minimalist ecclesiology as formulated classically by Melanchthon in article 7 of the Augsburg Confession, following previous texts of the young Luther and followed literally by Zwingli, Bucer, Calvin, and other Reformers, seem to buttress the ecclesiology practiced in the base ecclesial communities (*comunidades eclesiais de base*, normally referred to by the acronym CEBs). These communities are by and large Roman Catholic, that is, the people are gathered, the word is announced, and the sacraments administered. But it is precisely this definition of the church—the mantra of the Reformation—that has been evaded by theologians in Latin America. There is a remarkable ecclesiological deficit, particularly among Roman Catholics, except for Segundo and Boff. In 1968 Juan Luis Segundo published *Esa comunidad llamada Iglesia* before the expression "liberation theology" became an appellation for a theological movement born in Latin America.[15] Leonardo Boff's *Igreja, carisma e poder*,[16] published in 1982, came to the public when liberation theology was already known and was raising concerns to the Roman magisterium. The author was penalized with "obliging silence" by the Roman Congregation for the Doctrine of Faith. This ecclesiological issue remains to be addressed and acknowledged. Whoever takes up this

---

15. Segundo, *Esa comunidad llamada Iglesia* (*The Community Called Church*).
16. Boff, *Igreja, carisma e poder* (*Church, Charism and Power*).

challenge (at great risk) may unleash a process of reformation even more radical than what is already offered by liberation theology.

Nevertheless, contrary to the ecclesial situation at the time of the Reformation in the sixteenth century, the contemporary Latin American church is not a hegemonic institution, even as it still commands a certain amount of power. This accounts for part of the reason for the reluctance of theologians, mainly Roman Catholics, to engage this theological *locus*. It would not seem to be a central issue. Nonetheless, its importance is indisputable considering that the Vatican shows alarm at the slightest criticism of its ecclesial model. Examples are the two "Instructions" issued regarding liberation theology in 1984 and in 1986 in which this issue appears with prominence. This is not what Melanchthon once called "theological madness" (*rabies theologorum*), inconsequential to the cause of the gospel and its practice. But it is rather relevant.

When Luther re-elaborates the *notae ecclesiae*, the essential marks of the church (the Augsburg Confession, art. VII) in his text *On the Councils and the Church* (1539), he only repeats and unfolds Melanchthon's formulation of 1530. But he concludes with something that was not there before. And this is relevant for Latin American theology for it shows the potential merits of this minimalist ecclesiology. He adds a seventh *nota* (he calls them the holy possessions of the church) that was not there before. This seventh mark is cross and suffering. Luther's addition of the seventh *nota* to the *notae ecclesiae* is the point of reference here. It is not an addition but the evidence of a church that dares to be faithful to the marks of having a gathered assembly in which the word is proclaimed and the sacraments administered. Faithfulness to these will be evinced by cross and suffering. The importance of this ecclesiological vision calls for the examination of a church, any church—even if not hegemonic—that collaborates and benefits from the structure of a hegemonic system. Placing the cross and suffering as the necessary result of a church committed to the people demonstrates the importance of taking up the ecclesiological question as one way to address hardened systems of oppression. And this is no less true for the churches that claim the Reformation heritage in Europe, Latin America, or anywhere else in the world. Metaphorically phrased, while many Latin American Roman Catholics refuse the medication, Protestants take a placebo. But the true church that is on the side of those who suffer, suffers itself.

Cross. Reflections about the cross in relation to ecclesiology and about the theology of the cross abound in Latin America. Ignácio Ellacuría, Leonardo Boff, Jon Sobrino are some names easily associated with the most significant contemporary works on the theology of the cross. It is moving, at the popular level, to experience the spirituality of the cross (*mística da cruz*) when, for example, one goes through the spiritual exercise of the *via crucis* with the traditional stages of the cross, as developed in Franciscan spirituality, and connecting them with concrete situations in the lives of the people. In the theological elaborations, the cross linked to the suffering of the oppressed people comes through in stark critical contrast to its sacramental use as a repetition of the sacrifice in the eucharistic event as it so often happens in the official church. In this there are remarkable similarities to the theology of the cross developed by Luther. Jon Sobrino even laments having been accused of being a crypto-Lutheran for his theology of the cross.[17] Even so the interpretation of the theology of the cross is made through an "analogical principle."[18] The suffering of Christ is analogous to the suffering of the people. This explication is indeed similar to the theologies of the cross as developed by the Reformed theologian Jürgen Moltmann[19] or the Anglican Alister McGrath.[20]

However, the theology of the cross as formulated by Luther, in addition to rejecting the eucharistic repetition of the sacrifice, carries the argument further than is allowed by the "analogical principle" of Sobrino; it actually identifies the cross of Christ with suffering. In the same writing already alluded to, *On the Councils and the Church*, Luther presents his most elaborate interpretation of the Council of Chalcedon (451) on the doctrine of the two natures of Christ, affirming the incarnation of the *logos* in such a radical fashion that all of creation is subsumed in this incarnation, including nonliving matter, even death itself. He had already announced this position more than a decade earlier in his *Confession* of 1528 in which he speaks about the third mode of Christ's presence "according to his humanity," according to the flesh. In this mode, as already discussed, Christ is in anything, even if transcending all things as God transcends them.[21] For Luther, the third mode of Christ's presence is reason enough as to why suffering is not an alienation from God, but the affirmation of God's presence in the depth of suffering and even of death itself. Here is the affirmation of the resurrection as the insurrection of matter itself. One has to be materialist to believe in the resurrection. From this follows the *identification* of the cross of Christ with present suffering where it is happening, and not only an *analogy*! Boff gets closer to this in his most recent ecological reflections in a cosmic perspective. But he also does not get to connect this with the

17. Sobrino, *Jesus the Liberator*, 235.
18. Ibid., 270.
19. Moltmann, *The Crucified God*.
20. McGrath, *Theology of the Cross*.
21. See LW 37:216ff.

cross and suffering as implying the very presence of God in Christ in matter itself. This is a radicalizing perspective that Luther's theology of the cross offers. If this perspective were taken up, maybe the acclaimed formulation of the Episcopal Conference of Medellín (1968)—the "preferential option for the poor"—would be even radicalized as an identification of God in Christ and those who suffer. This means that the issue is not about God taking care of the poor first (and then the rich), but that in the depth of suffering of all creatures the presence of God in Christ (*parousia*) is made manifest.

These challenges are not to be used as trump cards by a theology that believes itself to be better equipped and thus can lecture Latin American theology. They are responsibilities that the theological heirs of the Reformation have toward establishing a fruitful dialogue for mutual growth. But this dialogue has been too timid and contaminated by prejudice, condescencion, and an incapability of engaging in a conversation in which all partners can learn and teach. This implies listening to the queries that Latin American theology has to those in the northern side of the Atlantic.

Contests from Latin American to European Theology

Structural Sin. The rootedness of sin and the free gift of grace are important to dismantle the system of penitence and victimization, which is decisive for the understanding of justification and justice. However, without invalidating this challenge that hails from the Reformation, there is a query coming from liberation theology and is addressed to theologies that see sin only in individual terms, missing its structural and systemic dimension. It is sad to say that in the theologies arising from the Reformation there are a few voices that have spoken about "corporate sin" (Schleiermacher) and "structures of evil" (Tillich). But the question of structural sin as raised by the Episcopal Conference of Medellín has mostly found deaf ears. There are not many resources in the theology of the Reformers, and Luther is no exception, to explain how sin structures itself in such a way as to make the "state of emergency" in which we live not an exception, but a rule.[22] If the heirs of the Reformation paid more attention to the fact that the Reformers eliminated the difference between sinful acts and concupiscence, they might acknowledge the immense difficulties twentieth-century European theology had in explaining *theologically* how citizens who abide by the law can still connive in systems that standardize evil. One is a sinner and a murderer not only by

22. Benjamin, *Illuminations*, 257. See also Agamben, *State of Exception*.

pulling the trigger but already by being part of a system that condones and promotes it.

Hannah Arendt talks about the "banality of Evil," after her write-up of the trial of Eichmann in Jerusalem.[23] Her point was that there is no radical evil; only love can be radical and go to the depth of being. Evil itself is banal. There was nothing extraordinary in Eichmann, the perverse Nazi executioner, that made him look like the devil incarnate. He was part of a machinery that made a state of emergency look like it was the rule, and thus laid bare "the lesson of the fearsome, word-and-thought defying *banality of Evil.*"[24] Surprising indeed it is that theologians in the tradition of the Reformation have been so inept in describing this "banality of Evil" in such a way as the Medellín Episcopal Conference was able to in coining the expression "structural sin." Medellin was saying about structures of evil what the Reformers said about concupiscence: it is sin itself.

God's Reign. Paul Tillich contrasted the "structures of evil" to structures of goodness ("angels" being the biblical and traditional metaphor for it).[25] Latin American theology normally does not make this quasi-symmetrical opposition between structures of evil and of good, even if we often find expressions such as "constructing the Kingdom" or giving "signs of the Kingdom." These expressions are to be seen as linguistic lapses. Conceptually there is no structural symmetry. This asymmetry is rather important to acknowledge. The Reign of God is not structured in terms *of* this world, but it happens *in* this world. It is an event, a fissure in the systems of this world; it is something that irrupts, but it does not become an alternative system. For example, in the Landless Peasant Movement the occupation of land can be considered a "sign" of the Kingdom. But this does not mean at all that in the new reality, after the occupation, a new system is going to solve the problems and a utopia is going to be instituted and goodness will systemically prevail. New levels of justice might be possible to attain because there is crack in what the "state of emergency" made normal. However there is no guaranty that the reshaped institutional spheres are going to deliver on their promise.

There is no visible reality to be acknowledged by the rules of the old. The new is not the reversal of the old; it is a *novum* whose dimensions cannot be measured by the old scales. The events that took place in connection to the breakdown of the Soviet Union and were symbolized by the fall of the Berlin Wall in 1989 was announced as the end of liberation theology.

23. Arendt, *Eichmann in Jerusalem.*
24. Ibid., 252.
25. Tillich, *Systematic Theology,* 1:260.

The supposition behind the prognostics was that the collapse of "real socialism" in east European countries left liberation theology without historical evidences of the "construction" of the Kingdom. The obituary was indeed premature because it was based on the false supposition of a structural alternative to the capitalist order responsible for the current state-of-emergency-made-normal and evil banal. The asymmetry is between structures of this world and the Reign of God as an event in the world, but not of this world. The motto of the World Social Forum—"another world is possible"—is also to be understood as a new reality in this world, but not of this world. *Pax mundi non speranda*, often celebrated in theologies that share the Reformation heritage, takes on a new meaning. Hope is not in the continuity of something of this world, but the irruption in the world of a peace that happens against all hope that structures itself as a system, a scheme.[26] This is *in nuce* Luther's apocalyptic vision, but often neglected. Instead Luther's eschatology has been read as an act of divine justification. His emphasis on materiality, if acknowledged, is only deferred to a distant future. This vision of the irruption of divine presence, *parousia*, as present event[27] offers a theological and pastoral perspective that the heritage of the Reformation should celebrate and embrace as its own. But, again, this has often been missed.

Contextuality. There are many other questions that Latin American theology could test European theology with. Even the critical tone of this questioning reveals simultaneously an outstanding theological debt to Europe. Many Latin American theologians studied in European universities. While this facilitates conversation, what is often lost in translation is the autochthonous language of the germinal phase of liberation theology at its grassroots. And this is difficult to explain. Richard Morse once observed that while Tocqueville, Weber, or Huizinga produced classical portrayals of North American society, nothing similar exists to describe Latin America. Intellects of no lesser caliber than Alexander von Humboldt or Saint-Hilaire, having stayed for even longer periods of time, were able to offer only glimpses of the character of the subcontinent.[28] Something similar happens when the theological landscape of Latin America is depicted. Only glimpses of its theology will emerge, and normally filtered by some selective affinities, conforming to a certain intellectual affection. Boff, for example, studied in a German university and receives there particular attention, eclipsing the likes of Gutiérrez, Segundo, Dussel, or Sobrino, who in other parts of the

---

26. Note the use of *mē syschēmatizesthe*, "do not be conformed" or "don't fall into schemes," in Rom 12:2.
27. See Richard, *Apocalypse*, 45.
28. Morse, *New World Soundings*, 157–58.

world are at the center of the theological spectrum. Yet, none of those really can represent Latin American theology, but a segment of it written "for export." So it is important to keep the perspectives in line. The reading of Latin America done in Europe is conditioned by cultural-linguistic elements as happens in any intercultural dialogue.

Henceforth the query to Europe is for it to understand that its theology and its venerable traditions are contextual. "We need to anthropologize the West," the North American anthropologist Paul Rabinow once said,[29] referring to the ethnographic practice of studying exotic cultures of the non-Western world and saying that it was time to turn the curious gaze toward oneself and find the exotic within. Latin American theology is asking something similar of European theology: European theology must be contextualized. The proposal is that European theology understand itself as contextual, as a genitive or adjectival theology. As Jean-Jacques Rousseau observed with pertinence more than two centuries ago: "For the past three or four hundred years the inhabitants of Europe have inundated the other parts of the world and continually published new collections of travels and stories; yet I am convinced that we know no other men but the Europeans."[30] What Latin Americans are expecting to hear from Europe is something like, "From where I stand, from my context, I understand the universal revelation of the Word as . . ." And thus the conversation may begin.

In 1976 German theologian Jürgen Moltmann published an open letter to Argentinian theologian José Míguez Bonino, criticizing some exponents of liberation theology at the time (in addition to Míguez Bonino, Brazilians Rubem Alves and Hugo Assmann, Uruguayan Juan Luis Segundo, and Peruvian Gustavo Gutiérrez).[31] In his critique he charges Latin American theology with not presenting its own face but inscribing it in the frame of some European thinkers (Kant, Hegel, and Marx, among them). In a perceptive and long response, Juan Luis Segundo asks him whether Moltmann wants exotic "stories" from Latin America so that he can gather them to write his "Universal theology" incorporating the Latin American "proper," while disavowing the latter's "occupation" of the intellectual territory of Europe. Segundo suggested that Moltmann wanted to extract the Latin American native produce, process it in the North Atlantic world, and barter it in the global market in which he was a theologian of fame. What Segundo was saying is that the German theologian was criticizing Latin American

---

29. Rabinow, *Essays on the Anthropology of Reason*, 36. Rabinow is commenting on Foucault's impact on Western anthropology.

30. Rousseau, *Basic Political Writings*, 110.

31. Moltmann, "On Latin American Theology."

theologians precisely because Latin American theologians admit to having learned from Europe![32] In fact, they have learned significantly from Europe. In Latin American theology we find conversations with, among others, Irenaeus of Lyon, Francis of Assisi, Thomas Aquinas, Luther, Rousseau, Hegel, Marx, as well as with Barth and Rahner, Sölle and Schüssler-Fiorenza, Metz and Moltmann. But we also find the Popol Vuh, Chilam Balam, Las Casas, Mariátegui, Franz Fanon, Arguedas, Paulo Freire, and so forth.

32. Segundo's response was never published in deference to the fact that Moltmann, not long after his critical letter, signed a letter of support for Latin American liberation theology, in the aftermath of a condemnation of it issued by German bishops.

18

Planet Luther

Challenges and Promises

A NEW TIME IS dawning on us.

Dawn! That time before sunrise, the twilight, when a change is waiting in the wings; when darkness is about to disappear and the sun is getting ready to peek out; when night makes way for the day. The dawn, as we know, announces a new day. What does the new day behold? What are its challenges? What does it promise? It is a new day making its appearance like a newborn baby without a name. It is up to us to give it a name—beautiful or . . .

Indeed a new time is dawning on us. The world around us, its aura and terrain, especially in the religious arena, are changing. And with change, invariably, come challenges as well as promises. As far as the Reformation, in general, and Lutheranism, in particular, are concerned the demographics impose contextual challenges and will increasingly do so to Lutheran theology as we have hitherto known it. Most of the traditional confessional families have migrated to the south of the planet. Catholics, Episcopalians, Methodists, and Presbyterians already have the majority of their membership outside of their original historical cradle. Lutherans are lagging behind, but already more than 40 percent of Lutherans are south (or in the Far East) of the North Atlantic axis, and in these new environments will soon become the majority of world Lutheranism. Luther is becoming planetary. But what seems more important is that the members of this soon-to-be majority—in the new contexts, in these nontraditional settings—are there as *minorities* surrounded not only by other Christian denominations and independent or nondenominational churches but also by other religions. New questions are being formulated for a theological response that conventional answers can no longer address. Answers to questions in the West—such as the challenge of works righteousness, secularization, and so forth—no longer fit the bill.

Luther Research and Lutheran Demographics—the Correlation

A cursory review of publications in Luther research will show that there is no correlation to this change in the demographics of Lutheranism by a long chalk. The authors are with few exceptions from Germany, Scandinavia, and some from the USA (an exception may be the LWF publication of annals of international conferences). And if experience is what makes a theologian, then context matters, for a context demarcates the scope of experiences one has; context challenges and changes texts. As the saying goes, "to each tribe its scribe." And this is precisely what Luther also says—that the Scriptures are indeed the word of God but we may not be the people.

The same is true where theology is concerned. We need to know the people and the word that speaks to them, the word that pertains to its situation. Obviously this creates a problem for those of us whose job description entails the charge to do systematic theology. And certainly we should apply Luther's advice on how to read the Bible to Luther's own text and say, "Yeah, this is Dr. Luther, but you are not the people to whom he is speaking." Certainly that has been done in abundance in Luther research, which has the merit of reading Luther as far from infallible. Such is the case in regard to Luther's words against the Jews, the Anabaptists, the Turks, and so forth, which Lutheran researchers even within Lutheranism have long decried. Some of these criticisms have come not only from theologians but also officially from the Lutheran World Federation or from particular Lutheran churches. There is also a gray area of what is often considered Luther's idiosyncrasies, as is often the case with his *scatological*, filthy, excremental, obscene language, his obsession with the devil, etc. Then there is an area that is not often touched, such as his criticism of usury (particularly in the later works[1]) or the "third mode" of Christ's presence as formulated in the *Confession* of 1528 (and quoted at length in articles VII and VIII of the Formula of Concord).[2]

---

1. To my knowledge, while almost everything of Luther has been translated into English, his long "Admonition to Pastors to Preach Against Usury" ("An die Pfarrhern wider den Wucher zu predigen," WA 51, 331–424) has never been translated. An exception has been the work of Ricardo Rieth; see, e.g., "Luther on Greed."

2. LW 37:216ff. See also Part Two, chapter 6.

God's *promissio* and the Promise of Luther

The question then is whether there are promises in Luther's or Lutheran theology that offer resources to face these changes and new challenges originating from new contexts. The word *promise* must be underlined here, for it etches itself in God's own *promissio*. It is the word that calls forth a new reality and addresses its creation with a dispatch, an illocutionary speech-act (the pragmatic force of an utterance) that calls for a response, becoming thus a perlocutionary effect (the effect produced in the one being addressed) that the promise produces in us.[3] To address the response to Luther's locution, particularly when it comes in languages and pre-understandings far beyond Luther's, his contemporaries, and even present-day Luther research (as represented, e.g., in the International Congress for Luther Research), requires new approaches that may not be conventional in most of Luther research. What is being responded to in Luther's own promise for us as he translated God's *promissio*? Or, in other words, what is the address that evokes a response? Better yet, what is the illocutionary act that produces a perlocutionary effect? And the answer may lie not only at the deeper levels of Luther research, but also at the surface when we consider the impact of his persona, its emblematic significance.

In an article published in 1988, titled "Teufelsdreck," Heiko Oberman issues the following criticism of the tendency in Luther research to zero in on the nodal point of the reformatory breakthrough, going deeper and deeper into a debate that has created factions in European Luther research:

> The history of Luther research in this century is the history of concentration by contraction, moving in ever smaller concentric circles from the large grasp of European Reformation history around the turn of the [twentieth] century to an increasing preoccupation with the German Reformation, then with Luther's thought, and finally with the Reformation breakthrough and the young Luther.[4]

This concentration by contraction is the attempt of locating the illocutionary speech-act that set in motion the reformatory movement and elicited the response that goes by that name. But in the case of the Reformation, as in many other historical events throughout history, the response exceeds what is prompted by the communicative act and saturates it with new meanings. Oberman has a point in criticizing the contraction of Reformation studies, but not because it moves "in ever smaller concentric

---

3. Austin, *How to Do Things with Words*, 109–32.
4. Oberman, "Teufelsdreck: Eschatology and Scatology in the 'Old' Luther."

circles," but simply because it digs too deep. The problem in this shrinkage of the research lies in what is obtained in ever deeper levels of meaning and specialized research, missing the fact that Luther became an emblematic figure to catalyze multifaceted dormant expectations and discontent with the church of Rome and its commerce of indulgences. Robert Scribner may have overdone his case, but he has a point when he argues that the Reformation "attained wider significance because it quickly outran Luther's ideas, and achieved a near revolutionary impetus of its own."[5] To use a contemporary analogy the "near revolutionary impetus" became a sort of "Occupy Rome" movement.

This dissociation between Luther's ideas, his prolific theological writings, and the emblematic figure he became is rather important and often missed as a topic in itself to be considered in Luther's research and the Reformer's significance as a catalyst of hopes of freedom in many places to this day. And this is the case even when complex and controversial issues in Luther's and Lutheran theology are paid no heed to.

Luther, a *Figura*

As exemplified earlier, the interpretative method developed in literary theory by Erich Auerbach in his influential essay titled "Figura"[6] helps explain this often overlooked aspect of the importance of the Reformer. *Figurae*, figures, as previously described, are emblematic characters or localized events. They are contextual with place, a time to which they belong. Yet they migrate! According to Auerbach, "A figural interpretation establishes a connection between two events or persons, the first of which signifies not only itself but also the second, while the second encompasses and fulfills the first."[7] The figural approach shows not only continuities but how a tradition is owned by incorporating historical circumstances and characters from other times and places. Such a procedure appeals to *figurae* in order to establish legitimacy, even when the content and meaning is not the same as the one of the original *typos* (the Greek equivalent of the Latin *figura*).[8] Much of

---

5. Scribner, *German Reformation*, 24.

6. Auerbach, "Figura," 11–76. The essay was first published in 1944, while Auerbach was in exile in Istanbul, and was then followed and applied in his influential *Mimesis*, originally published in 1946. See chapter 13 above.

7. Ibid., 53. Auerbach (a German Jew persecuted under Nazism) wrote this essay in the context of the German Christians' anti-Semitic attempt to dissociate the New Testament from the Old Testament. But figures of the Old Testament are ominous in the New Testament.

8. Ibid., 28, 36–38. *Typos, morphe*, or *schema* (1 Cor 7:31) are the Greek words often

Auerbach's research on the figural phenomenon was actually developed by considering how Old Testament *figurae* appear in the New Testament, regaining a significance that, on one hand, makes a claim of legitimacy, and, on the other hand, invests it with a new meaning as to bring the old one into completion.

Luther became such a *figura*, not only *of* David or Paul, but also *for* many that came after him. This is not meant against Luther scholarship, but as something to be understood before other, "deeper" aspects may be scrutinized and discerned. Can we understand that again? What was Luther if not a *figura* in the years that followed 1517, before the pamphlets of 1520 were widely recognized, not to mention before *The Bondage of the Will* of 1525, before the *Confession* of 1528, before his massive writings of the 1530s? The Reformer stood for something that was defined only by bare caricatured lines. But that is what helped decisively to launch a movement called the Reformation, way before any of the substantial issues defining differences between factions of the Reformation took place, from the early 1520s on. To read 1517 from the standpoint of 1525 (with the Anabaptist disputes), or 1529 (with Zwingli), or 1530 (with Melanchthon in Augsburg and Luther in Coburg), or from 2013, will never get one into some decisive features of the Reformation, because they are figural, and decisively so.

The examples can be multiplied, but the answer seems to be a simple one. The Reformer's impact and the Reformation movement as a whole was not read erstwhile starting from the dense texts of a Luther, a Zwingli, a Calvin, a Bucer, etc. Instead, and this is the crux, Luther stood and stands as a *figura* in and through which characters and events manifested themselves in concrete historical circumstances in which the figure of Luther intervenes to magnify the dimensions of characters and events relatively independent from the peculiar content of his theology, and simultaneously ground it contextually in new locations.[9]

Yet the figural approach is not phrenology, the analysis of the shape of the skull to determine the content of the mind—ridiculed by Hegel, but still held with respect by Goethe. The reason why the figure becomes so relevant

---

translated as *figura* as the dominant language of early Christianity was changing from Greek to Latin, beginning with Tertullian, one of the earliest Latin Fathers.

9. Not only is the *figure* of a person, but the legendary event of nailing ninety-five theses to the door of the Castle Church in Wittenberg is also the occasion for figural representation. At the Lutheran School of Theology at Chicago, where I have been teaching for the last two decades, a very militant group of students that advocates for LGBT people calls itself Thesis 96. There is also a group of international theologians, called Radicalizing Reformation, preparing a series of publications on the occasion of the five-hundredth commemoration of the Reformation, which is to culminate in the symbolic posting of a document titled "94 Theses."

is because there is some density underneath the surface that propelled the *figura* to appear. There is something more than Luther's silhouette profusely drawn in the legendary drawings and paintings of the nailing of the Ninety-Five Theses or his seclusion in the Wartburg Castle. These portrayals and representations of Luther are not something like Andy Warhol's *Campbell's Soup Cans*, and his future was something more than "fifteen minutes of fame," as the painter's celebrated catchphrase goes. There was indeed something deeper that prompted the figure to emerge, which is as important as the figure itself is; *figurae* are not figments.

The Construal

This is not to suggest that the surface analysis of the figural approach is the only thing that is left of Luther that is significant for Luther's planetary phenomenon as much as my intention to call attention to the figural importance and relevance. I therefore introduce some areas in which Luther's in-depth theological contribution might still, or again, have some relevance, even, and most importantly, in contexts outside of the ones directly and historically linked to the Reformation heritage.

Cross and Christ's Presence

Luther's celebrated phrase "the cross alone is our theology," and Regin Prenter's identification of the cross of Christ as identical to the cross we carry, lift up not only its intrinsic connection to our condition but also its social and ecological significance as well. And this is what is meant by the expression "there is one Cross. And it is plural."[10] This is in tune with Luther's understanding of the much-discussed "three modes of Christ's presence." The first and second modes—the historical Jesus and the sacraments—though often debated, were uncontestably received as representative of Luther's teaching on the real presence. But the third mode had some unforeseen consequences, not to mention some rousing possibilities, especially where it says "even according to his humanity."[11] This points to the fact that there is no presence without "stuff"—in other words, materiality. This third mode is what makes possible a theology in a planetary perspective. Christ is everywhere, and anywhere, embodied. And that, for Luther,

---

10. I am indebted to Neal Anthony for this expression in his endorsement of Philip et al., *Churrasco*.

11. LW 37:218.

is the crux of the matter. God is present in the very stuff of the world, in the living and nonliving, in the animate and the inanimate, wherever pain and death are at stake and the resurrection is a promise, a new creation. And this makes imperative the usage of the word "planet," for unlike "global," which refers to a self-contained totality, "planet" refers to a little piece of a stellar system, called the solar system, which in turn is a tiny piece of what is called a constellation, which is a small part of the dimensionless universe. Theodor Adorno might have learned something from his Lutheran mentor in Frankfurt, Paul Tillich, when he said that only a materialist can believe in the resurrection of the body.[12] Of course, he went beyond Tillich, who with his rounded-up system would never go so far, and be so faithful to this bold affirmation of someone who did not even confess the Christian faith (for he was a secular Jew). Or in the words of the Reformer himself: "No, comrade, wherever you place God for me, you must also place the humanity for me."[13]

Ecclesiology

In the Genesis lectures of 1535 and 1536 Luther offers a vision of the church that also entails promises. He discusses it in the context of the institution of the "orders." The first of them is the *ecclesia*, which is instituted with the establishment of the Shabbat. Since it precedes the *oeconomia* and the *politia*, Luther's image of the church is one, as he says, "without walls and without any pomp."[14] Some of Luther's speculations in his creative interpretation of the text are beyond anything that a contemporary critical reading of the text would allow.[15] And yet his imaginative reading underscores a theological vision of the church highly relevant for an ecclesiology today. The church established in paradise is an apophatic church. It is the tree of the knowledge of good and evil, which Luther equates with the tree of life (*arborvitae*). This was "Adam's church altar and pulpit."[16] But what is interesting in Luther's reading is an implicit ecumenical vision when Luther says that "it does not appear preposterous that . . . there stood several trees of the

12. Adorno, *Negative Dialectics*, 401.

13. LW 37:219.

14. LW 1:103.

15. I am not considering here the thesis of Peter Meinhold about glosses in the text added by a second generation of editors influenced by the emerging Lutheran orthodoxy. The concern here is with the imagery used and not with the dogmatic formulae that sometimes are of dubious origin as the discussion of the loss of the *imago* that sounds as if coming from Flacius Illyricus. See LW 1:60.

16. LW 1:95.

species arborvitae."[17] So these trees "would have been the church at which Adam, together with his descendants, would have gathered on the Sabbath day."[18] This vision of a multiplicity of trees for the worship of the descendants of Adam suggests first that there is not a single center to identify the true church. But even more, it implies also that the descendants of Adam are from all religions on the planet. Or to phrase it aphoristically: to each religious creed, its tree.

Running the risk of becoming too allegorical, the metaphor of the tree is for several reasons quite fitting for the church or the religious factor as such. Consider the following characteristics. Trees are freestanding organisms grounded on the earth. Among the living organisms they live the longest and grow the tallest always in search for light. They adapt to scarcity of space and through photosynthesis they transform carbon dioxide into oxygen, which after all is that which we require to be alive. Hence we have the importance of trees for the ecosystem. Not by chance has deforestation been emblematic of our sinful condition.

Of course, this idyllic vision of such apophatic church disappears with the fall, which in Luther's speculation happens on that first Shabbat. But it still remains in Luther's mind as an ideal of which the church, now with walls, policies, and pomp, dimly mirrors itself. Yet "the origin is the goal," in the celebrated expression of Karl Kraus. The difference that the fall represents is that now the church has to borrow from the spheres of the *oeconomia* and *politia* its specific functions to build and organize itself, and with them come along also the shortcomings that the fall impinged upon these institutions. And trees keep falling.

Between Economy and Politics

The cultural anthropologist Roberto DaMatta offers a terminology that is useful in reading Luther's view of the church as this place gripped between the other two institutional spheres. The terms *economy* and *politics* in their modern Western connotations really do not convey what Luther, following a long medieval tradition, called *oeconomia* and *politia*. The modern Western concepts of "economy" and "politics" have different connotations. Since the Industrial Revolution the concept of economy dissociates what in antiquity and medieval times was still housed in the domestic sphere, namely, production for the sustenance of life and its sexual reproduction. And since the American and French revolutions, politics gained emancipation from a

17. Ibid.
18. LW 1:105.

set order of flux of authority represented by monarchies in which the ruler is only bound to the rules he himself establishes.[19] Hence the coinage of the modern expression "political economy," a notion inconceivable in earlier times. But outside of the modern West there remains a distinction between these domains, even as modernization is a planetary phenomenon. This is why I believe the distinction DaMatta makes, in discussing Brazilian society, between "house" and "street" is important to understanding *oeconomia* and *politia*. The house is seen as a realm that controls the domains in which much of sexual reproduction takes place, and a significant amount of production of goods is allocated there. The street, on the other hand, serves as a metaphor for the space in which public affairs take place and human intersubjective matters are administered.[20]

This terminology seems to address rather well the way to understand Luther's distinction between *oeconomia* and *politia*, but also to address worldwide contexts in which the space of intimacy, sexuality, and often also of production for the sustenance of life, are protected from the public sphere, even architecturally so. The domestic space in those latitudes is often the space that in the modern West takes the form of health insurance and retirement pension. But such is not the case in many other contexts where "health insurance" and "pension" are still matters of the household. This helps to explain, for example, the dissension taken by some African churches of the Anglican and the Lutheran communions over the way the West takes its own position on questions of human sexuality and homo-affectivity. Even if morality plays a role in opposing the "liberal" Western position, it is not the primary cause of the strife; it is a question of how to keep the house in order, the *oiko-nomos*, and make it sustainable for generations to come. And this is done also by keeping one protected from what happens in the "street," in the public domain, often inimical, in some contexts, to the domain of intimacy, the domestic.

The Third Space

The way in which the economy became so much intertwined with politics is what accounts for a particular phenomenon characteristic of the West, called secularism. Secularism can be defined, to use the terminology I have suggested, as the street invading the house, or the other way around, the house invading the street. What disappears then is this "third space" that Luther called *ecclesia*, the church that keeps the economy and politics in

19. Morse, *New World Soundings*.
20. Matta, *A casa e a rua*.

relation, but still distinctly apart. Arguably no one understood this better than Walter Benjamin in his discussion of Parisian galleries, arcades, or *passages*. These are the architectural expression of the mingling of house and street, of economy and politics. In describing these recently created arcades, Benjamin offers the following comment:

> Already the inscriptions and signs on the entranceways (one could just as well say "exits," since, with these peculiar hybrid forms of house and street, every gate is simultaneously entrance and exit), already the inscriptions which multiply along the walls within . . . have about them something enigmatic.[21]

The recent instantiations of those early modern galleries are today's shopping centers and malls. Not by chance they have become the *ersatz* of the church for secularized societies.

Luther's distinction of the orders or "spheres of promise"[22] is no longer descriptive of modern and secularized Western societies, but it is a diagnostic tool to understand the Western peculiarity and, most importantly, other societies where Lutheranism is growing and in which even as modernization takes place secularism has not taken hold; the "house" and the "street" remain as discrete dimensions, and religion, to use a more generic word for *ecclesia*, is a space in-between, something like what Victor Turner called "betwixt and between"[23] and Homi Bhabha defined as a third space. It is an "interruptive, interrogative, and enunciative" space that blurs the limitations of traditional boundaries.[24] It is a hybrid space, which is not a result of two essences that combined to form a third. It is like a suspension and disruption, not a synthesis; something that is neither in nor out but both at the same time.

These three then—*oeconomia, politia,* and *ecclesia*—remain as foundational institutional realities that Aristotle, in the *Metaphysics* VI, described as the basic and discrete human faculties (*dianoia*): *poiēsis*, as the practice that creates objective realities, defines the order of the *oeconomia*; *praxis*, as the intersubjective communicative action with no material result, corresponds to *politia*; and *theōria*, the passive enduring of being an observant, defines the *ecclesia* or religious observance in general.

If the three spheres have been corrupted by the fall (the first to be corrupted, according to Luther, was the church, for the origin of sin took

---

21. Benjamin, *Arcades Project*, 871.

22. This rendition of the Lutheran notion of *Stände* is from German theologian Hans Ulrich and is also used by Swedish ethicist Elisabeth Gerle.

23. Turner, *Forest of Symbols*, 93–99.

24. Bhabha, *Location of Culture*, 37.

place on the first Shabbat[25]) they remain as divinely instituted as spheres of promise in which sanctification or holiness takes place. Luther stresses that with great emphasis when he distinguishes between being holy (*heilig*) and being blessed or saved (*selig*). "For to be holy and to be saved [or blessed] are two entirely different things. We are saved through Christ alone; but we become holy both through this faith and through these divine foundations and orders."[26] Now, if we connect this to Luther's third mode of presence, blessedness or salvation can be everywhere, for Christ may, according to his humanity, be there. It is not confined to a region or a particular religion, but embraces the entire planet. Sanctification, being holy, however, is the labor of love in the instituted spheres that everyone is called to serve in.

The Tree: A Planetary Metaphor

The tree or trees in paradise were, for Luther, an apt metaphor for the church because it pointed to the importance of seeing blessedness or salvation as embracing the entire planet. And the metaphor is even more fitting as the tree, as it grows in the front yard, stands between the house and the street. The church's ultimate goal is observant receptivity, which is proper to translate literally as *theōria*. But after the fall the church needs to borrow from the *oeconomia* its buildings and all the objective realities that make it up, and from the *politia* the rules of intersubjective actions that establish the liturgy as well as other interpersonal functions, such as counseling, parish counsel, and committee meetings. As an instituted reality it is dependent on the *oeconomia* and *politia*. This is why the church has this hybrid character and can be said to exist only as an event; it happens. It is not of our doing, as these lines of a poem, a *poiema*, by Joyce Kilmer say:

> I think that I shall never see
> A poem lovely as a tree.
> . . .
> A tree that looks at God all day,
> And lifts her leafy arms to pray
> . . .
> Poems are made by fools like me,
> But only God can make a tree.[27]

---

25. LW 1:70.
26. LW 37:365.
27. Kilmer, "Trees," in *Trees and Other Poems*, 18.

Part Four

Economy and Politics: The Paradigms

19

"The Third Bank of the River"

The Challenge of Modernity

> ... to a place where there is discord and cacophony under which there is a strange harmony ... the third bank of the river ... the land every soul craves for.
>
> —João Guimarães Rosa

Disembeddedness of Modernity

IN ONE OF GUIMARÃES Rosa's stories, "The Third Bank of the River,"[1] the dilemma of modernity is presented as a parable of a man whose existence was torn between the options he had to face inhabiting simultaneously the spaces of two worlds divided by a river. His existence was split into spaces he had to conform to and in neither was he able to find an authentic expression of his self. He missed the story, the myth that could situate him. He could not detect the territory of his being. In a desperate search for the answers he exiled himself for the rest of his life to a canoe forever floating in the middle of the river, in the third bank of the river.

The "disembedding"[2] of existence from its vital core, the loss of a foundational mythical nucleus, of a sense for location, or plainly the disenchantment with a world that has lost a texture that weaves together a sense of belonging have been different attempts to express the vertigo of living constantly on the edges of modern existence. Long before modern criticism of religion manifested itself with the Enlightenment, this sense of being exiled

---

1. Rosa, "Third Bank of the River."
2. The expression is Anthony Giddens'. See his *Modernity and Self-Identity*, 17–21.

from the house of being, the story that situates us, marked the emergence of the modern predicament.

Justification and justice, once united by the criterion of adjustment to the medieval institutions (in which the identity between the created order of things and providence, between *lex naturae* and *lex dei*, was embodied and expressed) are now disjointed. But let us consider what the modern disenchantment has liberated us from, lest we content ourselves to embark on the elusive quest for the third bank of the river. The thinking about two régimes to describe the paroxysm of our condition in Lutheran theology has to do with this modern predicament. It *signals* as much the irretrievable dream about times gone by, as it also intimates the triumph over an age that, even if it provided a house of being, was often enough also a prison.

The "Doctrine of the Two Kingdoms" was not formulated by Luther. It is a twentieth-century creation. Much less preoccupied with systematization than his twentieth-century followers, Luther's concern was to express the double-sided anthropological stance that simultaneously delineates human relations to what we would now call society on the one hand, and divine reality on the other: *coram mundo* and *coram deo*. The insight was an attempt to describe the "eccentric" character of the human condition: being open to the infinite and simultaneously closed to it by the immersion in the demands of quotidian experiences. It was about the recognition of being ultimately acted upon and the simultaneous concealment of such recognition by idolatrous misplaced dependence on and demonic mistrust in human instituted orders in the divinely established earthly régime.

Notwithstanding the judicious anthropological insight offered, Luther's concern was above all theological. The thinking regarding the two régimes made it possible to distinguish between the realm in which God works alone carrying forth the divine work of justification through faith and the realm in which human beings work with God as God's cooperators (*cooperatores dei*) in the continuing work of creation. One of Luther's preferred metaphors to describe this double agency of God was the anthropomorphic "hands of God." The institutions that God ordered for the maintenance of human welfare are in his "left hand," which following the common typology of his time were named: *oeconomia, politia, ecclesia*. In this realm the definite criterion for ethical decisions was the achievement of equity through dialogical reason.[3]

In the spiritual régime, located in God's "right hand," God's sovereignty worked through justification as *iustitia passiva*. Here no cooperation is

---

3. For the interpretation of how reason implies conversation and dialogue, see Honecker, *Sozialethik zwischen Tradition und Vernunft*.

allowed for. Synergism is ruled out. The human response is of a doxological and not ethical order. In the face of God's sole spiritual sovereignty, the human being can only render glory to whom glory is due. The spiritual principle precluded the possibility of reducing this realm to the heteronomous finitude of institutions. A doxological absence in this spiritual régime would correspond to the abjuration of reason and disregard of justice in the earthly régime. Secularism and autonomy are as much of an evil in one realm as idolatry and demonry is in the other.

The world in which Luther proposed these distinctions was in many respects a closed world, closed around its institutional formations, namely the economy or familial nucleus (as the pre-Industrial Revolution's basis of economic activity), the politics (that included all policy making) and the church (as the institutional form religion took). Luther did not challenge the divine foundation of these institutions as modernity would have done, but introduced the idea of the transient character of worldly institutions. The modern aspect of his thought was to relativize them in the face of a spiritual principle that would guarantee the freedom of human *conscience*. No human authority should take from the individual the right to books, one of the Reformer's metonymies for reason, and one's own faith. Making this distinction Luther could introduce the possibility of having a language, of speaking about the spiritual presence in grace through faith in a discourse that would not conform to or be subjected to the institutional demands of society. And, this for him, was because this presence was concealed *sub contraria specie*, under its opposite, and praise or lament was the only response to the Inscrutable Other. The ultimate mystery is here: we are condemned totally by the law, but simultaneously saved by the gospel. Even if in political, economic, or ecclesiastical matters he could at times be very conservative, he did not believe in the absolute character of such institutions and thus was often critical of them.

Justification and Justice

The distinction between the languages concerning justification and justice, namely doxological and ethical, had a liberating impact to the extent that it dismantled the belief in an institutional reality in which both justification and justice were supposed to be achieved by adjusting to the instituted order resulting in both a demise of the freedom of conscience and the absolutizing of order.

Once modernity finally and formally granted to individuals the right of freedom of conscience and recognized that institutions were not only relative but also transient, Luther's distinction lost its critical edge and fell into what was called a double morality. The distinction is now frequently made in terms of the separation between the public and the private realms in which the autonomy of the public sphere could be separated from the freedom of the private sphere, where conscience was entitled to make moral judgments. Hence the formulation of the modern political Kantian inspired motto: believe anything, but obey.[4] And Luther's creative distinction of the two discourses—the relative discourse of order that should reasonably rule everyday life and the absolute paradoxical discourse about the human condition of being *simul iustus et peccator*—received an authoritarian straitjacket against which so much criticism has been voiced.

The danger of such a development is one of splitting or separating the two realities so that autonomy is attributed to the institutionalized realm, whilst theological discourse hovers above the real concerns of everyday existence, addressing the conscience of an atomic individual (which Nietzsche called the "newest creation"). Lutheran orthodoxy was inclined to do this severance in the seventeenth century with the separation of ethics from dogmatics, removing the Christian imperative from social existence. The experiences gained from the Holocaust and from authoritarian political régimes in this century have made us aware of the dangers such an argument entails. Two well-known attempts to correct this problem have been made. They have received theological support beyond the circles from which they originally emerged and have influenced for example even many a liberation theologian.

One of the two attempts builds upon the Reformed tradition with its modern sensibilities proposing a "third use of the law" in addition to the "first" (the political use) and the "second" (the theological use). It bridges the gap between justification and justice, so that the former could be extended and positively recognized in the latter. This has been a legitimate concern and counteracts the tendency to regard society as an autonomous entity and ethics as something that can be decided on the basis of reason alone without any need to appeal to Christian values.

Another proposal came from so-called dialectical theology which calls for the radical understanding of the Lordship of Christ as God's command in the context of social existence. The difference between the defense of a "third use" of the law and the ethics of God's command is that the first entails a positive formulation of ethical axioms to be followed by Christians while the latter assesses the command of God as a negative word directed against *all hubris, all* human self-centered pretentiousness and will to power.

---

4. "Argue as much as you like and about whatever you like, but obey!" Kant, "What is Enlightenment," 55.

The problem with the first solution is that it aims at presenting a Christian option for social organization and will easily lead either to a renewed form of Christendom or to sectarianism. The conviction that there can be a Christian ethos that can be embodied and lived out as an alternative and challenging ethos with formative power over a culture has left a record of admirable witnesses and even martyrdom. However, it has also been easily transfigured into imposing, heteronomic attitudes of disregard, contempt, or even violation of cultures and civilizations as the history of colonialism only too often illustrated. Justification, then, is often measured by welfare, as Max Weber pointed out.

The second stance entails a negative approach to social issues on the basis of the radical affirmation of the Lordship of Christ. Christ's Lordship brings into awareness the demonic element in any exercise of earthly power, raising deep suspicion of the recurrent forms of idolatry besetting all power relations, in spite of all zealous and good intentions with which they might be invested. Between justification and justice there is no equation, no mediation: justice has no other criterion of its own but to subject oneself exclusively to God's command. However, this presupposes that the quest for justice will be a quest for power. This quest follows the failure to adequately recognize actual power relations in play. Needless to say, the power of the powerless ("counter-hegemony") has not only been a way to survive but also a way of resisting and limiting the tyrannical tendencies of hegemonic power. Oppressed and subaltern groups in society have regarded the negative approach to justice as being inadequate, if not suicidal, to bring about the necessary exercise of counter-hegemonic power (the empowerment of the powerless) for the achievement of justice.

This presents a double dilemma. On the one hand is the sheer rejection in attributing autonomy to the social sphere. In the absence of autonomy the problem lies in finding the theological criterion for justice without it being a positive expression of justification, which would result in some form of works righteousness. On the other, a sheer negative stance towards power in the face of the recognition of God's absolute and exclusive sovereignty fails to acknowledge not only the influence of secularism but of societies that are dominated by other religions. So, what is a way out of this mess? A glance back to Luther's insight might be helpful.

The Law-Gospel Asymmetry

In classical Lutheranism there is a curious asymmetry in the relation between the law and the gospel. While the law is divided into two uses (each corresponding to its function in each of the two régimes), the gospel is parallel only with the "theological" use. Even the designation "theological" leads one to suppose that the "political" is devoid of theological significance. This has led to a very pessimistic understanding of the worldly human condition, lived under the political use of the law that in itself would entail no hope for novelty (*pax mundi non speranda*). The gospel was turned into a universal category dissociated from common everyday experience where no novelty, no good news was to be expected. But why should we not speak theologically about quotidian hopes, about health, food, shelter, security, friendship, love, and so many everyday signs of good news that improve the quality of life, without the need to equate them with the ultimate values of the kingdom? In other words, can we not speak theologically about the divine signs of grace even if they are only contingent, particular and relative? Obviously the question *is* what criteria are we to be adopt for differentiating relative good from evil in the midst of everyday experience?

In the Christian tradition this has not been a forgotten dimension, but has frequently been undervalued, particularly in contemporary theology. H. Richard Niebuhr mocked contemporary theology overtaxed by christological dogmas as a "Unitarianism of the second article." This, along with secularism at the other end of the spectrum, has meant the loss of what James Gustafson called the "theocentric perspective."

This points to the need to recognize creation theology as a separate and distinct source of the theological evaluation of our way in the world. A creation theology is needed for at least two interconnected reasons. On the one hand, it allows for criteria to outline our experiences in the world positively. On the other, it provides for a common ground for dialogue with any culture which in its mythical nucleus will also have a story of the beginnings.

To say that creation is the first act of salvation tends to subsume creation into the ultimate language of redemption. Creation is not only to be seen in the perspective of a history of salvation, but of a worldly history in and through which we confess that God creates the space for human belonging.

The classical criteria can here be referred to without further elaboration. It suffices to point to the nucleus of the Judeo-Christian myth, the story that weaves our sense of belonging. It entails an organic and metabolic relation with nature (human beings cultivate the soil, the humus, from which the creature of earth is taken: labor is the continuation of the metabolism implied in the organic exchange between *adam*—human being—and *adamah*—humus, soil) and a dialogical relation with other human beings (the *imago Dei* is a profile recognized only in togetherness, the radical affirmation of egalitarianism). Both novelty and sin can be defined by whether they conform to or break with these two criteria. They are penultimate criteria, ambiguous ones, but nevertheless criteria that can provide a basis for discerning in everyday experience *signs* of life and death. It thus provides us with a working definition of justice, without compromising or separating from it the sense of awe and wonder in the face of the ultimate mystery that justification language brings about.

In pointing to these two criteria I have come full circle and am back at the point of departure: the quest for the third bank of the river. This "third bank" has always been with us in the stories we recount about where we come from, how old we are, and when fear arrived, even if these stories, the myths embedded in the world, have been distorted or covered by the high tide of disenchantment in the river of disembedded modernity.

20

Two Kingdoms Doctrine

When the Rubber Hits the Road

> Luther's Doctrine of the Two Kingdoms ... is like an ingenious labyrinth whose creator lost its plan in the middle of the work.
>
> —JOHANNES HECKEL[1]

THE SO-CALLED TWO KINGDOMS doctrine is the label under which a particular framing of the relationship between God's grace and everyday life in the midst of its institutional realities has been presented in twentieth-century Lutheranism. For half a century it has been the way Lutherans framed the relationship between justification and justice. How is it that this doctrine came to be regarded a central piece in Lutheran theology when it has such a remarkable short history as a "doctrine" and for the last decades has even faded into oblivion?[2] The reasons for this phenomenon are closely connected to a particular modern (Western) agenda fraught with the crisis of legitimacy of modern institutions.[3] And here we can be even more specific and locate the discussions within the German context from the end of the Weimar Republic through the post-World War II reconstruction. At the core of it lies the experience with Nazism. Regardless of the answer, the question

---

1. Heckel, "Im Irrgarten der Zwei-Reiche-Lehre," 317.
2. "For the last two or three decades, the 'doctrine of the two kingdoms' has been one of the most debated aspects of Luther's theology." Bornkamm, *Luther's Doctrine of the Two Kingdoms*, 1. Gerhard Ebeling sees in "the doctrine of the two kingdoms ... the fundamental problem of theology" being expressed (*Word and Faith*, 389).
3. See Habermas, *Communication and the Evolution of Society*, 178–205.

remains the same: In the face of the increasing awareness of the erratic and potentially volatile character of modern institutions how is the Christian faith to relate to them? The question has been one of legitimacy. Under which conditions can institutions claim the right to exercise dominion?[4] And many times the Lutheran answer to the legitimacy question was to grant these institutions autonomy vis-à-vis theological demands.[5] If the advantage of such a separation of competences is to avoid theocratic tendencies, exclusivism, and other "isms," it has also often proven disastrous under the particular conditions in which it was historically applied.[6] Further, its recent demise (who still discusses this doctrine today?[7]) is certainly linked with a thesis that dominated sociology of religion throughout most of the twentieth century, but is now generally accepted as wrong, namely, that modernization leads inevitably to secularization.[8] The clear distinction between the spiritual and the earthly was thought to be the articulation of a theology for a secularized world in which religion and everyday life could and should be kept apart.

The challenge is to address the question of justification and justice in the context of the "two kingdoms doctrine," and draw implications for its relevance in contemporary theology and ethics. To this end we must address the following questions. How and where did this doctrine emerge and what are its problems? Can these problems be traced back to Luther himself? Is there something that ought to be retained from this "doctrine"? And, finally, can it be relevant for a global multicultural reality?

The Genealogy of a "Doctrine"

The "two kingdoms doctrine" is a twentieth-century creation insofar as its formal status is concerned. As it is used in contemporary discussions,

---

4. It is important to notice that the question behind it was not one of authenticity (What are the practices by which subjects truly constitute themselves—*authenteo*?). See Habermas, *Legitimation Crisis*.

5. To focus its criticism on this point of the Lutheran heritage is the great merit of the Barmen Declaration.

6. This was the case not only in Germany but also in South Africa under Apartheid and in Chile under Pinochet, and some East European countries under the Soviet régime or influence. See Duchrow, *Zwei Reiche und Regimente: Ideologie oder evangelische Orientierung?*

7. To my knowledge few are the exceptions for over three decades. But see Dalferth, *Die Zweireichelehere Martin Luthers im Dialog mit der Befreiungstheologie*; and Montes, *Religión y nacionalismo: la doctrina luterana de los dos reinos como teología civil*. I thank John Stumme for calling my attention to this latter work.

8. Berger, "Protestantism and the Quest for Certainty," 782.

this concept was coined, as a *terminus technicus*, by Franz Lau in an essay published in 1933.⁹ The main thrust of the argument is the distinction between the spiritual reality, the *spiritualia*, and the earthly institutions, as the *carnalia* are defined. The *carnalia* are for Lau an *expression* of the *lex naturae*, but conditioned to change according to the *jus positivum*, the positive law that adjusts itself to changing circumstances for "time changes laws and customs" (*tempora mutant leges et mores*).¹⁰ Lau called this particular way of framing the issue in theological terms the "two kingdoms doctrine" (*Zweireichelehre*).

Lau's essay is an attempt to address and overcome the dispute, born along with the Luther Renaissance early in the twentieth century, between Ernst Troeltsch and Karl Holl on the question of Luther's understanding of the relationship between the divine law and natural law, and how they are institutionally embodied or positively expressed. For Troeltsch, the "early Protestantism" of Luther or Calvin was "simply a modification of Catholicism, in which the catholic formulation of the problems was retained, while a different answer was given."¹¹ Early Protestantism, argues Troeltsch, "exactly like the Middle Ages, everywhere subsumes under itself the *Lex Naturae* as being originally identical with the law of God."¹²

Holl, however, sees in Luther the opposite of what Troeltsch has found. For Holl, "Luther did not appeal to a natural law."¹³ Even if using terminology akin to natural law arguments, which admittedly causes some confusion, Luther is seen by Holl as a forerunner of Hume, setting apart the fundamental connection between *is* and *ought* that sustained the medieval doctrine of the natural law along the lines of Aristotelian entelechy.¹⁴ If Troeltsch's Luther is a "restored" relic of medieval Catholicism, Holl's is the beacon of modernity. Here the problem became one of adjustment or non-adjustment to the earthly stations (*Stände*) of the state, family, economy, and the church, as they were defined in medieval times, and by Luther himself. If Troeltsch saw in Luther a fundamental adjustment, Holl sustained a theonomic

---

9. Lau, *"Äusserliche Ordnung" und "weltlich Ding" in Luthers Theologie*. Others would date it to the publication of Harald Diem's seminal work on Luther's hermeneutics, "Luthers Lehre von den zwei Reichen untersucht von seinen Verständnis der Bergpredigt aus: ein Beitrag zum problem, Gesetz und Evangelium," in Sauter, *Zur Zwei-Reiche-Lehre Luthers*. See Honecker, *Soziallehre zwischen Tradition und Vernunft*, 176.

10. Lau, *"Äusserliche Ordnung"*, 38.

11. Troeltsch, *Protestantism and Progress*, 59.

12. Ibid., 45.

13. Holl, *Reconstruction of Morality*, 103.

14. Ibid., 145–47.

principle at work in Luther's understanding of Christian morality, for which the norm was *lex charitatis* and not by *lex naturae*.

However, in spite of the theonomic orientation of Holl's exposition of Luther, the way in which he insisted on Luther's break with the natural law tradition and on the separation between is and ought brought the suspicion that for Holl Luther would be defending the autonomy of institutions in the tradition of Kant's definition of the private use of reason by which one is compelled to accept their internal rules.[15] After this it became common to interpret the Lutheran theory of law along the lines of the notion of divine ordinances or mandates, but reject an abstract normative concept of natural law.[16] So the question became one of relating freedom with legal obligation in the sense of the "first (political) use of the law."

Lau's conceptualization of the "two kingdoms doctrine" was in fact an attempt at rescuing the uniqueness of the Reformation (over against medieval Catholicism) without succumbing to modern secular autonomy (*Eigengesetzlichkeit*). But if the solution seems so simple, how do we get to what a quarter of a century later was defined by Johannes Heckel as a maze? For Heckel, "Luther's Doctrine of the Two Kingdoms, as it has been articulated in Protestant theology, is like an ingenious labyrinth whose creator lost its plan in the middle of the work, so that [one] cannot find the way out."[17]

The Design of the Labyrinth

Fifty years of intense debate followed this initial argument. But the parameters of the debate would remain basically the same and would become, particularly in the 1970s, the litmus test for diagnosing a Lutheran's stance on any social issue. Flanked by the classical Reformed tradition of a "third use of the law," on the one side, and the Roman Catholic natural law tradition on the other, the two kingdoms doctrine became the Lutheran identifying badge. Yet within Lutheranism's own ranks the divisions were no less relevant. On the one side there were the "Barthians" in the Lutheran camp calling for the primacy of the lordship of Christ in dealing with questions of justification and justice. On the other side we find an array of liberal-inspired and confessionally framed theologies proclaiming a hands-off approach to

---

15. See Kant, "What is Enlightenment?," 5–7.

16. Hence there was a compromise; mandates and the "stations" (Stände) were neither under natural law, nor were they autonomous. Bayer, "Nature and Institution," 125–59, particularly 129–31. See also Pannenberg, *Ethics*, 26f.

17. Heckel, "Im Irrgarten der Zwei-Reiche-Lehre," 317.

Christian claims over what were regarded as autonomous spheres of public life. The issue was not settled; it was evaded by exhaustion.

Now, after four decades of only faint murmurs about it being heard, it might be time to revisit the issue in a different light, within different contexts and with a new agenda.[18] It was at the eclipse of the "two kingdoms" debate that two interrelated factors came into play in theological discussions and pertain to the issues and problems plaguing that debate. The first, briefly mentioned above, is that the parallelism between modernization and secularization is a particular and localized phenomenon, not a universal one. The second is that voices from around the world started to make their presence in the theological scenario. The traditional dissemination centers of theology have since become aware of their own location as a methodological and theological issue. And it is not by chance that these centers were largely the same in which the concomitance between modernization and secularization was being promoted. Christian theology in its Western northern manifestation has become aware of its particularity in a multi-religious world, albeit modernized and globalized. Under these circumstances, it is indeed interesting to probe how would one revisit the quandary plaguing the "two kingdoms doctrine."

Tracing the problem back to Luther, we can observe that it stems from two different theological models that are unevenly blended in Luther's own theological musings over some insights that neither he nor the Confessions framed as a doctrine as such. Luther was working simultaneously with two theological blueprints of very different origins; two informing theories, as the philosophers of science would call them. It was akin to the labor of an alchemist—trying to get orange juice by squeezing together apples and bananas. The first is related to Luther's understanding of the relationship between law and gospel. The gospel is the end of the law in the sense of bringing the power of the law to termination. The second was predicated upon the way earthly institutions (*carnalia*) were connected to natural (and divine) law. The gospel is seen here as restoring the law to its fullness, bringing it to fulfillment, which is the other sense of "end" or *telos*. Hence, out of these two sets of issues, efforts at a systematic reconstruction of Luther's understanding of the relationship between justification and justice have been attempted. In general, these two models are distinguished by a somewhat consistent use of terms in his German texts: "kingdoms" (*Reiche*) and "governances," or "regiments" (*Regimente*).[19] The first model (when "kingdom"

---

18. As indicative of the signs of the times, in February 2015 the Historical Commission of the German National Committee of the LWF sponsored a major symposium on "Luther's Two Kingdoms Doctrine in the Political Context of the 20th Century."

19. Even these terms are not consistently used by Luther. While in German *Reiche*

is the dominant category) goes back to the Augustinian tradition of the two cities (*civitates*) implying an axiological distinction, while the second (when "governance" language is more often used) retrieves the main elements of the medieval theory of two powers (*potestates*), or swords (*gladii*) implying a distinction of competences. But since in the Latin texts this distinction does not occur, the German distinction between *Reiche* and *Regimente* should be taken only as symptomatic of a search for a new language while revealing traces of different informing theories.

Depending on the way Luther is read, emphasis on one or the other of these informing theories is going to have a bearing on how the "two kingdoms doctrine" is interpreted and presented. Some will lean toward one end of the spectrum and could be characterized as having an "Augustinian" reading of Luther, with emphasis on the negative attitude toward institutions.[20] On the other end of the spectrum are the more conventional interpretations that see the "two kingdoms" mainly along the lines of the medieval understanding of the two swords, which emphasizes Luther's positive appreciation of the human institutions as founded in an original divine ordinance.[21] While the "Augustinian" emphasis sees Luther's concern in the efficacy of the gospel in instituting the law of Christ, in conforming reality to the lordship of Christ, the latter, medieval reading sets the emphasis on the adjustment of Christian life to the orders of creation. While the former entails christological emphasis, the latter has a social and institutional agenda. But both express the same concern with social ethical criteria that shape institutional commitments in politics, economy, the church, the family, etc. Both are concerned in defining how justification is related to justice.

The attempt to "edit" Luther out of what is perceived to be a methodological eclecticism suggests that there is a theoretical blunder that ought to be cleared of its unsystematic elements, or harmonized under one controlling paradigm only. However, we may contend that there is more to it than the apparent inconsistencies suggest. By combining the two traditions Luther was attempting to ensure two things simultaneously. First, to affirm the radical *crisis* that the Word represents in the midst of the world and its

---

and *Regimente* suggest a clear distinction between conceptual schemes, in Latin the term used for both is only *regnum*. For the best description of the formation of these two traditions, see Duchrow, *Christenheit und Weltverantwortung*, particularly his main thesis on 440.

20. See, e.g., Wolf, "Die 'lutherische Lehre' von den zwei Reichen in der gegenwärtigen Forschung," 255–73; Diem, "Luthers Predigt in den zwei Reichen," 175–214; Bornkamm, *Luther's Doctrine*.

21. See, e.g., Elert, *Morphologie des Luthertums*, vol. 2; Althaus, "Luthers Lehre von den beiden Reichen in Feuer der Kritik," 40–68; and Lau, "Äusserliche Ordnung."

régime;[22] second, to uphold also that this world with its ordinances, its institutions, is still part of God's good creation, regardless of its corruption by sin.[23] What once was an exception (the Fall) is now disguised as the rule and has spread itself from humans through their institutions to nature itself.[24]

So here we are in the midst of the maze or labyrinth that Heckel diagnosed in 1959. However, the term he used in German, *Irrgarten* may be also translated by "maze," which more properly describes what the discussion has become.[25] Luther tried to bring together apparently incompatible theological constructions, and ended up in a fossilized idea of the "orders" of creation, incompatible with modern day institutions, or in a system

---

22. For reasons that later will become clear, I find the word *régime* the best way to translate either *Regiment* or *Reich*, avoiding some of the connotations that "regiment," "governance," or "kingdom" carry. A "régime" is a regulated social system that includes institutions and also hegemonic patterns of thought. It combines power and knowledge.

23. In the case of the State (*politia*), unlike the other orders (*ecclesia* and *oeconomia*), some would defend the prelapsarian origin of the State. See Lau, "*Äusserliche Ordnung*", 13–14; Elert, *Morphologie des Luthertums*, 2:56f.; and, in a unique interpretation that will be discussed later, Törnvall, *Geistliches und weltliches Regiment bei Luther*, 38. Others, almost in a Hobbesian manner, would argue that it was an outer medicine (*externum remedium*) instituted as a result of the fall. See Diem, "Luthers Lehre von den zwei Reichen," 56–59, 70–72; Heckel, "Im Irrgarten der Zwei-Reiche-Lehre," 343–45; Bornkamm, *Luther's Doctrine of the Two Kingdoms*, 34–35; and Bayer, "Law and Morality," 64. Luther himself is ambivalent.

24. The metaphor of the mask (*larva*) Luther takes from the medieval carnival in which the mask was both a disguise and an allegory to unveil the real situation that in fact was more masked than the mask itself. Unlike Luther and his contemporaries, we suppose a divide between nature and institution. For Luther the distinction could be compared to the one between the buffoon and the costumes he wears, while the modern ditch corresponds to the crisis in natural law thinking since Hume. But for Luther such a distinction can no longer be taken for granted, even if Holl is right that he did not rely on the medieval concept of natural law. Nature and culture are both "institutions", and only as such are they also creation. For Luther the being of the world as creation is nature and institution, institution and nature, at the same time. (See Bayer, "Nature and Institution.") To put it still in other terms, nature was, for Luther, artificial, while the reverse then is also true: institutions are natural. The modern understanding of institutions, in the definition of Anthony Giddens, "create settings of action ordered in terms of modernity's own dynamics and severed from 'external criteria' . . . day-to-day social life tends to become separated from 'original' nature" (*Modernity and Self-Identity*, 8). Under these conditions the main question plaguing Lutheran social ethics has been the one of relating God's justifying word, cast in a forensic sense, to a reality of quotidian existence in which the juridical sense for even grasping the passive character that this justification implies is missing.

25. In everyday speech, both maze and labyrinth denote a complex and confusing series of pathways. Technically, however, the maze is distinguished from the labyrinth by its having paths that branch out into dead ends; labyrinths have a single path.

incapable of unfolding a social ethics out of its own premises, surrendering ethics and morality to autonomous spheres in secular existence.

The Mask and the Word

A careful examination of this problem and an insightful Ariadne's thread out of the labyrinth is offered by an unfortunately little known albeit important work by Gustav Törnvall.[26] Breaking with the dominant institutional approach to the "two kingdoms doctrine," Törnvall appeals to a functional interpretation of Luther's categories that refer to what is being discussed under "two kingdoms." Showing Luther's inconsistent use of terms to refer to these realities,[27] he argues that the institutional and substantive language that is used only reveals Luther's concern in being concrete in his imagery.[28] The two governances are fundamentally expressions of the Creator/creature theme in God's self-revelation, through the invisible Word of God (*verbum dei*) and the visible world as masks of God (*larvae dei*). The result, for Törnvall, is that the two kingdoms are two functional aspects of God's revelation: a kingdom of listening (*Hörreich*) and a kingdom of seeing (*Sehereich*). They are perspectives or dimensions of the single act of God's creation and revelation, and only derivatively institutional realities.[29] The question then is how to relate the visible with the audible in the midst of existence and recognize them in their relationship.

Hence, the basic distinction that is operative in Luther, at least since the Heidelberg Disputation of 1518,[30] is the one between the visible and the Word, between creature and Creator, the outer and the inner, between what the senses register and reason draws together, and what grace reveals to the spirit. Between these sets of categories there is a paradoxical and asymmetric relationship with which Luther operates to formulate his understanding of God's revelation.

It is "paradoxical" in the sense that one (the visible) points to the other (the Word), but is in it simultaneously negated. This implies the rejection of analogical reasoning while keeping the appearance of analogical

---

26. Törnvall, *Geistliches und weltliches Regiment*.

27. Ibid., 94–95. He quotes thirty-eight different couples of terms to frame the distinction.

28. Ibid., 38.

29. Cf. 17. In his interpretation of the law in Luther, Gerhard Forde follows a similar insight: "'law' is to be taken in a functional rather than a material sense." See his locus on "Christian Life," 2:400.

30. WA 1, 353–74; LW 31:39–70.

correspondence, that is, Luther's mode of argumentation entails elements of irony, the breakdown of analogical correspondence. It is impossible to read Luther without constantly being faced with ironic moves that break up continuities and systems of correspondence. It is "asymmetrical" because what appears to be the case in one set of categories that belong to one of the régimes (spiritual or earthly) is not simply reflected in the other, but is shaped in it in unexpected ways. Luther's use of two different theoretical models to articulate this issue of relating the Word to the mask and vice versa is what allows him to keep the ironic tone alive and not succumb to the dominant analogical method and yet keep the search for correspondences. His theology is neither synthesis nor a diastasis, yet simultaneously both. It is irony breaking into the tranquil realm of analogy. What the mask reveals is the very Word hidden in its cracks, to keep Luther's metaphor of the mask.

The Epistemological Turn

Between the mask and the Word, between what the eyes see and the spirit hear lies language; a strenuous search to convey a theological view for which there is not a grammar readily available (after all Luther believed that the Spirit has its own grammar). How would this help us to frame the question of God and justice?

The dramatic dimension of Luther's own anguish over a text of Paul on the justice of God comes to a sharp, if enigmatic, resolution in these words in his commentary on Isaiah 53: "Behold the new definition of justice (*definitionen novam iusticiae*): justice is the knowledge of Christ (*iusticia est cognicio Christi*)."[31] The insight to understand this comes once reading the Heidelberg disputation backwards, from the "philosophical" theses at the end to the theological ones at the beginning. Such a reading allows one to realize that, as Gustav Aulén and others already noticed,[32] Luther is struggling with language in order to bring to light something new, some good news, while being a child of his old world with its rhetoric in all the realms institutionally recognized.

His attack on philosophy (with its "reason"), the economic system (with its "markets"), jurisprudence (with its "justice"), the territorial states (with their "politics"), and the Church (with its "polities") was not to remodel

---

31. This is my translation from WA 31/2, 439, 19–20. The standard English translation (LW 17:230) reads: "You must therefore note this new definition of righteousness. Righteousness is the knowledge of Christ."

32. Nygren, *Meaning and Method*, 243–264; Bielfeldt, "Luther on Language," 195–220; see also chapter 1 above.

them. The Reformation was not about "reforming," as when one restores a building or remodels a house, but it is about a *new* formation. He was well aware of the inefficacy of interweaving the new with the old (Luke 5:36). He wanted to find or even provoke a crack, a crisis, in the systemic arrangements that controlled, ordered, and regulated those institutions that Luther took as basic following a general consensus: *ecclesia, oeconomia,* and *politia.* The "new" definition is not only redressing the old, mending the fractures; it is something new, a gift; it cracks the surfaces, opens up the wounds behind the mask and reveals the crisis. Luther's "new" definition sets itself against the old which he explicitly mentions in the same text: the proverbial *suum cuique* ("to each what to each is due"). The classical definition presumed a correspondence between the order of things (the *Stände*) and God's mercy toward us. The *cognicio Christi* is precisely this new knowledge, this new way of knowing that erupts through the very cracks of the systems of this world. The genitive in *cognicio Christi* means to know Christ, but it also means to have the *cognicio* of Christ, to have Christ's knowledge and Christ's mind; it is a double genitive. And this is a different knowledge of the order of things in the régimes of this world.

It is in the same context of the commentary on Isaiah 53 that Luther talks about how this is accomplished; it is a "wonderful exchange" (*mirabilem mutacionem*). For the Reformer, the danger in the interpretation of this expression is to make the "wonder" of this exchange into a temporary readjustment of relations into a new hegemonic arrangement, thus only reinstating the integrity of the old rule. For him this would be sophistry: "The sophists say that righteousness is the fixed will to render to each his own."[33]

Now the justice of Christ has then two interrelated aspects to it. It entails the grace of God toward us in the midst of our condition although it does so not by supplementing or even mending the systems in the world. It does it also by disclosing the fissures in the systems of knowledge and power. The new justice, the knowledge of Christ, is indeed foolishness. The power of Christ is indeed weakness. Paul's antitheses of 1 Corinthians 1 are an example of the search for this language that breaks through and breaks forth. Hence, it is not by chance the first "Philosophical" Thesis of the Heidelberg Disputation says: "The one who wishes to philosophize by using Aristotle without danger to his soul must first become thoroughly foolish in Christ." Luther himself could praise Aristotle on questions of ethics, which cannot entail the meaning that the philosophy of Aristotle per se is anti-Christian. This thesis makes only sense once one realizes that "Aristotle"

---

33. LW 17:229; *Iusticia est constans voluntas reddenti cuique, quod suum est.* WA 31/2 , 439, 5-6.

functions here as a metonymy for the standards of valid rationality, for the accepted régime of truth, which for the most it was.

While on our pursuit to be righteous, to have our due share and pay our dues, and yet not achieving it, the justice of Christ breaks in and fragments the systems of the world, its philosophy, ecclesial structures, legal rules, in short, economies and régimes of this world. The possibilities of justice in the midst of this world manifest themselves precisely where these economies and régimes break down. However, this is still a negative if not apocalyptic definition of justice. We need to know more than the power of fragmentation, and indeed also that that which brings about justice in the midst of everyday life in and in spite of the powers and the "knowledges" (*epistemes*) that rule the world.

The old quest for the Lutheran relation between justification and justice has been a search for a doctrine, when the very point is that ironically it is a "doctrine" that brings doctrines (insofar as they are human constructions) themselves into question. Addressed often from a moral theological standpoint (What ought we to do in society in accordance with our faith?), or then from an ontological standpoint (How is the creature related to the creator?), what is overlooked in the discussion is the epistemological question about the conditions of possibility for stating the problem (Where are we to look into to find the truth?). Luther's insight brings into question the relation between revelation and the régimes that control knowledge, establish rationalities, norm the market, and rule the church (the visible church is an earthly régime, just like the State or "economy"). This reading of the "two kingdoms doctrine" suggests that only when we understand that it is in the fissures and ruptures in the order of things that the formation of a new justice comes about, that the knowledge of Christ emerges. And this is a renewed, a newly formed justice, not a particular Christian justice, a Christian alternative to the world, but the alterity of Christ in the midst of the world.[34]

If there was a failure in the interpretations of Luther's thought on justification and justice it was not to recognize that when and where the two meet we are in an eschatological dimension.[35] The irruption of justice

---

34. The "third use of the law" is excluded. Although Luther can say that we can create new decalogues (WA 39/I, 47; LW 34:112–13) it is always within the context of the inherited tradition. Thus he writes from Coburg in 1530 a letter to Justus Jonas saying ... *et coepi judicare, decalogum esse dialeticam evangelii, et evangelium rhetoricam decalogi, habereque Christum omnia Mosi, sed Mosen non omnia Christi.* (" ... to begin with a distinction, the Decalogue is the logic of the Gospel, the Gospel the rhetoric of the Decalogue, so that we have in Christ all of Moses, but in Moses not all of Christ.") WA Br 5, 409, 28.

35. To stress Luther's eschatological thinking in connection with the "two

comes from the ends of this world (the outer ends, but also the ends in the midst of the world), exactly there where another world comes about and we have the courage not to disguise it for the sake of the old. The Kingdom of God, which Paul translated as justification, comes to us exactly at that point in time and space where our work, reasons, and régimes end or break down. There, where there is nothing, God creates. And this creation is also the introduction of another knowledge that comes through another way of reasoning, which Paul called the *apokalypsis Iesou Christou*.[36]

Justice as Difference

In its attempt at apologizing for the rightfulness of its order, the system hides its cracks. In the sermon on the "Two Kinds of Righteousness" (1518 or 1519),[37] Luther claims the priority of the alien justice of Christ over our justice that is also God's doing and can only be truly accomplished in divine–human cooperation. Later in the *Bondage of the Will*, the Reformer had worked with this distinction between the realm in which God works alone through grace, and the other one where we cooperate with God (*cooperatio homine cum Deo*) using our reason, work, and institutions.[38] However, there is a necessary logical priority between the first realm and the second. Luther's attack on works, as much as on reason (power and knowledge, as we would say it today), when framed in this context should be able to dispel the recurring suspicion of a Lutheran inherent quietism. And this is so because the earthly régimes (with their second form of justice according to Luther's sermon on the "Two Kinds of Righteousness") in which we are called to cooperate with God are a logical result of God's work in Christ conforming us to him and not displacing us into an alternative realm.[39] In the régimes of power and knowledge, of work and reason that are in place in this world, Luther's spiritual governance is a *difference*, a counter-point in the order of

---

kingdoms" is the merit of Ulrich Duchrow's comprehensive study, *Christenheit und Weltverantwortung*.

36. See Alexandra Brown, *Cross and Human Transformation* and the insightful epistemological study on the theology of the Cross by Mary Solberg, *Compelling Knowledge*.

37. WA 2, 145–52; LW 31:297–306.

38. WA 18, 754, 1–16; LW 33:242–43.

39. Here lies a further problem with the forensic understanding of justification. The first was to conform the logic of grace to juridical models. The additional problem is that it does not link causally and positively the work of redemption with human emancipation. At most it does it negatively by the fact the forgiven person is set free to act.

things; it is another régime in the sense of being a different régime and not an alternative one. In his late (1541?) sermon on Psalm 1 he phrased it like this: "When I say, 'Heaven' of the heaven of the Lord, I do not mean heaven as a site and a place in distinction to the Earth, I mean by it a régime."[40] Such a régime functions as an antithetical factor in the midst of the régimes that our reason and work erect, which are both part of God's good creation and also defiled by sin. Luther's understanding of revelation is indeed what in Greek apocalypse means. Luther's thinking on the two kingdoms motif is an invitation to recognize otherness, the difference that emerges in the midst of our platitudes, as the locus for the insurgence of justice.

What such a reading of the "two kingdoms" motif allows for is a theological practice in which the voices and knowledges of those who are subjugated will come to the fore. If justification is the Word embodying forgiveness, this forgiveness will produce words; it will authenticate the self-expression of those who have been defiled under the weight of sin and oppression. Justification is the word of the Author who authorizes. It authorizes the emergence of other voices dissonant from the prevailing régimes of truth and power. Justice begins here; it begins not by fulfilling the requirements of the prevailing régimes, but by setting other conditions, other parameters, which indeed sound very foolish or mad.

Instead of rejecting flat out the "two kingdoms doctrine" in its classical twentieth-century formulation as a useless relic of a superseded social and theological problem in the West, we can read it as a frail attempt of articulating Luther's own conviction that if justice is to be done it will have to come from the other, and every other is ultimately irreducibly an other.[41]

By this new definition, justice not only addresses the marginalized, heals the wounds of our world, and cares for the poor, but above all listens to their plea (the Pentecost is after all also a miracle of listening), sees the faces of the excluded ones. This is all the more relevant because their plea and faces reveal the fissures in the mask of God in the midst of the crude realities of this world that the régimes constantly try to hide, norm, and regulate. Hiding the margins is the oldest of strategies for maintaining power, for there is where the frailty of power is made manifest.

In sermon XLV of the "Homilies on the Acts"[42] Chrysostom illustrates what I am trying to explain here. The church, recognizes Chrysostom, has plenty of "money, and revenues." This was after all the early Constantin-

---

40. *Quando dico: Celum celi domini, non intelligo celum situ et loco distincto terra, sed ich meine das regiment mit.* WA 49, 224,30.

41. "Tout autre est tout autre" is the expression made famous by Jacques Derrida in his *The Gift of Death*, 82.

42. *The Nicene and Post-Nicene Fathers*, 272–77.

ian church. Institutions for the care of the poor and strangers were created. They were called *Xenodoxeion*. With his thundering golden mouth, Chrysostom launches an attack on them for they were being used by the now well-off Christians to avoid the face of the poor themselves. The incisiveness of Chrysostom's argument reveals someone who was ashamed of his fellow Christians. Chrysostom knew where justice started; it begins by allowing the other, the poor, the stranger to emerge, to have a voice, to have a face. The "two kingdoms doctrine" is not a doctrine. It is an epistemic principle that teaches the faithful that to know Christ is to know justice. And, conversely, where justice cries out there we find Christ. And so Luther: "Thus the world is full of God. In every alley, at your door you find Christ; stare not at heavens."[43]

---

43. *Also ist die welt vol vol Gott. In allen gassen, fur deiner thur findest du Christum. Gaff nicht ynn himel.* WA 20, 514, 27f.

21

Works, Law, and Faith

Régimes and Event in Luther

> It is the event alone, as illegal contingency, which causes a multiplicity in excess of itself to come forth and thus allows for the possibility of overstepping finitude. The subjective corollary . . . is that every law is the cipher of a finitude.
>
> —Alain Badiou[1]

Six months after the nailing of the 95 theses, in April of 1518, another disputation took place in the city of Heidelberg. The "Disputation of Heidelberg" is better known to this day for the famous theses distinguishing the theologian of glory from the theologian of the cross. This "Disputation," however, opens with these two theses that set the theoretical parameters for the whole:

1. The *law* of God, the most salutary doctrine of life cannot advance man on his way to righteousness, but rather hinders him.
2. Much less can human *works*, which are done over and over again with the aid of natural precepts, so to speak, lead to that end.[2]

Though in an unsystematic way, the initial (theological) 28 theses can be divided in the following way. The first 12 starts with the discussion

---

1. Badiou, *Saint Paul*, 81.
2. LW 31:39; WA 1, 353, 15–18 (emphasis added).

of "law" and then passes into the question of "works." The next six theses (13–18) are a criticism of free will. Theses 19–21 elaborate the distinction between the theologian of glory and the theologian of the cross. Theses 22–27 resume the discussion of law and work in the light of the theology of the cross. And the final theological thesis (28) is about love, divine and human. There are different ways to group the theses according to their emphases.[3] The grouping offered here points to the procedural difference that is often neglected. It is aimed at lifting up the significance of the fact that the theses that deal with law and with work mark a clear distinction in the *modus operandi* of the two. Although Luther himself also employs the Pauline expression "works of law," *work* and *law* point to distinct programmes.

There is an asymmetry in the operations of work and procedures of law. The work accomplishes something, produces an objective result for good or bad depending on the efficient cause operating (*operans*), as thesis 27 of the "Heidelberg Disputation" reads. If it is Christ through faith that operates, it is in God's sight good. The law, on the other hand, functions as the measuring rod and regulatory scale of the accomplishments as well as the gauge setting the demands for them to be done or prohibited. Work is determined by its relations to God and the world (*coram deo, coram mundo*), involving love and also desire. Meanwhile, law's procedures are constituted by their use in civil fora or in the divine realm through the theological use of the law, displaying human sociability but also selfish interests. This conceptual distinction has been obscured due to the peculiar development of Luther research in the past century with their concentration on the law–gospel dialectics and/or the two kingdoms motif.

Even while contributing his share to the confusion, the jurist and remarkable Luther scholar Johannes Heckel pointed in the right direction in diagnosing the problem when he remarked that "Luther used the vocabulary of medieval theology, but no one saw that his concept 'natural law' had a new content."[4] And in addition to this, "scholars dealt with the wrong Luther, questioning him as a philosopher of law; as his profession required, he answered, however, as a theologian. Both reasons together are the source of the confusion."[5]

A review of the development of the research on Luther is called for here, for the Reformer's corpus introduces new paradigms in the understanding of God and the word, as it invests old concepts with new meanings

---

3. See, e.g., Vercruysse, "Gesetz und Liebe"; Nestingen, "Luther's Heidelberg Disputation"; Forde, *On Being a Theologian of the Cross*.

4. Heckel, *Lex Charitatis*, 12.

5. Idem.

according to the semantic context in which they are employed or appear. We need also to find another or a new language to think with Luther about things that are disparate. The semantic fields do not relate to each other as entities relate to each other. They cannot be correlated, for the fields into which they are inserted proceed with different grammars. In one field there is a constellation of objective realities revealing some permanence, endurance, fidelity, constancy, and a certain logic of trajectories over time and space. In another dimension there is an eruption of subjectivity that has an eventual character that rouses a truth as subject that attests to an event, but a truth that precedes its logical demonstration. Not unlike Franciscan scholasticism of the thirteenth century (which shared Luther's contempt for Aristotle) this truth cannot separate the object from the subject and thus it is immediate in such a way that when it reveals itself it cannot be thought not to be. This is an event that can only be attested, for it depends on faith not on knowledge. In the field of permanence and constancy what we have are the traces denoted by the event. There they are analytically available, but one still has to believe in the originating event immersed in the depth of subjectivity of the one who attests to it. But how can we tell the story of this convoluted trajectory of Luther's thought on work and law? What follows is an attempt at it.

Régimes and Linguistic Domains

"All words are made new when they are transferred from their own [semantic] context to another."[6] This stance that Luther took during an academic disputation in 1537 was a position that he sustained throughout his life. Indeed Luther's own understanding of this transference is inevitable as he writes to Spalatin in 1519: " . . . (so it follows) in the midst of common language [vernacular] we have been battling."[7] This is, in the Reformer's estimation, not a happy event. "That we have to write books is already a great transgression and an infirmity of the spirit."[8] Yet this genitive should be read as both objectively as well as subjectively; the spirit is suffering infirmity, but also is the one who prompts the infirmity and transgression in order to administer a remedy. While many regret the fact that Luther's theology was not more systematic, it might be argued persuasively that the "unsystematic" nature of his writings cannot be dissociated from his theological program so pugnaciously expressed: "We must not, like these asses, ask the

6. WA 39/I, 231, 1ff.
7. . . . *mixtim (ut fit) vernacular lingua digladiabamur.* WA Br 1, 301, 16f.
8. WA 10/I, 657, 1f.

Latin letters how we are to speak German; but we must ask the mother in the home, the children in the street, the common man in the market place about this, and look them in the mouth to see how to speak, and afterwards do our translation."[9]

Luther's program of "looking people in the mouth" was to give back to them authentic words, stories that raise them out of silence and dissimulation, constantly transgressing disciplinary domains: "I don't know of any other ground than the one offered by the genius of languages [*die Art der Sprachen*] as God has created them."[10] This is succinctly expressed in the presentation of his treatise *To the Christian Nobility* (1520), "the time of silencing is over, the time to speak has come."[11] But what does this speaking accomplish?

The exodus from silence came as a hemorrhagic display of subjectivity, unstable and unregimented by the prevailing standards of legitimacy and systematic order. But no sooner than the movement was ignited came along the longing for stability to bring calm into the excess it unleashed. Luther himself, astounded by the impact of new words irrupting into ossified semantic domains, attempted to offer some hints to tame the chaos, but always leaving a door open for the spirit to stir it all up again. The movement unleashed by Luther was only coated by a plea for some order. Subsequent readings of the Reformer, however, were born already fossilized, with sanctimonious indignation against the stirrings of the spirit.

Luther's apparent lack of systematic discipline has led to a tendency to ignore him, as had been the case even in his own time, which he recognizes in his *Treatise on Good Works*:

> And although I know full well and hear every day that many people think little of me and say that I only write little pamphlets and sermons in German for the uneducated laity, I do not let that stop me. I believe that if I were of a mind to write big books of their kind, I could perhaps, with God's help, do it more readily than they could write my kind of little discourse . . . [12]

Another tendency is to recognize some of his insights, but bypass the corpus of his writings for more systematic and less compulsive elaborations of those insights, as in Calvin, e.g.[13] Or, then it was to take some concepts that play a pervasive role in the Reformer's theology and organize the rest

9. LW 35:190; WA 30/2, 638. See further discussion on chapter 1 above.
10. WA 18, 155, 4ff.
11. LW 44:123; WA 6, 404, 11f.
12. LW 44:22; WA 6, 203, 5ff.
13. A good example of this approach would be Torrance, *Kingdom and Church*.

of the material around these foci, relating them, and dismissing most of the rest as idiosyncratic expressions of an immature mind or of derailed musings of an old man.

The Lutheran "law and gospel" theme has been used in this dogmatic sense of serving as an organizing principle. The way it is used, the universal relationship between the law that condemns and the gospel that justifies and saves becomes the methodological principle for theological reflection. The law–gospel correlation is understood as a correlation between the theological use of the law dogmatically drawn from the universality of sin and the gospel. If the gospel is the response to the question raised by universal sin, then the word of grace is addressed to the individual in its universal sense: the sinner, defined independently from the content of particular sinful acts due to original sin. This individual stands along with the entire human race, all at the same level, before God (*coram Deus*). In the wordly realm (*coram mundo*) the civil use of the law is deprived of its theological significance, losing any correlation with the gospel, as if there were two different kinds of law.[14]

Henceforth, justification becomes an either-or and only an either-or. There is no modulation as to the civic aspect of the law. And this is the reason why good works are said to be necessary fruits of faith, but neither sufficient nor constitutive for salvation, and become even a source of condemnation if seen to be constitutive (good works are mortal sins, Luther often claimed). The logic here is paradoxical, but not preposterous. Works are particular acts with particular historical significance. If they were to be constitutive for salvation, they would in their particularity be also causative of justification! In this case, the scheme of law and gospel on the basis of general sin and universal grace would crumble. But then, why are works necessary? How do good works issue from faith? The response is unequivocal. It is not to conquer grace but to praise and give glory to God, the One who saves us unconditionally, not from social and historical determinations but from original sin. It is an eternal salvation without causal connection with everyday life.

On this topic we have the Lutheran conundrum of the so-called two kingdoms doctrine, a kingdom in the right hand of God and the other in the left that has already been explicated in the previous chapter. Ethics in Lutheran theology has been traditionally framed as a matter of the régime in the left hand of God, to use Luther's metaphor. It falls under the *regnum rationis*; it belongs to civil society where the criteria for vindicating an action

---

14. For a good criticism of this tendency see F. Edward Cranz, *An Essay on the Development of Luther's Thought on Justice, Law, and Society*, particularly 100–105.

is to know whether it is publicly accountable, reasonable, and able to enforce equity in society, economy, politics, and in the church. This is the realm in which human beings cooperate with God, as it is forcefully stated in *The Bondage of the Will*.[15] But why should this cooperation be important? Why should the achievement of equity and justice be of concern of the Christian *qua* Christian?

A commonly taken stance on this matter has defended that peace in the world is necessary for the proclamation of the saving grace, although in itself it accomplishes nothing: *pax mundi non speranda*. Such a view has been guilty of a helpless formalism that has translated "peace" into "order" and was able, in the name of order, to remain silent or even to justify outrageous political régimes. This has been underscored by the supposedly modern assumption about the autonomous character of secular institutions (*Eigengesetzlichkeit*) where theology would not have a say.

Behind this theological position is the theory of the double agency of God.[16] God is both the agent of salvation and the agent of preservation of the world's order. In this situation the discussion became so intractable that, as we have seen, Heckel suggested that the "two kingdoms doctrine" is a labyrinth whose author lost the plan in the midst of construction.[17] It has become indeed a dogmatic maze in which ethics is quite lost. Is it not cynical to justify ethics with the argument that we ought to join God in the task of preserving a helpless world while God saves our souls?

Since Harald Diem published his seminal work on the "two kingdoms" in 1938,[18] it has been argued that the first concern of the Reformer in formulating the distinction between the two régimes emerged out of the hermeneutical need to interpret the Scriptures without allegorizing them. Hence, we are talking about distinct genres or orders of discourse with a common reference: the experience of the will and agency of God. The distinguishing of doxology from ethics, jurisprudence, science, or philosophy found again support within theology to match Luther's high praise for the Psalter.[19] Such a distinction suggests sets of questions and answers that might employ different narratives according to distinct perspectives on the same issue requiring different literary devices all theologically praiseworthy

---

15. *Cooperatio homine cum deo,* WA 18, 754; LW 33:243.

16. See Althaus, "Luthers Lehre von der beiden Reichen," 40–68.

17. Heckel, "Im Irrgarten der Zwei-Reiche-Lehre," 3–39; cf. Heckel, *Lex Charitatis*, 145–75.

18. Diem, "Luthers Lehre von den zwei Reichen untersucht von seinen Verstandnis der Bergpredigt aus."

19. See, e.g., LW 35:254f.

when applied in its proper context (*foro*).²⁰ The doxological language, within which justification is a notion, implies the releasing of infinity, which molds speech, and yet the experiencing of the event will find a different form of expression when rendered in juridical, medical, economic, or philosophical lingo. Doxological language thus addresses the "breaking in of the *eschaton* in time."²¹ It is the occasion for the finite to bear the whole of infinity (*finitum capax infiniti*).

Rephrasing the Issue

Yet even with the insightful suggestion of Harald Diem, the problem still remains. What is the language to be spoken, where is its domain or what is the appropriate time to speak? The issue pertaining to the relationship between justice and justification unfolded into two related conjectures with followers in each camp. The first orders its grammar on the relationship between law and gospel and the second focuses the discussion on the way in which institutions are connected to natural law. Attempts at a systematic reconstruction of Luther's understanding of the relationship between justification and justice have been made accordingly. Nuances aside, one of these two is recognized by the emphasis on the two kingdoms or regiments,²² while the other focuses on Luther's institutional approach drawing on the instituted orders of creation.

The institutional approach that has focused on the "orders of creation" has received significant rejection, for it verged on divesting earthly institutions from theological import and regarding them as autonomous. A new emphasis began in the interpretation of this notion of "orders" or institutional spheres, and it has been lately stressed. It underscored the way Luther attempted to give *theological* significance to the traditional medieval doctrine of the hierarchies, or estates (*Stände*): *ecclesia, politia,* and *oeconomia*

---

20. Between the language spoken *coram deo* and the one *coram mundo* there is a profound difference.

21. Asendorf, *Eschatologie bei Luther*, 127. The author distinguishes the *Totalaspekt der Rechtfertigung* from the *Partialaspekt der Heiligung*. The Jesuit theologian Juan Luis Segundo grasps Luther's distinction when he speaks about the difference between "iconic" and "digital" language. See his *Faith and Ideologies*.

22 The terms to refer to these two realms are not consistently used by Luther. While in German *Reiche* and *Regimente* suggest a clear distinction between conceptual schemes, in Latin the term used for both is only *regnum*. For the best description of the formation of these two traditions, see Duchrow, *Christenheit und Weltverantwortung*. To avoid unnecessary dispute over nomenclature it is proper to call it a distinction of régimes.

(which in pre-capitalist times included labor, market, and—where the term comes from—household). They were categories of social orders that Luther inherited from medieval theology as a matter of course: "First, the Bible speaks and teaches about the works of God; no doubt about that. But these works are divided in three hierarchies: economy, politics, and church."[23] Around 1530, Luther's more general references to the worldly régime (*weltliche Regiment*) became nuanced with the underscoring of the "orders." He was already familiar and had used the popular medieval division of society into three "estates" or "hierarchies,"[24] distinguishing civil governance from the household (*oeconomia*) quite early on. The first time the three estates are mentioned in Luther was in 1519.[25] But the distinction became most prominent with and after his *Confession Concerning Christ's Supper* of 1528 and the *Catechisms* (1529).

While *ecclesia* and *oeconomia* could be easily assumed to belong to the prelapsarian condition as orders instituted by God, the fundamental problem of the theology of the orders of creation has to do with the place of the state and civil society, namely of *politia*. Although Luther did not want to recognize the political order as belonging to the prelapsarian condition, he also knew that politics is grounded in economy—resulting in an ambiguous treatment of the issue.[26] Twentieth-century theologians were divided in the interpretation of Luther's intention. While some would defend the prelapsarian origin of the state,[27] others would argue that for Luther it was an external medicine (*externum remedium*) instituted as a result of the fall.[28] What all agree on is that Luther is ambiguous on the issue and that a choice has to be made to understand the consequences of the human social and political engagements.

In the Middle Ages these hierarchies were often used in the sense of distinct classes, social strata, castes, or rank, and regarded as part and expression of the natural law. The division of these estates took many forms but they were all made in general reference to the clerics, the nobility, and

23. WA TR 5, nr.218.

24. Luther names them variously as *Orden, Stifte, Stände, Hierarchien, Ertzgewalten, fora, mandata,* etc. Cf. Duchrow, *Christenheit und Weltverantwortung*, 503f.

25. See his pamphlet "The Holy and Blessed Sacrament of Baptism." LW 35:38–41; WA 2, 734.

26. See in this connection WA 42, 79; LW 1:103–4.

27. See in this respect Lau, *"Ausserliche ordnung,"* 13–14; Elert, *Morphologie des Luthertums* 2:49–65; and, in a peculiar way, Törnvall, *Geistliches und weltliches Regiment bei Luther*, 38.

28. Diem, "Luthers Lehre," 56–59, 70–72; Heckel, "Im Irrgarten der Zwei-Reiche-Lehre," 343–45; Bornkamm, *Luther's Doctrine*, 34–35.

the commons, all united as the Persons of the Trinity for the sake of the earthly good of the *corpus christianum*, which was above it as the supernatural was to the natural as the *donum superadditum*. In the words of Ruth Mohl, rendering medieval convictions in *The Three Estates in Medieval and Renaissance Literature*,

> God created this threefold society, and so it must be right. He instituted the prayers of the clergy, the defense of knighthood, and the labor of the commons.... Moreover, Holy Church is depended on all of them and without any of them could not stand. Just as the Trinity would be inconceivable without Father, Son, and Holy Ghost, so the Church would be inconceivable without its three estates.[29]

The idea was clear that these estates were discrete parts of body of Christ that served as the natural infrastructure to its spiritual expression in the Holy Church, which was the head and the expression of the *corpus christianum*.[30]

Luther saw the church as an institution as one of the orders mandated by God since creation. It was the first one given to humans with the establishment of the Shabbat. The household and the civil government follow suit. As he writes in the Genesis commentary of 1535–36, "Here we have the establishment of the church [*ecclesia*] before there was any government of the home [*oeconomia*] and of the state [*politia*]."[31] The church is an instrument for the Word of God to be announced to the whole creation and for the human response to be expressed. So was the household or economy instituted to provide for sustenance or nourishment, while civil government was mandated for the sake of social order, defense, and protection. These institutions are by Luther called *larvae*, masks through and by which God works as if through instruments. In his words: "Three institutions (*Stände*) were ordained by God in which we live with God and good conscience. The first is the household; the other the political and worldly regime; the third the church or priestly order—all according to the three Persons of the Trinity."[32] For Luther they did not form classes, strata, or castes discretely separate from each other but are *functions* of human society in which all

---

29. Mohl, *Three Estates*, 330.

30. With his functional adoption of the three orders, Luther simultaneously discredited the medieval essentialist notion of the *corpus christianum*. See Küppers, "Luthers Dreihierarchienlehre," 370f.

31 LW 1:103; WA 42, 79

32. WA TR 6, 266 (nr. 6913). Such use of the *vestigia trinitatis*, common from Augustine through Scholastic theology, is unusual in Luther. See Bayer, "Nature and Institution," 125–59.

participate in one form or another, both passively and actively. So he regards the church not made only of the official priestly class, but of all who worship (priesthood of all believers), and the same is the case with the household and the civil government. The distinction between *vita activa* and *vita contemplativa* collapses as attributes of classes or castes.[33] With this Luther brings a dynamism into the static character of the hierarchies, even as he is still captive to its language and the imagery it evokes. Yet he pours new wine into old skins.

The Human Faculties

The medieval estates' typology relied on the Aristotelian distinction between the spheres of the house (*oikos, domus*) and of the public order (*polis, civitas*), to which the church (*ecclesia*) or the clergy completed the tripartite division.[34] In the tradition of Plato and Aristotle these correspond to the fundamental human vocations of nourishing life (Luther: *nehren*), protecting it (*wehren*) and teaching (*lehren*).[35] Important in Luther's adoption of the medieval three-estates typology are the functional or instrumental changes he brought about, particularly as it concerns the distinction between the household or economy and the political order. The choice of figures of speech, instruments, and masks he employs, and the reason for their choice, is noteworthy.

Luther then goes on to employ Aristotle's distinction of *poiēsis* and *praxis* to make his own distinction between *oeconomia* and *politia*. The distinctiveness of *poiēsis* and the verb *poieo* in contrast to *praxis* is that it designates an activity that results in a production of something, entailing an objective result, while *praxis* conveys a deed done that has an intersubjective effect but does not result in a positive and material outcome. The analogy to the Greek theater is fitting. *Poiēsis* describes the labor of those who built the theater, set the stage, and also wrote the play.[36] *Praxis*, in turn describes the

---

33. Cf. Küppers, "Luthers Dreihierarchienlehre," 361–74.

34. Duchrow, *Christenheit und Weltverantwortung*, 501f. Although the question of the particular conception of the church's institution that includes all humanity (it was instituted for Adam and his descendants) is in itself a topic that tempts me to dwell on for its implications, but this is not the task at hand.

35. This last vocation does not coincide with the church, but belongs to all three orders. See Schwarz, "Ecclesia, oeconomia, politia," 83.

36. The verb *poieo* is used in the Septuagint to translate God's creative activity, including the Hebrew *barah* of which God is the exclusive subject. From there it made it into the Nicene Creed which confesses the belief in God, *poieten ouranou kai ges*, the "poet" of heaven and earth. In the New Testament the verb is used to describe

activity of the actors performing the play. It is needless to add that theory is represented by the audience.

Aristotle's distinction between *praxis* and *poiēsis*, however, undergoes a convoluted history since its reception in the Latin world. These two faculties, through the Middle Ages and well into modernity, were subsumed into the notion of action (*actio*) or practice (*praxis*, since Duns Scotus). The distinction between *praxis* and *poiēsis* would only return explicitly to the philosophical and theological vocabulary with Hegel's *Phenomenology* in the section regarding the master and bondsman relation. There "work" (*Arbeit qua poiēsis*) is presented as the self-actualization of the human in transforming the material world in distinction to the interpersonal relation between the two exemplary figures.[37] The uniqueness of this conception of production as self-production was further developed by Marx's definition of "work" (*Arbeit*) as a metabolism (*Stoffwechsel*) between the worker and nature.[38] This metabolic relationship was distinguished from sociopolitical (intersubjective) relations, to which the term *praxis* was normally applied. *Praxis*, in its narrow sense, with its intersubjective structure, constitutes itself discursively as explanatory narrative and public communication. It is the medium of human communicative action, moral deliberation, and juridical legislation, and all that is required for procedural actions in the polis; it pertains to the life in the polis and the actions necessary to administer it—in short, politics. *Poiēsis*, on the other hand, describes all activity that aims at providing the objective means for the sustenance of life (including intellectual nourishment, hence the etymological root of the word *poetry*), as well as its preservation in the form of human biological reproduction—in short, "economy."

Oeconomia in medieval society, and also as Luther used the term, entailed basically domestic relations, relations of production and reproduction when the household and the economy, in the modern sense of the term, shared the same social space.[39] It was in this institutional reality with its distinctiveness that the Aristotelian *poietic* faculty, as opposed to the political

---

Jesus' healings. The unique acceptation of *poiēsis*, as opposed to *praxis*, was still held sharply by Basil in his *Hexameron* who delivering his lessons to an audience of artisans employed it analogically to connect human labor and divine creation, even as he recognizes the limits of the analogy.

37. Hegel, *Phenomenology of Spirit*, 111–19. See my articles "Theorie und Praxis III. Fundamentaltheologisch" (RGG4) and "Theory and Praxis III" (RPP).

38. Marx, *Das Kapital*, 1:192.

39. Bonhoeffer, recognizing the difficulty with the modern separation of the household from the means of production, divides Luther's *oeconomia* into two mandates: marriage (including family) and labor. Bonhoeffer, *Ethics*, 207–13, passim.

faculty, was preserved. And it is from this background that it should be read and understood.

The crucial point to be stressed is that when the Reformer uses the medieval set of order in doing it on the basis of the Aristotelian distinction of human faculties he reads these institutions in an anthropological key. The result is a phenomenological approach freeing the "orders" from being cast in immutable institutions. If they are "orders of creation" it is of a creation that God is bringing about in the fluidity of the present (*creatio continua*).

When Luther employs the distinction between *politia* and *oeconomia* he does it in order to stress two distinct forms in which these institutions offer differentiated manners through which humans cooperate with God,[40] where God does not work without us. This cooperation is carried out as through instruments or masks. Luther's use of these two metaphors, instrument (*Werkzeug/instrumentum*) and masks (*Larven/larvae*), even though he uses them most often interchangeably,[41] is revealing. *Werkzeug* is an instrument or a tool for a work or labor to be accomplished, a metaphor imported from the economic, or *poietic*, sphere, serving therefore as a *synecdoche* by which a part (tool) is taken for the whole (labor/*poiēsis*).[42] *Larva* is a mask taken from Greek theater by an actor to represent a given role a person plays, or from the medieval carnival to represent an impersonation. The mask is the metaphor appropriate to describe the political person, the one who speaks on behalf of a cause, a person or a group representing and communicating interests on account of the common good, functioning thus as a *metonymy*. However, for the Reformer it is clear that the agent behind the tool or the mask is either God or the devil and the final end is accordingly decided.

Although both *oeconomia* and *politia* are orders instituted by God, they are not autonomous or neutral. For Luther, natural law and divine law are one and the same, only *used* differently for distinct services to be accomplished through instruments or masks. The "supernatural" is not an *additum*, but lies in the depth of the "natural" as such, as he claimed regarding the third mode of Christ's presence according to his humanity in the *Confession* of 1528 (a passage quoted at length in the Solid Declaration, art. VII).[43] But the distinction between *oeconomia* and *politia* is what is decisive

---

40. LW 33:243.

41. See the use of these two terms used for politics in the *Lectures on Galatians* (LW 26:96; WA 40/I, 176).

42. For Luther's love of synecdoche as "a most sweet and necessary figure of speech," see LW 32:169; WA 8, 65, 8f.

43. LW 37:222-24; WA 26, 335, 29-336. See Kolb and Wengert, *Book of Concord*, 609-11 (art. VII).

here. Decisive it is because, in addition to being a receptacle of grace in *vita passiva*, it comprises two fundamental aspects of Luther's anthropology in *vita activa*: the human as a producer and as political animal.

Communication

As mentioned in the beginning of the book, Luther's as well as the Reformation's primary objective, to use the terminology of Gustavo Gutierrez,[44] was to pave the way for the underside of history to be privileged, to create a language that would enable the voiceless to have a voice. And as we saw the *communicatio idiomatum* was an effective tool to articulate this.

Luther's language game puts into practice his doctrine of the person of Christ, including the disputes over the Lord's Supper. Although the three *genera* of the *communicatio idiomatum* were not developed systematically by Luther himself, they were nevertheless deduced from his careful treatment of Chalcedon, particularly in the *Confession* of 1528 and *On the Councils and the Church* of 1539.[45] This communication of distinct idioms, dialects or facets of language developed for Christology is, however, read by early Lutherans in connection with the three modes of presence that correspond to the three medieval orders and cohere with the human faculties of Aristotle. The *genus idiomaticum* is that which translates for the sake of communicative action, when the will causes a deed (*praxis*) and thus is the mode of communication in *politia*. The *genus apotelesmaticum* is the one that denotes creation of objective reality (*poiēsis*). And the *genus majestaticum* is the characteristic of theological language that doxologically expresses how the finite is capable of the infinite (*finitum capax infiniti*). This is indeed a multilayered view of language which does not surrender the theological stimulus in discourses that do not belong to theology proper.

A further evidence of the distinct operational and procedural principles behind the distinction between the idioms used in *oeconomia* and *politia*, on the one hand, and theology, on the other, is to be found in *Disputatio de homine* of 1536.[46] In the initial nineteen theses on philosophy, Luther offers a revealing interpretation of the "four causes" of Aristotle in which he flatly denies philosophy and the sciences the capability of defining the efficient and the final cause for human existence, as he had just stated some months before

---

44. See Gutiérrez, *The Power of the Poor in History*, particularly chapter 7, "Theology from the Underside of History."

45. LW 37:209ff. and LW 41:103ff.

46. Ebeling, *Disputatio de homine*, 15–24.

in his first *Lectures on Genesis*: "God is the efficient and the final cause."[47] Theology alone is entitled to pronounce that, because they belong to God's own agency done apart from human cooperation. But as to the material and the formal cause Luther grants reason or philosophy some say, even if only at the level of the appearance of things in the case of the material cause or, in the case of the formal cause, as something that philosophers will dispute about but never agree upon (*nunquam conveniet inter philosophos*, thesis 15). Luther does not spend too much time discussing these two causes, but the distinction offers parallels to the one that we find at work in the institutions we are dealing with, and are directly related to the operational and procedural principles at work in *poiēsis* and *praxis*, respectively.

Blessed to Be Saints

The *causa materialis*, the material cause, is the one that presents the humans for what they are even in the midst of sin and of being a sinner,[48] which means one's own production and self-production and, therefore, shows what comes to be seen as the case (*satis videre*). The humans become "visible" by what they produce as the result of their labor or *poiēsis*.[49] The *causa formalis*, on the other hand, has to do with speech (*verbum vocale*) and communication;[50] it is about human re-presentation in the political sense of *praxis*. Yet it is proper for theology to address issues pertaining to human being as a whole, in a manner of speaking, in an idiom that calls to the fore efficient and final causes. This is theology's lingo. But as a Christian one is not excused from participating in any or all the divinely instituted orders as Luther states in the *Confession* of 1528: "But the holy orders and true religious institutions established by God are these three: the office of priest, the estate of marriage, the civil government. All who are engaged in . . . these are engaged in works which are all together holy in God's sight."[51] And he adds that "above these three institutions and orders is the common order of Christian love, in which one serves every needy person . . ."[52] All of this is indeed theological in *sensu latu* and apply to all. Strictly speaking, however, what makes a theologian is an experience that is bliss in the midst of trial

---

47. LW 1:127.

48. Ebeling, *Disputatio de Homine*, 347.

49. The use of the word *labor* for the delivery of a child is still a linguistic relic of the close association between human production and sexual reproduction.

50. Ebeling, *Disputatio de Homine*, 347f.

51. LW 37:364; WA 26, 504, 30ff.

52. LW 37:365; WA 26, 505, 10ff.

(*Anfechtung*): "For to be holy [*heilig*] and to be saved [blessed/*selig*] are two entirely different things."⁵³ This grammar of bliss, a.k.a. doxology, emanates from the gratuitous spring of the river of love, flowing even and because its banks give permanence and endurance to the stream..

Work is then the operational principle that organizes the household, labor, human reproduction, all of that which implies human drives, desires and appetites and concerns the human relationship with nature. The principles of work are concerned with metabolism that happens among organisms. They are constrained by constants—laws of the physical world, either organic or inorganic. In this realm of work the relationship between action and law is that the law establishes the condition of possibility for the work to be done. The knowledge of the physical or organic law confines the outcome of the "product," even as mutations happen, re-inscribing laws of physics and nature in general.

Law, in its juridical sense, is the procedural principle that organizes civil society, the state, and associations that aim at achieving what Luther regarded the goal of the first or civil use of the law: reason and equity (*Billigkeit*). Here the law is posited as the result of a social process, the aim of a process of socialization.

The asymmetry between these two dimensions as estates in regards to the law has been a source of considerable confusion, but they function differently in how they are related to God's grace. In terms of works, grace is superfluous for the object of one's love and adoration is believed to be construed by our own power to bring things into being. This is the essence of idolatry, and lies at the center of the *oeconomia* into which we are called to be co-operators with God. Idolatry entails acquisition, building or control of the objective world turning subjects into objects, bodies into merchandise, lured by the power of fetishism.

Now, in terms of law, in its juridical sense, it is not the love and attraction to the object that undermines the reception of grace. What undermines it is manifested in the human drive to legislate its own persona, to be subsumed under the mask required for social existence in conformity with the dominant ideology of the day. In other words we are justified by adjustment to the legal order. Here the good work is to create a fair, reasonable, and equitable society. Yet when this order or adjustment becomes an end in itself precluding the eruption of an eventual truth, sin manifests itself in terms of demonry, of legislating systems of privilege that prevents people access to the civil realm in which voices can be heard for justice to be done and the

---

53. LW 37:365; WA 26, 505, 18ff.

right of free speech is respected even and above all for the sake of a truth that defies order.

The intermingling of these two operational principles and their understanding of law, one natural and another positive and historical has been responsible for the outburst of some unprecedented violence not to establish a new law (as is the aim of any revolution) but to hasten its fulfilment. Nazism wanted to accelerate the dominance of the superior race by law of nature. Stalinism quickened historical law in creating the equality of all. As much as the former justified its politics as a historical necessity in its *poietic* endeavor, the latter saw history fulfilling in *praxis* a natural evolution. These two then, work and law, are discrete operations relative to each other, but should neither be mixed nor confused. Their mixing seems to be the occasion for the acclaimed autonomy of the secular order and the idolatrous and demonic claims to absoluteness and the simultaneous neglect of the third dimension (*ecclesia*),[54] which is still an institutional dimension of endurance and permanence. Yet the *ecclesia* is the proper space in which the doxological expression or response to the event through which we are blessed is housed. Sanctified, holy, we are by following in work and law the traces of the event.

---

54. As to *ecclesia*, it plays a significant role in this context, but it cannot be dealt with here. See Westhelle, *Church Event*, 31–46, 89–106.

22

Power and Politics

THE CONTRIBUTIONS OF LUTHER are varied, needless to say colorful, but the two kingdoms doctrine was one of the more notable ones. It soon became the litmus test to diagnose the Lutheran stance on social issues. And with it came its own promises and problems.

The two kingdoms doctrine dominated much of Luther research on power and politics following Franz Lau's essay of 1933,[1] already alluded to in chapter 20, and it continued to be discussed through the middle of the 1970s. From being one of the most debated issues in Luther's theology[2] and the fundamental problem of theology,[3] the two kingdoms doctrine was hardly in the LBC (Lutheran Broadcasting Corporation) news for the last three decades, there being almost a complete silence regarding this "doctrine." The "two kingdoms," born as a "doctrine" only in 1933, had indeed a short life.[4]

Did the concern about politics and power in Luther's theology fade accordingly with the malaise that brought to naught a once famous and highly debated doctrine? The answer is a qualified no! Qualified it is because the topic is not the same as it was raised before. Of the two kingdoms doctrine it can be said what was stated in graffiti on the wall of the University of Bogotá, Colombia, years ago: "When we had almost all the answers, the questions were changed." Indeed, the questions changed.

---

1. Lau, "Äusserlich Ordnung" und "weltlich Ding" in Luthers Theologie.
2. Bornkamm, *Luther's Doctrine of the Two Kingdoms*, 5.
3. Ebeling, "Necessity of the Doctrine of the Two Kingdoms," 389.
4. See chaper 20 above.

Migration and the Economy

More diverse issues came to the fore prompting new questions that were not there before. The reference of the graffiti at the wall of the University of Bogotá was a veiled reference to the changes that affected the world with the end of the Cold War, the dissolution of the Soviet Union, the fall of the Berlin Wall in 1989. But there are many other issues that have come into the agenda for which the year of 1989 stands as a symbol. For example, the growing diversity in feminism, and the gay movement that has an acronym that is ever increasing to accommodate different pleas, bringing the relationship between gender, human sexuality, and reproductive rights to a new plateau. In addition to these one must add immigration, which is considered one of the social markers of the century, particularly as it affects the traditional places where most Lutherans live—the US, central Europe, and Scandinavia. Most of these immigrants to these places come to find a source of livelihood. Strictly political refugees are among them a minority, even as the distinction between the two categories is imprecise. The most common cause of migration is the search for a place to ensure livelihood and to establish a household, to have an "economy." Politics and economics are indeed bundled together but they remain remarkably distinct. And it is only timely and salutary that we revisit Luther's theology with regard to this distinction, especially since it is an intricacy that the two kingdoms doctrine has not been effective in addressing. Indeed it tended to overlook this incisive yet nuanced distinction between politics and the economy.

The search for livelihood and the means to sustain and propagate life bring together what the West has strived so arduously to keep apart, the public and the private. Migrant workers in search for sustenance for themselves or their families raise issues about sexual ethos and reproductive rights that are closely intertwined with labor and the economy. This is not unknown where the means for survival are at their minimum. One does not need to search high and low for such instances. Consider the case of many places in the Third World where survival and reproduction are so closely linked together as to form an economic-political Gordian knot that defies unlacing. To attribute stances church leaders and politicians in these places take on issues pertaining to the aids pandemics or homosexuality to a moralistic pietism or political opportunism is not precisely helpful. It is not helpful insofar as it does not address the intimate relationship between sexual reproduction and the production of the means of sustenance, that is, the economy. The separation between production and reproduction can only be done in societies, as in modern Western societies, where the matters of the house or the bedroom have been privatized and economy moved out of the domain of the household. But it is not so in other parts of the world, mainly, but not exclusively, in the planetary south. For many of the poor in the world, raising children is their pension plan. The knot that intertwines sexual reproduction (and the moral problems it raises) with a sustainable livelihood, that is to say reproduction and production, can only be untangled when reasonable levels of international justice and economic equity is achieved.

Meanwhile, Lutheranism is moving south, to places where survival is often negotiated on a daily basis. In the last fifty years, the Lutheran majority on the North Atlantic axis has declined from about 90 percent to less than 60 percent. Lutheran churches in the South, particularly in Africa and Asia, are seeing a booming escalation in membership numbers, while these numbers are dwindling in Europe and the United States, projecting a near future with the majority of Lutherans in the southern hemisphere. This shift is not primarily the result of physical migration, yet it does indicate a symbolic change, a symbolic "migration," as it were. That this will change the agenda of Lutheran theology and ecclesial practice is indeed expected. Also expected is the reading of Luther to comply to this changing agenda, upsetting the hegemony that Germany, Scandinavia, and the United States have exercised (and still do) in Luther research.[5] With this, certainly the questions change, as much as they changed in regard to politics with the end of the Cold War. Changing *agenda* affects the *credenda*. In short, these issues addressed to church and theology are not only or primarily of a political nature; they pertain to the household in the broader sense of the term, to what was included in times prior to the emergence of financial capitalism and the Industrial Revolution in what was called the *oeconomia* in the etymological sense of the term, the rules and workings of the house.

The Material and Formal Causes

This brings us to address anew to Luther the question of power and politics with the question of the economy in mind, after the discussions about the two kingdoms has apparently faded to near oblivion. Around 1530, Luther's more general references to the worldly régime (*weltliche Regiment*) become more nuanced. By 1530, particularly after the *Confession* of 1528 and the *Catechisms* (1529) Luther's references to the earthly régime receives an analytical treatment with the incorporation of the popular medieval conception

---

5. Of symbolic significance is also the fact that since the first International Congress for Luther Research, held in Aarhus, Denmark, in 1956, for the first time the Congress was held in the planetary south, in Canoas, Brazil, in 2007.

of the three estates or hierarchies.[6] In Luther's usage these become distinct publics in which different anthropological faculties are employed for the sake of life in this world.[7] Of singular importance in Luther's adoption and revision of the medieval three estates' conception is the distinct demarcation between civil government (*politia*) and the household (*oeconomia*) and their attributions.

What is important in Luther's adoption of the medieval three estates typology already discussed above[8] are the functional or instrumental changes he brought about, particularly as it concerns the distinction between the household or economy and the political order. Aristotle in the *Politics*, influenced by Plato's *Republic*, and with his own regard for the natural state of slavery, distinguished between those who held responsibilities for the carrying out of the duties of the state, the citizens and the oligarchy, on the one hand, and, on the other, husbandmen, craftsmen, and laborers of all kind who "will of necessity be slaves or barbarians"—the latter fairly corresponding to what we would now call immigrants.[9]

We have already seen the distinctiveness of *poiēsis* and the verb *poieo* in contrast to *praxis*. The verb *poieo* is used in the Septuagint to translate God's creative activity, including the Hebrew *barah* of which God is the exclusive subject. From there it made it into the Nicene Creed which confesses the belief in God, *poieten ouranou kai ges*, the "poet" of heaven and earth. In the New Testament the verb is used to describe Jesus' healings. The unique acceptation of *poiēsis*, as opposed to *praxis*, was still held sharply by Basil in his *Hexameron* who while delivering his lessons to an audience of artisans employed it analogically to connect human labor and divine creation, even as he recognizes the limits of the analogy.

Luther's brief treatment of the two causes (formal and material), found in the initial nineteen theses of *Disputatio de Homine* of 1536[10] pertaining to human endeavor, reveal how close he was to the Aristotelian distinction of the human faculties of *poiēsis* and *praxis*. Among the four classical causes in Aristotle's theory, these two are the ground and foundation of the institutions of the *oeconomia* and *politia* as divine mandates through which humans present and represent themselves as instruments and masks of God.

---

6. Cf. Duchrow, *Christenheit und Weltverantwortung*, 503f.

7. The first time the three estates are mentioned in Luther is in 1519, in his pamphlet "The Holy and Blessed Sacrament of Baptism." LW 35:38–41; WA 2, 734, 24.

8. Supra chapter 20.

9. Mohl, *Three Estates*, 11.

10. This has been discussed above in chapter 21.

On the Councils and the Church from 1539 presents a summation of Luther's understanding of these institutions and its causes:

> Thus Psalm 127 says that there are only two temporal governments on earth, that of the city and that of the home.... The first government is that of the home, from which the people come; the second is that of the city, meaning the country, the people, princes and lords, which we call the secular government. These embrace everything—children, property, money, animals, etc. *The home must produce, whereas the city must guard, protect and defend.*[11]

There is no question as to the Reformer's own dependence on the static character of these medieval institutions. He did not know that the industrial revolution would move production out of the home. Nor did he know that the American and the French revolutions would do away with the entitlements of nobility. But what he did recognize are two fundamental anthropological dimensions that cannot be collapsed. And the distinction is what really matters.

On Keeping the Distinction

In the *Lectures on Genesis* Luther is not very consistent as to the origin of politics. Commenting on Genesis 2:9 he says that God had established in paradise "the administration of government and of the home."[12] But shortly thereafter, examining Genesis 2:16–17, he says that in paradise, unlike the church and the home, "there was no government of the state before sin, for there was no need for it. Civil government is a remedy required by our corrupted nature."[13] Despite this inconsistency, Luther normally held the opinion that civil government is demanded by the fall. Politics, as opposed to economics, is postlapsarian. It means that *politia* as such, even if mandated by God, is not an order of creation, in distinction to the economy and the church.[14] In the draft notations to the *Lectures on Genesis* Luther says,

> At this point [in the story about paradise] politics does not exist; it begins in the chapter on Cain [Gen 4]. Where politics is not in place, neither is the need for medicine or such things. All would be healthy; all would be right under the dominion of humans. Politics is the guard of fallen nature, economy is what remains of

11. LW 41:176f. (emphasis added).
12. LW 1:94.
13. LW 1:104
14. Bayer, "Nature and Institution," 128.

[original] nature, and the church is the redemption and restoration of nature.[15]

In his comments on Cain building a city for his "lust for ruling," Luther explicitly opposes it to the true church.[16] But what is more interesting still is that Cain, exiled to the land of Nod (homelessness or wandering), was sent off from his father's house, his *oeconomia*. Luther explains the difference in Genesis 2:14 between being driven from the face of the ground (*adamah*) where he had his dwelling and home, and being a wanderer on earth (*'aretz*).[17] Thus the curse on Cain was threefold:

> Thus one sin is punished by a threefold punishment. In the first place, Cain is deprived of spiritual or ecclesiastical glory. . . . In the second place, the earth is cursed, and this is a punishment that affects his domestic establishment. The third punishment—that he is to be a wanderer and is to find a permanent dwelling place nowhere—involves civil government.[18]

It is certainly not the case that the *oeconomia* has not been affected by sin, to the contrary. The point is that *politia* comes into existence when *oeconomia* is affected by sin. The latter requires the former for the defense of its own damaged integrity.[19] Cain himself constituted a household. But to the extent it has been affected by sin, it already entered into the realm of *politia* and indeed required it. This is seen in the example Luther offers in the preface to the *Small Catechism* counseling the teaching of the seventh commandment "to artisans and shoppers and even to farmers and household workers, because rampant . . . are all kinds of dishonesty and thievery."[20] The distinction being made is the one between self-expression in which human work produces and reproduces the means for the sustenance of life, from offspring to harvest, from the factory to the writers desk and pen, from the cook in the kitchen to the canvas of the painter. The other is the power of constraint to curb the effects of sin insofar as the second table of the Ten Commandments is concerned. And this can go from the discipline imposed to a child to waging war, from the work of legislation to police patrols, from

---

15. LW 1:314f. But notice that this is one of the passages in which *politia* is postlapsarian. Cf. WA 42, 22, 20–26; Ebeling, *Disputatio de homine*, 303. See also chapter 20 above.

16. LW 1:314.

17. LW 1:298.

18. LW 1:294.

19. Kolb and Wengert, *Book of Concord*, 349 (commentary on the seventh commandment).

20. Ibid.

regulating international trade to codes of social etiquette. All the structures for intersubjective and political deliberation are the necessary remedy for an economy that has been corrupted and labor alienated.

Luther's distinction of the two régimes, the spiritual and the earthly, has fallen short in addressing precisely the discrete character of economy and politics, and their relationship, which he himself often insisted on: "The will of God is to discern the orders" (*Vult Deus esse discrimina ordinum*).[21] The recognition that the church, qua *ecclesia*, has to be discerned as an order of creation and not what exclusively belongs to the spiritual régime is largely acknowledged. But the importance of the distinction between *oeconomia* and *politia* has often collapsed under the earthly régime in the so-called two kingdoms doctrine. Production and reproduction are different from praxis or politics. This allows us a qualified look into Luther's anthropology and, thereby, his view of power. More importantly, it establishes that the economic mandate has primacy over the political one. In the words of Oswald Bayer, "Luther was definitely aware that politics is grounded in economy."[22] And it is for the sake of the production and reproduction of life for all that politics is instituted.

Instruments and Masks: Equity and Reason

Although, as noted above, Luther uses the metaphors of "instrument" and "mask" interchangeably to describe the earthly institutions or mandates, they are also suggestive of distinct forms that the human *re*-presentation takes. And these correspond once more to the description of the human faculties of *poiēsis* and *praxis*, which ground the *oeconomia* and the *politia*, respectively. Under the condition of sin both are intertwined, but the distinction remains and one cannot be fully translated into the other. Hence in order to understand the human in her most clear profile or stature as *imago Dei*, one must attend to her capability of reproducing and producing the means for the sustenance of life. To be precise, she being this very means of reproducing and producing is conveyed by the word "instrument." This is the most fundamental form that power assumes and is not fully transferable to the political realm. In Luther's terms, it remains as a residue, a relic of uncorrupted nature (*reliquum naturae*).[23] The reformer's insistence in find-

21. See WA 44, 440, 25; 49, 613, 1ff.; 31/I, 399, 26ff. For further discussion of this and the different view of Melanchthon, see Elert, *Morphologie des Luthertums*, 2:49–65.
22. Bayer, "Nature and Institution," 128.
23. WA 42, 22, 24.

ing Christ among the poor, the laborers, the little ones, ought not to be read in a romantic tone. It is simply an epistemological gesture indicating that it is those whose labor has not produced the surplus necessary to have control and alienate the labor of others who best embody God's *poietic* mandate, and thus are the privileged expositors of Christ's presence.

The triune God is the *terminus a quo* and *ad quem* of this economy, the efficient and the final cause. In the interstice between the two, however, Christ is present, as Luther said, "as deep and as near to all created things as God is in them."[24] He adds that we do not know this from reason or from nature, but that from both reason and nature we can see and witness this presence of Christ in which we believe and through which God works and the human becomes *cooperator dei*. And in this earthly existence God operates through human labor and only through humans (*sed non operator sine nobis*).[25] This is why Luther can say that "labor is in itself pleasure,"[26] while politics is a function of its alienation, when unhappiness sets in, and the metabolism of labor is distorted.

Of course, one can understand such high value Luther put into labor, only if one brackets it from its political context in which, *post lapsum*, it is necessarily immersed into, but ought to be distinguished. Luther's own insistence that politics enters into the picture as a mandate of God after the Fall indicates that something happens to labor with human sin. Karl Marx, who called Luther "the oldest German political economist"[27] and discussed at length, in both the first and third volumes of *Das Kapital*, Luther's "Admonition to Pastors to Preach against Usury" (1540), insightfully remarked that "primitive accumulation [of capital] plays in political economy a role akin to the original sin [*Sündenfall*] in theology."[28]

As far as the *oeconomia* is concerned, *politia* emerges as the registry of sin and corruption, to which the very expression "political economy" testifies. Luther, in the *Lectures on Genesis* sees in the twofold mandates given to Adam, to work and watch, traces of the *oeconomia* and *politia* that after the fall have been distorted from their original intended end.[29] In the description of Adam tilling the fields and cultivating the garden, Luther notices that the human labors the very ground from which Adam was formed and

---

24. LW 37:223f. Cf. Solid Declaration, VII, in Kolb and Wengert, *Book of Concord*, 591–615.

25. LW 33:241–43

26. WA 6, 120, 25f. (*Labor est demum ipsa voluptas*); cf. LW 42:144–47.

27. Marx and Engels, *Collected Works*, 29:448.

28. Marx, *Kapital*, 1:741.

29. LW 1:102.

out of which nourishment is produced. To quote Marx again, labor consists in a metabolism (*Stoffwechel*) between the human and the rest of nature.[30] This is the foundation of the household and economy. The term metabolism is indeed very appropriate in its etymological sense (*meta-boleo*: bringing together), because its corruption or alienation is nothing else but *diabolic* (*dia-boleo*: throwing apart, the work of the devil). The *oeconomia* spells the material criterion for justice to be achieved. It offers the means and instruments or tools (*instrumentum*) for the material production for sustenance (*nehren*) and reproduction of life (*mehren*). The objective result is equity (*aequitas, Billigkeit*).[31]

Politia, grounded in the praxis of administering the *polis*, and guarding it against corruption can therefore be exercised only on the ground of restoring labor to its true metabolic function. Though the sword becomes a common trope for the way Luther describes politics and civil government, the actual formal cause for anything that happens in civil government is reason.

The distinction that is now obtained between the *homo oeconomicus vel poeticus* (in the Greek sense of *poiēsis*) and the *homo politicus* is that the former, as an instrument of the work of the triune God, presents God's continuing creation in and through us, while the latter does it so as a mask that reveals God's judgment of the world regarding the perversion of the *oeconomia*. This is why the political sphere does not have autonomy, and not because it fails to recognize the lordship of Christ,[32] but because its *nomos* is grounded in the *oikos*. And it is only for this end that it can be exercised, however complex and challenging to reason this task might be. If it is politics that administers the power relations, it is labor and the *oeconomia* that grounds it. Therefore, without seeking the achievement of justice according to the intrinsic right of the household, of labor and reproduction, politics is distorted and corrupted, the mask is fractured and its fissures expose only the unbearable sight of a hidden god that is at once the devil's own self.[33]

The distinction between *oeconomia* and *politia* are correlated to several other categories in which it reproduces itself. The argument at play here

---

30. Marx, *Kapital*, 1:192

31. Duchrow, *Christenheit und Weltverantwortung*, 498, 565ff.

32. Karl Barth and his followers, as reflected in the Barmen Declaration of 1934, defended the "lordship of Christ" over all dimensions of life as a critical principle directed against an understanding of the two kingdoms doctrine that would sponsor or tolerate a notion of the autonomy (*Eigengesetzlichkeit*) of secular spheres (see in particular article 2 of the Declaration).

33. "God cannot be God unless he first becomes a devil . . . the devil will not be the devil before being God." WA 31/1, 173–74; LW 26:95–96.

is that the Aristotelian distinction of the two human faculties that belong to *vita activa*, namely, *poiēsis* and *praxis*, are the operative principles. This distinction is reflected in Luther's apparently interchangeable use of "work" and "law," which are the faculties through which justice can be achieved. However they become idolatrous and demonic, respectively, when they pretend to move from the earthly régime to the spiritual, from the work of justice to justification. There is thus a corresponding relationship between the achievement of justice in the earthly régime and the reception of justification. Sin in its two manifestations, in idolatry and demonry, is then expressed in the ineptness to receive the gift and, simultaneously, to engage actively in the enforcement of justice with guidance of wisdom for equity to prevail.

The discussion in Luther research on the role of equity (*epieikeia*, *Billigkeit*) and its relationship to law is significant and highly controversial.[34] The texts normally appealed to are Luther's essay "Whether Soldiers, Too, Can Be Saved"[35] and his commentary on Genesis 19.[36] The first text has the classical expressions affirming the superiority of the equity over positive law, but still as an expression of natural law.[37] The difficulty in harmonizing the Reformer's thoughts on *epieikeia*, equity, with law without spiritualizing it,[38] may be solved by considering that while legislation (positive law) belongs to the reason of *politia*, equity pertains primarily to the *oeconomia*. The discussion of the theme in the Genesis commentary seems to corroborate this hypothesis. The context is the visitation of angels to Lot in Sodom. The whole story is framed by the tension between the city (*polis*) and the house (*oikos*). The house of Lot offered protection even as it contradicted the rule of the city. Lot's indecent offering of his daughters to the mob was illicit on all accounts, except that at the end, by offering protection to the angels, equity was served. But this could not be achieved in the city, only in the household by the decision of the head of the house. This suggests that operating in the Reformer's mind was precisely the distinction between the ruling of the household, the *oeconomia*, and the governance of the city, the *politia*. Equity was served when the door of the house could not be invaded by the city mob and the two orders were

---

34. Heckel, *Lex Charitatis*, 121–23; Duchrow, *Christenheit und Weltverantwortung*, 564–67.

35. WA 19, 61 6–662; LW 46:93–137.

36. WA 43, 62, 27ff.; LW 3:262.

37. WA 19, 631, 12, 25, and 632, 14ff.; LW 46:102f.

38. See Heckel, *Lex Charitatis*, 121f., footnote 622 for the adjudication of this debate between Lau and Holl, in favor of Lau's version that equity indeed belongs to the earthly regime.

kept apart and distinct. The text of Genesis 19 and Luther's commentary suggest two different paradigms in and through which humans cooperate with God in running the affairs of the world.

Contemporary Italian philosopher Giorgio Agamben[39] sustains that the "economic paradigm," not the "political" one, has been the grounding frame of the early Christian theology, and that these two could be discerned clearly. The patristic distinction between the immanent and the economic Trinity was thought of, as it is expressed explicitly, in economic terms and not in political terms. God's relation to the world is conceived as one that is framed primarily as the administration of *oikos*, and not of *polis*. This is the case, according to Agamben, already in Paul: "The lexicon of the Pauline *ekklēsia* is 'economic,' not political, and Christians are, in this sense, the first fully 'economic' men."[40] He further remarks with incisiveness that "the history of economic theology . . . has been left in the shadows not only by historians of ideas but also by theologians."[41]

The rediscovery of the "precise meaning of" economic theology and its significance for theology will necessitate a revisiting of Luther's *oeconomia* with its apparatuses that work in clear distinction, but not in exclusion, from *politia* and its apparatuses. The *oeconomia* is grounded in the faculty of *poiēsis*; its procedures involve a metabolic relationship with the matter that sustains and reproduces life in the world through work. *Oeconomia* employs tools for its sustenance and the reproduction of life in equity even on issues that the positive law does not cover. *Oeconomia* becomes distorted by idolatry, which is human fabrication and not divine donation.

This needs to be distinguished from the set of categories that belong to *politia*, which in turn is grounded in *praxis* employing reason for the achievement of justice, through the enforcement of legislation, the law that aims at protecting life and integrity of all persons (masks) in society. *Politia* becomes distorted by demonic possession that destroys personhood, violates the mask, rips one's shielding garment (*vestitus*, cf. Gen 3:21).

Both *oikos* and *polis* are descriptive of distinct dimensions that comprise *vita activa* in the pursuance of justice, but not justification. Justice expresses itself in the ordering of the *oeconomia* as equity (*epieikeia*), fairness even beyond or beneath the law. Justice expresses itself in the governance of the *politia* as equality of all in relationship to the law. But above all, the distinction of the spheres need to be acknowledged, especially considering the

---

39. Agamben, *The Kingdom and the Glory*.
40. Ibid., 24.
41. Ibid., 1.

fact that the "economic theology" and its distinctiveness has been neglected. On this subject the Reformer has valuable lessons to offer.

Marx was indeed right in his polemic acclamation of Luther as the first German economist, but how right was Luther in his perspicacity of the distinction between economy and politics? As seen in his exposition of Genesis and study of Aristotle's *Metaphysics*, his acumen is exceptional in discerning the unique distinction between the household or economy and the political. But alas the significance of this distinction has not been adequately attended to in the two kingdoms doctrine, and this does not suffice in a world or this earthly regime, as Luther would call it, where the dynamics, dialogue, and direction have taken on a different course, and in which the rules and workings of the house, so to speak, have changed considerably since the time of Luther. Two interrelated phenomena—immigrants from the South to the old bastions of Lutheranism and the increasing presence of Lutherans in the southern hemisphere—have brought the question of economy, as distinct from politics, to the Lutheran agenda in an altogether different perspective. But Luther's theological anthropology and his view of society offer resources that have not yet been fully explored. What has been offered in this essay is a roadmap, or better, an itinerary for this task by distinguishing economy from politics, according to two operational principles that are at work in Luther's work, which can be best expressed by the Aristotelian human faculties of *poiēsis* and *praxis* and how they can be recognized in the later Luther. Revisiting Luther on the distinction between economy and politics offers a view of power grounded on the economy, which politics should protect and defend. This seems to offer a venue through which Lutheranism, but not only, can move ahead to address the emerging question of the turn of the millennium.

23

Lutheran Social Ethics

A Sketch

Kairotic Events and Choratic Circumstances

CLOTHES GO IN AND out of fashion. Sometimes we keep our old clothes at the back of the wardrobe so that we can wear them again once they come back into fashion. The same happens to some concepts, ideologies, and philosophies which, after a while, are taken out of the wardrobe, are aired, given some sunlight and "worn" again. Such is the case with the word "development" that sounds sweet and gentle now. But this concept was definitely out of fashion in the mid-1970s in Brazil. The military régime had just completed a decade in power and would remain in control for another decade. It sustained itself with an ideological construct put together around the notion of development dubbed as "developmentism" (*desenvolvimentismo*). The notion was associated with an artfully constructed political coalition, designed by General Golbery do Couto e Silva, which brought into alliance the two main powerful classes in Brazil since colonial times, an agrarian and a clumsy but innovative emerging urban bourgeoisie, all to the exclusion of the vast majority of the Brazilian population. At the time, Antonio Delfin Netto, the powerful Finance Minister, said of development, "We need to let the cake rise before we bake it to be divided." That was development by exclusion. Holistic was the capital that prospered, not the citizens. The Brazilian version of the infamous adage attributed to Marie Antoinette in response to the plea of the poor for bread, "let them eat cake."

Should we wait for the time when the notion of development would once again be unfashionable? The word development has a sweeter ring now than it did then, and it would not be preposterous to nurture some expectations and see signs of the time when development is redefined in a way that it sustains all. In other words, it is high time to think of development as holistic; a time when the adjectives "sustainable" and "holistic" used in connection with development would be redundant. I propose that in a Lutheran verve, with its enigmatic apocalyptic overtones that simultaneously put no hope in the order of this world, and yet invest it simultaneously with abundant expectations. The orders of this world should be erected on the idea of love and happiness, for it is in this world, "according to the flesh," insists Luther, that the Christ is present, as in the now and here that Christ chooses, and that is his *parousia*, or presence.[1]

There is no doubt that Luther significantly impacted economy and politics. It is not by chance that Karl Marx called him "the first German economist," Heinrich Heine referred to Robespierre as the "Luther of the French Revolution," and Engels said of Adam Smith that he was "the Luther of political economy." While this certainly is anecdotal, it is still significant for a theological thinker whose theology is drenched by apocalyptic storms.[2] How can one whose thought is guided by the impending end of the world contribute something to the advancement of the secular orders? Commenting on Johannes Weiss's and Albert Schweitzer's theses that the message of Jesus was an imminent, consistent (*konsequente*) eschatological vision, the Lutheran theologian and phenomenologist of religion Rudolf Otto draws attention to a problem that could also apply to Luther. Making the following observation regarding Schweitzer's attributing of a "marvelous ethics" to Jesus, Otto writes: "In doing so he seems not to realize that these two understandings [imminent eschatology and ethical responsibility], when put together, reveal something inconsistent, if not an irrationalism inherent to a genuine eschatology."[3]

Indeed, it would be an unintelligible rationality if, but only if, the eschatological reality is conceived as a chronological *telos*, mysteriously scheduled for a specific day. Nevertheless, it is not inconsistent if eschatology is understood as an event that comes into time as an indentation, an intervention that consumes time in itself and in it cannot be inscribed except

---

1. When Walter Benjamin writes, "The order of the profane should be erected on the idea of happiness" (*Reflections*, 312), he has the Apostle Paul in mind (particularly Rom 8), argues Jacob Taubes (*Political Theology of Paul*, 72f.). I would add that he could also have had Luther in mind.

2. See, e.g., Oberman, *Luther: Man between God and the Devil*. For the view that the apocalyptic motif in Luther is only a dependent variable in the Reformer's theology, see Lohse, *Martin Luther's Theology*. The position championed by Oberman among others has generally prevailed. See Part Two, chapter 11 above.

3. Otto, *Kingdom of God*, 59.

narrated retrospectively. Examples for this abound and include Mount Horeb, the Jabbok river, the Transfiguration event, the gathering in the Upper Room, Pentecost, the Road to Damascus, the Tower Experience, and so on down to our own personal experiences in the life of prayer, meditation, reading, and trial. The point of Otto is to show not incongruence in Jesus teaching, but the problem with the idea of a "consistent eschatology" to which ethics would indeed be extraneous. "For without this irrationality an ethic, just in as far as it is marvelous, and even as an 'interim-ethic,' would be inherently inconsistent with teaching that the end is at hand."[4] And so he continues his argument:

> This irrational quality is repeated in every place where genuine eschatological feeling exists.... It is rationalized away if we rob it of one of its antithetic elements by explaining that the eschatological order does not belong to the sphere of time. Its irrational quality is obscured when we speak of a consistent eschatology, and yet include a marvelous ethic in spite of the inner contradiction between the two elements.[5]

Otto's point, which he had further elaborated in his classic *The Idea of the Holy*,[6] is to show that in genuine religious experience eschatology is not a limit *ad extra rationis*, something beyond the realm of what reason can encompass, but rather *in profundis rationis*, in the very depths of reason itself.

These are *kairotic* events that took place in a given setting (a mountain, a river, a room, a road), which means that these events happened in liminal places, under *choratic* circumstances, which take place in sites that are neither in nor out, yet both at once. The word *chōra* in Greek denotes these occurrences as taking place between places. Hence, the apocalyptic attitude toward a decaying world is seen as the result of the work of the apocalyptic naysayer, the apostate, the enemy, the Antichrist, against whom the messianic presence, the *parousia*, is an event that intervenes in the order of the world, revealing things for what they really are. But how is this then related to the betterment of the world, to the achievement of a good life, happiness, and contentment (*eudaimonia*)? We must search for the answer to this question first in Luther's concept of the two régimes, or the well-known two kingdoms doctrine as discussed above.

---

4. Ibid.
5. Ibid., 63.
6. Otto, *The Idea of the Holy*.

Thinking on Two Régimes

Luther's teachings on the two régimes, the worldly and the spiritual, is something that he eventually shared with other reformers such as Zwingli, Melanchthon, Bucer, Calvin and others. It has been interpreted in several ways. For example, in German theology, in response to its abuse during the Nazi period, there was a tendency to read it as an extension or even foundation of the law/gospel distinction. In the USA, with its indebtedness to the Hobbesian/Lockean type of liberalism, it has been almost equated with the separation of church and state. With the publication in 1970 of Ulrich Duchrow's work, *Christenheit und Weltverantwortung*,[7] an amazing amount of research on the topic since the 1930s was put to rest. Some of its lessons have been ignored, others have been learned. Among those learned was that the spiritual régime (or kingdom, regiment) is not a symmetrical figure of the earthly, in which the earthly would be the shadowy Platonic projection of the spiritual. It is also not Augustine's two divergent roads offering the pilgrim a choice of which to follow, to bliss or to gloom. Neither is it a distinction between content and form as the "Barthian" Lutherans would frame it. It is even less in any sense a direct expression of the relationship between church and state (a penchant of US interpreters). Finally, it is also not what post-Vatican II progressive Roman Catholic theologians consider it to be: a post *corpus christianum* revision of the two planes theory, the natural and the supernatural. In sum, it is not as if two vectors ran parallel to each other to meet only in the future eschatological horizon, and were occasionally related through the ministry (*Amt*), proclamation, sacraments and charity. Positively stated, the two régimes describe asymmetric dimensions that do not concur, but where the spiritual produces incidents in the earthly order and is subjectively apprehended[8] as something that happens and breaks through the order of things and, in that, reveals the masks under which the divine is hidden. Through these masks shines the light that convicts the world and promises a good life in the midst of the ordeal of a perennially decaying world.

But how does this happen? How it happens is concretely predicated on a peculiar Lutheran teaching and interpretation of the Chalcedonian *communicatio idiomatum* as the union and not mixing of the two natures in Christ. Luther's interpretation of one of its propositions, which was later dubbed the *genus majestaticum*, started to mark the difference between the

---

7. Duchrow, *Christenheit und Weltverantwortung*.

8. This is what Luther meant by the affirmation that "experience makes a theologian." WA TR 1, 16, 13 (nr. 46); LW 54:7.

Lutheran and the Reformed traditions.[9] A year before, Luther, who thought that he did not have much time left in life, decided to write his theological *Confession Concerning Christ's Supper*.[10] As discussed in chapter 8, the text is better known for setting up the argument that at Marburg would underscore the Lutheran stance on real presence,[11] where he goes even further than affirming the real presence. His elucidation of the three modes of Christ's presence—the historical Jesus; the sacramental presence in the visible elements entailing a promise; and the third, where Christ is indivisible with God and present everywhere—says that Christ is inseparable from God (or indivisible, as Luther would say), and "wherever God is, he must be also, otherwise our faith is false."[12]

This is the crucial aspect of Luther's theology. Christ is present where the right hand of God is (to use the creedal metaphor discussed at Marburg), which is to say, everywhere—yet in a clothed or masked way that is the outward matter we see and our senses detect. Luther expressed this wrapping of God with a series of metaphors: mask (*larva*), clothing (*vestitus*), wrapping (*involucrum*),[13] which are the external manifestations or representations of God's presence in Christ, according to the flesh, that means in nature, in "majestic matter," as Luther qualified it. This third mode of presence should not surprise those familiar with his *Sermon on the Sacrament of the Body and Blood of Christ* of 1526, where, presupposing the real presence in the sacrament, he states, "If it were possible and I should measure all creatures and describe them in words, you would see wonders just as great, nay, even greater, than in this sacrament."[14]

But how is this to be conceived? Here Luther appeals to ordinary experience,[15] as he often does. He suggests the analogy of a crystal with many facets that display a spark or a bubble inside the crystal even as it appears in every one of the many facets to be there at the surface of the facet, when in fact it is in the middle of it. So he applies the analogy:

---

9. This as early as the dispute with Zwingli at the Marburg Colloquy of 1529.

10. WA 26, 261–509; LW 37:151–372.

11. This, incidentally, was the only point of discord between Zwingli and Luther after the two expressed agreement on the other fourteen theses bearing the position of the Reformation, but it was strong enough for the editors of WA to regard its formulation in the *Confession* of 1528 the "shibboleth of the genuine Lutheran." WA 26, 249. See also Part Two, chapter 6.

12. WA 26, 336, 15–19; LW 37:223.

13. In earlier chapters I refer to Luther's various uses of the metaphor of the mask.

14. WA 19, 487; LW 36:338.

15. WA 26, 337; LW 37:224: "I am not speaking now from Scripture," he says.

> If Christ also sat at one place in the center of the universe, like the bubble or spark in a crystal, and if a certain point in the universe were indicated to me ... by the Word, should I not be able to say, "See there is the body of Christ ...," just as I say, when a certain side of the crystal is placed before my eyes, "See, there is the spark in the very front of the crystal"?[16]

Indeed it looks to be on the surface of the facet while in fact it is at its core. Here Luther plays with words in his spelling of crystal as *Christall* (modern German *Kristall*); a strict transmutation would render it as "Christ-All" in English.[17]

But before we fall into a deification of nature, we need to pause, because now comes Luther's apocalyptic move. As in early Jewish apocalyptic, the presence (*parousia*) of the Messiah is accompanied by the manifestation of the Anti-Christ, an entity that does not come from above but is at work in the midst of the "orders of creation," or institutional spheres, the economy, politics, and the church. As sin is a universal condition (*peccatum originale originatum*), it is also always at work (*peccatum originale originans*) "because all have sinned" (Rom 5:12). And what does sin accomplish? To carry on Luther's metaphor, the work of the devil is the one that cracks the mask, tears the clothing, rips the wrappings of the divine, effaces the facets of the crystal. In other words, it destroys nature, and corrupts the institutions ordered for its protection. And this protection, the mask, the clothing, the wrapping shields us from the exposure to the *deus nudus*, the ominous *tremendum* of Otto. At this point, Luther's disconcerting paradoxes again throw us off balance, because this is precisely also the point in which messianic presence is at hand. The *parousia* of Christ becomes manifest showering us with faith, love, and hope. And for what? To rapture us to heaven? Or, is it to throw us into the abysmal black hole of a naked god? No, neither! Rather, it is to darn the ripped clothing, to mend the mask, to restore the wrapping. This he expresses in theological concepts, but in paradoxical terms: *ad deum contra deum confugere*, "to flee from and find refuge in God against God."[18]

An Admonition

This can be illustrated using the last of Luther's three writings against usury (in 1519/20, 1524, and this last from 1540). The language exemplifies

---

16. WA 26, 337, 15–20; LW 37:224.

17. See the excellent reflection on this passage, even as he borders with good reason on a "panchristism," in Gregersen, "Natural Events as Crystals of God," 143–55.

18. WA 5, 204, 26f.

Luther's use of apocalyptic verbiage and imagery, channeling at times motifs not unlike the description of the Beast of the Sea (i.e., the market[19]) of Revelation 13.

Further, Luther does not abandon the concrete ground of addressing a socioeconomic problem; he is adamant in not allowing a "spiritualization" of the issue. And last, but decisively, he is tackling what he regards as a superlative manifestation of evil at the time—the practice of usury, which was the main tool in the implementation of the emerging financial capitalism. The usurer is the primate of the *homo pecuniosus*, our contemporary capitalist. The choice of this text was not made on the basis of its moral implications, as if it could provide us with anachronistic criteria to pass judgment on late-modern capitalism. The treatise is titled "An Admonition to Pastors to Preach against Usury" and, interestingly, is one of Luther's texts that has not been translated into English.[20]

Luther starts by exposing misconceptions regarding the practice of usury, namely, the presumption that by lending money the usurer is actually providing a service to the people. Foreshadowing the modern criticism of ideology he writes:

> Whoever takes more or better than he gives is doing usury and this is no service at all, but wrong done to his neighbor as when one steals and robs. All is not service and benefit to a neighbor that is called service and benefit. For an adulteress and adulterer do one another a great service and pleasure. . . . The devil himself does his servant inestimable service.[21]

To make his case, the Reformer does not appeal to dogmatic or ecclesial authority. He draws on classical philosophy (Seneca, Aristotle, among others) to demonstrate his point: "We must spare our theology hereupon."[22] At the court of reason and for the sake of equity,[23] he pleads his case that usury is an unnatural (*wider die Natur*, i.e., not part of the relationship of humans with the rest of nature) mode of producing value.[24] This would not be a problem in itself if it were not for the fact that usury cannot create value

---

19. For the use of the imagery as an allegory for the market, see Westhelle, "Revelation 13," 183–99.

20. This text has not been translated, to my knowledge (at least, it is not part of the most complete English edition of the Reformer's works).

21. WA 51, 338, 32–339, 25.

22. WA 51, 344, 30f.

23. WA 52, 344, 25f.

24. For Aristotle's argument, see *Treatise of Government*, Book 1, ch. 10.

without (mis-)appropriating "alien labor."[25] And the verdict is peremptory: "Even if we were not Christian reason alone would tell us all the same that a usurer is a murderer."[26]

After having argued so far without appealing to theology he starts to address Christian folk: "The heathen were able by the light of reason, to conclude that the usurer is a double-dyed thief and murderer. We Christians, however, hold them in such honor, that we fairly worship them for the sake of their money."[27] And the attack goes on with apocalyptic zest:

> Therefore is there, on this earth, no greater enemy of man (after the devil) than a gripe-money, and usurer, for he wants to be God over all men . . . a usurer and money-glutton . . . he may have the whole world to himself, and everyone may receive from him as from God and be his serf forever. . . . The usurer wants to condemn the whole world to hunger, suffering and misery.[28]

And what are we to do? The language becomes shocking and appalling: "And since we break on the wheel and behead highwaymen, murderers and housebreakers, how much more should we break on the wheel and kill . . . hunt down, curse and behead all usurers."[29] And Luther refuses to make the spiritual leap from the concrete political order to the universal condition of human sinfulness as a palliative by which sin is denounced while the sinner is justified. Is this not a problem to be solved by sincere repentance alone, knowing that, after all, justification is for the sinner qua sinner? The response resounds clearly and coherently:

> They say that the world could not be without usury. This is certainly true. For so strong and stiff can no government in the world ever be and has never been. . . . And even if a government could prevent all sin, there would still be original sin. . . . But if with this [argument] they think they are excused, let them see.[30]

Preachers who fail to raise their voice from the pulpit against usury and usurers and even associate with them "make a comedy of their preaching office . . . and turn themselves against the truth. . . . Such people cannot promote the gospel."[31]

25. WA 51, 351, 21–27.
26. WA 51, 361, 34–361, 17.
27. WA 51, 261, 30–32.
28. WA 51, 396, 28–397, 19.
29. WA 51, 421, 24–26.
30. WA 51, 353, 32–354, 28.
31. WA 51, 409, 19–22.

Sin is not to be fought in a disembodied piety, but it is always to be fought where it appears: in the flesh, in matter because that is where the gates to condemnation as well as redemption open themselves. Or Luther again:

> If our gospel is the true light, then it must truly shine in the darkness.... If we do not want suffering, if we want to transform the world [*die Welt anders haben*] then we must go out into the world [*zur Welt hinaus gehen*] or create [*schaffen*] another world which will do whatever we, or God wants.[32]

And Luther adds, "God's marvelous power and wisdom must have its signs [*Spuren*] and must be grasped herein [*hierin*]." And what are these traces, these signs that may be grasped in here? The answer is straight forward in the same text: "earthly peace to increase and sustain [*mehren und nehren*] the human race."[33] And this peace that promotes development and sustainability is concretely undermined by the practice of usury, which for the Reformer at the time rated with singular highest prominence among the manifestations of sin.[34]

However, there remained a logical inconsistency in the Reformer, the same one that Otto denounced in Schweitzer, who maintained a "marvelous ethics" alongside a thoroughgoing (*konsequente*) eschatology, which is indeed echoed by Jesus' saying, "Occasions for stumbling are bound to come, but woe to anyone by whom they come!" (Luke 17:1; Matt 18:7). How can this combination of an apocalyptic stance (the world is going to hell in a handcart) and a vigorous defense of justice, reason, and fairness for the promotion of the common good be explained?

The grounds for the so-called inconsistency can be elucidated either by some circumstantial peculiarities or deeply felt theological convictions. Although Luther had said that there was no saint that was not well versed in politics and economy, his temperament (notwithstanding his "sainthood") did not thrive in those fields, even if his impact on them has been colossal. His base remained in theology, with frequent incursions into those other fields, but never on their own autonomous grounds. To say it differently, if the young Luther would be placed in the second half of the twentieth century, alas, he would be a dismal failure in *Realpolitik* and would not be admitted to study monetarism at the School of Economics of the University of Chicago. In spite of having been exposed and influenced by the nominalism of the *via moderna*, his understanding of the exchange value of merchandise

---

32. WA 51, 409, 27–32.
33. WA 51, 354, 29–31.
34. See Rieth, *"Habsucht" bei Martin Luther*.

was that of a realist. He followed the prevailing medieval Aristotelian theory of the sterility of money, and saw value determined and imbued in merchandise by labor. In that he was even less refined than the late medieval Roman moralists who, under the spell of money's sterility, could come up with a justification for a quasi-interest principle of charging a fee for a loan on account of depreciation due to currency handling.

Luther was light years away from his younger reformation colleague, John Calvin, who recognized the economic validity of earning interest for lending money. The interest rates charged would have to be subject to strict and reasonable regulation. As Richard Tawney remarked when comparing Calvin to Luther, "The significant feature in his [Calvin's] discussion of the subject [of usury and interest] is that he assumes credit to be a normal and inevitable incident in the life of a society."[35] Max Weber, who begins his *Protestant Ethic and the Spirit of Capitalism* with the importance of Luther's understanding of vocation (*Beruf*) for the ensuing development of a worldly asceticism, has hardly anything to say in favor of Luther as far as his contribution to development of capitalism is concerned: ". . . it is hardly necessary to point out that Luther cannot be claimed for the spirit of capitalism in the sense in which we have used that term above, or for that matter in any sense whatever."[36] Indeed, Luther's home base was theology. If, however, he did not contribute much to capitalism as such, it is because his sway in economy, politics, and society was grounded in a theology not subjected to political negotiations or economic calculations. So, is there an inconsistency between an apocalyptic attitude and a call for world responsibility? What follows will show that this so-called inconsistency is a misplaced diagnosis.

Luther's scathing attack on usury is due to the misery it engenders, thus disturbing the earthly peace necessary for the pursuance and advancement of the common good. And this good is predicated on the result of labor, which, for Luther, was the source of earthly, material value for the promotion and sustenance of life sustained by God's promise to Adam before the Fall.[37] If we consider what Luther has written about the "third mode of presence" of Christ, "according to the flesh," labor, as the human engagement with nature, plays a critical role. The disregard for and exploitation of labor undermines a "metabolism"[38] that takes place when *adam*, the creature of the earth, cultivates *adamah*, the fertile soil producing and

---

35. Tawney, *Religion and the Rise of Capitalism*, 95. It should be noted that later in his career, Luther admitted some flexibility on the question of regulated interests as insurance for a debtor's insolvency. See zur Mühlen, "Arbeit VI."

36. Weber, *Protestant Ethic*, 82.

37. See Rieth, *"Habsucht" bei Martin Luther*, 217f.; Bayer, "Nature and Institution," 125–59.

38. *Stoffwechsel*, metabolism, is how Karl Marx explains labor in *Das Kapital*, 1:192.

reproducing itself, participating and transforming human beings and the rest of nature in which the majestic presence of God in Christ, in matter dwells. Therefore, Luther describes the labor performed in the three institutional spheres (*ecclesia, oeconomia, politia*) as bringing forth "God's gifts," adding "These [gifts] are masks of God, behind which He wants to remain concealed and do all things."[39] The use of the "mask" motif is significant in the imagery that the metaphor evokes. Usury (or sin in general) destroys the dignity of labor and damages the masks of God, exposing thus the reality of the abyss of the *deus nudus*. This is why labor itself—and the peace, protection, sustenance and procreation it provides—is of no soteriological import. It goes without saying—*sola fide*. But labor is the means through which the promises embedded in the earthly divinely instituted orders come to fruition: protection, sustenance, and growth (*wehre, nehre, mehre*). This is why if we say *pax mundi non speranda*, we also must add *pax mundi exspectare est*. The peace of the world is not a function of hope, but it is a longing for, a looking forward to, what can be attained herein.

In the awake of neo-developmentalism does Luther's theology contribute to a holistic model of development? At best, Luther triggered a chain of events to which, if compared to Calvin for instance, he contributed preciously little in terms of how to control and administer political and economic affairs with realistic programs and viable projects. As the gospel is not spiritualized, it must leave its imprints in this material world. What these signs look like and how they are to be discerned remains vague. The Reformer denounced with prophetic incisiveness what he considered a pervasive manifestation of sin at his time—money and the practice of usury. He did it mostly in theological terms. But when he was arguing not as a theologian ("We must spare our theology hereupon," said Luther) his appeal to the classic Aristotelian notion of "sterile money" sounded as an informed political and economic analysis of the inception of the capitalist mode of production and the market economy in the sixteenth century.

Rippling Effects

Before we finish with a sophism in saying that the helpful aspect of Luther's theology is his theology of aspects, we need to add a final point. When Ernst Troeltsch wrote his influential essay, "The Historical and Dogmatic Method in Theology" (1898),[40] he raised three criteria by which to evaluate the reli-

---

39. WA 31/1, 434, 7–11; LW 14:114f.

40. Troeltsch, *Gesammelte Schriften*, 2:729–53; cf. Harvey, *Historian and the Believer*, 14–33.

ability of a historical claim. The first was criticism (a claim should be judged by its internal consistency and independent corroboration and degree of probability), analogy (if an event should find correspondence, or analogous to contemporary attested events) and, thirdly, correlation. This last one is the most intriguing, for it does not want to establish the objective factuality of the event itself, but of its effect in a constellation of interconnected events achieving measurable outcomes even if the originating cause is beyond critical inquiry. Ernst Käsemann seems to have relied on this criterion to launch the "New Quest for the Historical Jesus." Looking at the way in which the event of Christ is reported—clothed in embarrassment and debasement of a convicted criminal and legally executed by crucifixion—there must have been something there that was enough of an objective ground to produce the historical chain of effects that shaped the history and culture of a significant part of the world.

What is called for here is a similar quest for the significance of Luther and Lutheranism in defining economic and political programs that surfaced out of a Lutheran religious ethos, even without explicit help from Luther's works. Until recently, works on the religious roots of modern societies have focused on the contrast between Roman Catholicism and the Reformation heritage. Such is the theme of the classical studies by Max Weber and Richard Tawney. Luther appears only to set the stage for Calvin, Calvinists, and the Puritans. The method was to establish the theoretical sources of social practices.

The sociologist Sigrun Kahl took a different approach. She decided to do a comparative study not on the progress of the capitalist spirit, but to explore the religious roots of modern poverty policies in countries whose major religious constituencies belong to three distinct confessional families, the Catholic, Lutheran, and Reformed Protestant traditions.[41] She warns against the temptation of generalization, particularly of different religious formations in Western societies due to the progressive admixture of traditions, and rejects the claim that the religious factor is the independent variable of sociopolitical diversity in Western modernity (although she gets very close to such a claim). She presents a typological distinction of profiles in countries shaped more typically by each of the three traditions. These are some of her conclusions after an exhaustive documentation pertaining to poverty policies:

> Catholic social doctrine continued to view the beggar as closest to Christ. Therefore, poverty did not carry stigma, and good works, especially almsgiving, guaranteed salvation; in Calvinism

41. Kahl, "The Religious Roots of Modern Poverty Policy," 91–126.

> it is a mark of lacking grace; and in Lutheranism poverty itself says nothing about one's state of grace....
>
> Catholic poor relief remained a responsibility of the hospitals and private charity. Lutheran poor relief was predominantly organized as outdoor relief, to be financed out of the common chest and later on a poor tax. Reformed Protestant poor relief for the able-bodied was institutionalized in the workhouse.... Catholic subsidiarity and Reformed Protestant individualism and voluntarism both attribute a negative role to the state.... In countries under Catholic or Reformed Protestant dominance, poor relief was not secularized as early and as comprehensively as in the Lutheran countries....
>
> The fundamental tension in poor relief is that between granting economic support *and* ensuring that everybody who can work in fact does. Each tradition has solved this goal conflict differently.... Each strategy creates particular problems within the work-welfare trade-off: integration strategies historically rooted in Catholicism provide social assistance benefits or other local support but permanently exclude the long-term unemployed from work. Integration strategies rooted in Lutheranism prevent economic hardship and provide work but institutionalize an inferior kind of work outside the labor market. Integration strategies historically rooted in Reformed Protestantism promote (low wage) labor market integration at the expense of guaranteeing an economic and social minimum.[42]

After several disclaimers regarding some generalizations she concludes, "Despite the immense changes the welfare state brought about, much of the national continuities in attitudes towards, and policies against, poverty can be traced back to religious roots."[43]

To presume a direct causality between facets of Luther's theology, and his theology of facets, would be an inappropriate affectation. But conjectures are justifiably elicited. And one wonders with a certain amount of perplexity whether the distinctive course that poverty policies took in predominantly Lutheran countries might be somehow, at the end of the day, related to the crystal, the Christ-All, grafted in the social, political, and economic masks of God. This should provide an interesting point of departure, but only a point of departure, for a comparative evaluation of the importance of each tradition for contributing toward an equitable developmental paradigm.

---

42. Ibid., 120–23.
43. Idem.

Conclusion

Inconclusive Final Notes

> The two poles of a figure are separated in time, but both, being real events or persons, are within temporality. They are both contained in the flowing stream which is historical life, and only the comprehension, the *intellectus spiritualis*, of their interdependence is a spiritual act.
>
> —Erich Auerbach[1]

A THEOLOGICAL BOOK IS worth its completion when it discloses a threshold, a passage across its own bounds, a gate through its end; it is not the *telos* of a work accomplished. Its cover is not a closure, but an overture offering vistas of a beyond yet uncharted, of a *presence* that its pages *represent*. Such a work needs to be anticlimactic. As in the Gospel of John, after all has been definitely accomplished (*tetelestai*) the tomb is closed, the story continues and presence is unleashed. The *figura*, with which we have been concerned, passes away (*praeterit enim figura*, 1 Cor 7:31); it is transfigured. But in passing, in its passage, glimpses of presence flash through. To comprehend this is a spiritual act.

The approaching jubilee of the Reformation provides the occasion for the revisiting of Luther with an inundation of publications to which the present volume adds itself and would likely be diluted or run over, as by

---

1. Auerbach, "Figura," 54.

an avalanche. But studying the Reformer's figure, as it is transfigured into diverse contexts absorbing new contents, as is the intention of this volume, is not a revisiting Luther. The point was to observe how he, as a figure, comes himself to visit new contexts, being by them hosted, fed, and clothed. The celebrated words of Anders Nygren, said in closing his keynote to the first Assembly of the Lutheran World Federation (Lund, 1947), "Forward to Luther," were certainly meant as a rhetorical watchword that pointed to the future significance of the Reformer. But his words may entail not only a dispatch to the future. "Forward to Luther" is also an invitation to find his figure visiting unexpected contexts, being there endowed with elements alien in its original habitat. This reconfiguration gives to the Reformer a peculiar and uncanny character, its very identity questionable and its appearance illegitimate.

The present volume stops short of supplying a road map with addresses and locations of these visitations; yet it offers an itinerary that point to directions to these places that figures of the Reformer and events associated with his person visit. The focus of the multifaceted enquiry into which his studies immersed themselves probed the result of this pergerination; it was not intended as a study of the figural method of interpretation. The figural method examines the migration of a character or event from one place and time to another and the changes it undergoes being both historically concrete. And even as the figure's historical veracity is contaminated by legend, it is real as long as it is taken as historical. The point is that between two historically rooted factors, alleged or not, this study took on a third element, the *spiritual* bond between them. The union without surrendering difference, the disparity of identities takes place by a spiritual principle that holds together the nonidentity of an identity. This was called the "spirit of Protestantism" by Hegel, or the "Protestant principle," in a similar fashion, by Tillich.

Four perspectives offered insights into probing this connection. The medieval distinction of the *trivium*—grammar, rhetoric, and logic or dialectic (which added to the *quadrivium* forms the lower level of the seven liberal arts)—is adopted. The first two parts presented above—"The Genius of Language" and "Theology Matters"—are comprised of studies written from perspectives of grammar. If theology is the art of making discernments on the use and employment of language and the rules of communication, Luther's use and application of language in context (*forum*) is examined as a spiritual procedure connecting the Word to the words, and in the words finding the dwelling of the Word, its cradle, to use Luther's image. The second part, dealing with substantive theological doctrines from the doctrine of justification to the Reformer's apocalyptic eschatology, going through his

Archimedean point, the *theologia crucis*, presents the core of the rendition of the gospel, which belongs to the art of rhetoric. After the use and the procedural functions of language is examined, and the theological core of the gospel is described, Part Three applies the interface of grammar and rhetoric to practical cases in which the figural method exhibits itself; a planetary dispensation of a figure is displayed. Finally, in Part Four, the use of logic or dialectic, charts the concrete relationship that faith and love assume in the asymmetric relationship between *vita passiva* and *vita activa*. The emphasis in this part, however, lies in the logical, or dialectical, unfolding of love in the human engagement with the world, according to the workings and rationalities of worldly institutions, which are social expressions of anthropological faculties subjacent to Luther's view of *vita activa*.

Luther was not a theoretician of Protestantism, but a practitioner of protest. Destined, then and now, to be a minority and marginal occurrence, in no sense is his *figura* negligible or frivolous, as one would not regard the minimal quantitative presence of the yeast insignificant for the bulk of the dough. Luther research has often dealt with the Reformer's program as an immodest claim for modesty, but it may be better described as a modest call for immodesty. While many an attempt is aimed at raising him as a fixed and stable star, his figure speaks to an erratic planet disturbing and destabilizing the neat orderliness of systemic orbits.

Bibliography

Adorno, Theodor W. *Negative Dialectics*. New York: Continuum, 1997.
Aesop. *Aesop's Fables*. Illustrated by Heidi Holder. New York: Viking, 1981.
Agamben, Giorgio. *The Kingdom and the Glory: For a Theological Genealogy of Economy and Government*. Translated by Lorenzo Chiesa (with Matteo Mandarini). Stanford: Stanford University Press, 2011.
———. *State of Exception*. Translated by Kevin Attell. Chicago: University of Chicago Press, 2005.
Althaus, Paul. "Luthers Lehre von der beiden Reichen." *Lutherjahrbuch* 14 (1957) 40–68.
Altmann, Walter. *Luther and Liberation: A Latin American Perspective*. Translated by Mary M. Solberg. Minneapolis: Fortress, 1992.
Alves, Rubem A. *Protestantismo e repressão*. São Paulo: Editora Ática, 1979.
Andrade, Oswald de. "Manifesto Antropófago." In *An Anthology of Brazilian Prose (from the Beginnings to the Present Day)*, edited by R. L. Scott-Buccleuch and Mário Teles de Oliveira, 387–90. São Paulo: Editôra Ática, 1971.
The Ante-Nicene Fathers. Edited by Alexander Roberts and James Donaldson. 10 vols. 1885–87. Reprint, Peabody, MA: Hendrickson, 1994.
Anthony, Neal J. *Cross Narratives: Martin Luther's Christology and the Location of Redemption*. Eugene, OR: Pickwick, 2010.
Arendt, Hannah. *Eichmann in Jerusalem: A Report on the Banality of Evil*. New York: Penguin, 2006.
———. *The Human Condition*. Chicago: University of Chicago Press, 1958.
Aristotle. *The Metaphysics*. Translated by Hugh Tredennick. 2 vols. Cambridge: Harvard University Press, 1933.
Arnold, Martin. *Handwerker als theologische Schriftsteller: Studien zu Flugschriften der frühen Reformation (1523–1525)*. Göttingen: Vandenhoeck & Ruprecht, 1990.
Asendorf, Ulrich. *Eschatologie bei Luther*. Göttingen: Vandenhoeck & Ruprecht, 1967.
Athanasius. *On the Incarnation of the Word*. Translated by Archibald Robertson. In *Christology of the Later Fathers*, edited by Edward Rochie Hardy, 55–110. Philadelphia: Westminster, 1954.
Auerbach, Erich. *Mimesis: The Representation of Reality in Western Literature*. Translated by Willard R. Trask. Princeton: Princeton University Press, 1953.
———. *Scenes from the Drama of European Literature: Six Essays*. New York: Meridian, 1959.
Aulen, Gustaf. *Christus Victor*. London: SPCK, 1956.

Austin, J. L. *How to Do Things with Words*. Oxford: Clarendon, 1962.
Bacon, Francis. *Novum Organum*. Edited by Joseph Devey. New York: Collier, 1901.
Badiou, Alain. *Saint Paul: The Foundation of Universalism*. Translated by Ray Brassier. Stanford: Stanford University Press, 2003.
Bakhtin, M. M. *A cultura popular na Idade Média e no Renascimento: o contexto de François Rabelais*. Translated by Yara Frateschi Vieria. São Paulo: Hucitec, 1999.
———. *The Dialogic Imagination: Four Essays*. Edited by Michael Holquist. Translated by Caryl Emerson and Michael Holquist. Austin: University of Texas Press, 1981.
Barth, Karl. *Die kirchliche Dogmatik*. Bd. 1. Zollikon-Zürich: Evangelischer Verlag, 1952.
Basil. *On the Spirit*. In vol. 8 of *The Nicene and Post-Nicene Fathers*, Series 2. Edited by Philip Schaff and Henry Wace. Reprint, Peabody, MA: Hendrickson, 1999.
Bastian, Jean Pierre. *Protestantismo y sociedad en México*. México: CUPSA, 1984.
———. *Protestantismos y modernidad latinoamericana: historia de unas minorías religiosas activas en América Latina*. México: Fondo de Cultura Económica, 1994.
Bauer, Walter. *Rechtgläubigkeit und Ketzerei im ältesten Christentum*. Tübingen: Mohr, 1934.
Bayer, Oswald. *Gott als Autor: zu einer poietologischen Theologie*. Tübingen: Mohr Siebeck, 1999.
———. "Nature and Institution: Luther's Doctrine of the Three Orders." *Lutheran Quarterly* 12 (1998) 125–59.
———. *Promissio: Geschichte der reformatorischen Wende in Luthers Theologie*. Göttingen: Vandenhoeck & Ruprecht, 1971.
———. *Theology the Lutheran Way*. Translated by Jeffrey G. Silcock and Mark C. Mattes. Grand Rapids: Eerdmans, 2007.
Benjamin, Walter. *The Arcades Project*. Translated by Howard Eiland and Kevin McLaughlin; prepared on the basis of the German volume edited by Rolf Tiedemann. Cambridge: Belknap Press of Harvard University Press, 1999.
———. *Illuminations*. Edited by Hannah Arendt. Translated by Harry Zohn. New York: Schocken, 1969.
———. *Reflections: Essays, Aphorisms, Autobiographical Writings*. Translated by Edmund Jephcott. Edited by Peter Demetz. New York: Harcourt Brace Jovanovich, 1978.
———. "The Work of Art in the Age of Mechanical Reproduction." In *Illuminations*, edited by Hannah Arendt, translated by Harry Zohn, 217–51. New York: Schocken, 1968.
Berger, Peter L. "On Lutheran Identity in America." *Lutheran Quarterly* 20, no. 3 (2006) 337–347.
———. "Protestantism and the Quest for Certainty." *The Christian Century* 115 (1998) 782.
Bhabha, Homi K. *The Location of Culture*. London: Routledge, 1994.
Bielfeldt, Dennis. "Luther, Metaphor, and Theological Language." *Modern Theology* 6 (1990) 121–35.
———. "Luther on Language." *Lutheran Quarterly* 16 (2002) 195–220.
Blaumeiser, Hubertus. *Martin Luthers Kreuzestheologie: Schlüssel zu seiner Deutung von Mensch und Wirklichkeit; eine Untersuchung anhand der Operationes in Psalmos, 1519–1521*. Paderborn: Bonifatius, 1995.
Boff, Leonardo. *Igreja, carisma e poder: ensaios de eclesiologia militante*. Petrópolis: Vozes, 1981.

Bonhoeffer, Dietrich. *Christ the Center*. Translated by John Bowden. New York: Harper, 1966.

———. *Ethics*. Translated by Neville Horton Smith. New York: Macmillan, 1955.

Bornkamm, Heinrich. *Luther im Spiegel der Deutschen Geistesgeschichte*. Heidelberg: Quelle & Meyer, 1955.

———. *Luther's Doctrine of the Two Kingdoms in the Context of His Theology*. Translated by Karl H. Hertz. Philadelphia: Fortress, 1966.

Braaten, Carl E. *Mother Church: Ecclesiology and Ecumenism*. Minneapolis: Fortress, 1998.

Braaten, Carl E., and Robert W. Jenson, eds. *Union with Christ: The New Finnish Interpretation of Luther*. Grand Rapids: Eerdmans, 1998.

Brandt, Hermann. *Gottes Gegenwart in Lateinamerika: Inkarnation als Leitmotiv der Befreiungstheologie*. Hamburg: Steinmann & Steinmann, 1992.

Brecht, Martin. *Luther als Schriftsteller: Zeugnisse seines dichterischen Gestaltens*. Stuttgart: Calwer Verlag, 1990.

Buchwald, Reinhard. "Martinus Eleutherius." *Deutsche Monatschrift* 12 (1912) 421–24.

Bultmann, Rudolf. *Das Urchristentum im Rahmen der antiken Religionen*. Zurich: Artemis, 1954.

———. *The Presence of Eternity: History and Eschatology*. The Gifford Lectures 1954–55. New York: Harper, 1957.

Burke, Kenneth. *Attitudes toward History*. 2 vols. New York: New Republic, 1937.

Camus, Albert. *The Myth of Sisyphus and Other Essays*. Translated by Justin O'Brien. New York: Vintage, 1955.

Casaldáliga, Pedro. *Creio na justiça e na esperança*. Rio de Janeiro: Civilização Brasileira, 1978.

Collingwood, R. G. *The Idea of Nature*. New York: Oxford University Press, 1960.

Cranz, F. Edward. *An Essay on the Development of Luther's Thought on Justice, Law, and Society*. 1959.

Dalferth, Silfredo Bernardo. *Die Zweireichelehre Martin Luthers im Dialog mit der Befreiungstheologie Leonardo Boffs*. Frankfurt: Peter Lang, 1996.

Derrida, Jacques. *The Gift of Death*. Translated by David Willis. Chicago: University of Chicago Press, 1995.

———. *Given Time. I, Counterfeit Money*. Translated by Peggy Kamuf. Chicago: University of Chicago Press, 1992.

———. *Mal d'archive*. Paris: Editions Galilée, 1995.

Dibelius, Martin. *Die Formgeschichte des Evangeliums*. Tübingen: Mohr (Siebeck), 1959.

Dickens, Arthur G. *The German Nation and Martin Luther*. London: Fontana, 1976.

Diem, Harald. "Luthers Lehre von den zwei Reichen untersucht von seinen Verstandnis der Bergpredigt aus: ein Beitrag zum problem 'Gesetz und Evangelium.'" In *Zur Zwei-Reiche-Lehre Luthers*, edited by Gerhard Sauter, 1–173. Munich: Kaiser, 1973.

Diem, Hermann. "Luthers Predigt in den zwei Reichen." In *Zur Zwei-Reiche-Lehre Luthers*, edited by Gerhard Sauter, 175–214. Munich: Kaiser, 1973.

Duchrow, Ulrich. *Christenheit und Weltverantwortung: Traditionsgeschichte und systematische Struktur der Zweireichelehre*. Stuttgart: E. Klett, 1970.

———. *Zwei Reiche und Regimente: Ideologie oder evangelische Orientierung?* Gütersloh: Mohn, 1977.

Ebeling, Gerhard. *Introduction to a Theological Theory of Language*. Translated by R. A. Wilson. Philadelphia: Fortress, 1973.

———. *Luther: An Introduction to His Thought*. Translated by R. A. Wilson. Philadelphia: Fortress, 1970.

———. *Lutherstudien*. Vol. 2, *Disputatio de homine*. Tübingen: Mohr, 1982.
———. "The Necessity of the Doctrine of the Two Kingdoms." In *Word and Faith*, 386–406. Philadelphia: Fortress, 1963.
———. *Word and Faith*. Philadelphia: Fortress, 1963.
Edwards, Mark U., Jr. *Luther's Last Battles: Politics and Polemics, 1531–46*. Minneapolis: Fortress, 2005.
Elert, Werner. *Morphologie des Luthertums*. Vol. 2. Munich: Beck, 1932.
Forde, Gerhard O. *A More Radical Gospel: Essays on Eschatology, Authority, Atonement, and Ecumenism*. Edited by Mark C. Mattes and Steven D. Paulson. Grand Rapids: Eerdmans, 2004.
———. *On Being a Theologian of the Cross: Reflections on Luther's Heidelberg Disputation, 1518*. Grand Rapids: Eerdmans, 1997.
———. *Theology Is for Proclamation*. Minneapolis: Fortress, 1990.
France, Anatole. *The Garden of Epicurus*. Translated by Alfred Allinson. London: J. Lane, 1908.
Freire, Paulo. *Pedagogy of the Oppressed*. Translated by Myra Bergman Ramos. London: Penguin, 1972.
Frenz, Helmut. *Mi vida chilena: solidaridad con los oprimidos*. Translated by Sonia Plaut. Santiago: LOM, 2006.
García Márquez, Gabriel. *O general em seu labirinto*. Rio de Janeiro: Editora Record, 1989.
Gerrish, B. A. "'To the Unknown God': Luther and Calvin on the Hiddenness of God." *The Journal of Religion* 53 (1973) 263–92.
Giddens, Anthony. *Modernity and Self-Identity: Self and Society in the Late Modern Age*. Stanford: Stanford University Press, 1991.
Goethe, Johann Wolfgang von. *Faust: eine Tragödie*. Munich: Deutscher Taschenbuch Verlag, 1972.
———. *Maximen und Reflexionen*. With notes and introduction by Max Hecker. Frankfurt am Main: Insel, 1976.
González Montes, Adolfo. *Religión y nacionalismo: la doctrina luterana de los dos reinos como teología civil*. Salamanca: Universidad Pontificia, 1982.
Gramsci, Antonio. *The Gramsci Reader: Selected Writings, 1916–1935*. Edited by David Forgacs. New York: New York University Press, 2000.
Gregersen, Niels Henrik. "Deep Incarnation: The Logos Became Flesh." In *Transformative Theological Perspectives*, edited by Karen L. Bloomquist, 167–82. Minneapolis: Lutheran University Press, 2009.
———. "Natural Events as Crystals of God—Luther's Eucharistic Theology and the Question of Nature's Sacramentality." In *Concern for Creation: Voices on the Theology of Creation*, edited by Viggo Mortensen. Uppsala: Tro & Tanke, 1995.
Grosshans, Hans-Peter. "Lutheran Hermeneutics." In *"You Have the Words of Eternal Life": Transformative Readings of the Gospel of John from a Lutheran Perspective*, edited by Kenneth Mtata, 23–46. Minneapolis: Lutheran University Press, 2012.
Gutiérrez, Gustavo. *The Power of the Poor in History: Selected Writings*. Translated by Robert R. Barr. Maryknoll, NY: Orbis, 1983.
Habermas, Jürgen. *Communication and the Evolution of Society*. Translated by Thomas McCarthy. Boston: Beacon, 1979.
———. *Legitimation Crisis*. Translated by Thomas McCarthy. Boston: Beacon, 1975.

Haraway, Donna Jeanne. *Simians, Cyborgs, and Women: The Reinvention of Nature.* New York: Routledge, 1991.

Harss, Luis, and Barbara Dohmann. *Into the Mainstream: Conversations with Latin-American Writers.* New York: Harper & Row, 1967.

Harvey, Van Austin. *The Historian and the Believer: The Morality of Historical Knowledge and Christian Belief.* Philadelphia: Westminster, 1966.

Heckel, Johannes. "Im Irrgarten der Zwei-Reiche-Lehre: Zwei Abhandlungen zum Reichs- und Kirchenbegriff Martin Luthers." *Theologische heute* 55 (1959) 343–46.

———. *Lex Charitatis: A Juristic Disquisition on Law in the Theology of Martin Luther.* Translated and edited by Gottfried G. Krodel. Grand Rapids: Eerdmans, 2010.

Heen, Erik M. "The Distinction 'Material/Formal Principles' and Its Use in American Lutheran Theology." *Lutheran Quarterly* 17 (2003) 329–54.

Hegel, Georg Wilhelm Friedrich. *Phänomenologie des Geistes.* Frankfurt am Main: Suhrkamp, 1977.

———. *Phenomenology of Spirit.* Translated by A. V. Miller; with analysis and foreword by J. N Findlay. Oxford: Clarendon, 1977.

———. *Werke in zwanzig Bänden.* Frankfurt am Main: Suhrkamp, 1971.

Heidegger, Martin. *Being and Time.* New York: Harper, 1962.

———. *Existence and Being.* Chicago: H. Regnery, 1949.

Heller, Ágnes. *Renaissance Man.* London: Routledge & Kegan Paul, 1978.

Helmer, Christine, ed. *The Global Luther: A Theologian for Modern Times.* Minneapolis: Fortress, 2009.

Hesse-Biber, Sharlene, et al., eds. *Feminist Approaches to Theory and Methodology: An Interdisciplinary Reader.* New York: Oxford University Press, 1999.

Holl, Karl. *The Cultural Significance of the Reformation.* Translated by Karl and Barbara Hertz and John H. Lichtblau. New York: Meridian, 1959.

———. *The Reconstruction of Morality.* Edited by James Luther Adams and Walter F. Bense. Translated by Fred W. Meuser and Walter R. Wietzke. Minneapolis: Augsburg, 1979.

Holm, Bo Kristian. "Luther's Theology of the Gift." In *The Gift of Grace: The Future of Lutheran Theology,* edited by Niels Henrik Gregersen et al., 78–86. Minneapolis: Fortress, 2004.

Honecker, Martin. *Sozialethik zwischen Tradition und Vernunft.* Tübingen: Mohr, 1977.

Ianni, Octávio. *Dialética e capitalismo.* Petrópolis: Vozes, 1982.

Irenaeus. *St. Irenaeus of Lyons Against the Heresies.* Translated by Dominic J. Unger; with further revisions by John J. Dillon. New York: Paulist, 1992.

Jenkins, Philip. *The Next Christendom: The Coming of Global Christianity.* Oxford: Oxford University Press, 2002.

John of Damascus. "Exposition of the Orthodox Faith." In vol. 9 of *The Nicene and Post-Nicene Fathers,* Series 2. Edited by Philip Schaff and Henry Wace. Reprint, Peabody, MA: Hendrickson, 1994.

Kahl, Sigrun. "The Religious Roots of Modern Poverty Policy: Catholic, Lutheran, and Reformed Protestant Traditions Compared." *European Journal of Sociology* 46 (2005) 91–126.

Kant, Immanuel. *Critique of Pure Reason.* Translated by J. M. D. Meiklejohn. London: Bell, 1881.

———. *On History.* Edited by Lewis White Beck. Translated by Lewis White Beck et al. Indianapolis: Bobbs-Merrill, 1963.

Käsemann, Ernst. *Jesus Means Freedom*. Translated by Frank Clarke. Philadelphia: Fortress, 1969.

———. "Ketzer und Zeuge: Zum johanneischen Verfasserproblem." *Zeitschrift für Theologie und Kirche* 48 (1951) 292–311.

———. *New Testament Questions of Today*. Translated by W. J. Montague. Philadelphia: Fortress, 1969.

Keller, Catherine. "The Flesh of God: A Metaphor in the Wild." In *Theology That Matters: Ecology, Economy, and God*, edited by Darby Kathleen Ray, 91–108. Minneapolis: Fortress, 2006.

Kierkegaard, Søren. *Works of Love*. Translated by Howard and Edna Hong. New York: Harper & Row, 1962.

Kilmer, Joyce. *Trees and Other Poems*. New York: Doran, 1914.

Kilpp, Nelson. *Teologia do Antigo Testamento*. São Leopoldo, Brazil: Mimeo, 1988.

Kittelson, James Matthew. "Luther on Being 'Lutheran.'" *Lutheran Quarterly* 17 (2003) 99–110.

Kolb, Robert. *Bound Choice, Election, and Wittenberg Theological Method: From Martin Luther to the Formula of Concord*. Grand Rapids: Eerdmans, 2005.

Kolb, Robert, and Timothy J. Wengert, eds. *The Book of Concord: The Confessions of the Evangelical Lutheran Church*. Translated by Charles Arand et al. Minneapolis: Fortress, 2000.

Koutzii, Flávio. *Pedaços de morte no coração*. Porto Alegre, Brazil: L & PM Editores, 1984.

Küppers, Jürgen. "Luthers Dreihierarchienlehre als Kritik an der mittelalterlichen Gesellschaftsauffassung." *Evangelische Theologie* 19 (1959) 361–74.

Lau, Franz. *"Ausserliche ordnung" und "weltlich ding" in Luthers theologie*. Göttingen: Vandenhoeck & Ruprecht, 1933.

———. *Luther*. Berlin: de Gruyter, 1959.

Laube, Adolf. *Flugschriften der Frühen Reformationsbewegung (1518–1524)*. Vaduz: Topos, 1983.

Lessing, Gotthold Ephraim. *Lessing's Theological Writings: Selections in Translation*. Stanford: Stanford University Press, 1957.

Lindbeck, George A. *The Nature of Doctrine: Religion and Theology in a Postliberal Age*. Philadelphia: Westminster, 1984.

Loewenich, Walther von. *Luther's Theology of the Cross*. Translated by Herbert J. A. Bouman. Minneapolis: Augsburg, 1976.

Löfgren, David. *Die Theologie der Schöpfung bei Luther*. Göttingen: Vandenhoeck & Ruprecht, 1960.

Lohse, Bernard. *Martin Luther's Theology: Its Historical and Systematic Development*. Translated and edited by Roy A. Harrisville. Minneapolis: Fortress, 1999.

Ludolphy, Ingetraut. "Luther und die Astrologie." In *"Astrologi Hallucinati": Stars and the End of the World in Luther's Time*, edited by Paola Zambelli, 101–7. Berlin: de Gruyter, 1986.

Luther, Martin. *D. Martin Luthers Werke. Kritische Gesamtausgabe*. 73 vols. Weimar: Herman Böhlaus Nachfolger, 1883–2009.

———. *D. Martin Luthers Werke. Kritische Gesamtausgabe. Briefwechsel*. 18 vols. Weimar: Hermann Böhlaus Nachfolger, 1930–85.

———. *D. Martin Luthers Werke. Kritische Gesamtausgabe. Tischreden*. 6 vols. Weimar: Hermann Böhlaus Nachfolger, 1912–21.

----------. *Luther—Selected Political Writings*. Edited by J. M. Porter. Philadelphia: Fortress, 1974.
----------. *Works*. Edited by Jaroslav Pelikan and Helmut T. Lehmann. American ed. 55 vols. Philadelphia: Muehlenberg and Fortress; St. Louis: Concordia, 1955–86.
Lutheran World Federation Assembly. *In Christ, a New Community: The Proceedings of the Sixth Assembly of the Lutheran World Federation*. Edited by Arne Sovik. Geneva: LWF, 1977.
----------. *Sent Into the World: The Proceedings of the Fifth Assembly of the Lutheran World Federation*. Edited by LaVern K. Grosc. Minneapolis: Augsburg, 1971.
Martins, José de Souza. *Caminhada no chão da noite: emancipação política e libertação nos movimentos sociais no campo*. São Paulo: Editora Hucitec, 1989.
Marx, Karl. "Critique of Hegel's Philosophy of Right." In *Karl Marx, Frederick Engels: Collected Works*, translated by Richard Dixon et al. New York: International Publishers, 1975.
----------. *Das Kapital: Kritik der politischen Ökonomie*. Vol. 1. Berlin: Dietz, 1962.
Matta, Roberto da. *A casa e a rua: espaço, cidadania, mulher e morte no Brasil*. Rio de Janeiro: Rocco, 1997.
Mattes, Mark C. *The Role of Justification in Contemporary Theology*. Grand Rapids: Eerdmans, 2004.
McGrath, Alister E. *Luther's Theology of the Cross: Martin Luther's Theological Breakthrough*. Oxford: Blackwell, 1985.
Melanchthon, Philipp. *Menlanchthon deutsch*. Edited by Michael Beyer et al. 2 vols. Leipzig: Evangelische Verlagsanstalt, 2011–.
Metz, Johannes Baptist. "Theology as Biography." In *Faith in History and Society: Toward a Practical Fundamental Theology*, translated and edited by J. Matthew Ashley, 219–28. New York: Crossroad, 2004.
Mohanty, Chandra Talpade. "Women Workers and Capitalist Scripts." In *Feminist Approaches to Theory and Methodology: An Interdisciplinary Reader*, edited by Sharlene Hesse-Biber et al., 362–88. New York: Oxford University Press, 1999.
Mohl, Ruth. *The Three Estates in Medieval and Renaissance Literature*. New York: Columbia University Press, 1933.
Moltmann, Jürgen. *The Crucified God: The Cross of Christ as the Foundation and Criticism of Christian Theology*. Translated by R. A. Wilson and John Bowden. Minneapolis: Fortress, 1993.
----------. "On Latin American Liberation Theology: An Open Letter to José Míguez Bonino." *Christianity and Crisis* 36 (1976) 57–63.
Morse, Richard M. *New World Soundings: Culture and Ideology in the Americas*. Baltimore: Johns Hopkins University Press, 1989.
Mortensen, Viggo, ed. *Concern for Creation: Voices on the Theology of Creation*. Uppsala: Svenska kyrkan. Forskningsråd, 1995.
Nelson, Benjamin. *The Idea of Usury: From Tribal Brotherhood to Universal Otherhood*. Princeton: Princeton University Press, 1949.
Nestingen, James. "Luther's Heidelberg Disputation: An Analysis of the Argument." In *All Things New: Essays in Honor of Roy A. Harrisville*, edited by Arland J. Hultgren et al., 147–54. St. Paul: Word & World, Luther Northwestern Theological Seminary, 1992.
Niebuhr, H. Richard. *The Social Sources of Denominationalism*. New York: H. Holt, 1929.

Nietzsche, Friedrich Wilhelm. *The Birth of Tragedy, and The Case of Wagner*. Translated with commentary by Walter Kaufmann. New York: Vintage, 1967.

———. *Werke in zwei Bänden*. Selected and introduced by August Messer. Leipzig: A. Kröner, 1930.

Nilsson, Kjell Ove. *Simul: Das Miteinander von Göttlichem und Menschlichem in Luthers Theologie*. Göttingen. Vandenhoeck & Ruprecht, 1966.

Noll, Mark. "American Lutherans Yesterday and Today." In *Lutherans Today: American Lutheran Identity in the Twenty-First Century*, edited by Richard P. Cimino, 337–47. Grand Rapids: Eerdmans, 2003.

Nygren, Anders. *Meaning and Method: Prolegomena to a Scientific Philosophy of Religion and a Scientific Theology*. Translated by Philip S. Watson. Philadelphia: Fortress, 1972.

Oberman, Heiko Augustinus. *Forerunners of the Reformation: The Shape of Late Medieval Thought*. Translated by Paul L. Nyhus. New York: Holt, Rinehart and Winston, 1966.

———. *Luther: Man between God and the Devil*. New York: Image, 1992.

———. "Teufelsdreck: Eschatology and Scatology in the 'Old' Luther." *The Sixteenth Century Journal* 19 (1988) 435–50.

Otto, Rudolf. *The Kingdom of God and the Son of Man: A Study in the History of Religion*. Translated by Floyd V. Filson and Bertram Lee-Woolf. New and rev. ed. London: Lutterworth, 1943.

———. *The Idea of the Holy: An Inquiry into the Non-rational Factor in the Idea of the Divine and Its Relation to the Rational*. London: Oxford University Press, 1923.

Pagels, Elaine. *Adam, Eve, and the Serpent*. New York: Random House, 1988.

Pannenberg, Wolfhart. *Ethics*. Translated by Keith Crim. Philadelphia: Westminster, 1981.

Pauck, Wilhelm. "Luther and Melanchthon." In *Luther and Melanchthon in the History and Theology of the Reformation*, edited by Vilmos Vajta, 13–31. Philadelphia: Muhlenberg, 1961.

Paulson, Steven D. "Lutheran Assertions Regarding Scripture." *Lutheran Quarterly* 17 (2003) 373–85.

Paz, Octavio. *La otra voz: poesía y fin de siglo*. Barcelona: Seix Barral, 1990.

———. *Posdata*. Mexico: Siglo Veintiuno Editores, 1970.

Peura, Simo. *Mehr als ein Mensch? Die Vergöttlichung als Thema der Theologie Martin Luthers von 1513 bis 1519*. Mainz: P. von Zabern, 1994.

Philip, Mary, et al. *Churrasco: A Theological Feast in Honor of Vítor Westhelle*. Eugene, OR: Pickwick, 2013.

Prenter, Regin. *Luther's Theology of the Cross*. Philadelphia: Fortress, 1971.

———. "Zur Theologie des Kreuzes bei Luther." *Lutherische Rundschau: Zeitschrift des lutherischen Weltbundes* 9 (1959) 270–83.

Preston, Ronald H. *Religion and the Ambiguities of Capitalism*. London: SCM, 1991.

Proceedings of the Fourth Assembly of the LWF, Helsinki, July 30–August 11, 1963. Berlin: Lutherisches, 1965.

Proceedings of the LWF Assembly, Lund, Sweden, June 30–July 6, 1947. Philadelphia: United Lutheran Publishing House, 1948.

Proceedings of the Second Assembly of the LWF, Hannover, Germany, July 25–August 3, 1952. Gunzenhausen: Riedel, 1952.

Proceedings of the Third Assembly of the LWF, Minneapolis, Minnesota, August 15–25, 1957. Geneva: LWR, 1958.
Rabinow, Paul. *Essays on the Anthropology of Reason*. Princeton: Princeton University Press, 1996.
Ray, Darby Kathleen. *Theology That Matters: Ecology, Economy, and God*. Minneapolis: Fortress, 2006.
Reimarus, Hermann Samuel. *Fragments from Reimarus: Consisting of Brief Critical Remarks on the Object of Jesus and His Disciples as Seen in the New Testament*. Translated from the German of G. E. Lessing. Edited by Charles Voysey. London: Williams and Norgate, 1879.
Richard, Pablo. *Apocalypse: A People's Commentary on the Book of Revelation*. Maryknoll, NY: Orbis, 1995.
Rieth, Ricardo. *"Habsucht" bei Martin Luther: ökumenisches und theologisches Denken, Tradition und soziale Wirklichkeit im Zeitalter der Reformation*. Weimar: Hermann Böhlaus Nachfolger, 1996.
———. "Luther on Greed." *Lutheran Quarterly* 15 (2001) 336–51.
Rilke, Rainer Maria. *Die Gedichte*. Frankfurt am Main: Insel, 1997.
Romano, Ruggiero. *Os mecanismos da conquista colonial: os conquistadores*. São Paulo: Perspectiva, 1973.
Rosa, João Guimarães. *The Third Bank of the River, and Other Stories*. Translated by Barbara Shelby. New York: Knopf, 1968.
Rosen, Stanley. *Hermeneutics as Politics*. New York: Oxford University Press, 1987.
Rousseau, Jean-Jacques. *The Basic Political Writings*. Translated and edited by Donald A. Cress. 2nd ed. Indianapolis: Hackett, 2011.
Roy, Arundhati. *An Ordinary Person's Guide to Empire*. Cambridge: South End, 2004.
Ruge-Jones, Philip. *Cross in Tensions: Luther's Theology of the Cross as Theologico-Social Critique*. Eugene, OR: Pickwick, 2008.
Ruokanen, Miikka. *Doctrina divinitus inspirata: Luther's Position in the Ecumenical Problem of Biblical Inspiration*. Helsinki: Luther-Agricola Society, 1985.
Saarinen, Risto. "Communicating the Grace of God in a Pluralistic Society." In *The Gift of Grace: The Future of Lutheran Theology*, edited by Niels Henrik Gregersen et al., 67–77. Minneapolis: Fortress, 2005.
Said, Edward W. *Culture and Imperialism*. New York: Vintage, 1994.
Saler, Robert C. *Between Magisterium and Marketplace: A Constructive Account of Theology and the Church*. Minneapolis: Fortress, 2014.
Sauter, Gerhard, ed. *Zur Zwei-Reiche-Lehre Luthers*. Munich: Kaiser, 1973.
Scaer, David P. *The Lutheran World Federation Today*. Saint Louis: Concordia, 1971.
Scheler, Max. *Man's Place in Nature*. Translated by Hans Meyerhoff. Boston: Beacon, 1961.
Schillebeeckx, Edward. *Jesus: An Experiment in Christology*. Translated by Hubert Hoskins. New York: Crossroad, 1981.
Schjørring, Jens Holger, et al., eds. *From Federation to Communion: The History of the Lutheran World Federation*. Minneapolis: Fortress, 1997.
Schleiermacher, Friedrich. *The Christian Faith*. Edited by H. R. Mackintosh and J. S. Stewart. Edinburgh: T. & T. Clark, 1989.
———. *Der christliche Glaube nach den Grundsätzen der evangelischen Kirche im Zusammenhange dargestellt*. Bd. 2. Berlin: de Gruyter, 1960.

Schmitt, Carl. *The Concept of the Political.* Translated by George Schwab; with comments on Schmitt's essay by Leo Strauss. New Brunswick, NJ: Rutgers University Press, 1976.
Schütze, Christian von. "Waldgeschichte und Weltgeschichte auf dem Weg in die Wüste?" *Der Überblick* 3 (1989) 5–8.
Schwantes, Milton. *Projetos de esperança: meditações sobre Gênesis 1–11.* Petrópolis: Vozes, 1989.
Schwarz, Reinhard. "Ecclesia, oeconomia, politia: Sozialgeschichtliche und fundamentalethische Aspekte der protestatischen Drei-Stände-Theorie." In *Protestantismus und Neuzeit,* edited by Horst Renz and Friedrich W. Graf, 78–88. Güttersloh: Gerd Mohn, 1984.
Scott, Joan W. "The Evidence of Experience." In *Feminist Approaches to Theory and Methodology: An Interdisciplinary Reader,* edited by Sharlene Hesse-Biber et al., 79–99. New York: Oxford University Press, 1999.
Scribner, Robert W. *For the Sake of Simple Folk: Popular Propaganda for the German Reformation.* Cambridge: Cambridge University Press, 1981.
———. *The German Reformation.* Atlantic Highlands, NJ: Humanities Press, 1986.
Segundo, Juan Luis. *Esa communidad llamada Iglesia.* Buenos Aires: Carlos Lohlé, 1968.
———. *Faith and Ideologies.* Translated by John Drury. Maryknoll, NY: Orbis, 1984.
Shakespeare, William. *The Tempest.* London: Dent, 1935.
Sobrino, Jon. *Jesus the Liberator: A Historical-Theological Reading of Jesus of Nazareth.* Translated by Paul Burns and Francis McDonagh. Maryknoll, NY: Orbis, 1993.
Solberg, Mary M. *Compelling Knowledge: A Feminist Proposal for an Epistemology of the Cross.* Albany: State University of New York Press, 1997.
Sölle, Dorothee. *Suffering.* Translated by Everett R. Kalin. Philadelphia: Fortress, 1975.
Spener, Philipp Jakob. *Pia Desideria.* Translated and edited by Theodore G. Tappert. Philadelphia: Fortress, 1964.
Spivak, Gayatri Chakravorty. "Can the Subaltern Speak?" In *Marxism and the Interpretation of Culture,* edited by Cary Nelson and Lawrence Grossberg, 271–313. Urbana: University of Illinois Press, 1988.
———. *A Critique of Postcolonial Reason: Toward a History of the Vanishing Present.* Cambridge: Harvard University Press, 1999.
Springer, Carl P. E. *Luther's Aesop.* Kirksville, MO: Truman State University Press, 2011.
Steiger, Johann Anselm. "The *communicatio idiomatum* as the Axle and Motor of Luther's Theology." *Lutheran Quarterly* 14 (2000) 125–58.
Stolt, Birgit. "Luther's Faith of 'the Heart': Experience, Emotion, and Reason." In *The Global Luther: A Theologian for Modern Times,* edited by Christine Helmer, 131–50. Minneapolis: Fortress, 2009.
———. *Studien zu Luthers Freiheitstraktat: mit besonderer Rücksicht auf das Verhältnis der lateinischen und der deutschen Fassung zueinander und die Stilmittel der Rhetorik.* Stockholm: Almqvist Wiksell, 1969.
Taubes, Jacob. *Occidental Eschatology.* Translated by David Ratmoko. Stanford: Stanford University Press, 2009.
———. *The Political Theology of Paul.* Translated by Dana Hollander. Stanford: Stanford University Press, 2004.
Tawney, R. H. *Religion and the Rise of Capitalism: A Historical Study.* New York: New American Library, 1954.

Theology in the LWF: Legacy Document of the Commission on Studies. Edited by Paul Rajashekar and Götz Planer-Friedrich. Geneva: Lutheran World Federation, 1989.

Tillich, Paul. *The Interpretation of History*. Part one translated by N. A. Rasetzki; parts two, three, and four translated by Elsa L. Talmey. New York: Scribner's, 1936.

———. *Systematic Theology*. Vol. 1. Chicago: University of Chicago Press, 1951.

———. *Theology of Culture*. Edited by Robert C. Kimball. New York: Oxford University Press, 1964.

Törnvall, Gustaf. *Geistliches und weltliches Regiment bei Luther: Studien zu Luthers Weltbild und Gesellschaftsverständnis*. Munich: C. Kaiser, 1947.

Torrance, Thomas F. *Kingdom and Church: A Study in the Theology of the Reformation*. Edinburgh: Oliver and Boyd, 1956.

Tracy, David W. "Form and Fragment: The Recovery of the Hidden and Incomprehensible God." In *The Concept of God in Global Dialogue*, edited by Werner G. Jeanrond and Aasulv Lande, 98–114. Maryknoll, NY: Orbis, 2005.

———. "The Hidden God: The Divine Other of Liberation." *Cross Currents* 46 (1996) 5–16.

Troeltsch, Ernst. *Glaubenslehre*. Munich: Duncker & Humblot, 1925.

———. *Protestantism and Progress: A Historical Study of the Relation of Protestantism to the Modern World*. Translated by W. Montgomery. Boston: Beacon, 1958.

Turner, Victor W. *The Forest of Symbols: Aspects of Ndembu Ritual*. Ithaca: Cornell University Press, 1967.

Twesten, August Detlev Christian. *Vorlesungen über die Dogmatik der evangelisch-lutherischen Kirche: nach dem Compendium des Herrn Dr. W. M. L. de Wette*. Hamburg: F. Perthes, 1834.

Työrinoja, Reijo. "Nova vocabula et nova lingua: Luther's Conception of Doctrinal Formulas." In *Thesaurus Lutheri*, edited by Tuomo Mannermaa et al., 221–36. Helsinki: Vammala, 1987.

Vercruysse, Jos E. "Gesetz und Liebe." *Lutherjahrbuch* 48 (1981) 7–43.

Wabel, Thomas. *Sprache als Grenze in Luthers theologischer Hermeneutik und Wittgensteins Sprachphilosophie*. Berlin: de Gruyter, 1998.

Weber, Max. *The Protestant Ethic and the Spirit of Capitalism*. Translated by Talcott Parsons. New York: Scribner's, 1958.

Wengert, Timothy J., ed. *Harvesting Martin Luther's Reflections on Theology, Ethics, and the Church*. Grand Rapids: Eerdmans, 2004.

Westermann, Claus. *Creation*. Translated by John J. Scullion. Philadelphia: Fortress, 1974.

Westhelle, Vítor. "Apresentação." *Estudos Teológicos* 31 (1991) 119–20.

———. *The Church Event: Call and Challenge of a Church Protestant*. Minneapolis: Fortress, 2010.

———. "Communication and the Transgression of Language in Martin Luther." *Lutheran Quarterly* 17 (2003) 1–27.

———. "Considerações sobre o Etno-Luteranismo Latino-Americano." *Estudos Teológicos* 18 (1978) 77–94.

———. "The Dark Room, the Labyrinth, and the Mirror: On Interpreting Luther's Thought on Justification and Justice." In *By Faith Alone: Essays on Justification in Honor of Gerhard O. Forde*, edited by Joseph A. Burgess and Marc Kolden, 316–31. Grand Rapids: Eerdmans, 2004.

———. *Eschatology and Space: The Lost Dimension in Theology Past and Present.* New York: Palgrave Macmillan, 2012.

———. "Hybridity and Luther's Reading of Chalcedon." In *Gudstankens aktualitet: Bidrag om teologiens opgave og indhold og protestantismens indre spændinger; Festskrift til Peter Widmann,* edited by Else Marie Wiberg Pedersen et al., 233–53. Copenhagen: ANIS, 2010.

———. "Idols and Demons: On Discerning the Spirits." *Dialog* 41 (2002) 9–15.

———. "Justification as Death and Gift." *Lutheran Qaurterly* 24 (2010) 249–62.

———. "Luther and Liberation." *Dialog* 25 (1986) 51–58.

———. "'The Noble Tribe of Truth': Etchings on Myth, Language, and Truth Speaking." Presentation given at Aarhus University, Denmark.

———. "Os Sinais dos Lugares: As Dimensões Esquecidas." In *Peregrinação: Estudos em homenagem a Joachim Fischer,* edited by Martin N. Dreher, 255–68. São Leopoldo, Brazil: Sinodal, 1990.

———. "Power and Politics: Incursions in Luther's Theology." In *The Global Luther: A Theologian for Modern Times,* edited by Christine Helmer, 284–300. Minneapolis: Fortress, 2009.

———. "Revelation 13: Between the Colonial and the Postcolonial; a Reading from Brazil." In *From Every People and Nation: The Book of Revelation in Intercultural Perspective,* edited by David Rhoads, 183–99. Minneapolis: Fortress, 2005.

———. "Theological Education: *Quo Vadis?*" *Currents in Theology and Mission* 24 (1997) 273–85.

———. "Theorie und Praxis, III. Fundamentaltheologisch." In vol. 8 of *Die Religion in Geschichte und Gegenwart,* edited by Hans Dieter Betz et al. 4th ed. Tübingen: Mohr Siebeck, 2005.

———. "'The Third Bank of the River': Thoughts on Justification and Justice." In *Justification and Justice,* edited by Viggo Mortensen, 29–36. Geneva: Lutheran World Federation, 1992.

White, Lynn, Jr. "The Historical Roots of Our Ecological Crisis." *Science* 155 (1967) 1203–7.

Wiberg Pedersen, Else Marie. "Can God Speak the Vernacular?" In *The Vernacular Spirit: Essays on Medieval Religious Literature,* edited by Renate Blumenfeld-Kosinski et al., 185–208. New York: Palgrave, 2002.

Widmann, Peter. "'Reformation' as Common Faith." In *The Gift of Grace: The Future of Lutheran Theology,* edited by Niels Henrik Gregersen et al., 243–49. Minneapolis: Fortress, 2004.

Wolf, Ernst. "Die 'lutherische Lehre' von den zwei Reichen in der gegenwärtigen Forschung." *Zeitschrift für evangelisches Kirchenrecht* 6 (1959) 255–73.

Wolin, Sheldon S. *Politics and Vision: Continuity and Innovation in Western Political Thought.* Boston: Little Brown, 1960.

Yeats, William Butler. *The Collected Poems.* Edited by Richard J. Finneran. Rev. 2nd ed. New York: Scribner's, 1996.

Zur Mühlen, Karl-Heinz. "Arbeit VI: Reformation und Orthodoxie." In vol. 3 of *Theologische Realenzyklopädie,* 635–39. Berlin: de Gruyter, 1978.

Author Index

Aristotle, 9, 10, 78n28, 112, 148, 250, 271, 278, 285–86, 288, 295, 303, 310
Athanasius, 103
Auerbach, Erich, ix, 6, 114, 187, 244, 317
Augustine, 12, 32, 98, 120, 143, 189–90, 200–201, 232, 284n32, 307
Aulén, G. 270

Bakhtin, Mikhail, 25, 30–33, 34n59, 35–36, 39
Barth, Karl, 104, 114, 124, 240, 300n32
Basil of Caesarea, 43–44, 285–86n36, 295
Bayer, Oswald, 45, 86n11, 111n4, 112n7, 114n13, 121n44, 123n51, 265n16, 268n23, 268n24, 298
Benjamin, Walter, 7, 60–61, 163, 186, 226, 236n22, 250, 305n1
Bonhoeffer, Dietrich, 119n34, 199n8, 286n39

Calvin, Jean, 313

Diem, Harald, 69–70, 264n9, 281–82
Duchrow, Ulrich, 76n24, 263n6, 266–67n19, 272–73n35, 282n22, 283n24, 285n34, 295n6, 300n31, 301n34, 307

Ebeling, Gerhard, 20, 28–29, 155, 262n2, 297n15

Forde, Gerard, 45, 111, 161, 269n29, 277n3,
Flacius Illyricus, Matthias, 97, 247n15

Goethe, Johann Wolfgang von, 6, 17, 85, 245
Gregory Nazianzen, 19, 103

Heckel, Johannes, 262, 265, 268, 277, 281, 283n28, 301n38
Hegel, G. W. F., 2, 37, 49, 84, 92–93, 95–96, 140, 213, 231, 239–40, 245, 286, 318
Heidegger, Martin, 24, 36, 113, 208
Holl, Karl, 34, 264–65, 268n24, 301n38

Irenaeus, 44–45, 47, 90, 101, 209, 240

Lau, Franz, 25, 264, 292
Lessing, Gotthold Ephraim, 41–42, 63n19, 112n6, 158, 208
Lindbeck, George, 28–29
Loewenich, Walter von, 116–17, 119
Luther, Martin, ix–xi, 1, 3, 6, 8, 17, 23, 25n27, 103n19, 114n13, 142, 181, 206n28, 226–27, 263n7, 305n2, 312n34

Marx, Karl, 2, 46n19, 131, 134, 141–42, 206, 213, 239–40, 286, 299–300, 303, 305, 313n38
Melanchthon, Philipp, 20, 33, 59, 87, 123n53, 151, 157, 160, 228, 233–34, 245, 298n21, 307

Müntzer, Thomas, 2, 10

Nietzsche, Friedrich, 26, 32, 98, 141, 258
Nygren, Anders, 21, 170, 318

Oberman, Haiko, 33n55, 43n5, 243, 305n2

Pelikan, Jaroslav, 69n4
Prenter, Regin, 114–16, 122n48, 125, 131, 160, 246

Schleiermacher, Friedrich, 96–97, 183, 208, 236

Sobrino, Jon, 115–16, 228, 234–35, 238

Tillich, Paul, 102, 121n45, 200, 220, 231, 236–37, 247, 318
Tracy, David, viii, 120, 161–62
Troeltsch, Ernst, 32n51, 132, 232, 264, 314

Wittgenstein, Ludwig, 12, 21n12, 21n13, 24, 63n18
Wolf, Ernst, 276n20

Zwingli, Ulrich, 18n1, 158–59, 228, 233, 245, 307, 308n9, 308n11

Subject Index

antinomianism, 55–6
apocalypse, 13, 66, 102, 133, 155–63, 227–28, 238, 272, 274, 305–6, 309–13, 318, 331
Augsburg Confession, 56, 151, 174, 193, 233–34
autos-da-fé, 4, 196, 198, 200, 203

blessed/saved/*selig*, 65, 77, 154, 251, 290
Bondage of the Will 44, 112–13, 119–20, 149, 197, 245, 273, 281
Book of Concord 4, 18n1, 56n39, 56n41, 65n24, 105n26, 122n46, 130n12, 131n15, 191n17, 287n43, 297n19, 299n24, 328

catechism, 2, 51–52, 283, 294, 297
Chalcedon 5, 12, 18, 62–3, 95, 97, 99, 104–8, 122, 159, 235, 288, 307, 334
Christ's presence, mode of, 64, 87, 106–7, 122, 130, 158–59, 235, 242, 246, 251, 287, 308, 313
christology, 18, 62, 64, 77, 100, 107, 109, 119n34, 122, 159, 288
church event, 148, 154
communicatio, 12, 18, 62, 64, 72, 77, 105–6, 109, 288, 307, 332
communication, 11–12, 17–19, 21–23, 28, 30–32, 36, 39, 55, 62, 101, 105–7, 148, 167, 170, 186, 191, 211, 221–22, 224, 262, 286, 288–89, 318, 326, 333

Confession (Concerning Christ's Supper), 64–65, 77, 105, 122, 158, 235, 242, 245, 283, 287–89, 294, 308
Cooperatio, cooperation 89, 256, 273, 281, 287, 289
*coram deo, mundo, hominibus, meipso,*8, 20, 31, 72, 76, 256, 277, 280, 282
Councils and the Church, 62, 73, 107, 123, 151, 159, 234–35, 288, 296
cross of Christ, 114–116, 121, 130–31, 160, 191, 235, 246
culture, modern, 169–70
culture, popular, 22, 33–34
Culture, Lutheranism and, vi, 195, 204
culture, theology and, 169

Decalogue, 51–52, 54, 214, 272
Demons, 23, 94, 162, 334
desire, 91–94, 203, 232, 277, 290
dialect, 48–51, 53–54, 56, 190, 215
dialectics, 46, 49–52, 54, 92, 167, 192, 277, 318–19; dialectical 32, 53, 158, 161, 167, 258, 319
Dreiständelehre, 9

*ecclesia,*9, 18, 38, 55, 65, 73, 75, 87, 90, 93, 119, 132, 148–49, 154, 191, 199, 201–2, 247, 249–50, 256, 268, 271, 282–85, 291, 294, 298, 314, 332
ecclesial principle, 44
ecology, 134, 138, 171–72, 208, 328

335

SUBJECT INDEX

economy, v, 5, 7, 9, 20–21, 38, 46, 69, 72, 76–77, 83, 90–92, 105, 215, 141–42, 148–50, 153–54, 187, 199, 248–50, 257, 264, 267, 272, 281, 283–86, 293–296, 298–300, 303, 305, 309, 312–14

equity, 11, 38, 40, 53–54, 92, 154, 256, 281, 290, 294, 298, 300–2, 310

eschatology, 133–34, 155–57, 163, 218, 238, 243n4, 305–6, 312, 318, 325–26, 330, 332, 334

exemplum, 29n43, 49, 74n14, 114

experience, 19, 24, 29–31, 39, 58, 70, 86–87, 89–90, 115, 117, 120–23, 127, 129, 131, 133, 144, 147, 156, 173, 175, 179, 185–86, 188, 190–93, 205, 207, 211, 214–16, 218–22, 224–25, 227–228, 234, 242, 256, 258, 260–62, 281, 289, 306, 307n8, 308, 332

faith, x, 27, 29, 37, 39, 42–43, 45–46, 48, 52, 55, 58, 64–66, 68, 71–74, 76–80, 86, 88–89, 96–98, 112–13, 117, 122, 126, 137, 139, 143–44, 147, 152, 156, 162, 169, 173, 183, 189, 199, 201, 216, 224, 227, 247, 256–57, 276–78, 280, 308–9, 319, 326–27, 329, 331–34

fragmentation, 3, 167–69, 175–77, 180, 272

Freedom of a Christian, 2, 230

freedom, 2–7, 20, 40, 89–90, 98n11, 141, 146, 153, 174, 186, 197–98, 203, 205, 230–31, 244, 257–58, 265

gift, 46–47, 49–50, 55, 69–74, 79, 83–86, 88–89, 91, 94, 105, 109, 114, 117–18, 122, 137, 163, 180, 194, 202, 204–6, 215, 222, 225, 232, 236, 271, 274n41, 301, 314

globalization, 168–69, 170, 172, 180

governance, 187, 266–267, 268n22, 269, 273, 283, 301, 302

grammar, 15, 21, 23, 29–30, 38–39, 49, 51, 210, 224, 270, 278, 282. 290, 318–19

Heidelberg Disputation, 93, 111–12, 269–71, 277

hiddenness, 118–20, 161–62

holy (*heilig*), 65, 77, 251

hybridity, 95–96, 98, 100–104, 106–9, 213

idols, 23n19, 51, 63, 93, 222, 224

imago, 101–2, 139, 247n15, 260, 298

interest, 10, 91–94, 204, 313

involucrum (see also wrapping), 33, 89n21, 126, 143, 308

justice, ix–xi, 8, 10–12, 52, 78, 91–92, 117–18, 136, 141–42, 171, 236–37, 256–59, 261–63, 265–67, 270–75, 281–82, 290, 294, 300–302, 312

justification, vii–viii, 8–9, 11–13, 38, 43, 53, 55, 83–94, 105, 116–17, 121, 138, 168, 172–73, 176–77, 185, 191–94, 201, 206, 223, 232, 236, 238, 256–59, 261–63, 265–68, 272–74, 280, 282, 301–2, 311, 313, 318

labor (see also work), 9, 70, 75, 78, 80, 86, 91–93, 141–42, 144, 148–49, 199n8, 202, 206, 251, 260, 266, 283–87, 289–90, 293, 295, 298–300, 311, 313–14, 316

language, 11–13, 17–40, 45, 50, 54, 60–63, 65, 74–75, 79, 85, 93, 109, 152, 156, 160, 168, 193, 205, 214, 216, 238, 242, 257, 260–61, 267, 270–71, 278–79, 282, 288, 318–19

law and gospel, 50, 55, 95, 266, 280, 282

law, use of, 53, 56n41, 93, 258, 260, 265, 272n34, 277, 280, 290, 301

Lectures on Genesis, 66, 147, 148, 202, 289, 296, 299

love of the enemy, 70–73, 75–76, 79–80

mask, *larva(e)*, 33–34, 38–39, 70, 89–90, 119, 126, 128–31, 143–44, 159, 162, 191, 268n24, 269–71, 274,

284–85, 287, 290, 295, 298, 300, 302, 307–9, 314, 316
materialism, 66, 159
matter, 66, 77, 122, 127, 140, 142, 159–60, 199, 235–36, 302, 308, 312, 314
Moses, 47, 51–55, 65, 74, 162, 188–92, 210, 213–214, 216, 220, 272n34
myth, 26, 85, 139–42, 167, 212n5, 255, 260

Notae ecclesiae, 234

oeconomia, 9, 38, 55, 65, 73, 75, 90–93, 112, 119, 132, 148–49, 151, 153–54, 199, 202, 206, 247–51, 256, 268n23, 271, 282–88, 290, 294–95, 297–302, 314
oppression, viii, 9, 11, 20–22, 24, 91, 177, 184, 189, 212, 216, 231, 234, 274

Paul, 7, 19, 37, 48, 54, 63, 66, 86–7, 89n20, 104, 150n12, 151n14, 159, 184, 189–90, 210, 218, 220, 224, 245, 270–71, 273, 302, 305n1
peasant, x, 3, 10, 40, 70, 115, 192, 219–20, 227, 237
piety, 32, 96, 138, 141–42, 144, 147, 184, 232, 312
politia, 9, 38, 55, 65, 73, 75, 90–93, 112, 119, 132, 148–49, 151, 154, 199, 202, 206, 247–51, 256, 268n23, 271, 282–85, 287–88, 295–302, 314
politics, 5–6, 8, 20–21, 41, 76, 79, 148–151, 153–54, 174, 199–200, 203, 215, 248–50, 257, 267, 270, 281, 283, 286, 291–96, 298–300, 303, 305, 309, 312–313
poiēsis, 90, 202, 250, 285–89, 295, 298, 300–303
 theōria, 9, 112, 250–51
praxis, 9, 90, 112, 171, 180, 202, 250, 285–86, 288–89, 291, 295, 298, 300–303

priesthood, 52, 145–46, 154, 199, 230–31, 285
Protestant, 10, 29n43, 41, 44, 96, 112, 114, 124, 183, 198, 227, 229–31, 233–34, 264, 313, 315–16, 318
Psalter, 58–66, 69, 281

Reformed, 173, 178, 183, 205n25, 235, 258, 265, 308, 315–16
régime/s, 8, 11–12, 20–22, 29, 38–40, 69, 74, 76, 79–80, 95, 103, 119, 145, 149, 199, 204, 211–12, 233, 256–58, 260, 266, 268, 270–74, 276, 278, 280–81, 283–84, 294, 298, 301, 303–4, 307
Regiment, 76, 263n6, 266–69, 282–83, 294, 307
reich, 69, 76, 262n1, 263n6, 264n9, 265n17, 266–68, 281n16, 282n22
representation, 12–13, 59, 83, 91–93, 103, 127, 143, 149, 158, 174–77, 184–87, 189, 199–200, 202–5, 211–13, 218, 221–22, 224, 245n9, 246, 308
re-presentation, 11, 93–94, 156, 289, 298
revelatio sub contraria, 119

sacrament, *sacramentum,* 11, 29n43, 49, 51, 64, 74, 87, 114, 123, 130, 150–52, 160, 191, 199, 202, 206, 233–34, 246, 307–8
saved/blessed/*selig,* 65, 77, 154, 251, 290
selig/saved/blessed 65, 77, 154, 251, 290
spheres of promise, 66, 91, 231, 250–51
solus Christus, x, 2, 8, 43, 46, 95
sola fide, x, 2, 8, 43, 46, 78, 314
sola gratia, x, 2, 8, 43, 46, 95
sola scriptura, 41–43, 46, 120, 230

theologia crucis, 111–13, 117, 121, 318
theology of the cross, vii–viii, 111, 113–19, 121–23, 125, 130–32, 160, 234–236, 273, 277
theologian of the cross, 111–12, 121, 143, 276–77

transfiguration, ix–x, xii, 5, 9, 13, 187–92, 209–11, 214, 218, 306
translation, 17, 20, 36–37, 40, 45, 48–49, 53, 60–62, 64, 123, 186, 199, 206, 229, 238, 279
two kingdoms doctrine, 11, 69, 76, 192, 205, 256, 262–69, 272, 274–75, 277, 280–82, 292–94, 298, 300n32, 303, 306

vernacular, 12, 18–20, 22, 24–26, 28n39, 36–38, 41, 60–62, 191, 278
vestitus (garment), 89, 127, 302, 308
vita active, 71, 85–86, 87n14, 121, 201, 285, 288, 301–2, 319
vita contemplative, 285

Wittenberg, 1, 40, 162, 190, 245n9
Word of God, 10–11, 18–19, 21, 48, 52, 63, 74, 113n11, 119, 121, 147–48, 154, 213, 215, 228, 230, 242, 269, 284
work (as labor), 21, 91–93, 122, 163, 199n8, 274, 286–87, 289–90, 299–300, 302, 316
work/s and law, 76, 78, 89, 112, 119, 121–22, 163, 242, 259, 273, 276–78, 280, 291, 301, 315
work of God, 115, 122, 128–29, 131, 144, 149, 163, 256, 283–4, 273
wrapping, 33, 89–90, 126, 140, 143, 308–9

Zweireichelehre, 264

www.ingramcontent.com/pod-product-compliance
Lightning Source LLC
Chambersburg PA
CBHW020109010526
44115CB00008B/759